A DUAL APPROACH TO OCEAN GOVERNANCE

Ashgate International Law Series

Series Editor: Alex Conte, OECD, Paris

The Ashgate International Law Series brings together top-quality titles, principally in the area of public international law but also in private international law, under the label of a single international series. Each title represents work which is the result of high-level research, aimed at both the professorial and postgraduate academic market as well as the expert practitioner.

Also in the series

Terrorism, War and International Law
The Legality of the Use of Force Against Afghanistan in 2001
Myra Williamson
ISBN 978 0 7546 7403 0

A Dual Approach
to Ocean Governance

The Cases of Zonal and Integrated Management in
International Law of the Sea

YOSHIFUMI TANAKA
University of Westminster, UK

ASHGATE

Published by
Ashgate Publishing Limited
Wey Court East
Union Road
Farnham
Surrey GU9 7PT
England

Ashgate Publishing Company
Suite 420
101 Cherry Street
Burlington, VT 05401-4405
USA

www.ashgate.com

British Library Cataloguing in Publication Data
Tanaka, Yoshifumi
    A dual approach to ocean governance : the cases of zonal
    and integrated management in international law of the sea.
    - (The Ashgate international law series)
    1. Marine resources conservation - Law and legislation
    2. Law of the sea
    I. Title
    341.4'5

Library of Congress Cataloging-in-Publication Data
Tanaka, Yoshifumi.
    A dual approach to ocean governance : the cases of zonal and integrated management in international law of the sea / by Yoshifumi Tanaka.
        p. cm. -- (The Ashgate international law series)
    Includes bibliographical references and index.
    ISBN 978-0-7546-7170-1 (hardback) 1. Marine resources conservation--Law and legislation. 2. Law of the sea. I. Title.

    K3485.T36 2008
    346.04'695616--dc22

                                                                    2008022336

ISBN 978 0 7546 7170 1

Mixed Sources
Product group from well-managed
forests and other controlled sources
www.fsc.org Cert no. SA-COC-1565
© 1996 Forest Stewardship Council
FSC

Printed and bound in Great Britain by
MPG Books Ltd, Bodmin, Cornwall.

Contents

To Akiko

List of Figures and Tables

Figures

Tables

The author wishes to thank the OSPAR Commission and the IMO for its permission to reproduce the figures.

Table of Cases

Table of Treaties

The major treaties referred to in this book are listed here.

Acknowledgements

This book is the result of a research project undertaken by the author for the Programme for Research in Third Level Institutions in the Republic of Ireland. First and foremost, I wish to acknowledge the support of the Higher Education Authority in Ireland under this programme, which provided me with a fellowship to develop this project at the Marine Law and Ocean Policy Centre, Martin Ryan Marine Science Institute, National University of Ireland, Galway. Equally, I would like to thank Dr Ronan Long, Director of the Marine Law and Ocean Policy Centre, for his support and suggestions for this study. Furthermore, I wish to thank Professor Michael Guiry, Director of the Martin Ryan Marine Science Institute, for his encouragement. A debt of gratitude is also owed to the members of the Marine Law and Ocean Policy Centre, Professor Clive Symmons and Dr Ann-Marie O'Hagan, for their suggestions and friendship. Moreover, I should like to express my sincere gratitude to Dr Michael Johnstone for proofreading my drafts. In addition, I appreciated very much the constructive comments I received from the anonymous reviewers. I am also grateful to the University of Westminster School of Law for giving me research remissions to complete this project.

Some parts of Chapter 1 appeared in the *International Journal of Marine and Coastal Law*, Vol. 19, 2004, and Chapter 6 is the revision of my article appearing in *Zeitschrift für ausländisches öffentliches Recht und Völkerrecht (ZaöRV)*, Vol. 65, 2005. I am grateful to the *International Journal of Marine and Coastal Law*, Martinus Nijhoff Publishers, and *ZaöRV* for permission to use these previously published materials.

Finally, I would like to express my gratitude to my wife, Akiko, for all her support and prayer throughout my study.

Y.T.
London

List of Abbreviations

AFDI	*Annuaire français de droit international*
AJIL	*American Journal of International Law*
ASDI	*Annuaire suisse de droit international*
BYIL	*British Yearbook of International Law*
COP	Conference of the Parties
CYIL	*Canadian Yearbook of International Law*
EEZ	Exclusive Economic Zone
EFP	Experimental Fishing Programme
EFZ	Exclusive Fishing Zone
EJIL	*European Journal of International Law*
FAO	Food and Agriculture Organisation of the United Nations
GYIL	*German Yearbook of International Law*
ICCAT	International Commission for the Conservation of Atlantic Tunas
ICES	International Council for the Exploration of the Sea
ICJ	International Court of Justice
ICLQ	*International and Comparative Law Quarterly*
IJECL	*International Journal of Estuarine and Coastal Law*
IJMCL	*International Journal of Marine and Coastal Law*
ILC	International Law Commission
ILM	*International Legal Materials*
ILR	*International Law Reports*
IMO	International Maritime Organisation
INSC	International North Sea Conference
IOTC	Indian Ocean Tuna Commission
ITLOS	International Tribunal for the Law of the Sea
IUCN	International Union for the Conservation of Nature
IUU	Illegal, Unreported and Unregulated Fishing
LOSC	United Nations Convention on the Law of the Sea
MPAs	Marine Protected Areas
MSY	Maximum Sustainable Yield
NAFO	North-West Atlantic Fisheries Organisation
NEAFC	North-East Atlantic Fisheries Commission
ODIL	*Ocean Development and International Law*
PSSAs	Particularly Sensitive Sea Areas
RCADI	*Recueil des cours de l'Académie de droit international*
RECIEL	*Review of European Community and International Environmental Law*

RGDIP	*Revue générale de droit international public*
TAC	Total Allowable Catch
UN	United Nations
UNCED	United Nations Conference on Environment and Development
UNCLOS	United Nations Conference on the Law of the Sea
UNTS	*United Nations Treaty Series*
YILC	*Yearbook of International Law Commission*
ZaöRV	*Zeitschrift für ausländisches öffentliches Recht und Völkerrecht (Heidelberg Journal of International Law)*

Chapter 1
A New Perspective on Ocean Governance

'Be fruitful and increase in number and fill the water in the seas, ...' (Genesis 1:22)

Introduction – Traditional Approach of Law of the Sea and Its Problems[1]

Formation of the Zonal Management Approach in International Law of the Sea

The ocean is one unity in a physical sense. From a legal viewpoint, however, the ocean has been divided by States. It may be said that the history of international law of the sea is that of the division of the ocean. Indeed, contemporary international law of the sea divides the ocean into multiple jurisdictional spaces, such as internal waters, territorial seas, contiguous zone, EEZ, archipelagic waters, continental shelf, high seas and the deep seabed (the Area) which is the common heritage of mankind. In principle, the law of the sea regulates human activities in the ocean according to the legal category of ocean spaces. This is sometimes referred to as the sector or zonal management approach.

This approach is deeply rooted in the history of the law. That history has been dominated by two principles, that is, the principle of sovereignty and the principle of freedom.[2] The principle of sovereignty promoted the extension of coastal States' jurisdiction, while the principle of freedom ensured the non-appropriation of the ocean as well as freedom of use. On the basis of two opposing principles, the ocean has been largely divided into two categories.[3] The first category is marine

---

1 The basic idea of this chapter was expressed in Y. Tanaka, 'Zonal and Integrated Management Approaches to Ocean Governance: Reflections on a Dual Approach in International Law of the Sea' (2004) 19 *IJMCL*, pp. 483–514. This chapter is partly drawn from this article with some modifications.

2 D.P. O'Connell (I.A. Shearer, ed.), *The International Law of the Sea*, Vol. I, (Oxford, Clarendon Press, 1982) p. 1. T. Scovazzi, 'The Evolution of International Law of the Sea: New Issues, New Challenges' (2000) 286 *RCADI*, p. 54.

3 An analysis of the history of law of the sea in detail is beyond the scope of this study. On this issue, see in particular Scovazzi, *ibid.*, pp. 55–87; O'Connell, above note 2, pp. 1–28; L. Juda, *International Law and Ocean Use Management: The Evolution of Ocean Governance* (London and New York, Routledge, 1996) pp. 8–92; R.P. Anand, *Origin and Development of the Law of the Sea: History of International Law Revisited* (The Hague, Nijhoff, 1983); T.W. Fulton, *The Sovereignty of the Sea* (Edinburgh and London, William Blackwood and Sons, 1911); P.C. Jessup, *The Law of Territorial Waters and Maritime Jurisdiction* (New York, G.A. Jennings Co., Inc, 1927) (in particular Chapter I); H. Takabayashi, *Ryokai Seido no Kenkyu* (Study of Territorial Sea, in Japanese) 3rd edn (Tokyo, Yushindo, 1987).

space adjacent to coasts which is subject to territorial sovereignty. The second type concerns marine space beyond States' sovereignty where the principle of freedom is applied. The former crystallised into territorial seas and the latter was embodied in the high seas.

A dichotomy between the narrow territorial sea and the vast high seas, which represented a prototype of the zonal management approach, was formulated with the emergence of the modern State. It has been considered that the notion of the modern State was formulated by Vattel;[4] and that the modern concept of the territorial sea was also clearly presented by the same writer.[5] In his book published in 1758, Vattel stated that:

> When a nation takes possession of certain parts of the sea, it takes possession of the empire over them, as well as of the domain, on the same principle which we advanced in treating of the land (205). These parts of the sea are within the jurisdiction of the nation, and a part of its territory: the sovereign commands there; he makes laws, and may punish those who violate them; in a word, he has the same rights there as on land, and, in general, every right which the laws of the state allow him.[6]

On the other hand, Vattel denied that the high seas could be appropriated by States. In his words:

> The earth no longer furnishing, without culture, the things necessary or useful to the human race, who were extremely multiplied, it became necessary to introduce the right of property, in order that each might apply himself with more success to the cultivation of what had fallen to his share, and multiply, by his labour, the necessaries and conveniences of life. [...] But this is not the case with the open sea, on which people may sail and fish without the least prejudice to any person whatsoever, and without

---

4 Albert de Lapradelle stated that Vattel was the first writer who had the clear and complete conception of the modern State. Albert de Lapradelle, 'Introduction' to M. de Vattel, *Le droit des gens ou principes de la loi naturelle, Appliqués à la conduite et aux affaires des Nations et des Souverains* (The Classics of International Law, Washington, Carnegie Institution of Washington, 1916) p. xlvi.

5 Takabayashi, above note 3, p. 43.

6 Emmerich de Vattel, *The Law of Nations; or Principles of the Law of Nature, Applied to the Conduct and Affairs of Nations and Sovereigns* (translated by Joseph Chitty, Philadelphia, T and JW Johnson and Co., Law Booksellers, 1863) p. 130, section 295. The original phrase is: 'Quand une Nation s'empare de certaines parties de la mer, elle y occupe l'Empire, aussi bien que le Domaine, par la même raison que nous avons alléguée en parlant des terres (§ 205). Ces parties de la mer font de la Juridiction, du Territoire de la Nation; le Souverain y commande, il y donne des Lois & peut réprimer ceux qui les violent; en un mot, il y a tous les même droits qui lui appartiennent sur la terre, & en général tous ceux que la Loi de l'Etat lui donne.' Vattel, above note 4, p. 253, section 295.

putting any one in danger. No nation, therefore, has a right to take possession of the open sea, or claim the sole use of it, to the exclusion of other nations.[7]

In so stating, Vattel clearly distinguished the high seas from the territorial sea.

Later on, the dualism between the territorial sea and the high seas was consolidated through State practice. It is safe to assert that the distinction between territorial seas where the coastal States possessed sovereignty, and the high seas, which were governed by the freedom of the seas, was clearly confirmed in the Hague Conference for the Codification of International Law of 1930.[8] The division of the ocean was further promoted after the Second World War.[9] Undoubtedly the Truman Proclamations of 1945 regarding the continental shelf as well as the fisheries zone were a landmark promoting the division of the ocean by coastal States. Since then, as typically shown in the 1952 Santiago Declaration[10] and the 1952 Presidential Proclamation of the Republic of Korea,[11] coastal States have extended national jurisdiction over the seabed beyond their territorial seas as well as superjacent waters of the seabed, with a view to controlling marine natural resources.[12] Against that background, the zonal management approach was, for the first time in the history of international law, codified in the 1958 Geneva Conventions as *lex scripta*.[13] Article 1 of the Convention on the High

---

7 *Ibid.*, p. 125, section 281. The original phrase is: 'La terre ne fournissant plus sans culture toutes les choses nécessaires ou utiles au Genre – humain extrêmement multiplié, il devint convenable d'introduire le droit de propriété, afin que chacun pût s'appliquer avec plus de succès à cultiver ce qui lui était échu en partage, & à multiplier par son travail les diverses choses utiles à la vie. [...] Mais ce n'est point le cas de la pleine mer, dans laquelle on peut naviger & pêcher, sans porter de prejudice à qui que ce soit, & sans mettre personne en peril. Aucune Nation n'a donc le droit de s'emparer de la pleine mer, ou de s'en attribuer l'usage, à l'exclusion des autres.' Vattel, above note 4, p. 244, section 281.

8 Bases of Discussion No. 1 confirmed sovereignty over the territorial seas, by stating that: 'A State possesses sovereignty over a belt of sea round its coasts; this belt constitutes its territorial waters.' Reproduced in S. Rosenne (ed.), *League of Nations, Conference for the Codification of International Law (1930)*, Vol. 2 (New York, Oceana, 1975) p. 235. See also G. Gidel, *Le droit international public de la mer: Le temps de paix*, Tome 3, Fascicule I (Paris, Duchemin, reprinted in 1981) p. 169. O'Connell, above note 2, pp. 75–80.

9 *Cf.* W. Friedmann, 'Selden Redivivus: Toward a Partition of the Seas?' (1971) 65 *AJIL*, pp. 757–70.

10 Reproduced in M.M. Whiteman, *Digest of International Law*, Vol. 4 (Washington, Department of State Publication, 1965) pp. 1089–90; S. Oda, *The International Law of the Ocean Development* (Leiden, Sijthoff, 1972) pp. 345–6.

11 Presidential Proclamation of Sovereignty over Adjacent Seas, 18 January 1952, in United Nations Legislative Series, *Laws and Regulations on the Regime of the Territorial Sea* (New York, United Nations, 1957) p. 30. See also 'Chronique des faits internationaux' (1959) 63 *RGDIP*, pp. 300–303.

12 Juda, above note 3, pp. 113–16.

13 The First United Nations Conference on the Law of the Sea (UNCLOS I), which was convened in Geneva on 24 February 1958, adopted four conventions, as well as an

Seas stipulates that: 'The term "high seas" means all parts of the sea that are not included in the territorial sea or in the internal waters of a State.' It follows that the 1958 Geneva Conventions divided the ocean into three main categories: internal waters, territorial sea and high seas. As internal waters and territorial seas are under the territorial sovereignty of the coastal States, it is arguable that the 1958 Geneva Conventions still maintained the traditional dualism in the oceans.[14]

Under the zonal management approach, the spatial ambit of the territorial sea *prima facie* coincides with the monopoly of marine resources by the coastal State. Accordingly, it was not surprising that the breadth of the territorial seas was a matter of important concern for every State with fishery interests.[15] Owing to the sharp division of opinions among States on this issue,[16] however, UNCLOS I failed to reach an agreement with respect to the breadth of the territorial sea. Thus Article 6 of the Convention on the Territorial Sea and the Contiguous Zone merely provides that: 'The outer limit of the territorial sea is the line every point of which is at a distance from the nearest point of the baseline equal to the breadth of the territorial sea.' Although UNCLOS II was convened on 17 March 1960 in Geneva in order to discuss this issue, the efforts to fix the outer limit of the territorial seas proved once again in vain.[17] Consequently, a fundamental question with the zonal

---

optional protocol on dispute settlement:
- The Convention on the Territorial Sea and the Contiguous Zone,
- The Convention on the High Seas,
- The Convention on Fishing and Conservation of the Living Resources of the High Seas,
- The Convention on the Continental Shelf, and
- The Optional Protocol of Signature Concerning the Compulsory Settlement of Disputes.

With respect to the analysis of the Geneva Conventions, see, for instance, J.H.W. Verzijl, 'The United Nations Conference on the Law of the Sea, Geneva, 1958 (I) and (II)' (1959) 6 *NILR*, pp. 1–42; 115–39; R-E. Charlier, 'Résultats et enseignements des conférences du droit de la mer' (Genève 1958 et 1960) (1960) 6 *AFDI*, pp. 63–76.

14 Furthermore, with respect to the seabed, the institution of the continental shelf was enshrined in the 1958 Convention on the Continental Shelf. In addition, the contiguous zone which may not extend beyond twelve miles from the baseline was also embodied in the Convention on the Territorial Sea and the Contiguous Zone. Yet the contiguous zone is part of the high seas under Article 24 (1) of the 1958 Convention on the Territorial Sea and the Contiguous Zone. Thus, arguably the contiguous zone cannot be regarded a main category of marine spaces.

15 S. Oda, *International Control of Sea Resources* (Dordrecht, Nijhoff, 1989) p. 13.

16 With respect to the discussion in UNCLOS I on this issue, see in particular Oda, *ibid.*, pp. 97–111; Verzijl, above note 13, pp. 22–9.

17 It is acknowledged that the joint Canada–US proposal of six-mile territorial sea plus six-mile fishery zone was defeated by a single vote. See Oda, above note 15, p. 104.

management approach was left unsettled. This failure encouraged the further extension of the coastal State's jurisdiction toward the high seas.[18]

After the Third United Nations Conference on the Law of the Sea (UNCLOS III), the oceans were divided into multi-jurisdictional zones. Article 86 of the UN Convention on the Law of the Sea (hereafter the 1982 LOSC) sets out that:

> The provisions of this Part [VII] apply to all parts of the sea that are not included in the exclusive economic zone, in the territorial sea or in the internal waters of a State, or in the archipelagic waters of an archipelagic State. This article does not entail any abridgement of the freedoms enjoyed by all States in the exclusive economic zone in accordance with article 58.

The above provision shows that the 1982 LOSC distinguishes five basic categories of marine spaces: internal waters, territorial seas, archipelagic waters, the exclusive economic zone and the high seas. Furthermore, the Convention establishes other regimes concerning marine spaces such as the contiguous zone (Article 33),[19] the continental shelf (Part VI)[20] and the Area (Part XI). It follows that the ocean was divided into multiple maritime spaces under the LOSC; and that the zonal management approach was transformed from dualism to multilateralism. An innovation of the LOSC is that it finally resolved the essential question associated with the zonal management approach, that is to say, the breadth of territorial seas. States reached an agreement that the maximum seaward limit of the territorial sea was 12 miles.[21] Thus it may be said that the zonal management approach was established in the 1982 LOSC in its true sense. In this regard, it is important to note that the question relating to the maximum breadth of territorial seas could be resolved by institutionalising a new resource-oriented zone under the coastal

---

18 W.T. Burke, *The New International Law of Fisheries: UNCLOS 1982 and Beyond* (Oxford, Clarendon Press, 1994) p. 11.

19 A contiguous zone is a part of the high seas if a coastal State does not claim an EEZ. When a coastal State established an EEZ, a contiguous zone constitutes a part of the EEZ.

20 Should a coastal State not establish an EEZ, the adjacent waters of the continental shelf are the high seas. When a coastal State establishes an EEZ, the continental shelf constitutes the seabed part of EEZ, since the concept of EEZ includes seabed as well as superjacent waters and airspace (Articles 56 (1) and 58 (1) of the LOSC).

21 Article 3. It is arguable that at present the 12-mile breadth of territorial sea has been accepted by the majority of States as customary law. T. Treves, 'Codification du droit international et pratique des Etats dans le droit de la mer' (1990) 223 *RCADI*, pp. 66–74. With respect to the analysis of State practice on the seaward limit of the territorial sea, see R. Churchill, 'The Impact of State Practice on the Jurisdictional Framework Contained in the LOS Convention', in Alex G. Oude Elferink (ed.), *Stability and Change in the Law of the Sea: The Role of the LOS Convention* (Leiden and Boston, Nijhoff, 2005) pp. 109–10; J.A. Roach and R.W. Smith, *United States Responses to Excessive Maritime Claims*, 2nd edn (The Hague, Nijhoff, 1996) pp. 147–61.

State's jurisdiction: the 200-mile EEZ.[22] In other words, States could agree the maximum breadth of the territorial sea only by changing the traditional dualism in the oceans.[23]

Problems with the Traditional Approach in Law of the Sea

It is now apparent, however, that the traditional zonal management approach is insufficient to resolve the problems encountered in the management of ocean space. The first problem concerns the divergence of the law and nature. Under the zonal management approach, marine spaces in international law are in principle defined *spatially*, based on distance from the coast, irrespective of the nature of the ocean and the natural resources within it.[24] By using the distance criterion, the ecological interactions between marine species as well as the ecological conditions of the physical surroundings are ignored. Science shows that, frequently, maritime delimitation lines do not respect the uniqueness of marine ecosystems.[25] Indeed, due to their nature, several species, such as straddling and highly migratory species, do not respect artificial boundaries. Hence, a clear-cut distinction between marine spaces under the coastal State's jurisdiction and marine spaces beyond such a jurisdiction is not always suitable for the management of those species.[26]

---

22 Concerning the EEZ, the ICJ, in the *Tunisia/Libya* case of 1982, has ruled that the EEZ 'may be regarded as part of modern international law'. ICJ Reports 1982, p. 74, para. 100. Equally, the ICJ, in the *Libya/Malta* case of 1985, has clearly stated that: 'the institution of the exclusive economic zone, with its rule on entitlement by reason of distance, is shown by the practice of States to have become a part of customary law.' ICJ Reports 1985, p. 33, para. 34.

23 Takabayashi, above note 3, p. 9.

24 See Articles 3, 33, 57, 76 (1) of the LOSC. However, internal waters and archipelagic waters constitute exceptions. The former are located on the landward side of the baseline of the territorial sea (Article 8 of the LOSC), and the latter consist of the waters enclosed in the archipelagic baselines drawn in accordance with Article 47 (Article 49 of the LOSC). Thus the two institutions do not rely on the spatial distance from the baseline. Furthermore, the high seas are defined residually as 'all parts of the sea that are not included in the exclusive economic zone, in the territorial sea or in the internal waters of a State, or in the archipelagic waters of an archipelagic State' (Article 86 of the LOSC).

25 L. Juda, 'Considerations in Developing a Functional Approach to the Governance of Large Marine Ecosystems' (1999) 30 *ODIL*, pp. 93–4. See also, by the same author, 'Changing Perspectives on the Oceans: Implications for International Fisheries and Oceans Governance', in D.D. Caron and H.N. Scheiber (eds), *Bringing New Law to Ocean Waters* (Leiden, Brill, 2004) p. 20.

26 Scovazzi, above note 2, p. 131. D. Freestone, 'The Conservation of Marine Ecosystems under International Law', in C. Redgwell and M. Bowman (eds), *International Law and the Conservation of Biological Diversity* (The Hague, Kluwer, 1996) pp. 94 and 102; E.A. Kirk, 'Maritime Zones and the Ecosystem Approach: A Mismatch?' (1999) 8 *RECIEL*, pp. 68–9. Limitations of the traditional approach to conservation of marine living resources will be examined in Chapter 2 in some detail.

As the ocean is a dynamic natural system, it is logical that international law of the sea must take the dynamics of nature into account. Nevertheless, the law of the sea based on the zonal management approach has not yet sufficiently considered the fluid and dynamic nature of the ocean as well as the intricate relationship of marine ecosystems and the environments that support them.

Secondly, law of the sea has traditionally adopted a sectoral approach, thereby ignoring interrelationships between marine issues. As reflected in the Preamble of the 1982 LOSC,[27] however, it is important to recognise that the problems pertaining to ocean space are closely interrelated. For instance, protection of the marine environment is essential for the effective management of marine living resources as well as marine biological diversity. Furthermore, regulation of fishing activities is required in order to conserve marine biological diversity. Moreover, safety of navigation and protection of the marine environment, including marine ecosystems, are linked since measures for maritime traffic security usually prevent environmental hazards as well. Thus, it is becoming apparent that there is a need to focus on the interplay between marine issues from holistic viewpoints.

Thirdly, it should be noted that the two traditional principles supporting the zonal management approach are currently in need of reconsideration. With respect to marine living resources, in particular, the freedom of the seas appears to lose its validity. Indeed, as many writers have suggested, the overexploitation and the exhaustion of fisheries are critical problems. Accordingly, it is arguable that the *laissez-faire* system of freedom is no longer valid for the management of living resources in the high seas.[28] In this regard, it should be recalled that, as early as 1974, the ICJ in the *Fisheries Jurisdiction* case has already stated that:

> It is one of the advances in maritime international law, resulting from the intensification of fishing, that the former laissez-faire treatment of the living resources of the sea in the high seas has been replaced by a recognition of a duty to have due regard to the rights of other States and *the need of conservation for the benefit of all.*[29]

---

27 The Preamble states that: 'the problems of ocean space are closely interrelated and need to be considered as a whole.'

28 C. Floit, 'Reconsidering Freedom of the High Seas: Protection of Living Marine Resources on the High Seas', in J.M. Van Dyke, D. Zaelke and G. Hewison (eds), *Freedom for the Seas in the 21st Century: Ocean Governance and Environmental Harmony* (Washington, DC, Covelo, California, Island Press, 1993) p. 310 ff. See also R.P. Anand, 'Changing Concepts of Freedom of the Seas: A Historical Perspective,' in *ibid.*, pp. 72–86; T. Scovazzi, 'La liberté de la mer: vers l'affaiblissement d'un principe vénérable?' (1998) 3 *Annuaire du droit de la mer*, pp. 13–29 (in particular pp. 21–25).

29 Emphasis added. ICJ Reports 1974, p. 31, para. 72 of the judgment between the United Kingdom and Iceland, and at 200, para. 64 of the judgment between the Federal Republic of Germany and Iceland.

Concerning the principle of sovereignty, an attempt to extend a national jurisdiction toward the high seas has not completely ceased.[30] Nevertheless, it appears doubtful that the extension of coastal State jurisdiction could resolve problems relating to marine pollution and the conservation of living resources. Such an extension could produce international disputes threatening the integrity of the 1982 LOSC. The recent disputes between Canada and Spain relating to the arrest of the *Estai* illustrate this problem.[31] Furthermore, it would be difficult in practice for coastal States to enforce their regulations thousands of miles from their coasts.[32] In sum, at least in some respects, it is necessary to review the validity of traditional principles in international law of the sea. It is against this background that a new approach to ocean governance is required.

Quest for an Integrated Management Approach in the Opinions of Writers as well as in International Instruments

Argument by José León Suárez

The problems with the zonal management approach were not unknown. Some writers have already stressed the need for a holistic approach in ocean governance. On this issue, Mr José León Suárez submitted a report on the exploitation of the

---

30 Some States, such as Chile, Argentina and Canada, have attempted to extend their jurisdiction beyond their EEZ. Francisco Orrego Vicuña has argued that future extensions of coastal State authority cannot be ruled out if international arrangements fail. Francisco Orrego Vicuña, 'The International Law of High Seas Fisheries: From Freedom of Fishing to Sustainable Use', in O.S. Stokke (ed.), *Governing High Seas Fisheries: The Interplay of Global and Regional Regimes* (Oxford, Oxford University Press, 2001) p. 45. See also by the same author, *The Changing International Law of High Seas Fisheries* (Cambridge, Cambridge University Press, 1999) pp. 107–18; 'The "Presential Sea": Defining Coastal States' Special Interests in High Seas Fisheries and Other Activities' (1992) 35 *GYIL*, pp. 264–92. Nevertheless, the policy of those States invited many criticisms from academics. See, for instance, Scovazzi, above note 2, pp. 133–7; J.G. Dalton, 'The Chilean Mar Presencial: A Harmless Concept or a Dangerous Precedent?' (1993) 8 *IJMCL*, pp. 397–418; C.C. Joyner and P.N. de Cola, 'Chile's Presential Sea Proposal: Implications for Straddling Stocks and the International Law of Fisheries' (1993) 24 *ODIL*, pp. 99–121; B. Labat, 'Le concept chilien de "Mer presencielle" et ses conséquences sur le régime de la pêche dans la partie de la haute mer adjacente à la limite des 200 milles marins' (1997) 2 *Annuaire du droit de la mer*, pp. 29–52.

31 With respect to this case, see, for instance, Louise de la Fayette, 'The Fisheries Jurisdiction Case (Spain v Canada), Judgment on Jurisdiction of 4 December 1998' (1999) 48 *ICLQ*, pp. 664–72; P.A. Curran and R.J. Long, 'Fishery Law, Unilateral Enforcement in International Waters: the Case of the "Estai"' (1996) 5 *Irish Journal of European Law*, pp. 123–63. See also Chapter 2 of this study.

32 R.R. Churchill, 'Legal Uncertainties in International High Seas Fisheries Management' (1998) 37 *Fisheries Research*, p. 236.

products of the sea before the Experts Committee for the Progressive Codification of International Law in 1927. In this report, Suárez observed that the treaties in relation to certain species had not always taken the point of greatest importance to humanity and the biologico-economic aspect into account.[33] Thus, Suárez stressed the need for a new treaty on the basis of biological characteristics. In his view:

> [A]s, if we consider the life of all the species in the animal kingdom, biological solidarity is even closer among the denizens of the ocean than among land animals, the disappearance of certain species would destroy the balance in the struggle for existence and would bring about the extinction of other species also. […] The majority of aquatic animals are essentially migratory, and it is this characteristic which creates the biologico-geographical solidarity of species, which should find its counterpart in a legal solidarity in the sphere of international law in which we are working.[34]

It is important to note that José León Suárez pointed to the parallelism between 'biologico-geographical solidarity' and 'legal solidarity'. Suárez then suggested that the marine living resources, and whales in particular, should be considered as part of the heritage of mankind. In his words: 'The riches of the sea, and especially the immense wealth of the Antarctic region, are the patrimony of the whole human race.'[35] Thus, Suárez proposed the establishment of a reserved zone in the high seas on the basis of what was known already or may be discovered with regard to the habitat and migration of whales. It is interesting to note that, in 1927, he already presented a similar concept to the common heritage of mankind.[36]

The Concept of 'domaine public international'

Argument by Georges Scelle Even after the establishment of the zonal management approach, some writers did not renounce the quest for a holistic approach. In this respect, one may note with interest that Georges Scelle presented another perspective on the law of the sea, which was totally different from the zonal management approach. Scelle regarded the ocean as a whole as part of the 'domaine public international'.[37] According to Scelle, all organised societies need a

---

33 S. Rosenne (ed.), *League of Nations, Committee of Experts for the Progressive Codification of International Law (1925–1928)*, Vol. 2 (New York, Oceana Publications, 1972) p. 151.

34 *Ibid.*, p. 147.

35 *Ibid.*, p. 149.

36 Scovazzi stated that Mr Suárez could be considered as an antecedent for the concept of the common heritage of mankind. Scovazzi, above note 2, pp. 93 and 118.

37 The *Dictionnaire de la terminologie du Droit international* gives two definitions of the 'domaine public international'. According to the first definition, which was based on Scelle's view, '*domaine public international*' means '*Expression employée par certains auteurs pour désigner un espace qui ne relève de la souveraineté territoriale d'aucun Etat et est ouvert à l'utilisation par les divers membres de la Communauté internationale,*

'domaine public'. With respect to such a 'domaine public',[38] private appropriation shall be limited for common usage or for public services. Thus, certain goods and spaces are to be classified into the rubric of 'domaine public' because of the necessity of the usage for all (that is, 'nécessité sociale'). States have such a 'domaine public'. Similarly, international law could also classify certain goods or spaces into the category of 'domaine public international'. The ocean, including both territorial and high seas, is an example of the 'domaine public international'.[39] In this regard, Scelle stressed the unity of the ocean by saying that:

> It is impossible to find a natural limit between the territorial waters and the high seas and both the territorial waters and the high seas form necessarily part of the '*domaine public international*', since if the access to the territorial seas were not free, no navigation would be possible on the sea. There is no navigation without stops, refuges and supplying, and, consequently, there is no international commerce without the unity of the sea. It remains or should remain obvious that the concept of the territorial sea is a legal *fiction*: at best, a complementary method of using the high seas.[40]

---

selon des règles de droit international'. Yet, as will be seen in the text, Scelle considered that spaces under territorial sovereignty could also be classified into the '*domaine public international*'. In accordance with the second and broad definition, '*Le domaine public international comprend les biens dont l'usage ou la jouissance appartient à tous les peuples tout qui sont affectés à un service public international tels les océans, les mers libres, les palais de la Société des nations, de la Commission européenne du Danube, etc.*' Paul Négulesco took this view. *Dictionnaire de la terminolgie du droit international, publié sous la direction de J. Basdevant* (Paris, Sirey, 1960) p. 220.

38 In France, the term '*domaine public*' is defined, for instance, as '*ceux des biens appartenant à l'Etat ou à une autre collectivité territoriale, qui ne sont pas susceptibles d'appropriation privée en raison de leur nature ou de la destination qui leur est donnée, c'est-à-dire pratiquement tous les biens affectés à l'usage du public ou à un service public*'. Mme S. Cornit (ed.), *Dictionnaire de droit*, Tome I, 2nd edn (Paris, Dalloz, 1966) pp. 600–601. Yet, the concept of '*domaine public international*' in international law relates, in essence, solely to spaces. Although Scelle referred to '*biens*' (goods), his examples concerned only spaces. On this point, '*domaine public*' in French law and '*domaine public international*' in international law should be distinguished.

39 G. Scelle, *Manuel élémentaire de droit international public (avec les Textes essentiels)* (Paris, Les éditions Domat-Montchrestien, 1943) p. 276.

40 Our translation. The original phrase is: '*Il est impossible de trouver une limite naturelle entre les eaux territoriales et la Haute Mer et les unes et les autres font nécessairement partie du domaine public international, car si l'accès de la mer territoriale n'était pas libre, il n'y aurait aucune navigation possible sur la mer elle-même. Il n'y a pas de navigation sans escales, refuges et ravitaillement, ni par conséquent de commerce international, sans unicité de la mer. Mais il reste, ou devrait rester, évident que la notion de mer territoriale est une fiction juridique, mieux: un procédé complémentaire de l'utilisation de la Haute Mer.*' G. Scelle, 'Plateau continental et droit international' (1955) 63 *RGDIP*, p. 52. See also Scelle, above note 39, p. 279.

In Scelle's view, therefore, territorial seas are also part of the '*domaine public international*'. Similarly, Scelle criticised the concept of the continental shelf on the ground that it would be unrealistic to deal separately with the continental shelf and the superjacent waters.[41] In short, it may be said that the focus of Scelle's theory is the unity of the ocean as well as its common usage for all. Needless to say, Scelle knew that the territorial sea was part of the territory of the coastal State in positive international law. Nevertheless, Scelle criticised this rule since it was contrary to the unity of the ocean. Hence Scelle was, as *lex ferenda*, supportive of the theory of servitude presented by de Lapradelle.[42] In Scelle's view, the coastal State exercises its jurisdiction as an organ of the international community in accordance with the '*dédoublement fonctionnel*'.[43]

Experience has shown, however, that Scelle's view has not been supported by State practice. One explanation may be that the exclusive rights to marine natural resources were highly important to the coastal State, and were to become increasingly important. The '*obsession du territoire*' of the coastal State was so strong that his theory could not be supported by many States extending their jurisdiction toward the high seas.

Arguments by Ruzié, Bastid and Nguyen Quoc Dinh   Later, however, the theory of 'domaine public international' was to be advanced by other French writers.[44] In this respect, Ruzié defined the 'domaine public international' as 'a unity of spaces whose utilization concerns the international community as a whole, or at least the population of several States. Whether or not they are subject to territorial sovereignty, their legal regime is governed by particular rules because of the common interest.'[45] As examples of the 'domaine public international',

---

41 Scelle, above note 40 (*RGDIP*), p. 18.

42 Scelle, above note 39, pp. 319–20. For the servitude theory in the territorial sea, see A.G. de Lapradelle, 'Le droit de l'État sur la mer territoriale' (1898) 5 *RGDIP*, pp. 264–84; pp. 309–47.

43 In the context of law of the sea, Scelle often referred to this theory. See above note 39, p. 283, 318, 334, 336. With respect to *dédoublement fonctionnel*, see G. Scelle, 'Le phénomène juridique du dédoublement fonctionnel', in *Rechtsfragen der internationalen Organisation, Festschrift für Hans Wehberg zu seinem Geburtstag* (Frankfurt am Main, Vittorio Klostermann, 1956) pp. 324–42; A. Cassese, 'Remarks on Scelle's Theory of "Role Splitting" (*dédoublement fonctionnel*) in International Law' (1990) 1 *EJIL*, pp. 210–31; M. Nishiumi, 'Dédoublement fonctionnel de l'Etat et droit international contemporain: d'après la pensée de Georges Scelle' (in Japanese) (2001) 20 *Yearbook of World Law*, pp. 77–106.

44 With respect to the analysis of the concept, see T. Kuwahara, 'La notion de domaine public international' (in Japanese) (1987) 97 *The Hitotsubashi Review*, pp. 867–77.

45 Our translation. The original phrase is: '*un ensemble d'espaces dont l'utilisation intéresse la communauté internationale, dans son entier, ou du moins la population de plusieurs Etats. Qu'ils soient soumis, ou non, à une souveraineté territoriale, leur régime juridique est régi par* des règles particulières en raison de cet intérêt commun' (original emphasis). D. Ruzié, *Droit international public*, 7th edn (Paris, Dalloz, 1987) p. 82.

Ruzié enumerated the ocean, river, air space and extra-atmospheric space.[46] It is important to note that Ruzié focused on the common interest in spaces, which characterises the law of 'domaine public international'. According to this theory, all spaces that are used by the international community as a whole are regarded as 'domaine public international', independent of territorial sovereignty.[47] It follows that the ocean as a whole, including internal waters as well as territorial seas, could be regarded as 'domaine public international'. In this sense, this theory is totally different from the traditional zonal management approach. Similarly, in the first edition of his textbook published in 1975, Nguyen Quoc Dinh considered the ocean, international canals, international rivers and air and outer spaces as part of 'domaine public international'.[48] Furthermore, in the lecture series of 1976–77 at the University of Paris, Mme Bastid presented the notion of 'espaces d'intérêt international', which was essentially the same concept as 'domaine public international'. According to Bastid, 'espaces d'intérêt international' are spaces which affect the international community as a whole or which directly concern the people of several States.[49] Thus, Mme Bastid categorised the ocean, international river, air space and outer space as 'espaces d'intérêt international'.[50]

At the same time, it should be stressed that that theory did *not* purport to completely deny the zonal management approach. Differing from Scelle, the three authors Ruzié, Nguyen Quoc Dinh and Bastid clearly recognised that internal waters and territorial seas were subject to the territorial sovereignty of the coastal State.[51] In this respect, Nguyen Quoc Dinh stressed that there were fundamental differences between the regime regarding '*domaine public*' in municipal law and that of '*domaine public international*' in international law. Specifically, the regime in international law protected not only general interests but also exclusive national interests; while, in international order, certain '*domaines*', such as the territorial seas, are used by all States (for innocent passage), they are connected to State

---

46 *Ibid.*

47 For instance, territorial seas are also a part of the '*domaine public international*' since innocent passage is permitted there.

48 Nguyen Quoc Dinh, *Droit international public*, 1st edn (Paris, L.G.D.J., 1975) p. 525. His textbook continues to be revised by P. Daillier and A. Pellet. Although the term '*domaine public internationale*' was not used in the revised editions, it appears that the basic idea of that concept was not totally abandoned. Kuwahara, above note 44, p. 872.

49 Mme P. Bastid, *Cours de droit international public* (*Les Cours de Droit*, Paris, Université de Paris, 1976–1977) p. 1221.

50 *Ibid.*, pp. 1221–8. As with Mme Bastid, writers tend to avoid the term '*domaine public international*', probably because that concept is different from the municipal law concept of '*domaine public*'. Kuwahara, above note 44, pp. 873–4. In addition, one will note with interest that Virally categorised the ocean, air space and outer space into '*les espaces ouverts*'. M. Virally, 'Panorama du droit international contemporain: Cours général de droit international public' (1983-V) 183 *RCADI*, p. 151.

51 Nguyen Quoc Dinh, above note 48, p. 526. See also, Ruzié, above note 45, pp. 96 and 100; Bastid, above note 49, p. 1262.

territory and are subject to the territorial sovereignty of the State; hence, the regime regarding their common use must take the principle of exclusivity of the sovereignty into account. For this reason, Nguyen Quoc Dinh stated that the law of '*domaine public international*' reflected two principal and contradictory considerations.[52] It may be said that the theory of the '*domaine public international*' is characterised by holistic viewpoints reflecting the general interests of common use as well as the protection of national interests, which concerns the zonal management approach. In this sense, it appears that this theory provides in essence a dialectical viewpoint in law of the sea.

Concept of the Common Heritage of Mankind

Another attempt at presenting a holistic approach is the concept of the common heritage of mankind.[53] In law of the sea, the concept of the common heritage of mankind was embodied under Part XI of the LOSC.[54] Article 136 of the LOSC clearly stated that: 'The Area and its resources are the common heritage of mankind.'[55] Article 137 then provides for the non-appropriation of the Area and its resources. Furthermore, Article 140 (1) stipulates that activities in the Area shall be carried out for the benefit of mankind as a whole. Moreover, Article 141 states that the Area shall be open to use exclusively for peaceful purposes by all States. In sum, it could be said that the principle of the common heritage of mankind in the 1982 LOSC is composed of three sub-principles, that is, the non-appropriation of the Area and its resources, the benefit of mankind and the use of the Area exclusively for peaceful purposes. It should be noted that these elements remain intact in the 1994 Agreement relating to the Implementation of Part XI of the LOSC.[56] It is true that, under the 1982 LOSC, the application of the common

---

52 Nguyen Quoc Dinh, above note 48, pp. 525–6.

53 With respect to the concept of the common heritage of mankind, there are a number of articles and it is impossible to enumerate those studies here. For a recent comprehensive study, including bibliography in detail, see K. Baslar, *The Concept of the Common Heritage of Mankind in International Law* (The Hague, Martinus Nijhoff Publishers, 1998).

54 With respect to the legislative history of relevant provisions in the 1982 LOSC, see UNDOALOS, *The Law of the Sea: Concept of the Common Heritage of Mankind, Legislative History of Articles 133 to 150 and 311 (6) of the United Nations Convention on the Law of the Sea* (New York, United Nations, 1996).

55 'Area' means the sea-bed and ocean floor and subsoil thereof, beyond the limits of national jurisdiction (Article 1 (1) of the UN LOSC).

56 In this regard, Article 311 (6) of the LOSC stipulates that: 'States Parties agree that there shall be no amendments to the basic principle relating to the common heritage of mankind set forth in article 136 and that they shall not be party to any agreement in derogation thereof.' Furthermore, the second paragraph of the Preamble of the 1994 Agreement reaffirms that 'the seabed and ocean floor and subsoil thereof, beyond the limits of national jurisdiction [...], as well as their resources of the Area, are the common heritage of mankind'.

heritage of mankind is limited to the Area.[57] Nevertheless, the introduction of that concept in law of the sea was particularly important for three reasons.

First, it may be argued that the term 'mankind' is a trans-spatial and transtemporal concept. It is trans-spatial because 'mankind' includes all people of the planet. At the same time, it is transtemporal because 'mankind' includes both present and future generations.[58] Thus, it may be said that the concept of 'mankind' in itself contains an element for integration.[59]

Secondly, one should note that 'mankind' is not a merely abstract concept. So far as the 1982 LOSC is concerned, 'mankind' has an operational organ, that is, the International Seabed Authority. In this respect, Article 137 (2) provides that: 'All rights in the resources of the Area are vested in mankind as a whole, on whose behalf the Authority shall act.' In accordance with Article 153 (1), activities in the Area shall be organised, carried out and controlled by the Authority on behalf of mankind as a whole. Hence, exploration and exploitation of natural resources in the Area are under the control of the International Seabed Authority on behalf of 'mankind'. To this extent, it may be argued that 'mankind' is appearing as a subject in international law.[60] It should also be noted that the deep seabed regime

---

57 Yet it should not be forgotten that, originally, the 1971 draft Ocean Space Treaty elaborated by Malta prepared for a more holistic system than the existing Part XI of the LOSC. Article 2 of the 1971 draft treaty stressed the unity of the ocean, by saying that: 'the seas and the oceans constitute a single ecological system vital to life and that all States have a common interest in the maintenance of the quality of the marine environment.' The draft treaty then suggested that all natural resources, whether living or non-living, located in the area beyond the 200-mile limit were to be managed by the International Ocean Space Institutions (Articles 66 and 75 of the draft treaty). This draft was reproduced in S. Oda (ed.), *The International Law of the Ocean Development: Basic Documents* (Leiden, Sijthoff, 1972) pp. 149–93. Regarding the analysis of the idea of Ambassador Pardo, see L.B. Sohn, 'Managing the Law of the Sea: Ambassador Pardo's Forgotten Second Idea', in J.I. Charney, D.K. Anton and M.E. O'Connell (eds), *Politics, Values and Functions: International Law in the 21st Century. Essays in Honor of Professor Louis Henkin* (The Hague, Kluwer, 1997) pp. 275–93.

58 R-J. Dupuy, 'La notion de patrimoine commun de l'humanité appliquée aux fonds marins', in R-J. Dupuy, *Dialectiques du droit international: souveraineté des Etats, communauté internationale et droits de l'humanité* (Paris, Pedone, 1999) pp. 189–94. In particular, Kiss stressed the transtemporal dimension of the concept of the common heritage of mankind. A-C. Kiss, 'La notion de patrimoine commun de l'humanité' (1982) 175 *RCADI*, p. 240.

59 R-J. Dupuy stated that 'mankind' is a concept of integration. *Ibid.*, p. 191. With respect to the significance of the emerging concept of 'mankind', see P-M. Dupuy, 'Humanité, communauté et efficacité du droit', in *Humanité et droit international, Mélanges René-Jean Dupuy* (Paris, Pedone, 1991) pp. 133–48.

60 T. Kuwahara, *Introduction to International Law of the Sea* (in Japanese) (Tokyo, Shinzansha, 2002) pp. 214–17. In his General Course at the Hague Academy of International law, Antônio Augusto Cançado Trindade explicitly states that: 'humankind as such has also emerged as a subject of International Law.' A.A.C. Trindade, 'International

purports to promote the benefit of mankind as a whole. Hence it may be said that the regime based on the concept of the common heritage of mankind is a major departure from the traditional law of the sea, balancing the everlasting conflict between the principle of sovereignty and the principle of freedom.[61]

Thirdly, some writers argue that, as *lex ferenda*, the concept of the common heritage of mankind might be applicable to living resources or even the ocean as a whole. For instance, Oda stated that: '[I]n the future, almost without doubt, this concept [of the common heritage of mankind] will also apply to fishery resources or even to protection of the marine environment.'[62] Furthermore, Van Dyke indicated the concept of common heritage of mankind as a principle for a comprehensive regime of ocean governance, by stating that: 'it should be noted that the resources of the high seas are the common heritage of humanity, to be shared equitably.'[63] Baslar also maintained that the status of fish stocks and marine pollution should be considered from the viewpoints of the concept of the common heritage of mankind.[64] Considering that the concept of 'mankind' contains the element for integration, it is arguable that opinions of these writers are also in line with a holistic approach.

The above brief review reveals that several writers have considered the possibility of a holistic approach. Although those arguments were not fully supported in positive international law, it is important to note that the need for a holistic approach has been considered by several writers focusing on the common interests of the international community.

Law for Humankind: Towards a New *Jus Gentium*' (2005) 316 *RCADI*, p. 318. See also J. Combacau, *Le droit international de la mer, Que sais-je?* (Paris, PUF, 1985) p. 88.

61 Scovazzi, above note 2, p. 121. In Japan, Kuwahara was also supportive of that view. T. Kuwahara, *International Law of the Sea* (in Japanese) (Tokyo, Kokusaishoin, 1992) pp. 164–6.

62 S. Oda, 'Sharing of Ocean Resources: Unresolved Issues in the Law of the Sea' (1981) 3 *Journal of International and Comparative Law*, p. 13. See also by the same author, above note 15, p. xxvi. Mann-Borgese is also supportive of this view. E. Mann-Borgese, 'The Common Heritage of Mankind: From Non-Living To Living Resources and Beyond', in N. Ando, E. McWhinney and R. Wolfrum (eds), *Liber Amicorum Judge Shigeru Oda* (The Hague, Kluwer, 2002) p. 1319. However, Hayashi is prudent on this point. He considered that it would be some time before the common heritage concept would replace the principle of freedom of fishing on the high seas, however limited the scope of its application would become. M. Hayashi, 'New Developments in International Fisheries Law and the Freedom of High Seas Fishing' (in Japanese) (2003) 102 *The Journal of International Law and Diplomacy*, pp. 176 and 205.

63 Van Dyke continued that 'recognizing that the ocean is a common heritage can also help in determining how to allocate its limited resources'. J.M. Van Dyke, 'International Governance and Stewardship of the High Seas and Its Resources', in Van Dyke *et al.*, above note 28, p. 19.

64 Baslar, above note 53, pp. 228–42.

Integrated Management Approach in International Instruments

Integrated Management Approach as an Emerging Concept

It is of particular interest that recently, international documents tend to stress the importance of a holistic approach by referring to the concept of 'integrated management approach' or 'integrated ocean management'. For instance, Paragraph 17.1 of Agenda 21 adopted in the United Nations Conference on Environment and Development (UNCED/the Earth Summit) stated that:

> The marine environment – including the oceans and all seas and adjacent coastal areas – forms an integrated whole that is an essential component of the global life -support system and a positive asset that presents opportunities for sustainable development. [...] This requires *new* approaches to marine and coastal area management and development, at the national, subregional, regional and global levels, *approaches that are integrated in content and are precautionary and anticipatory in ambit*, as reflected in the following programme areas.[65]

It is worth noting that Agenda 21 considered that the unity of the ocean would be a starting point for a new approach to international law of the sea.

Furthermore, the UN General Assembly Resolution of 28 November 2001 explicitly used the words 'integrated ocean management'. In that resolution, the General Assembly recommended that, in view of the forthcoming World Summit on Sustainable Development, the Consultative Process should discuss the issues of: 'Capacity-building, regional cooperation and coordination, and *integrated ocean management*, as important cross-cutting issues to address ocean affairs, such as marine science and the transfer of technology, sustainable fisheries, the degradation of the marine environment and the safety of navigation.'[66] Similarly, in 2002, the Report of the Meeting of the UN Informal Consultative Process on Oceans stated that: '*An integrated, interdisciplinary, interzonal and ecosystem-based approach to oceans management*, consistent with the legal framework provided by UNCLOS and the goals of chapter 17 of Agenda 21, is not just desirable, it is essential.'[67] The UN General Assembly Resolution 60/30 adopted

---

65 Emphasis added. Agenda 21 is available at <http://www.un.org/esa/sustdev/documents/agenda21/english/agenda21toc.htm>. With respect to the UNCED, see A-C. Kiss and S. Doumbe-Bille, 'La conférence des Nations Unies sur l'environnement et le développement (Rio de Janeiro, 3–14 Juin 1992)' (1992) 38 *AFDI*, pp. 823–43. See also H. Naeve and S.M. Garcia, 'The United Nations System Responds to Agenda 21.17: Oceans' (1995) 29 *Ocean and Coastal Management*, pp. 23–33.

66 Emphasis added. UN General Assembly Resolution 56/12, *Ocean and the Law of the Sea*, A/RES/56/12, Distr. 13 December 2001, para. 48.

67 Emphasis added. United Nations, *Report on the Work of the United Nations Open-ended Informal Consultative Process Established by the General Assembly in Its Resolution*

in the 56th plenary meeting of 29 November 2005 also concurs with the above approach, by stating that they were:

> *Conscious* that the problems of ocean space are closely interrelated and need to be considered as a whole through an *integrated*, interdisciplinary and intersectoral approach, and reaffirming the need to improve cooperation and coordination at national, regional and global levels, in accordance with the Convention, to support and supplement the efforts of each State in promoting the implementation and observance of the Convention, and the *integrated management* and sustainable development of the oceans and seas.[68]

The need for an integrated management approach is also stressed at the regional level. For instance, on 20 December 2002, the UN General Assembly adopted Resolution 57/261, entitled 'Promoting an Integrated Management Approach to the Caribbean Sea Area in the Context of Sustainable Development'.[69] Owing to the unique biodiversity and highly fragile ecosystem of the Caribbean Sea, this resolution recognised 'the importance of adopting *an integrated management approach* to the Caribbean Sea area in the context of sustainable development' and encouraged the further promotion of that approach.[70]

Integrated Management Approach at Three Levels

It is worth noting that the above documents repeatedly emphasised the need for 'integrated ocean management' or 'an integrated management approach'. The emergence of the concept of the 'integrated management approach' is of particular importance in the sense that it may lead to a new perspective relating to the law, that is to say, *the law of the sea as a dual legal system between the zonal and the integrated management approaches.* Considering that the law of the sea has been essentially based on the zonal management approach, these dialectical viewpoints may involve a structural change in the law. The problem is, however, that the concept of the 'integrated management approach' remains obscure in international law. Indeed, it appears that international instruments tend to use the term loosely. In order to clarify the concept, it is necessary to consider what elements should be 'integrated' under this approach.

Although there is no clear definition of the integrated management approach in law, it is obvious at least that the principal purpose of the integrated management

---

54/33 in Order to Facilitate the Annual Review by the Assembly of Developments in Ocean Affairs at Its Third Meeting, A/57/80, 2 July 2002, p. 4, para. 4.

68 Emphasis added. UN General Assembly, *Oceans and the Law of the Sea*, A/RES/60/30, Distr. 8 March 2006, Preamble. A similar view is also expressed in UN General Assembly, *Oceans and the Law of the Sea*, A/RES/57/141, 21 February 2003, Preamble.

69 A/RES/57/261, 27 February 2003.

70 *Ibid.*, p. 4, paras 2–4.

approach is to overcome the problems which cannot be easily solved under the traditional law of the sea.[71] In so doing, it is conceivable that a certain degree of integration should be required in at least three levels: ecological, normative and implementation levels. These three levels of integration are interlinked.

First, the integrated management approach is particularly at issue in the conservation of marine living resources and biological diversity. It is becoming apparent that the intricate relationship of marine ecosystems and the environments that support them are important elements in establishing an effective ocean management regarding marine living resources as well as marine biological diversity. Thus, the integrated management approach focusing on ecological interaction is required. In this respect, it would seem that the ecosystem approach is of central importance.[72] While the term 'ecosystem approach' has been variously defined in different settings, the Biodiversity Committee of the Convention for the Protection of the Marine Environment of the North-East Atlantic (hereafter the OSPAR Convention) of 1992 defined this approach as:

> the comprehensive integrated management of human activities based on the best available scientific knowledge about the ecosystem and its dynamics, in order to identify and take action on influences which are critical to the health of marine ecosystems, thereby achieving sustainable use of ecosystem goods and services and maintenance of ecosystem integrity.[73]

---

71 It is interesting to note that there is a similar notion of 'integrated coastal zone management (ICZM)'. This concept concerns the coastal area, including the interface of the land and sea, under national jurisdiction, although its spatial scope is obscure. On the other hand, the integrated management approach discussed in this study relates to the use of *the ocean as a whole* in international law. Hence, the exercise of the integrated management approach concerns all members of the international community, including both coastal and non-coastal States as well as international organisations. In this sense, the integrated management approach addressed in this study should be distinguished from the concept of ICZM. With respect to the concept of ICZM, see in particular B. Cicin-Sain and R.W. Knecht, *Integrated Coastal and Ocean Management: Concepts and Practices* (Washington, D.C., Island Press, 1998); R. Beckman and B. Coleman, 'Integrated Coastal Management: The Role of Law and Lawyers' (1999) 14 *IJMCL*, pp. 491–522.

72 The need for an ecosystem approach is often stressed by writers, particularly in the context of the management of marine living resources. See, for instance, E.J. Molenaar, 'Ecosystem-Based Fisheries Management, Commercial Fisheries, Marine Mammals and the 2001 Reykjavik Declaration in the Context of International Law' (2002) 17 *IJMCL*, pp. 561–95; L. Juda, 'Rio Plus Ten: The Evolution of International Marine Fisheries Governance' (2002) 33 *ODIL*, pp. 109–44 (in particular, pp. 131–2).

73 Meeting of the Biodiversity Committee (BDC), Dublin, 20–24 January 2003, Summary Record BDC 2003, BDC 03/10/1-E, Annex 13, p. 1. Furthermore, the Report of the UN Secretary-General defines a marine ecosystem as: 'the sum total of marine organisms living in a particular sea area, the interactions between those organisms and the physical environment in which they interact. A vulnerable marine ecosystem could be defined as one that is particularly susceptible to disruption, to damage or even to destruction

In accordance with this definition, the ecosystem approach focuses on biological interactions between all marine species in the same, as well as in neighbouring, zones, and the ecological conditions of the physical surroundings.[74] In other words, the conservation of ecosystem structure and functioning as a whole constitutes a priority purpose of the ecosystem approach.[75] In this respect, the Report of the UN Secretary-General stated that:

> The distinguishing feature of the ecosystem approach is that it is *integrated and holistic*, taking account of all the components of an ecosystem, both physical and biological, of their interaction and of all activities that could affect them. All human activities that could affect the oceans should be managed in a *comprehensive and integrated manner*, on the basis of a scientific assessment of the state of the ecosystem, the interaction of its components and the pressures upon it.[76]

Thus, as will be seen, it is arguable that the ecosystem approach will be at the heart of the integrated management approach at the ecological level.[77]

Secondly, the integrated management approach is also becoming important at the normative level. In this respect, one should note that the problems of ocean space are closely interrelated and need to be considered as a whole.[78] Thus, focus should be on the interrelationship between marine issues. Indeed, the words in Chapter 17 of Agenda 21, 'approaches that are integrated in content', appear to suggest that the integrated management approach is cross-sectoral in nature. It may be said that the interdisciplinary approach focusing on the interaction between ocean questions is at the heart of this approach.[79] In this regard, it is welcome that a dynamic treaty network is currently becoming established with respect to a variety of marine affairs. On the other hand, it is undeniable that the growing numbers of treaties may run the risk of producing overlaps or conflicts of relevant rules,

---

due to its physical characteristics, the activities and interactions of the organisms therein and the impacts they suffer from human activities and the surrounding environment.' United Nations, *Report of the Secretary-General, Oceans and the Law of the Sea*, A/58/65, 3 March 2003, p. 53, para. 172.

74 N. Matz, 'The Interaction Between the Convention on Biological Diversity and the UN Convention on the Law of the Sea', in P. Ehlers, E. Mann-Borgese and R. Wolfrum (eds), *Marine Issues: From a Scientific, Political and Legal Perspective* (The Hague, Kluwer, 2002) p. 208.

75 The Conference of the Parties, Decision V/6. *Ecosystem Approach*, UNEP/CBD/COP/5/23, 15–16 May 2000, p. 106.

76 Emphasis added. United Nations, *Report of the Secretary-General, Ocean and the Law of the Sea*, A/61/63, 9 March 2006, p. 38, para. 136.

77 The ecosystem approach will be addressed in Chapter 3 of this study.

78 Preamble of the 1982 LOSC.

79 In fact, Juda clearly stated that: 'The identification of existing and projected uses and contemplation of their interactions and compatibility are key components of "integrated" management.' Above note 3, p. 286.

owing to the close interrelationship between marine issues.[80] Hence, the focus on the interplay between marine issues inevitably produces the question how it is possible to avoid duplication or conflicts between relevant rules. It follows that the integrated management approach is also required with a view to harmonising relevant rules concerning ocean governance. In this respect, coordination of relevant rules of treaties through the Conference of the Parties (COP) as well as the establishment of inter-treaty linkage through COP will become particularly important.[81]

Thirdly, it is necessary to consider the question of how it is possible to implement relevant rules in an integrated manner.[82] This question relates to the integrated management approach at the implementation level. It is true that, as with other domains of international law, there is no central organisation for implementing relevant rules concerning ocean affairs. In this sense, it is an inevitable conclusion that international law of the sea remains in essence a decentralised system. Even so, it is worth noting that some mechanisms concerning the implementation of the law are developing. It is of particular interest that international supervision through international institutions and non-flag States' enforcement are increasingly important in order to secure the compliance with treaties in this field.[83] It is also notable that the functions of international organisations are expanding in a variety of domains in international law, and the law of the sea is no exception. This point is illustrated by the fact that specialised UN agencies, such as IMO,[84]

---

80 With respect to the examination of possible conflicts between relevant rules, see in particular R. Wolfrum and N. Matz, *Conflicts in International Environmental Law* (Berlin, Springer, 2003). In particular, the normative relationship between the Rio Convention and the 1982 UN Convention on the Law of the Sea has been discussed in some studies. See, for instance, M. Chandler, 'The Biodiversity Convention: Selected Issues of Interest to the International Lawyer' (1993) 4 *Colorado Journal of International Environmental Law and Policy*, pp. 141–75 (in particular, pp. 152–3); R. Wolfrum and N. Matz, 'The Interplay of the United Nations Convention on the Law of the Sea and the Convention on Biological Diversity' (2000) 4 *Max Planck Yearbook of United Nations Law*, pp. 445–80; Matz, above note 74, pp. 203–20.

81 See Chapter 4 of this study.

82 'Implementation' is a word with more than one meaning. Churchill indicated four meanings of this word. R. Churchill, 'Levels of Implementation of the Law of the Sea Convention: An Overview', in D. Vidas and W. Østreng (eds), *Order for the Oceans at the Turn of the Century* (The Hague, Kluwer, 1999) p. 317. In the narrow sense, the word means the putting into effect by States of their rights and obligations under a treaty. *Ibid.* In this study, however, the word is used in a broad sense, that is, the adoption of relevant rules, standards and guidelines as well as furthering the aims and rules of a treaty by means of subsequent action.

83 This issue will be addressed in Chapter 3.

84 With respect to IMO, see M.H. Nordquist and J.N. Moore (eds), *Current Maritime Issues and the International Maritime Organization* (The Hague, Nijhoff, 1999).

FAO,[85] UNESCO/IOC, together with UNEP, are playing an important role in ocean management. It should also be noted that there are a number of regional organisations relating, in particular, to fisheries.[86] For the purpose of this study, the integrated management approach can be understood as an approach comprising these three levels of integration.

Dual Approach to Ocean Governance in International Law of the Sea

In light of the above consideration, as a theoretical framework for analysis, one may point to two basic approaches to ocean governance in international law: the zonal and integrated management approaches.[87] These approaches show clear contrasts in at least four respects.[88]

First, with respect to the basic presumption, the zonal management approach reflects the confirmation of the sovereign State system arguably derived from the Peace of Westphalia.[89] On the other hand, due to its nature, the integrated management approach presupposes the 'international community' based on common interests.[90] Without the awareness of common interests of the 'international

---

85 Regarding the activities of FAO on law of the sea, see M.H. Nordquist and J.N. Moore (eds), *Current Fisheries Issues and the Food and Agriculture Organization of the United Nations* (The Hague, Nijhoff, 2000).

86 Regarding the role of regional organisations in general, see B. Kwiatkowska, 'The Role of Regional Organizations in Development Cooperation in Marine Affairs', in A.H.A. Soons, *Implementation of the Law of the Sea Convention Through International Institutions, Proceedings of the 23rd Annual Conference of the Law of the Sea Institute*, 12–15 June 1989 (Honolulu, University of Hawaii, 1990) pp. 38–138. With respect to regional fishery organisations, see R. Barston, 'The Law of the Sea and Regional Fisheries Organisations' (1999) 14 *IJMCL*, pp. 333–52; R. Wolfrum, 'Fishery Commissions', in R. Bernhardt (ed.), 11 *Encyclopedia of Public International Law* (Amsterdam, Elsevier, 1989) pp. 117–21; Juda, above note 72, pp. 123–8.

87 This does not mean that the integrated management approach is already well established in positive international law. At this stage, the integrated management approach is a concept which constitutes a framework for analysis in this study.

88 Tanaka, above note 1, pp. 512–14.

89 With respect to the Peace of Westphalia, see L. Gross, 'The Peace of Westphalia 1648–1948' (1948) 42 *AJIL*, pp. 20–41.

90 With respect to the concept of international community, see in particular, 'Communauté internationale', in R-J. Dupuy, *Dialectiques du droit international; souveraineté des Etats, communauté internationale et droit de l'humanité* (Paris, Pedone, 1999) pp. 309–14; B. Simma and A.L. Paulus, 'The "International Community": Facing the Challenge of Globalization' (1998) 9 *EJIL*, pp. 266–77; C. Tomuschat, 'Obligations Arising for States Without or Against Their Will' (1993) 241 *RCADI*, pp. 209–40; P-M. Dupuy, 'L'unité de l'ordre juridique international: Cours général de droit international public (2000)' (2002) 297 *RCADI*, pp. 24568.

community',[91] the integrated management approach will not function. In relation to this, it is important to note that the reference to the 'international community' is increasingly seen in international decisions, treaties and UN Resolutions. With respect to international decisions, it is common knowledge that the ICJ in the *Barcelona Traction* case characterised obligations *erga omnes* as the obligations of a State towards 'the international community as a whole'.[92] Ten years later, the Court in the *United States Hostages in Tehran* case again referred to its duty to draw the attention of the 'entire international community'.[93] At the treaty level, Article 53 of the 1969 Vienna Convention on the Law of Treaties refers to the 'international community' in conjunction with *jus cogens*.[94] Furthermore, Article 6 of the 1972 Convention for the Protection of the World Cultural and Natural Heritage recognises the duty of the 'international community as a whole' to co-operate in the protection of a world heritage.[95] The 1988 International Convention for the Suppression of Unlawful Acts Against the Safety of Maritime Navigation states that the occurrence of unlawful acts against the safety of maritime navigation is a matter of grave concern to 'the international community as a whole'.[96] And again, the 1998 Rome Statute of the International Criminal Court provides jurisdiction concerning 'the most serious crimes of concern to the international community as a whole'.[97] It is notable that unlike Article 53 of the Vienna Convention on the Law

---

91 In this respect, Antônio Augusto Cançado Trindade clearly states that: 'The growing consciousness of the need to bear in mind common values in pursuance of common interests has brought about a fundamental change in the outlook of International Law in the last decade.' Above note 60, p. 35. See also V. Gowlland-Debbas, 'Judicial Insights into Fundamental Values and Interests of the International Community', in A.S. Muller, D. Raič and J.M. Thuránszky (eds), *The International Court of Justice: Its Future Role after Fifty Years* (The Hague, Nijhoff, 1997) pp. 327–66.

92 ICJ Reports 1970, p. 32, para. 33.

93 ICJ Reports 1980, p. 43, para. 92. See also P-M. Dupuy, above note 90, pp. 251–2.

94 'A treaty is void, if at the time of its conclusion, it conflicts with a peremptory norm of general international law. For the purposes of the present Convention, a peremptory norm of general international law is a norm accepted and recognized by the international community of States as a whole as a norm from which no derogation is permitted and which can be modified only by a subsequent norm of general international law having the same character.' In this respect, Tomuschat argues that the concept of *jus cogens* 'denotes an overarching system which embodies a common interest of all States and, indirectly, of mankind.' Tomuschat, above note 90, p. 227.

95 In addition, the Preamble of the Convention states that: 'it is incumbent on the international community as a whole to participate in the protection of the cultural and natural heritage of outstanding universal value.' For the text of the Convention, see P.W. Birnie and A. Boyle (eds), *Basic Documents on International Law and the Environment* (Oxford, Oxford University Press, 1995) pp. 375–89.

96 For the text of the Convention, see E.D. Brown, *The International Law of the Sea*, Vol. II (Aldershot, Dartmouth, 1994) pp. 203–11.

97 For the text of the Statute, see M.D. Evans (ed.), *Blackstone's International Law Documents*, 6th edn (Oxford, Oxford University Press, 2003) pp. 463–515.

of Treaties, no mention was made with respect to 'States'.[98] Arguably this point implies that the concept of 'the international community as a whole' is no longer limited to the community of States. The concept of the 'international community' can also be detected in various UN General Assembly Resolutions.[99] In the context of the law of the sea, for instance, the UN General Assembly Resolution 44/225 on Large-Scale Pelagic Driftnet Fishing calls upon 'all members of the international community' to strengthen their co-operation in the conservation and management of living marine resources.[100] Overall it is becoming apparent that the concept of the international community is currently enshrined in positive international law.[101] It would appear that increasing attention to the integrated management approach to ocean governance should be considered in conjunction with the growing awareness of common interests of the international community as a whole.[102]

Secondly, regarding the task assigned to each approach, the zonal management approach purports in essence to *divide* the ocean into several jurisdictional spaces balancing the principle of sovereignty and the principle of freedom. In the international society, one of the principal functions of international law concerned the spatial distribution of States' jurisdiction.[103] Hence it is not surprising that

---

98 P-M. Dupuy, above note 90, p. 255. In this respect, Trindade argues that 'the conception of international community encompasses today all subjects of international law – States, international organizations, individuals, and humankind'. Above note 60, p. 219.

99 Tomuschat, above note 90, pp. 228–30; P-M. Dupuy, above note 90, pp. 252–4.

100 The formal title is: General Assembly Resolution 44/225 of 22 December 1989 on Large-Scale Pelagic Driftnet Fishing and Its Impact on the Living Marine Resources on the World's Oceans and Seas. For the text, see Brown, above note 96, pp. 241–3.

101 P-M. Dupuy, above note 90, pp. 257–8. In relation to this, Simma stated that: 'a rising awareness of the common interests of the international community, a community that comprises not only States, but in the last instance all human beings, has begun to change the nature of international law profoundly.' B. Simma, 'From Bilateralism to Community Interest in International Law' (1994) 250 *RCADI*, p. 234. Such awareness can also be detected in international law of the sea. See José Antonio Pastor Ridruejo, 'Le droit international à la veille du vingt et unième siècle: Normes, faits et valeurs: Cours général de droit international public' (1998) 274 *RCADI*, p. 254.

102 On the other hand, the concept of common interests of the international community is an issue which needs further clarification. In this respect, Simma argues that the identification of common interests does not derive from scientific abstraction but rather flows from the recognition of concrete problems. In his view, examples of common interests include: international peace and security, solidarity between developed and developing countries, protection of the environment, the common heritage of mankind and the protection of human rights. Simma, above note 101, pp. 235–43. It would appear that conservation of marine living resources as well as marine biological diversity may be added to the list of common interests of the international community.

103 G. Scelle, 'Obsession du territoire', *Symbolae Verzijl* (The Hague, Nijhoff, 1958) p. 349. See also J.L. Brierly, *The Outlook for International Law* (Oxford, Clarendon Press, 1944) p. 9; C. Tomuschat, 'International Law: Ensuring the Survival of Mankind on the Eve of A New Century' (1999) 281 *RCADI*, p. 57.

traditional law of the sea on the basis of the zonal management approach has also focused mainly on the spatial distribution of States' jurisdiction by dividing the ocean into several sectors. It may be said that traditional law of the sea based on the zonal management approach is a typical example of the international law of co-existence.[104] By contrast, the integrated management approach purports to create a scheme for the common usage of the ocean focusing on common interests of the international community. In so doing, the integrated management approach aims to bring members of the international community actively together with a view to enhancing international co-operation. In this sense, it appears that the integrated management approach reflects the international law of co-operation.

Thirdly, the zonal management approach is essentially spatial in nature, in the sense that the ocean is divided on the basis of distance from the coast. By relying on the objective criterion of distance, the law of the sea based on the zonal management approach succeeded in distributing the State's jurisdiction in the ocean. On the other hand, the integrated management approach focuses on the unity of marine ecosystems. Thus, it may be said that this is an ecology-oriented approach.

Fourthly, with respect to the implementation of rules governing marine issues, the traditional law of the sea was essentially self-regulation on the basis of reciprocity.[105] Under the zonal management approach, the implementation of relevant rules remains non-institutional. As the main purpose of the zonal management approach is to separate State jurisdiction, it is not surprising that the traditional approach did not develop the institutional mechanisms of the law of the sea. However, the integrated management approach is in essence institutional. Considering that international co-operation is essential to advance the integrated management approach, institutionalised mechanisms for ensuring such co-operation, such as an international supervision through international institutions, become particularly important.

---

104 G. Abi-Saab, 'Cours général de droit international public' (1987) 207 *RCADI*, p. 320. In this regard, it is well known that Friedmann pointed to the expansion of international law from international law of co-existence and international law of co-operation. The latter is further categorized into the international law of co-operation at universal level and one at regional level. Regarding this formula, W. Friedmann, *The Changing Structure of International Law* (London, Stevens and Sons, 1964) pp. 60–71; by the same author, 'General Course in Public International Law' (1969) 127 *RCADI*, pp. 91–109. With respect to Friedmann's thought, see, in particular, G. Abi-Saab, 'Whither the International Community?' (1998) 9 *EJIL*, pp. 250–54; K. Obata, '"Stratification of International Law" as the Construction of a World Public Sphere: The Legal Project of Wolfgang Friedmann in His Later Period' (in Japanese) (2001) 20 *Yearbook of World Law*, pp. 151–76.

105 With respect to reciprocity in international law, see B. Simma, 'Reciprocity', in R. Bernhardt (ed.), *Encyclopedia of Public International Law*, Vol. 4 (Amsterdam, North-Holland Elsevier, 2000) pp. 29–33; M. Virally, 'Le principe de réciprocité dans le droit international contemporain' (1967-III) 122 *RCADI*, pp. 5–105.

The principal thesis of this study is that the contemporary law of the sea should be considered as a dual legal system between the zonal and integrated management approaches. On the one hand, there is no doubt that law of the sea is dominated by the zonal management approach. Considering that the world is divided into sovereign States, the main role of the zonal management approach – spatial distribution of national jurisdiction – will in no way lose its importance. On the other hand, as will be seen, it is becoming apparent that the zonal management approach is insufficient for ocean management in some respects, and, thus, the new integrated management approach is needed in international law of the sea. Hence, two different approaches must coexist in international law of the sea *at the same time*.[106] Indeed, the purpose of the integrated management approach is *not* to replace the zonal management approach, but to resolve the problems that cannot be resolved under the zonal management approach.

Plan of This Study

Against that background, this study seeks to address the dual approach to ocean governance in international law. It would seem that among various marine issues, interaction between the zonal and the integrated management approaches may be most vividly at issue with respect to conservation of marine living resources as well as marine biological diversity. Accordingly, the focus of this study will be mainly on the interaction between the two approaches in this field. Currently there are relatively many treaties addressing conservation of marine species as well as marine biological diversity at the global and regional levels. Owing to the limited space, however, it is beyond the scope of this study to examine each and every regional treaty on this subject. Hence, concerning regional practice, we will take the North-East Atlantic as an example.[107] As will be seen, State practice in this region provides an interesting insight into this issue. In accordance with Article 1 of the 1992 OSPAR Convention, the geographical scope of the North-East Atlantic comprises five sub-regions: the (Greater) North Sea, Arctic Waters, the Celtic Seas, the Bay of Biscay and Iberian Coast, and the Wider Atlantic. The

---

106 It is interesting to note that R-J. Dupuy considered international law in general as a dialectical legal system between the relational order ('*l'ordre relationnel*') and the institutional order ('*l'ordre institutionnel*'). In his view, an important point is that the institutional order does *not* take the place of the relational order and, thus, the two types of order coexist in international law. It appears that the dialectic approach may also be useful in the context of the law of the sea. R-J. Dupuy, 'Communauté internationale et disparités de développement: Cours général de droit international public' (1979) 165 *RCADI*, pp. 9–232 (in particular, pp. 39–44, 46). With respect to the dialectical approach to international law in general, see, by the same author, *Le droit international public, (Que sais-je?)* 11th edn (Paris, PUF, 2001).

107 This region was selected for the purposes of the research project carried out under the Programme for Research in Third Level Institutions in the Republic of Ireland.

Baltic Sea and the Mediterranean Sea are not included.[108] With respect to the geographical scope of the North-East Atlantic, we will follow the definition of the OSPAR Convention.

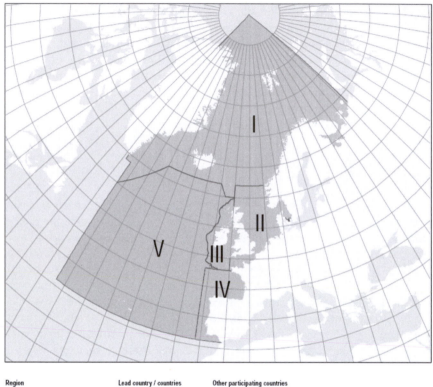

Region	Lead country / countries	Other participating countries
I – Arctic Waters	Norway	Denmark (including Faroe Islands) and Iceland
II – Greater North Sea	Netherlands	Belgium, Denmark, France, Germany, Norway, Sweden and UK
III – Celtic Seas	Ireland and UK	
IV – Bay of Biscay and Iberian Coast	France and Spain	Portugal
V – Wider Atlantic	Iceland and Portugal	Belgium, Denmark, France, Germany, Ireland, Netherlands, Norway, Spain, Sweden and UK

Figure 1.1   The OSPAR Maritime Area

Source: OSPAR Commission, *Quality Status Report 2000* (London, OSPAR Commission, 2000) p. 2.

---

108 See Figure 1.1.

This study is composed of three parts. Part One consists of two chapters that will address the dual approach to the conservation of marine living resources. Chapter 2 will examine essential features of the traditional zonal management approach as well as its limits. Chapter 3 will consider whether and to what degree elements for the integrated management approach exist in contemporary international law relating to the conservation of marine living resources. Part Two will be devoted to analysing the conservation of marine biological diversity. Chapter 4 will examine the global legal frameworks in this field as well as regional State practice in the North-East Atlantic. Further to this, Chapter 5 will examine marine protected areas as a possible tool for the integrated management approach to the conservation of marine biological diversity. Part Three will consider marine scientific research as a basis for ocean governance. To this end, Chapter 6 will address the obligation to co-operate in marine scientific research in international law. Finally, the general conclusion will be presented in Chapter 7.

PART I
The Dual Approach to Conservation of Marine Living Sources

Chapter 2

Limits of the Zonal Management Approach to Conservation of Marine Living Resources

Introduction

Nature of the Problem

In 2005, the FAO published a document reviewing the state of the world marine fishery resources. According to the FAO, of the 441 stock or species group where assessment information was available, an estimated 52 per cent of the world stocks were fully exploited, and, thus, they were already at or very close to their maximum sustainable production limits, with no room for further expansion. Approximately 17 per cent were currently over-exploited, 7 per cent depleted and 1 per cent recovering, all of which offer no room for further exploitation. Only 3 per cent are currently under-exploited and 20 per cent are moderately exploited. The FAO also suggested that the stocks of seven of the top ten species that account for 30 per cent of the world total marine capture fisheries production were either fully exploited or over-exploited; and that no sustainable increases in catches could be expected from these species.[1] The situation is even worse in some regions. In the North-East Atlantic as well as the Western Indian Ocean, for instance, 100 per cent of stocks were already fully exploited or over-exploited.[2] According to the Report of the UN Secretary-General of 2004, many scientists considered that if current levels of exploitation were maintained, not only would the commercial extinction of fish stocks soon become a reality, but the long-term biological sustainability of many fish stocks would also be threatened.[3] Thus, the UN General Assembly Resolution 58/240 reiterated '*its deep concern* at the situation of many of the world's fisheries'.[4] As marine living resources are an important source of protein

---

1 FAO Fisheries Department, *Review of the State of World Marine Fishery Resources*, FAO Fisheries Technical Paper 457 (Rome, FAO, 2005) p. 6.

2 *Ibid.*, p. 11. State of fishery resources by region is displayed in Figure A.2.2. of the FAO's Review, p. 10.

3 United Nations, *Report of the Secretary-General, Oceans and the Law of the Sea*, A/59/62, 4 March 2004, p. 53, para. 206.

4 Emphasis original. UN General Assembly Resolution 58/240. *Oceans and the Law of the Sea*, A/RES/58/240, 5 March 2004, para. 12 of the Preamble.

in a situation of food shortage at the global level, there is a great need to pursue conservation policies in order to prevent depletion of these resources.[5]

It must also be noted that destructive fishing practices significantly damage marine biological diversity at the three levels. At the genetic level, fisheries change population characteristics, such as age distribution, reproduction, stocks structure, which result in alterations to the genome. At the species level, fishing activities affect species composition and interactions by selectively removing target species, by-catch of unwanted species, physical disturbance and discards. At the ecosystem level, fishing impacts the diversity of marine habitats and ecosystem function. In fact, certain fishing gears, such as trawling, may physically alter and in some cases destroy habitats within the marine environment.[6] Thus, attention should be drawn to the relation between fishing and marine biological diversity.

Against this background, Part One will address the zonal and integrated management approaches to conservation of marine living resources. To this end, it will be appropriate to commence our study with an examination of essential issues concerning the traditional zonal management approach in Chapter 2. This chapter is composed of four sections. After briefly examining the concept of conservation in the first section, the second section will review the *Bering Sea Fur-Seals* arbitration, since fundamental questions associated with the zonal management approach may be identified in this award. The third section will address limitations of this approach in the global legal frameworks in this field, that is to say, the 1958 Geneva Convention on Fishing and the Conservation of Living Resources of the High Seas, as well as the 1982 UN Convention on the Law of the Sea (Hereafter the LOSC). Finally, conclusions will be presented in the fourth section.

The Concept of Conservation

As a preliminary consideration, it will be appropriate to examine the concept of conservation in international law. Article 2 of the 1958 Geneva Convention on Fishing and Conservation of the Living Resources of the High Seas (hereafter the High Seas Fishing Convention) defines conservation as: 'the aggregate of the measures rendering possible the optimum sustainable yield from those resources so as to secure a maximum supply of food and other marine products.' Article

---

5 According to FAO, overall fish provided more than 2.6 billion people with at least 20 per cent of their average per capita animal protein intake. FAO, *The State of World Fisheries and Aquaculture* (Rome, FAO, 2004) p. 3. See also C.A. Fleischer, 'Fisheries and Biological Resources', in R-J. Dupuy and D. Vignes (eds), *A Handbook on the New Law of the Sea*, Vol. 2 (Dordrecht, Nijhoff, 1991) p. 992.

6 G.W. Boehlert, 'Biodiversity and the Sustainability of Marine Fisheries' (1996) 9 *Oceanography*, pp. 28 and 32; A. Rieser, 'International Fisheries Law, Overfishing and Marine Biodiversity' (1997) 9 *The Georgetown International Environmental Law Review*, p. 254; G. Rose, 'Marine Biodiversity Protection through Fisheries Management: International Legal Developments' (1999) 8 *RECIEL*, p. 284.

2 further provides that: 'Conservation programmes should be formulated with a view to securing in the first place a supply of food for human consumption.' This definition clearly shows that conservation is an anthropological concept; and that it does not directly mean a moratorium or prohibition of exploitation of marine living resources.[7] In this regard, for example, the 1980 Convention on the Conservation of Antarctic Marine Living Resources explicitly states that 'the term "conservation" includes rational use'.[8] Similarly, the 1982 LOSC requires the coastal State to promote the objective of optimum utilisation of the living resources in the EEZ and to conserve those resources at the same time.[9] With respect to the concept of conservation, three points should be noted.

A first point concerns repercussions of economic, political and social elements in determining conservation measures. In this respect, Article 2 of the High Seas Fishing Convention makes it clear that '[c]onservation programmes should be formulated with a view to securing in the first place a supply of food for human consumption'. It is conceivable that the 'supply of food for human consumption' will be determined on the basis of economic and social needs. It would seem that in certain circumstances, economic needs for controlling the market and price will also require various fishing regulations. In reality, it appears difficult to distinguish regulations of fishing only for conservation purposes based on scientific data from the controls governing marked possibilities of the specific State.[10] Hence, it must be pointed out that conservation is not a purely scientific or biological concept, but is qualified by economic, political and social elements.

A second point pertains to the close interrelationship between conservation and allocation. It has been argued that allocation of finite amounts of marine living resources has been the question at the heart of the international law governing fisheries. On this point, Oda argued that:

> The most important question to be solved at present is not concerned with the desirability or possibility of conservation measures, but rather with the distribution of resources among nation-states. In other words, we are confronted with the questions: how can marine resources, the exploitation of which must be limited with a view to conservation, be shared among states which naturally want to maximize their own portion?[11]

---

7 D. Vignes, 'La formation historique du droit international de la pêche', in D. Vignes, G. Cataldi and R.C. Raigón (eds), *Le droit international de la pêche maritime* (Bruxelles, Bruylant, 2000) p. 34.

8 Article II (2).

9 Article 63 (1) and Article 61.

10 S. Oda, 'The 1958 Geneva Convention on Fishing and Conservation of the Living Resources of the High Seas: Its Immaturities' (1960) 55 *Die Friedens-Warte*. Reproduced in S. Oda, *Fifty Years of the Law of the Sea* (The Hague, Kluwer, 2003) p. 143.

11 S. Oda, 'New Trends in the Regime of the Seas: A Consideration of the Problems of Conservation and Distribution of Marine Resources II' (1957–58) 18 *ZaöRV*, p. 285.

In light of limited amounts of marine living resources, there is little doubt that allocation of those resources is a central question underlying international law in this field. Given that approximately 77 per cent of the world fish stocks have already been fully exploited or over-exploited, however, there seems to be a general sense that proper conservation of marine living resources is a prerequisite for the equitable distribution of those resources. Thus, it has to be stressed that the conservation and equitable allocation of finite amounts of marine living resources are intimately intertwined.[12]

Thirdly, it should be noted that conservation of marine species may often be characterised by national interest. It seems probable that States introduce conservation measures with a view to safeguarding the national fishing industry.[13] An example may be furnished by the 1945 Truman Proclamation with respect to coastal fisheries in certain areas of the high seas. The Truman Proclamation stated that '[i]n view of the pressing need for conservation and protection of fishery resources', the United States would establish conservation zones in which fishing activities shall be subject to its regulation and control.[14] Nonetheless, the factual situation suggested that the need to alleviate future threats and to respond to the political demands of American salmon interests led the United States to issue the Truman Proclamation.[15] There appeared to be little doubt that the real purpose of the Truman Proclamation was to control offshore living resources by excluding foreign fishing vessels.[16] Similarly, in the 1952 Santiago Declaration, three Andean States, Chile, Ecuador and Peru, stressed the need to preserve for and make available to their respective peoples the natural resources in the sea adjacent to their coasts. In the words of the Declaration:

1. Governments are bound to ensure for their people access to necessary food supplies and to furnish them with the means of developing their economy.

---

12 L. Juda, *International Law and Ocean Use Management: The Evolution of Ocean Governance* (London and New York, Routledge, 1996) p. 82.

13 The marine policy of the Korean Government gave rise to a serious dispute between Japan and the Republic of Korea. In the end, the Republic of Korea and Japan concluded the Korea–Japanese Fisheries Convention in 1965. With respect to the analysis of the Rhee Line, see in particular S. Oda, *International Control of Sea Resources* (Dordrecht, Nijhoff, 1989) pp. 26–8.

14 Proclamation by President Truman of 28 September 1945 on Policy of the United States with respect to Coastal Fisheries in Certain Areas of the High Seas (Presidential Proclamation No. 2668).

15 Juda, above note 12, p. 109. In fact, in the late 1930s, the United States began to realise the need to exclude Japanese vessels from the fishing of salmon or king crab in the Gulf of Alaska or the Bering Sea. Oda, above note 13, p. xiv.

16 Unlike the 1945 Truman Proclamation on the Continental Shelf, however, the United States itself did not act to implement the Truman Proclamation on Fisheries until the mid-1960s. H.N. Scheiber, 'U.S. Policy, the Pacific Tuna Economy, and Ocean Law Innovation: The Post-World War II Era, 1945 to 1970', in D.D. Caron and H.N. Scheiber (eds), *Bringing New Law to Ocean Waters* (Leiden, Brill, 2004) p. 34.

2. It is therefore the duty of each Government to ensure the conservation and protection of its natural resources and to regulate the use thereof to the greatest possible advantage of its country.[17]

These phrases highlighted a close linkage between the development of national economy and the conservation of natural resources. In relation to this, it should be noted that at that time, Chile, Ecuador, Peru and some other Latin American States did not have the technical capacity and capital investments sufficient to effectively exploit marine living resources in the vast marine area. Accordingly, it could be assumed that those States expected foreign fishing vessels to engage themselves in fishing in the area on the conditions specified by these States, instead of exploiting marine living resources on their own.[18] Indeed, Article 6 of the Peruvian Regulation of 1956 required foreign vessels engaged in fishing in the waters off the Peruvian coast to pay $200 as a registration fee for every year, and $12 per registered ton as a permit fee for every 100 days, starting from the date of issuance.[19] Hence, it would seem that the real purpose of their claims was to increase national benefit by imposing fishing fees upon nationals of other fishing States.[20]

Essence of the Zonal Management Approach – The *Bering Sea Fur-Seals* Case (Great Britain v. USA, 1893) Revisited

The conservation of marine living resources is not a novel issue in international law. Since the 1890s, the dangers of over-fishing had already become a serious concern in international society.[21] In particular, the great development of trawl-

---

17 Reproduced in M.M. Whiteman, *Digest of International Law*, Vol. 4 (Washington, Department of State Publication, 1965) pp. 1089–90; S. Oda, *The International Law of the Ocean Development* (Leiden, Sijthoff, 1972) pp. 345–6. The Santiago Declaration invited strong objection from Denmark, Sweden, the Netherlands, Norway, the United Kingdom and the USA. With respect to the Santiago Declaration and reaction by other States, see Oda, above note 13, pp. 21–4; J.A. de Yturriaga Barberan, *The International Regime of Fisheries: From UNCLOS 1982 to the Presential Sea* (The Hague, Nijhoff, 1997) pp. 7–10.

18 Oda, above note 10, pp. 154–5.

19 Regulations concerning the Issuance of Fishing Permits for Foreign Vessels in Peruvian Waters, 1956. Reproduced in S.A. Bayitch, *Interamerican Law of Fisheries: An Introduction with Documents* (New York, Oceana, 1957) pp. 32–5.

20 Oda, above note 10, p. 155.

21 For an overview of the historical legal background to international law of fisheries, see in particular Vignes, above note 7, pp. 11–45; F. Orrego Vicuña, 'The International Law of High Seas Fisheries: From Freedom of Fishing to Sustainable Use', in O. Schram Stokke (ed.), *Governing High Seas Fisheries: The Interplay of Global and Regional Regimes* (Oxford, Oxford University Press, 2001) pp. 23–5; J.F. Caddy and K.L. Cochrane, 'A Review of Fisheries Management Past and Present and Some Future Perspectives for the Third Millennium' (2001) 44 *Ocean and Coastal Management*, pp. 654–7.

fishing from steamers highlighted the question of the inadequacy of the ordinary three-mile limit for the regulation of fisheries.[22] Consequently, the coastal State has been impelled by the need to extend their jurisdiction over fishing beyond the limit of three miles.[23] In relation to this, the coastal State has encountered a difficult question: *the regulation of fisheries of migratory species.* This issue invites serious consideration since it concerns an inherent limitation with the zonal management approach. On this issue, it is of particular interest that essential questions associated with the zonal management approach were already raised in the *Bering Sea Fur-Seals* case between Great Britain and the United States of America of 1893.[24] Although this case is well known, some of the important points of the case should therefore be identified below.

The Course of the Litigation

Facts   By a convention signed at Washington on 30 March 1867, Russia ceded to the USA the territory which was known as Alaska for some $7.2 million. Immediately after the US acquisition of Alaska, indiscriminate and massive hunting

---

22   T.W. Fulton, *The Sovereignty of the Sea* (Edinburgh and London, William Blackwood and Sons, 1911) pp. 698–700.

23   D.P. O'Connell (I.A. Shearer ed.), *The International Law of the Sea*, Vol. I (Oxford, Clarendon Press, 1982) p. 21 and pp. 524–5; Fulton, above note 22, p. 694. In fact, *Institut de droit international* generally agreed, at the meeting in Paris in 1894, that the territorial sea extended for six marine miles measured from the low-water mark along the whole coast lines. Article 2 of 'Règle adopté par l'Institut de droit international, à Paris, le 31 mars 1894, sur la définition et le régime de la mer territorial' (1894–95) 13 *Annuaire de l'Institut de droit international* (Session de Paris) p. 329.

24   For the documents relating to the Bering Fur Seal Arbitration, see Fur Seal Arbitration, *Proceedings of the Tribunal of Arbitration Convened at Paris under the Treaty between the United States of America and Great Britain, Concluded at Washington, February 29, 1882, for the Determination of Questions between the Two Governments Concerning the Jurisdictional Rights of the United States in the Waters of the Bering Sea*, 16 Vols, (Washington, DC, Government Printing Office, 1895). For the text of the Award, see *ibid.*, Vol. 1, pp. 75–84. The Award, together with summary of facts and arguments in detail, is reproduced in J.B. Moore, *History and Digest of the International Arbitrations to Which the United States Has Been a Party*, Vol. I (Washington, DC, Government Printing Office, 1898) pp. 755–961; C.A.R. Robb (ed.), *International Environmental Law Reports*, Vol. 1 (Cambridge, Cambridge University Press, 1999) pp. 43–88. This study will not address each and every issue of this case. With respect to the analysis of this case, see F. de Martens, 'Le Tribunal d'Arbitrage de Paris et la mer territoriale' (1894) 1 *RGDIP*, pp. 32–43; E.D. Engelhardt, 'De l'exécution de la sentence arbitrale de 1893 sur les pêcheries de Behring' (1898) 5 *RGDIP*, pp. 193–207; Editorial Comment, 'The Fur Seal Question' (1907) 1 *AJIL*, pp. 742–9; W. Williams, 'Reminiscences of the Bering Sea Arbitration' (1943) 37 *AJIL*, pp. 562–84; C.P.R. Romano, *The Peaceful Settlement of International Environmental Disputes: A Pragmatic Approach* (The Hague, Kluwer, 2000) pp. 133–50.

of seals occurred. It was reported that at least 240,000 seals were killed in 1868.[25] In response to this problem, between 1868 and 1873, the USA adopted a series of statutes which included a prohibition on the killing, without authorisation, of any otter, mink, marten, sable, fur-seal or other fur-bearing animal, within the limits of Alaskan territory, or in the waters thereof.[26] By the act of 1 July 1870, entitled 'An Act to Prevent the Extermination of Fur-Bearing Animals in Alaska', it was made 'unlawful to kill any fur-seal upon the islands of St Paul and St George, and in the waters adjacent thereto, except during the months of June, July, September, and October or to kill such seals at any time by the use of firearms, or use other means tending to drive the seals away from said islands'.[27] On 3 August 1870, in pursuance of the act of 1 July 1870, the Secretary of the Treasury leased the privilege of taking fur-seals on the islands of St Paul and St George to the Alaska Commercial Company. Yet the number of seals to be taken was limited to a total of 100,000 per annum.[28]

In September and November 1886, three British Columbian sealing schooners, the *Carolena*, *Onward* and *Thornton*, were seized by the American authorities. According to the depositions of the officers and men, the vessels were all in the open sea in the Bering Sea, more than 60 miles from the nearest land. Indeed, the evidence given by the officers of the revenue cutter *Corwin* showed that one of the schooners, *Thornton*, was seized 60 or 70 miles southeast of St George's Island for the offence of hunting and killing seals in part of the Bering Sea. Both the master and mate were convicted and sentenced to a period of imprisonment and a fine. The masters and mates of the other two schooners were believed to have suffered a similar penalty.[29] In 1889, further seizures of vessels by the US Authority occurred, and Great Britain protested that such seizures were wholly unjustified by international law. In response to these protests, the US Secretary of State stated that the vessels in question had been engaged in a pursuit that was *contra bonos mores* (immoral), a pursuit which of necessity involves a serious and permanent injury to the rights of the Government and the people of the United States.[30] Furthermore, he asserted that the fisheries of the Bering Sea had been exclusively controlled by the Russian Government, without interference or without question, from their original discovery until the cession of Alaska to the United Sates in 1867.[31]

On the issue, the British Foreign Secretary argued that it was an axiom of international maritime law that such action was admissible only in the case of piracy or in pursuance of special international agreement. He also questioned whether

---

25 Fur Seal Arbitration, Vol. IV, p. 78. See also Juda, above note 12, p. 30; Romano, above note 24, p. 135.

26 Moore, above note 24, pp. 763–4.

27 *Ibid.*, pp. 764 and 767.

28 *Ibid.*, p. 767. See also Fur Seal Award, above note 24, Vol. II, p. 153.

29 Moore, above note 24, pp. 770–71.

30 Argument by Mr Blaine, *ibid.*, p. 785.

31 *Ibid.*, p. 786.

the killing of seals could of itself be regarded as *contra bonos mores*, unless and until for special reasons it had been agreed by international arrangement to forbid it.[32] After negotiations, on 29 February 1892, Great Britain and the United States signed, in Washington, the Treaty for Submitting to Arbitration the Questions Relating to the Seal Fisheries in Bering Sea.[33]

Arguments by the Parties A principal issue of the arbitration related to the question of whether or not the United States had 'any rights, and, if so, what right, of protection or property in the fur-seals frequenting the islands of the United States in Bering Sea when such seals are found outside the ordinary three-mile limit'.[34] The United States asserted that it had 'a right of protection and property in the fur-seals frequenting the Pribilof Islands when found outside the ordinary three-mile limit, based upon the established principles of the common and civil law, upon the practice of nations, upon the laws of natural history, and upon the common interests of mankind'.[35] It is interesting to note that the United States referred to the concept of 'the common interests of mankind' since, theoretically at least, this concept contained an idea which would lead to the concept of the common heritage of mankind. Nevertheless, there appears to be little doubt that overall the real purpose of the United States was to protect its national interests concerning fur-seal fisheries.[36] In fact, in other parts, the United States strongly asserted the right to protect their sealing interests and industry, by referring to the concept of a property interest in the herd:

> All that is needed for their [the United States'] purposes is that their property interest in the herds should be so far recognized as to justify a prohibition by them of any destructive pursuit of the animal calculated to injure the industry prosecuted by them on the islands upon the basis of their property interest. The conception of a property interest in the herd, as distinct from a particular title to every seal composing the herd, is clear and intelligible; and a recognition of this would enable the United States to adopt any reasonable measures for the protection of such interest.[37]

---

32 Lord Salisbury's Argument, *ibid.*, p. 793.

33 *Ibid.*, p. 799. The Arbitral Tribunal was composed of seven arbitrators: J.M. Harlan, J.T. Morgan (the United States), Lord Hannen, Sir John Thompson (the United Kingdom), Baron Alphonse de Courcel (France), Marquis Emilio Visconti Venosta (Italy), Gergers Gram (Sweden and Norway). *Ibid.*, p. 805.

34 Article VI (5) of the 1892 Treaty Submitting to Arbitration the Questions Relating to the Seal Fisheries in Behring Sea. Reproduced in *ibid.*, p. 801.

35 *Ibid.*, p. 811.

36 Romano, above note 24, p. 148. It appears inconceivable that these concepts had a basis in positive international law at that time. It would appear that the resort to the extra-legal concepts indicated the lack of precedents that could support the attitude of the United States.

37 Emphasis original. Argument by Mr Carter, Moore, above note 24, pp. 837–8.

Furthermore, the United States claimed that once the national industry was created, the nation had the right to protect against the attempts of the citizens of another nation, for their own temporary benefit, to come and break it.[38] In this relation, the United States asserted that: '[T]he sea is free only for innocent and inoffensive use, not injurious to the just interests of any nation which borders upon it; that to the invasion of such interests, for the purposes of private gain, it is not free.'[39] Thus, the United States claimed that it may exercise, on the high seas, the right of self-defence which could extend to all the material interests of a nation that were important to defend. According to the United States, the right of self-defence was subject to no territorial line.[40]

On the other hand, Great Britain advocated the strict application of the freedom of the high seas. In the view of Great Britain, the United States' claim was entirely without precedent and in contradiction of the position assumed by the United States in analogous cases on more than one occasion.[41] Great Britain maintained that: 'The sea now known as Behring Sea is an open sea, free to the vessels of all nations, and the right of all nations to navigate and fish in the waters of Behring Sea, other than the territorial waters thereof, is a natural right.'[42] According to Great Britain, '[t]he United States have not, nor has any subject of the United States, any property in fur-seals until they have been reduced into possession by capture, and the property so acquired endures so long only as they are retained in control'.[43] Hence, Great Britain claimed that: 'Fur Seals are animals *feræ naturæ*, and the United States has no right of protection or property in fur seals when found outside the ordinary 3-mile limit, whether such seals frequent the islands of the United States in Behring Sea or not.'[44]

In summary, it may be said that the *Bering Sea Fur-Seals* dispute concerned in essence a conflict between the absolute application of the freedom of the high seas, which was asserted by Great Britain, and the protection of national interests of the coastal State (the United States) in conservation of fisheries of migratory species. Here one may detect a prototype of fishery disputes under the zonal management approach.

Award by the Arbitral Tribunal   The Arbitral Tribunal rejected, by a majority of five to two, the right of the United States on the ocean beyond the ordinary three-

---

38 Mr Carter's Argument, *ibid.*, p. 864. In this regard, Mr Carter stated that 'we [the United States] have the right to carry on the industry upon the islands; and having that right, when the carrying of the industry is prevented by wrongful acts in other places, we have the right to protect ourselves by repressing those acts'. *Ibid.*, p. 865.

39 Mr Phelps's Written Argument, *ibid.*, p. 839.

40 *Ibid.*, pp. 839–44.

41 The British Case, *ibid.*, p. 819. See also p. 827.

42 Fur Seal Arbitration, above note 24, Vol. IV, p. 120.

43 *Ibid.*, p. 122.

44 *Ibid.*, p. 122.

mile limit. In the words of the Tribunal: 'The United States has not any right of protection or property in the fur-seals frequenting the islands of the United States in Bering Sea, when such seals are found outside the ordinary three-mile limit.'[45] In so ruling, the Arbitral Tribunal made it clear that the legal status of the oceans differed within and outside the three-mile limit. Thus, the dichotomy of the ocean was explicitly confirmed by the Arbitral Tribunal.

On the other hand, Article 7 of the Treaty of Arbitration provided that if the determination of the foregoing questions as to the exclusive jurisdiction of the United States shall leave the subject in such position that the concurrence of Great Britain was necessary to the establishment of regulations for the proper protection and preservation of the fur-seal in the Bering Sea, the arbitrators shall then determine what concurrent regulations outside the jurisdictional limits of the respective governments were necessary, and over what waters such regulations should extend.[46] As the Arbitral Tribunal rejected the United States' property rights over the fur-seals, the arbitrators were required to establish regulations for their protection. Thus, the Arbitral Tribunal determined regulations applicable to both Parties in the mode provided by the Treaty. Article 1 of the regulations required the Parties to: 'forbid their citizens and subjects respectively to kill, capture or pursue at any time and in any manner whatever, the animals commonly called fur seals, within a zone of sixty miles around the Pribilov Islands, inclusive of the territorial waters.'[47] It must also be noted that this regulation was to be applied outside the jurisdictional limits of the respective government and extended over the waters of the Bering Sea.[48] In so doing, it appears that the Arbitral Tribunal attempted to protect fur-seals from destructive exploitation on the high seas.

Essential Issues of the Zonal Management Approach

On the basis of the analysis of the *Bering Sea Fur-Seals* arbitration, it is possible to point to at least three essential issues concerning the zonal management approach.

---

45 *Ibid.*, Vol. I, p. 78; Moore, above note 24, p. 949.

46 *Ibid.*, p. 801.

47 Fur Seal Arbitration, above note 24, Vol. I, p. 79; Moore, above note 24, p. 949.

48 Article 2 of the regulation stipulates that: 'The two Governments shall forbid their citizens and subjects respectively to kill, capture or pursue, in any manner whatever, during the season extending, each year, from the 1st of May to the 31st of July, both inclusive, the fur seals on the high sea, in the part of the Pacific Ocean, inclusive of the Bering sea, which is situated to the North of the 35th degree of North latitude, and eastward of the 180th degree of longitude from Greenwich till it strikes the water boundary described in Article 1 of the Treaty of 1867 between the United States and Russia, and following that line up to Bering straits.' Fur Seal Arbitration, above note 24, Vol. 1, p. 79; Moore, above note 24, p. 949.

The Expansive Nature of the Coastal State's Jurisdiction   A first issue relates to the breadth of marine spaces under national jurisdiction of the coastal State. Arguably the validity of the zonal management approach for the coastal State depends on whether or not spatial ambit of marine spaces under the coastal State's jurisdiction is sufficient to safeguard its national interest. The coastal State will accept existing rules of international law only if these rules adequately reflect its national interest. Once the spatial ambit of the coastal State's jurisdiction becomes inadequate to safeguard its national interest, it is almost inevitable that the coastal State will extend its national jurisdiction towards the high seas. Hence, the breadth of marine spaces under national jurisdiction becomes the question at the heart of the zonal management approach. In this respect, an issue arising is that the adequate width of marine spaces under national jurisdiction can change with the development of technology. Experience has shown that, usually, the development of technology as well as increasing competition over marine resources prompts the coastal State to extend its national jurisdiction toward the high seas with a view to controlling offshore living resources. In this sense, it may be said that the coastal State's jurisdiction is essentially expansive in nature.

In fact, since the *Bering Sea Fur-Seals* dispute, the extension of the coastal State's jurisdiction has been a central issue in case law relating to conservation of marine living resources. In the *Mortensen v Peters* case of 1906,[49] for instance, a dispute was raised with respect to the validity of the arrest of a Danish fisherman named Mortensen, who was operating a Norwegian vessel in a part of the Moray Firth five miles or so northeast of Lossiemouth. In this case, the Scottish court upheld the conviction of Mortensen on the basis of the 1889 Act. This case was appealed to the High Court of Justiciary, but the Court unanimously upheld the conviction in 1906.[50] The High Court of Justiciary found that the 1889 Act was applicable to foreign-flag vessels in areas beyond the three-mile limit. Accordingly, the validity of three-mile limit was challenged by the High Court of Justiciary.

After the Second World War, unilateral expansion of the coastal State's jurisdiction beyond the limits of the territorial sea became a subject of dispute in the two *Fishery Jurisdiction* cases, between the United Kingdom and Iceland, and between the Federal Republic of Germany and Iceland respectively.[51] Like the

---

49 Reproduced in K.R. Simmonds (ed.), *Cases on the Law of the Sea*, Vol. III (Dobbs Ferry, New York, Oceana, 1980) pp. 288–96.

50 *Ibid.*, p. 291.

51 As the Court's decision in each case is essentially very similar, all references to its judgment as well as Opinions of Judges will be quoted from the *Fishery Jurisdiction* judgment between the United Kingdom and Iceland. With respect to this case, see R. Churchill, 'The Fisheries Jurisdiction Cases: The Contribution of the International Court of Justice to the Debate on Coastal States' Fisheries Rights' (1975) 24 *ICLQ*, pp. 82–105; E. Langavant and O. Pirotte, 'L'affaire des pêcheries islandaises: L'arrêt de la Cour international de Justice du 25 juillet 1974' (1976) 80 *RGDIP*, pp. 55–103; L. Favoreu, 'Les affaires de la compétence en matière de pêcheries (Royaume-Uni c. Islande et Allemagne fédérale c. Islande): Arrêts du 25 juillet 1974 (fond)' (1974) 20 *AFDI*, pp. 253–85; Romano,

Bering Sea Fur-Seals arbitration, a principal question in the *Fishery Jurisdiction* cases related to the conflict between unilateral expansion of the coastal State's jurisdiction (Iceland's claim for the 50 miles fishery zone) toward the high seas and the principle of the freedom of the high seas.[52] Unlike the *Bering Sea Fur-Seals* Award, however, the ICJ in the *Fishery Jurisdiction* cases (Merits) of 1974 accepted the jurisdiction of the coastal State to regulate fishing activities beyond the limit of the territorial sea. The Court regarded two concepts as customary international law: the exclusive fishery zone up to a 12-mile limit, as well as the preferential rights of the coastal State.[53] The concept of the exclusive fishery zone, which exists as a *tertium genus* (*une troisième catégorie*) between the territorial sea and the high seas, signalled a change from the traditional dualism at the customary law level.[54] In fact, after the judgment, the concept of the EEZ was very soon established through State practice.

Nonetheless, the establishment of the 200-mile EEZ did not stop a unilateral expansion of the coastal State's jurisdiction toward the high seas. This fact was clearly demonstrated by the 1998 *Fishery Jurisdiction* dispute between Spain and Canada. This dispute related to the arrest of the *Estai*, a fishing vessel flying the Spanish flag and manned by a Spanish crew, by the Canadian Authority some 245 miles from the Canadian coast in 1995.[55] The vessel was seized and its master arrested on charges of violations of the Coastal Fisheries Protection Act as well as its implementing regulations.[56] The arrest of the *Estai* invited protest from Spain[57]

---

above note 24, pp. 151–76; Juda, above note 12, pp. 171–80. Iceland did not appear before the ICJ, rejecting the jurisdiction of the Court.

52 ICJ Reports 1974 (United Kingdom *v.* Iceland), p. 16, para. 31.

53 *Ibid.*, p. 23, para. 52. See also p. 26, para. 58. On the other hand, the customary law character of the exclusive fishery zone up to a twelve-mile limit maximum was not free from controversy. It appeared problematic that the majority opinion failed to clarify the existence of consistent and widespread State practice as well as *opinio juris* in this matter. In his article of 1975, Churchill argued that there seemed to be sufficient evidence to justify the claim that an exclusive fishing zone up to twelve miles from the coastal State's baselines was recognised as being a rule of customary international law. Thus Churchill showed useful data on State practice relating to 12-mile exclusive fishing zones. Churchill, above note 51, pp. 88–9. It would appear, however, that the existence of *opinio juris* in this matter remained obscure.

54 See also Joint Separate Opinion of Judges Forster, Bengzon, Jiménez de Aréchaga, Nagendra Singh, and Ruda, ICJ Reports 1974, p. 46, para. 6.

55 The point of arrest was in Division 3L of the NAFO Regulatory Area (Grand Banks area).

56 ICJ Reports 1998, p. 443, para. 19.

57 On 10 March 1995, the Spanish Ministry of Foreign Affairs sent a Note Verbale to the Canadian Embassy in Spain, saying that: 'In carrying out the said boarding operation, the Canadian authorities breached the universally accepted norm of customary international law codified in Article 92 and articles to the same effect of the 1982 Convention on the Law of the Sea, according to which ships on the high seas shall be subject to the exclusive jurisdiction of the flag State.' *Ibid.*, para. 20.

and the European Community as well as its Member States.[58] In its turn, however, on 10 March 1995 the Canadian Department of Foreign Affairs and International Trade responded that 'the arrest of the *Estai* was necessary in order to put a stop to the overfishing of Greenland halibut by Spanish fishermen'.[59] Thus, once again, a dispute arose with respect to the validity of the unilateral extension of the coastal State's (Canada's) jurisdiction toward the high seas for the conservation of marine living resources. It appears that the *Estai* dispute shows an interesting similarity with the *Bering Sea Fur-Seals* arbitration as well as the *Fishery Jurisdiction* cases of 1974. In light of Canada's reservation,[60] the ICJ, in the *Estai* case, found that it had no jurisdiction to adjudicate upon this dispute;[61] and thus, the Court did not examine the validity of the conduct of Canada.[62] Even so, the *Estai* dispute has proven that spatial scope of the coastal State's jurisdiction remains an essential issue under the zonal management approach.

Question over the Absolute Application of the Freedom of the High Seas A second issue relates to the validity of an absolute application of the freedom of the high seas to conservation of marine living resources. The *Bering Sea Fur-Seals* dispute has demonstrated that the absolute application of the principle of freedom of the high seas would run a risk of exhausting marine species. As explained earlier,

---

58 *Ibid.*, p. 444, para. 20.

59 *Ibid.*, p. 443, para. 20.

60 On 10 May 1994, Canada accepted the compulsory jurisdiction of the ICJ over all disputes other than:

(d) disputes arising out of or concerning conservation and management measures taken by Canada with respect to vessels fishing in the NAFO Regulatory Area, as defined in the Convention on Future Multilateral Co-operation in the Northwest Atlantic Fisheries, 1978, and the enforcement of such measures.

Ibid., p. 439, para. 14.

61 *Ibid.*, p. 468, para. 89. On this issue, see in particular P. Weil, 'Le principe de la jurisdiction consensuelle à l'épreuve du feu: à propos de l'arrêt de la Cour internationale de Justice dans l'affaire de la compétence en matière de pêcheries (Espagne c. Canada)', in C.A. Armas Barea, J.A. Barberis, J. Barboza, H. Caminos, E. Candioti, E. de La Guardia, H.D.T. Gutiérrez Posse, G. Moncayo, E.J. Rey Caro and R.E. Vinuesa (eds), *Liber Amicorum 'Im Memoriam' of Judge José Maria Ruda* (The Hague, Kluwer, 2000), pp. 157–78.

62 It would appear, however, that the unilateral extension of the coastal State's jurisdiction beyond the limit of the EEZ would be contrary to positive international law. In this respect, Judge Oda stated that: 'I have no doubt that Canada believed that it had a legitimate right to adopt and enforce certain fisheries legislation, but that it also believed in the light of the development of the law of the sea, that that right may belong to the area of *lex ferenda* and, in this belief, Canada wishes to avoid any judicial determination by the International Court of Justice.' Separate Opinion of Judge Oda, ICJ Reports 1998, p. 484, para. 21. On the other hand, Judge Bedjaoui expressed his misgivings, by stating that: 'the Court in no way endorses Canada's conduct by declaring that it lacks jurisdiction in regard to that conduct. That is true, but psychologically the impact is disastrous.' Dissenting Opinion of Judge Bedjaoui, *ibid.*, p. 537, para. 54.

the United States argued that no part of the high sea was, or ought to be, open to individuals for the purpose of accomplishing the destruction of national interests. This argument represented an important idea that the freedom of the high seas must be exercised with due regard for the interests of the coastal States.[63] In this respect, it must be noted that the Arbitral Tribunal did not admit unconditional freedom of hunting of fur-seals; and that it determined regulations, including the prohibition of the hunting of fur-seals within 60 miles. In so doing, it would appear that the Arbitral Tribunal attempted to reconcile the need for conservation of marine living resources and the interest of the distant-water fishing States on the basis of the principle of freedom of the high seas.[64]

It is interesting to note that later on, a similar approach was taken in the *Fishery Jurisdiction* case between the United Kingdom and Iceland. In this case, the ICJ concluded that a unilateral extension of the exclusive fishing rights of Iceland to 50 nautical miles from the baselines was not opposable to the United Kingdom.[65] This did not mean, however, that the United Kingdom could enjoy the freedom of fishing in the disputed waters in the 12-mile to 50-mile zone in an absolute manner. 'On the contrary,' the Court continued, 'both States have an obligation to take full account of each other's rights and of any fishery conservation measures the necessity of which is shown to exist in those waters.'[66] Hence, the Court placed an obligation upon both Parties to keep under review the fishery resources in the disputed waters and to examine together, in the light of scientific and other available information, the measures required for the conservation and development, and equitable exploitation, of those resources, taking into account any international agreement in force between them.[67] In relation to this, it is notable that the Court stressed the importance of an 'equitable solution' or 'equitable exploitation'. Indeed, in the operative part of the judgment, the Court placed a mutual obligation upon the Parties to undertake negotiations in good faith for the equitable solution of their difference concerning their respective fishery rights.[68] Thus, it may be argued that the Court attempted to reconcile the preferential rights of Iceland and the traditional fishery rights of the United Kingdom with a view to reaching an 'equitable solution'. The *Bering Sea Fur-Seals* Arbitration and the *Fishery Jurisdiction* case appear to show that the principle of the freedom of the high seas

---

63 *Cf.* T. Scovazzi, 'The Evolution of International Law of the Sea: New Issues, New Challenges' (2000) 286 *RCADI*, pp. 84–5.

64 Scovazzi stressed the importance of the Tribunal's solution, by stating that: 'Without encroaching upon the principle of freedom of the high seas, the decision of the Tribunal constitutes a precedent for the formation of the rule that States which exploit a living resource on the high seas have an obligation to co-operate to prevent its destruction.' *Ibid.*, p. 87. See also P. Birnie and A. Boyle, *International Law and Environment*, 2nd edn (Oxford, Oxford University Press, 2002) p. 650.

65 ICJ Reports 1974, p. 34, para. 79 (1).

66 *Ibid.*, p. 31, para. 72.

67 *Ibid.*

68 *Ibid.*, p. 34, para. 79 (3). See also para. 79 (4) (c)(d).

is not absolute in its nature; and the freedom must be reconciled with the need to conserve marine living resources.

The Importance of International Co-operation   Thirdly, in light of the mobile nature of marine species, the zonal management approach encounters a considerable difficulty as to regulation of migratory species. Thus international co-operation among relevant States becomes a prerequisite to effectively conserve migratory marine species. In fact, the *Bering Sea Fur-Seals* dispute highlighted the importance of international co-operation in this matter. Following the arbitration, legislation to implement the regulations was enacted by Great Britain and the USA in 1894.[69] Nonetheless, such regulations were ineffective for various reasons.[70] One reason was that the regulation did not cover the whole fur-seal occurrence area, that is to say, the whole North Pacific. Admittedly the Arbitral Tribunal could not create a regulation applicable to the whole Pacific north of 35° N, since that would have included seal herds dwelling on Japanese and Russian territories. Yet such a geographical limit had reduced the effectiveness of the regulation, displacing sealing to other areas of the Pacific during the restricted periods.[71] Another reason concerned the presence of free-riders, such as Japan and Russia. The refusal by Japan and Russia to agree to similar regulations for their vessels and citizens made the regulations largely ineffective. This question was eventually resolved by the conclusion of the 1911 Convention respecting Measures for the Preservation and Protection of Fur Seals in the North Pacific Ocean.[72] This factual situation suggested that the regulation of migrating species could not be effective unless all relevant States participated to an international regulation scheme. This underscores the importance of the establishment of an international framework for regulation of migrating species on the basis of international co-operation.[73]

On the basis of the above considerations, the next section will examine whether and to what extent those issues have been addressed in global treaties with respect to conservation of marine living resources.

---

69 J.B. Moore, *A Digest of International Law*, Vol. I (Washington, DC, Government Printing Office, 1906) p. 922. See also Robb, above note 24, p. 83.

70 On this point, see Romano, above note 24, pp. 144–5.

71 *Ibid.*, pp. 145 and 149.

72 The text of the treaty was published by His Majesty's Stationery Office, Cd. 5971; Robb, above note 24, p. 83; Romano, above note 24, pp. 145–6.

73 *Cf.* W.T. Burke, *The New International Law of Fisheries: UNCLOS 1982 and Beyond* (Oxford, Clarendon Press, 1994) p. 5.

Limits of the Zonal Management Approach in the Global Legal Framework

The 1958 Geneva Convention on Fishing and Conservation of the Living Resources of the High Seas

The Concept of a Special Interest of the Coastal State At the global level, an obligation relating to conservation of marine living resources on the high seas was, for the first time, enshrined in the 1958 High Seas Fishing Convention.[74] The Preamble of this Convention makes explicit the need for conservation of those resources on the high seas, by stating that:[75]

> Considering that the development of modern techniques for the exploitation of the living resources of the sea, increasing man's ability to meet the need of the world's expanding population for food, has exposed some of these resources to the danger of being over-exploited, [...] the nature of the problems involved in the conservation of the living resources of the high seas is such that there is a clear necessity that they be solved, whenever possible, on the basis of international co-operation through the concerted action of all the States concerned.

Thus the High Seas Fishing Convention required States to apply conservation measures to their own nationals in accordance with Articles 3 and 4.[76] Given that the high seas fisheries may have adverse effects upon marine species in the territorial seas of the coastal State, the protection of interest of the coastal State is of particular importance in this field.[77] Accordingly, Article 1 (1) of this Convention sets out that:

> All States have the right for their nationals to engage in fishing on the high seas, subject (a) to their treaty obligations, (b) to the interests and rights of coastal States as provided for in this Convention, and (c) to the provisions contained in the following articles concerning conservation of the living resources of the high seas.

---

74 With respect to the analysis of this Convention in some detail, see A. Gros, 'La convention sur la pêche et la conservation des ressources biologiques de la haute mer' (1959) 97 *RCADI*, pp. 5–89; Oda, above note 10, pp. 139–62; Nguyen Quoc Dinh, 'La revendication des droits préférentiels de pêche en haute mer devant les Conférences des Nations Unies sur le droit de la mer de 1958 et 1960' (1960) 6 *AFDI*, pp. 77–110; L. Lucchini and M. Vœlckel, *Droit de la mer, Tome 2, Vol. 2 Navigation et Pêche* (Paris, Pedone, 1996) pp. 426–38.

75 Preamble.

76 Oda, above note 13, p. 112. Accordingly, the obligations to conserve marine living resources do not alter the principle of the exclusive jurisdiction of flag State.

77 With respect to this issue, see Gros, above note 74, p. 43.

It is important to note that Article 1 (1) (b) explicitly accepted that the right of fishing is subject to the interests and rights of coastal States. It appears that this may be an important qualification of the principle of freedom of fishing on the high seas.[78]

Furthermore, it is worth noting that the High Seas Fishing Convention introduced a new concept of the 'special interest' of the coastal State. Article 6 of the High Seas Fishing Convention is worth quoting in full:

> 1. A coastal State has a special interest in the maintenance of the productivity of the living resources in any area of the high seas adjacent to its territorial sea.
>
> 2. A coastal State is entitled to take part on an equal footing in any system of research and regulation for purposes of conservation of the living resources of the high seas in that area, even though its nationals do not carry on fishing there.
>
> 3. A State whose nationals are engaged in fishing in any area of the high seas adjacent to the territorial sea of a State shall, at the request of that coastal State, enter into negotiations with a view to prescribing by agreement the measures necessary for the conservation of the living resources of the high seas in that area.
>
> 4. A State whose nationals are engaged in fishing in any area of the high seas adjacent to the territorial sea of a coastal State shall not enforce conservation measures in that area which are opposed to those which have been adopted by the coastal State, but may enter into negotiations with the coastal State with a view to prescribing by agreement the measures necessary for the conservation of the living resources of the high seas in that area.

Thus, Article 7 empowered the coastal State to take unilateral measures, by providing that:

> 1. Having regard to the provisions of paragraph 1 of Article 6, any coastal State may, with a view to the maintenance of the productivity of the living resources of the sea, adopt unilateral measures of conservation appropriate to any stock of fish or other marine resources in any area of the high seas adjacent to its territorial sea, provided that negotiations to that effect with the other States concerned have not led to an agreement within six months.
>
> 2. The measures which the coastal State adopts under the previous paragraph shall be valid as to other States only if the following requirements are fulfilled:

---

78 F. Orrego Vicuña, *The Changing International Law of High Seas Fisheries* (Cambridge, Cambridge University Press, 1999) p. 19. Later on, Article 1 became the basis for Article 116 of the 1982 LOSC. Burke, above note 73, p. 13.

(a) That there is a need for urgent application of conservation measures in the light of the existing knowledge of the fishery;

(b) That the measures adopted are based on appropriate scientific findings;

(c) That such measures do not discriminate in form or in fact against foreign fishermen.

It appears that these provisions are innovative in the sense that they attempt to prevent adverse impacts arising from high seas fishing by accepting special interests of the coastal States. On the other hand, it would seem that the provisions leave some room for discussion.

First, it needs to be stressed that the notion of special interest of the coastal State does not mean that the coastal State acquires the exclusive or preferential rights of fisheries in the area concerned.[79] Article 7 should not be construed in such a way as to entitle the coastal State to directly apply its measures to nationals of other States. Rather, it should be interpreted to mean that fishing States are obliged to apply the measures unilaterally adopted by the coastal State to its own nationals. In this sense, Article 7 (1) does not disturb the exclusivity of the flag State jurisdiction over vessels flying its flag.[80]

Secondly, it appears problematic that the spatial extent of the area 'adjacent to its territorial sea' is not identified. It is probable that such an area adjacent to its territorial sea may be extended toward the high seas in accordance with the development of marine technology of the coastal State. If this is the case, these provisions will be beneficial to the coastal State.[81] Furthermore, a difficult question may be raised when a coastal State wishes to enact regulations in an area which is also adjacent to the coasts of other States. In such a case, the application of the measures will depend upon an agreement between the coastal States concerned.[82]

Thirdly, a serious dispute may be raised when a coastal State takes unilateral measures of conservation in accordance with Article 7 (1). In this respect, Article 7 (4) provides that when the measures taken by the coastal State are not accepted by the other States concerned, 'any of the parties may initiate the procedure contemplated by Article 9'.[83] Arguably the criteria to be applied by the special

---

79   J.H.W. Verzijl, 'The United Nations Conference on the Law of the Sea, Geneva, 1958, II' (1959) 6 *NILR*, p. 125. Oda, above note 13, p. 116.

80   S. Oda, 'Fisheries under the United Nations Convention on the Law of the Sea' (1983) 77 *AJIL*, p. 740.

81   Oda, above note 13, p. 117.

82   United Nations, *Report of the International Law Commission, Official Records, Eighth Session*, 23 April–4 July 1956, p. 36.

83   Article 9 stipulates that: 'Any dispute which may arise between States under Articles 4, 5, 6, 7, and 8 shall, at the request of any of the parties, be submitted for settlement to a special commission of five members, unless the parties agree to seek a solution by another method of peaceful settlement, as provided for in Article 33 of the Charter of the United Nations.' The special commission is to render its decision within a period of five months from the time it is appointed (Article 9 (5)). Decisions of the commission shall be

commission are limited to the three requirements which are provided in Article 7 (2).[84] Under Article 7 (4), the measures adopted shall remain obligatory pending the decision of the special commission subject to Article 10 (2). In accordance with Article 10 (2), the measures taken by the coastal State 'shall only be suspended when it is apparent to the commission on the basis of *prima facie* evidence that the need for the urgent application of such measures does not exist'. To this extent, it would seem that this provision is beneficial to the coastal State. Furthermore, the special commission does not deal with every kind of dispute relating to the high seas fisheries. For instance, disputes concerning the distribution of marine resources do not fall within the competence of the special commission.[85]

Obligation of Newcomer States   As explained earlier, the presence of free-riders undermines the effectiveness of regulatory measures necessary for the conservation of marine species. In this respect, it is of particular interest that the High Seas Fishing Convention provides an obligation concerning newcomer States. Article 5 provides that:

> 1. If, subsequent to the adoption of the measures referred to in Article 3 and 4, nationals of other States engage in fishing the same stock or stocks of fish or other living marine resources in any area or areas of the high seas, the other States shall apply the measures, which shall not be discriminatory in form or in fact, to their own nationals not later than seven months after the date on which the measures shall have been notified to the Director-General of the Food and Agriculture Organisation of the United Nations. The Director-General shall notify such measures to any State which so requests and, in any case, to any State specified by the State initiating the measure.
> 2. If these other States do not accept the measures so adopted and if no agreement can be reached within twelve months, any of the interested parties may initiate the procedure contemplated by Article 9. Subject to paragraph 2 of Article 10, the measures adopted shall remain obligatory pending the decision of the special commission.

Article 5 further stipulates that the other States (the newcomer States) shall apply the measures 'to their own nationals'. Hence this provision should not be construed as allowing the fishing State or States to exercise jurisdiction over the nationals of the newcomer States.[86] While the duties of newcomer States appear to be desirable with a view to enhancing the effectiveness of conservation measures, Article 5 is not free of controversy.

A first question arising pertains to the identification of newcomer States. In this regard, a commentary of the ILC states that 'the regulation should be applicable

---

by majority vote (Article 9 (7)). The decision of the special commission is binding on the States concerned (Article 11).

84 Oda, above note 10, p. 151.

85 *Ibid.*, p. 152.

86 *Ibid.*, p. 113.

to newcomers only if they engage in fishing on a scale which would substantially affect the stock or stocks in question'.[87] Nevertheless, there is no mechanism to determine whether newcomer States are *substantially* fishing on this scale in the High Seas Fishing Convention.[88] In light of the difficulty associated with the identification of newcomer States, it is questionable whether those obligations may be effectively implemented by relevant States.

Secondly, it would appear that the High Seas Fishing Convention places a heavy obligation upon the newcomer State which adheres to this Convention. It is true that in accordance with Article 4, the newcomer State that cannot accept the existing conservation measures may commence negotiations with the State or States adopting these measures; and that the newcomer State may submit a dispute to a special commission where no agreement can be reached within twelve months. Nevertheless, unless otherwise agreed upon by negotiation or decision by the special commission, the newcomer State is not released from the duty of applying the existing measures.[89]

Conservation of Migratory Species　Last but not least, it should be recalled that since the *Bering Sea Fur-Seals* dispute, conservation of migratory species has represented an important challenge to the zonal management approach. Nonetheless, the High Seas Fishing Convention contains no specific rule in this matter. In this respect, UNCLOS I merely adopted a resolution on co-operation in conservation of migratory species:

> [The Conference] Recommends to the coastal States that, in the cases where a stock or stocks of fish or other living marine resources inhabit both the fishing areas under their jurisdiction and areas of the adjacent high seas, they should co-operate with such international conservation organizations as may be responsible for the development and application of conservation measures in the adjacent high seas, in the adoption and enforcement, as far as practicable, of the necessary conservation measures on the fishing areas under their jurisdiction.[90]

This resolution merely requires, however, an obligation to co-operate in the conservation of migratory species in an abstract manner. Thus, we may be forced to conclude that the 1958 Geneva Convention failed to address the real issue of migratory species.[91] Overall the above discussions can be summarised in the following way:

87　United Nations, *Report of the International Law Commission*, above note 82, p. 35.

88　Oda, above note 13, p. 114.

89　*Ibid.*

90　United Nations Conference on the Law of the Sea, *Official Records*, Vol. II, Plenary Meetings (Geneva 24 February–27 April 1958) p. 144.

91　R-E. Charlier, 'Résultats et enseignements des conférences du droit de la mer' (1960) 6 *AFDI*, p. 72.

(i)   The High Seas Fishing Convention is innovative in the sense that it provides the concept of special interest of the coastal State as well as the obligation of newcomer States. In so doing, the High Seas Fishing Convention attempts to ensure effectiveness of conservation of marine species.

(ii)   It should be noted, however, that the concept of special interest neither accepted the preferential rights of the coastal State nor exception of the exclusivity of the flag State jurisdiction over vessels flying its flag. In this sense, the High Seas Fishing Convention still maintains the traditional dualism in international law of the sea.

(iii)   The High Seas Fishing Convention did not adequately address conservation of migratory species. Consequently, an important issue relating to the zonal management approach was left unresolved.

(iv)   Despite some innovative provisions, States were not fully supportive of this Convention.[92] The factual situation shows that so far only 38 States are Parties to it.[93]

The 1982 UN Convention on the Law of the Sea

As explained in Chapter 1, the zonal management approach was established in its true sense in the 1982 LOSC.[94] It may be said that the LOSC made an important contribution to establishing legal order in the oceans. On the other hand, although the Convention explicitly recognises its aim of promoting the conservation of marine living resources,[95] the fact that nearly 80 per cent of fish stocks are over-exploited demonstrates that the LOSC has not been successful in this field. While this may be due to a lack of will on the part of States Parties to implement relevant provisions of the Convention, it is arguable that the LOSC itself contains some limitations in this matter. In this respect, at least three principal limitations with the LOSC must be pointed out: inadequacy of rules relating to the conservation of marine living resources in the EEZ as well as in the high seas, and weakness of rules concerning migratory species.[96]

---

92 Vignes, above note 7, p. 33; Birnie and Boyle, above note 64, p. 651.

93 The data is available at the website of Multilateral Treaties Deposited with the Secretary-General of the UN <http://untreaty.un.org/ENGLISH/bible/englishinternetbible/bible.asp>.

94 See Chapter 1, p. 5.

95 Paragraph 4 of the Preamble.

96 *Cf.* E. Hey, 'Global Fisheries Regulations in the First Half of the 1990s' (1996) 11 *IJMCL*, pp. 460–62.

Limits of the Conservation of Marine Living Resources in the EEZ[97]   With the establishment of the 200-mile EEZ, a vast area of the ocean was placed under the national jurisdiction of the coastal State.[98] Considering that approximately 90 per cent of all commercially exploitable fish stocks are caught within 200 miles of the coast,[99] coastal States have a considerable role to play in conservation of those resources in their EEZs. Thus Article 61 (2) of the LOSC obliges the coastal State to ensure through proper conservation and management measures that the maintenance of the living resources in the EEZ is not endangered by over-exploitation, by taking into account the best scientific evidence available to it. In taking such measures, the coastal State is required to take into consideration the effects on species associated with or dependent upon harvested species by virtue of Article 61 (4). Furthermore, Article 193 requires States to exercise the sovereign right to exploit their natural resources in accordance with their duty to protect and preserve the marine environment. Arguably, conservation of those resources in the EEZ is based mainly on two key elements.

A first element concerns the notion of allowable catch. Article 61 (1) requires the coastal State to determine the allowable catch of the living resources in its EEZ. Article 62 (2) further provides that where the coastal State does not have the capacity to harvest the entire allowable catch, it shall, through agreements or other

---

97 The legal framework of the LOSC concerning the EEZ has already been examined by a large number of writers, including H. Caminos, 'The Regime of Fisheries in the Exclusive Economic Zone', in F. Orrego Vicuña (ed.), *The Exclusive Economic Zone, A Latin American Perspective* (Boulder, Colo., Westview Press, 1984) pp. 143–58; J. Carroz, 'Les problèmes de la pêche dans la convention sur le droit de la mer et la pratique des Etats', in D. Bardonnet and M. Virally (eds), *Le nouveau droit international de la mer* (Paris, Pedone, 1983) pp. 177–229; P. Mengozzi, 'Fishing and International Cooperation in the Light of New Developments in the Law of the Sea', in B. Vukas (ed.), *Essays on the New Law of the Sea* (Zagreb, Sveučilišna naklada Liber, 1985) pp. 261–75; L. Caflisch, 'Fisheries in the Exclusive Economic Zone: An Overview', in U. Leanza (ed), *The International Legal Regime of the Mediterranean Sea* (Milan, Giuffrè, 1987) pp. 149–71; D. Attard, *The Exclusive Economic Zone in International Law* (Oxford, Clarendon Press, 1987) pp. 146–91; B. Kwiatkowska, *The 200 Mile Exclusive Economic Zone in the New Law of the Sea* (Dordrecht, Nijhoff, 1989) pp. 45–102; F. Orrego Vicuña, *The Exclusive Economic Zone: Regime and Legal Nature under International Law* (Cambridge, Cambridge University Press, 1989); Fleischer, above note 5, pp. 989–1126; Lucchini and Vœlckel, above note 74, pp. 449–544; G. Cataldi, 'La pêche dans les eaux soumises à la souveraineté ou à la juridiction des Etats côtiers', in Vignes, Cataldi and Raigón (eds), above note 7, pp. 47–116 (in particular, pp. 63–116).

98 Article 56 (1). It is suggested that the universal establishment of 200-mile EEZs would embrace about 36 per cent of the total oceans. R.R. Churchill and A.V. Lowe, *The Law of the Sea*, 3rd edn (Manchester, Manchester University Press, 1999) p. 162.

99 P. Malanczuk, *Akehurst's Modern Introduction to International Law*, 7th revised edn (London, Routledge, 1997) p. 183; P.G.G. Davies and C. Redgwell, 'The International Legal Regulation of Straddling Fish Stocks' (1996) 67 *BYIL*, p. 200; Churchill and Lowe, above note 98, p. 162.

arrangements, give other States access to the surplus of the allowable catch. The allowable catch is a key concept with respect to the conservation of marine living resources in the sense that other consequential decisions relating to access to the fish in the EEZ depend basically on the amount of the allowable catch determined by the coastal States.[100]

A second factor concerns maximum sustainable yield (MSY). This concept may be defined as the largest average catch or yield that can continuously be taken from a stock under existing environmental conditions.[101] In this regard, Article 61 (3) requires that conservation measures in the EEZ shall be:

> designed to maintain or restore populations of harvested species at levels which can produce the maximum sustainable yield as qualified by relevant environmental and economic factors, including the economic needs of coastal fishing communities and the special requirements of developing States, and taking into account fishing patterns, the interdependence of stocks and any generally recommended international minimum standards, whether subregional, regional or global.

Furthermore, Article 61 (3) obliges the coastal State to take into consideration the effects on species associated with or dependent upon harvested species with a view to maintaining or restoring populations of such associated or dependent species above levels at which their reproduction may become seriously threatened. Overall it may be said that proper conservation of marine living resources under the 1982 LOSC relies on the effective implementation of those obligations by the coastal State.

However ideal they may appear, it would seem that provisions relating to conservation of marine living resources represent considerable difficulties in their implementation. In particular, four obstacles should be noted.

A first difficulty relates to the determination of the allowable catch. The 1982 LOSC seemingly presupposes that the resources considered are only affected by

---

100 Burke, above note 73, p. 44. An exception in this matter may be the right of developing land-locked and geographically disadvantaged States to participate in the exploitation of marine living resources of the EEZ of coastal States of the same subregion or region (Articles 69 (1) and 70 (1) of the LOSC). Where certain conditions are fulfilled, the participation of developing land-locked or geographically disadvantaged States is not limited to the surplus of the living resources in accordance with Article 69 (3) as well as 70 (4). L. Caflisch, 'La Convention des Nations Unies sur le droit de la mer adoptée le 30 avril 1982' (1983) 39 *ASDI*, p. 73. The terms and modalities of such participation are to be established by the States concerned through international agreements in conformity with Articles 69 (2) and 70 (3). Under Article 71, however, Articles 69 and 70 do not apply in the case of a coastal State whose economy is overwhelmingly dependent on the exploitation of the living resources of its EEZ. A typical example is provided by Iceland. .

101 FAO Glossary, which is based on W.E. Ricker, 'Computation and Interpretation of Biological Statistics of Fish Populations' (1975) 191 *Bulletin of the Fisheries Research Board of Canada*, pp. 2–6. See FAO's home page <http://www.fao.org>.

the coastal State's harvest. This could be the case if those resources exist only in the EEZ of that State. Nonetheless, a difficult question arises where a population of fish occurs both in the waters of the coastal State and in other areas, and where harvesting can also take place in those other areas. In this case, it appears imperative that the allowable catch should be determined for the population in its entirety. It is logical that the coastal State's determination of the allowable catch within its zone must take due account of the harvesting that takes place beyond the limits of its jurisdiction, be it within the zones of another State or on the high seas.[102] Yet there is no mechanism to do so in the LOSC. Hence, it will be difficult for the coastal State to properly determine the allowable catch of a straddling and highly migratory species because of its high mobility. Furthermore, as there are various species in the oceans, it is likely that, in practice, fishermen will simultaneously capture various fish including associated species. Accordingly, it appears difficult to keep precisely the amount of the allowable catch. Should fishermen capture by accident species which are not part of their quota or are prohibited from exploitation, for instance, one wonders whether such species must be returned to the oceans.[103] Moreover, it has to be stressed that reliable scientific data is a prerequisite to determining the allowable catch. In reality, however, the collection and analysis of relevant data are frequently inadequate, and costly, particularly for developing States.[104] Considering that knowledge of marine ecosystems in the EEZ is inadequate, it appears difficult for the coastal State to fulfil this obligation.[105]

Secondly, the LOSC gives the coastal State a large discretion to determine the allowable catch. Apart from the single qualification not to endanger living resources by over-exploitation, it would seem that the coastal State may in fact set the allowable catch as it wishes.[106] Thus, there is a concern that the coastal State emerges with a zero surplus and thereby evades its duty to allocate surpluses in its EEZ by manipulating the allowable catch.[107] In this respect, it is to be noted that the coastal State's capacity to harvest living resources does not depend solely

---

102 Fleischer, above note 5, p. 1073.

103 Vignes, above note 7, p. 40.

104 Churchill and Lowe, above note 98, p. 283; Burke, above note 73, p. 45.

105 *Ibid.*, p. 58; R. Churchill, '10 Years of the UN Convention on the Law of the Sea: Towards a Global Ocean Regime? A General Appraisal' (2005) 48 *GYIL*, p. 107. In fact, a study of the United Nations states that: '[t]here do not appear, […], to be many cases where such legislation contains specific provisions regarding the concepts of total allowable catch and optimum utilization of resources and the access of third States to the surplus.' United Nations Division for Ocean Affairs and the Law of the Sea (UNDOALOS), Office of Legal Affairs, *The Law of the Sea: Practice of States at the Time of Entry into Force of the United Nations Convention on the Law of the Sea* (New York, United Nations, 1994) p. 11. See also Cataldi, above note 97, p. 87.

106 Burke, above note 73, pp. 47–8.

107 Yet such manipulations would be contrary to the obligation of optimum utilisation as well as the obligation not to abuse rights by virtue of Article 300 of the LOSC. Caflisch, above note 97, p. 161.

on the capital and technology of its own national economy. It is possible for the coastal State to introduce foreign capital and technology. If this is the case, the coastal State may always have the capacity to harvest the entire allowable catch. Hence, it would appear that conclusion of agreements concerning third States' access to surplus would be difficult in reality.[108] In sum, it would seem that the obligation to establish the allowable catch is more apparent than real.[109]

A third obstacle concerns the absence of a dispute settlement mechanism with respect to the conservation of marine living resources in the EEZ.[110] In accordance with Article 297 (3) (a), any disputes relating to a State's sovereign rights with respect to the living resources in the EEZ or their exercise, including its discretionary powers for determining the allowable catch, its harvesting capacity, the allocation of surpluses to other States and the terms and conditions established in its conservation and management laws and regulations, are exempted from the compulsory settlement procedure embodied in Part XV of the LOSC.[111] It is true that these disputes are to be submitted to conciliation under Annex V of the LOSC. Yet it would be highly difficult for the third party to prove the manifest breach of the coastal State's obligation concerning the conservation and management of living resources in the EEZ as well as the determination of allowable catch.[112] Furthermore, the Conciliation Commission cannot substitute its discretion for that of the coastal State by virtue of Article 297 (3) (c). In any case, the report drawn up by the Commission shall not be binding upon the Parties under Article 7 (2) of Annex V. The conclusion seems inevitable that the coastal State possesses a broad discretion in setting the allowable catch;[113] and that it is highly difficult for a third party to challenge the decision by the coastal State.

A fourth difficulty relates to the concept of MSY. It has been suggested that the validity of this concept is questionable as a conservation objective since it fails to take into account not only economic objectives but also the ecological relationships of species, the quality status of that habitat, the limits of the given area's biomass,

---

108 Oda, above note 80, p. 744.

109 Burke, above note 73, p. 44.

110 On this issue, see R. Barnes, 'The Convention on the Law of the Sea: An Effective Framework for Domestic Fisheries Conservation?', in D. Freestone, R. Barnes and D. Ong (eds), *The Law of the Sea: Progress and Prospects* (Oxford, Oxford University Press, 2006) p. 239; Carroz, above note 97, p. 189; R.C. Raigón, 'Règlement des différends', in Vignes *et al.*, above note 7, pp. 316–65. With respect to the dispute settlement mechanism in the LOSC, see, for instance, A.E. Boyle, 'Dispute Settlement and the Law of the Sea Convention: Problems of Fragmentation and Jurisdiction' (1997) 46 *ICLQ*, pp. 37–54; T.A. Mensah, 'The Dispute Settlement Regime of the 1982 United Nations Convention on the Law of the Sea' (1998) 2 *Max Planck Yearbook of United Nations Law*, pp. 307–23; N. Klein, *Dispute Settlement in the UN Convention on the Law of the Sea* (Cambridge, Cambridge University Press, 2005).

111 Article 297 (3) (a).

112 Cataldi, above note 97, p. 86.

113 Barnes, above note 110, p. 245.

and factors disturbing the environment.[114] The various methods of calculating the MSY have been criticised on the ground that they rely on incomplete or speculative assumptions and data.[115] Furthermore, given that knowledge and understanding of marine ecosystems are still inadequate, it appears difficult to make the proper calculation of MSY taking ecological factors into account.[116] Even if the concept of MSY itself is not wrong, it is said that its determination is rarely, if ever, correct and the administrative measures taken with a view to its adoption have been and generally still are inadequate and inappropriate.[117] Overall there appears to be a risk that the coastal State's jurisdiction over natural resources in the EEZ may be approaching *grosso modo* to that in the territorial sea, even though there are some limitations on the exercise of its jurisdiction.[118]

Limits of the Conservation of Marine Living Resources in the High Seas   Traditionally conservation of living resources on the high seas has attracted little attention. As a result of the establishment of the 200-mile EEZ, however, fishing vessels of distant

---

114 For problems concerning the concept of MSY, see Birnie and Boyle, above note 64, pp. 551–2.

115 Attard, above note 97, p. 153.

116 S.B. Kaye, *International Fisheries Management* (The Hague, Kluwer, 2001) pp. 52–3. In relation to this, Kesteven suggests that rather than a single MSY figure, there are a large number of possibilities in an array of at least four dimensions: within-year variations of abundance and composition, short- and long-term environmental favourability, year-to-year fluctuations in abundance and composition, and socio-economic evaluation of catch. Furthermore, it should be noted that the greatest MSY is likely to occur only once in many years. G.L. Kesteven, 'MSY Revisited: A Realistic Approach to Fisheries Management and Administration' (1997) 21 *Marine Policy*, pp. 73 and 75. On the other hand, O'Connell points to two approaches toward the calculation of MSY. One approach is to project on a global basis the yields established in practice in such heavily fished areas as the Humboldt Current; the other approach is to calculate the amount of phytoplankton which is naturally produced in the oceans, and on which the fishery stocks depend. Yet there is a wide discrepancy in the results reached by these methods. O'Connell, above note 23, p. 564. It would seem that the scientific evaluations are inconclusive and, thus, political and economic considerations will strongly affect the determination of MSY.

117 Kesteven, above note 116, p. 73.

118 In this respect, Judge Oda in the *Tunisia/Libya* case has stated that: 'the mode of exercise of jurisdiction is no different from that exercised by the coastal State within its territorial sea and, so far as the development of the natural resources of the sea is concerned, its competence in the Exclusive Economic Zone is equivalent to that it enjoys in the territorial sea.' Dissenting Opinion of Judge Oda, ICJ Reports 1982, p. 230, para. 124. R-J. Dupuy also argued that a State would promote the territorialisation of the EEZ by taking the form of a two-stage process: in the first stage, sovereignty could be broken down into specialised rights or competences; then the second stage, spread over repeated and generalised actions, could progressively reconstitute the sovereignty of the coastal State over the 200 miles previously considered. R-J. Dupuy, 'The Sea Under National Competence', in Dupuy and Vignes, above note 5, pp. 292 ff.

fishing States increasingly go to fish in the remaining high seas, leading to exhaustion of living resources. Consequently, the conservation of living resources on the high seas is becoming a matter of important concern in the international community. In this respect, the 1982 LOSC places obligations upon States to conserve these resources. Article 87 (1) (e) of the 1982 LOSC clearly sets out that the freedom of fishing is subject to conditions laid down in section 2, Part VII.[119] Furthermore, Article 116 provides that all States have the right for their nationals to engage in fishing on the high seas subject to (a) their treaty obligations; (b) the rights and duties as well as the interests of coastal States provided for, inter alia, in Article 63, paragraph 2, and Articles 64 to 67; and (c) the provisions of this section. The obligations concerning the conservation of living resources on the high seas are further elaborated in Articles 117, 118 and 119. Article 117 imposes upon 'all States' to take, or to co-operate with other States in taking, such measures for their respective nationals as may be necessary for the conservation of the living resources of the high seas. This provision is basically the same as Article 1 (2) of the High Seas Fishing Convention. Furthermore, Article 118 places a clear obligation upon States to co-operate with each other in the 'conservation and management' of living resources in the areas of the high seas. Article 118 further obliges States whose nationals exploit identical living resources, or different living resources in the same area, to negotiate with a view to take the measures necessary for the conservation of the living resources concerned.[120] Article 118 requires States to co-operate as appropriate to establish subregional or regional fisheries organisations to this end. Arguably participation in regional fisheries bodies is one method of fulfilling the obligation to co-operate in conservation of the living resources on the high seas.[121]

Moreover, Article 119 provides specific measures relating to the conservation of the living resources of the high seas. Article 119 (1) imposes States to take measures which are designed to maintain or restore populations of harvested species at levels which can produce the 'maximum sustainable yield' in determining the allowable catch and establishing other conservation measures for the living resources in the high seas. To this end, Article 119 (1) (a) requires States to consider the following factors:

(i)   the best scientific evidence available,
(ii)   relevant environmental and economic factors,
(iii)   the requirements of developing States,
(iv)   fishing patterns and the interdependence of stocks, and
(v)   any generally recommended international minimum standards.

---

119 On this point, the following study is of particular interest. UNDOALOS, *The Law of the Sea: The Regime for High-Seas Fisheries, Status and Prospects* (New York, United Nations, 1992) pp. 1–48 (in particular, pp. 6–12).

120 Unlike in the first sentence, there is no reference to the word 'management' in the second sentence of Article 118.

121 UNDOALOS, above note 119, p. 26, para. 78.

These requirements parallel Article 61 (3) concerning the conservation of the living resources in the EEZ.[122] Also, States are required to 'take into consideration the effects on species associated with or dependent upon harvested species with a view to maintaining or restoring populations of such associated or dependent species above levels at which their reproduction may become seriously threatened'.[123] States are obliged to exchange available scientific information relevant to the conservation of fish stocks on the high seas.[124] In addition, the States concerned shall ensure that conservation measures and their implementation do not discriminate against the fishermen of any State.[125] There is little doubt that the obligation to co-operate is a prerequisite in the conservation of living resources on the high seas. Nevertheless, it would seem that these provisions of the LOSC contain some issues which need further consideration.[126]

First, the obligation to co-operate in Articles 117 and 118 is too vague to be very useful.[127] For instance, there is no specific guidance describing how the co-operation shall be performed, and how it is possible to judge whether or not such an obligation was breached. Furthermore, Article 118 does not explicitly require States to pursue negotiations until an agreement is reached, nor does it specify the consequence of a failure in these negotiations.[128] In this relation, it should be recalled that the ICJ, in the *North Sea Continental Shelf* cases, emphasised the duty to negotiate, although the context is different: '[T]hey [the parties] are under an obligation so to conduct themselves that the negotiations are meaningful, which will not be the case when either of them insists upon its own position without contemplating any modification of it.'[129]

Secondly, concerning Article 119, it should be recalled that the validity of the concept of MSY is now a matter of discussion. It should also be noted that, unlike Article 2 of the 1958 High Seas Fishing Convention and Article 62 (1) of the LOSC, there is no reference to 'optimum utilisation' of the living resources in connection with high seas resources.[130]

Thirdly, unlike the 1958 High Seas Fisheries Convention, there is no provision relating to new entrants fishing on the high seas in the 1982 LOSC. Thus, even if some States reach agreement with respect to the conservation of living resources

---

122 Yet Article 61 (3) contains one more element, of 'economic needs of coastal fishing communities'. On the other hand, Article 119 contains an element which is lacking in Article 61 (3), that is to say, the requirements of developing States.

123 Article 119 (1) (b).

124 Article 119 (2).

125 Article 119 (3).

126 Oda, above note 13, p. xxii.

127 *Ibid.*

128 UNDOALOS, above note 119, p. 26, para. 77. See also Davies and Redgwell, above note 99, p. 229.

129 ICJ Reports 1969, p. 47, para. 85.

130 Oda, above note 13, p. xxii.

on the high seas, the accord may be at the mercy of new entrants. In this respect, a study of the UNDOALOS argued that:

> Even though outsiders are not parties to the specific instrument or to the subregional or regional commission that established the moratorium, nevertheless their obligations of cooperation and conservation under the 1982 Convention would compel them to comply unless they could establish that the moratorium was a measure that could not be justified under article 119 of the LOSC.[131]

Yet it is debatable whether the LOSC imposes such a strong obligation upon a newcomer State. In relation to this, it should be remembered that there is no obligation for States to reach an agreement under Article 118.

Finally, with respect to compliance with and enforcement of relevant rules, the 1982 LOSC relies essentially on the exclusive jurisdiction of the flag State. Nonetheless, State practice shows that the flag State, in particular the flag of convenience, does not adequately regulate fishing activities by vessels flying its flag due to a lack of will of flag States.[132] It must also be noted that many developing States lack the necessary capability to prevent illegal fishing by foreign fleets.[133] Hence, further consideration should be given to mechanisms ensuring the compliance with and enforcement of relevant rules in this field.

Limits of Conservation of Migratory Marine Species   A third limit of the 1982 LOSC concerns the inadequacy of rules with respect to conservation of migratory marine species. Concerning the regulation of shared fish stocks,[134] Article 63 (1) provides that:

> Where the same stock or stocks of associated species occur within the exclusive economic zones of two or more coastal States, these States shall seek, either directly or through appropriate subregional or regional organisations, to agree upon the measures

---

131 UNDOALOS, above note 119, p. 29.

132 This issue will be discussed in Chapter 3.

133 Churchill, above note 105, pp. 107–8.

134 There is no agreed terminology for fish stocks migrating or being distributed between the EEZs of two or more States. Although the term 'shared stocks' is not used in the LOSC, for the purpose of this study, it may be appropriate to use this term to describe stocks provided in Article 63 (1). In this respect, see R.R. Churchill, 'The Management of Shared Fish Stocks: The Neglected "Other" Paragraph of Article 63 of the UN Convention on the Law of the Sea', in A. Strati, M. Gavouneli and N. Skourtos (eds), *Unresolved Issues and New Challenges to the Law of the Sea: Time Before and Time After* (Leiden and Boston, Nijhoff, 2006) p. 3. On the other hand, some writers use the term 'transboundary stocks'. See, for instance, R. Lagoni, 'Principles Applicable to Living Resources Occurring Both Within and Without the Exclusive Economic Zone or in Zones of Overlapping Claims', in International Law Association, *Report of the Sixty-Fifth Conference at Cairo in 1992* (1993) p. 255; M.H. Nordquist, S.N. Nandan and S. Rosenne (eds), *United Nations Convention on*

necessary to co-ordinate and ensure the conservation and development of such stocks without prejudice to the other provisions of this Part.

In accordance with ordinary meaning, 'the same stock' means a group of the same species present in an area, independent of whether or not it forms shoals or lives discrete, whereas 'stocks of associated species' may be defined as groups of species of fish in the same area which prey upon or are preyed upon by the harvested species or prey upon the same food as the harvested species.[135] It is apparent that a lack of consistency in the conservation and management measures between States concerned could render those measures ineffective. Thus, there is a need to co-ordinate national measures with respect to the shared stocks. In this respect, three points should be noted.

First, whereas Article 63 (1) places an obligation upon States to negotiate in good faith with a view to concluding an agreement, the word 'seek' suggests that there is no obligation that States shall reach agreement.[136] Should no agreement be concluded, each State is to manage shared fish stocks occurring in its EEZ in accordance with international law governing marine living resources of this zone.[137] In such a case, however, it is likely that a shared stock may be mismanaged owing to the lack of co-ordination.[138]

Secondly, in order to establish co-ordinated conservation measures relating to a shared stock, it is necessary to establish a more positive international co-operation in the exchange of scientific data as well as concerted marine scientific research. To this end, it is arguable that regional fishery organisations or arrangements will have an important role to play.[139]

Thirdly, it should be noted that Article 63 (1) cautiously adds the words 'without prejudice to the other provisions of this Part'. This means that the States are bound by their conservation duties embodied in Articles 61 and 62 of the LOSC when managing a shared stock. Arguably these duties include promotion of the optimum utilisation of the stock, prevention of its over-exploitation, the maintenance of the

---

the Law of the Sea 1982: A Commentary (hereafter *Virginia Commentary*), Vol. II (The Hague, Nijhoff, 1993) p. 640; Attard, above note 97, p. 182.

135 Lagoni, above note 134, p. 257. In practice, the identification of shared stocks is not free from difficulty. In the late 1970s, for instance, the EC took the view that the western mackerel stock was an exclusive EC stock, while Norway argued that the stock was indeed shared. According to Churchill, it was only in the late 1980s that the EC acknowledged that the western mackerel was shared, and not until the early 1990s that Norway and the EC recognised that the stock was not only shared but was also a straddling one. Churchill, above note 134, p. 7.

136 Lagoni, above note 134, p. 258. However, it has to be stressed that States are under the obligation to negotiate in good faith.

137 Churchill and Lowe, above note 98, p. 294; Lagoni, above note 134, p. 262.

138 Churchill, above note 134, pp. 8–9; Guifang Xue, *China and International Fisheries Law and Policy* (Leiden and Boston, Nijhoff, 2005) p. 24.

139 Churchill, above note 134, p. 8.

MSY, the setting of an allowable catch, and the taking into account of the best scientific evidence available.[140] In relation to this, a question arising is how it is possible to reconcile 'conservation' and 'development' of those stocks. Although Article 63 (1) contains no guidance on this issue, a reasonable interpretation may be that obligations of conservation embodied in Article 61 are also applicable to the 'development' of shared stocks.[141] It may be argued that the exploitation of shared stocks in a deteriorating manner would be contrary to the obligation to negotiate in good faith under Article 63 (1). Overall it may be concluded that Article 63 (1) provides only a minimum rule relating to the conservation and management of shared stocks.[142]

With respect to straddling fish stocks, Article 63 (2) provides that:

> Where the same stock or stocks of associated species occur both within the exclusive economic zone and in an area beyond and adjacent to the zone, the coastal State and the States fishing for such stocks in the adjacent area shall seek, either directly or through appropriate subregional or regional organisations, to agree upon the measures necessary for the conservation of these stocks in the adjacent area.[143]

In light of the similarity of language with Article 63 (1), similar criticisms will be applied to Article 63 (2). Indeed, as with Article 63 (1), Article 63 (2) contains no specific recourse in the case of inability to reach agreement.[144] Thus the failure to agree conservation measures concerning straddling fish stocks leads neither to a suspension of fishing nor to the provisional application of national or regional measures.[145] A difficulty in reaching a conservation agreement will be increased where the number of potential fishing States remains indeterminate.[146] Even if the coastal States and high seas fishing States reach agreement in accordance with Article 63 (2), there is a risk that the accord may be undermined by new entrants.[147] It should also be noted that the conservation of straddling stocks extends only to conservation of such stocks 'in the area beyond and adjacent to' the EEZ, and not within their whole geographic range in areas under national jurisdiction and

---

140 *Ibid.*, p. 11.

141 *Virginia Commentary*, above note 134, p. 647.

142 Lagoni, above note 134, p. 259. See also Churchill, above note 134, p. 11.

143 With respect to the analysis of this provision, see J.L. Meseguer, 'Le régime juridique de l'exploitation de stocks communs de poissons au-delà des 200 milles (article 63, paragraphe 2, de la Convention sur le droit de la mer)' (1982) 28 *AFDI*, pp. 885–99.

144 Davies and Redgwell, above note 99, p. 236.

145 *Ibid.*

146 O. Thébaud, 'Transboundary Marine Fisheries Management: Recent Developments and Elements of Analysis' (1997) 21 *Marine Policy*, p. 241.

147 W.T. Burke, 'Unregulated High Seas Fishing and Ocean Governance', in J.M. Van Dyke, D. Zaelke and G. Hewison (eds), *Freedom for the Seas in the 21st Century: Ocean Governance and Environmental Harmony* (Washington, DC, Island Press, 1993) p. 240.

areas beyond such jurisdiction.[148] Thus the importance will be underscored of the establishment of a regime including all States fishing the straddling stocks in relevant areas. Moreover, Article 63 (2) provides no guidance as to how it is possible to allocate those resources between vessels fishing for such stocks in the EEZ and vessels fishing for those stocks on the high seas.[149] This point shows a clear contrast with the provision for anadromous species, in that States in whose rivers anadromous stocks originate shall have the primary interest in and responsibility for such stocks, and fisheries for anadromous stocks shall be conducted only in waters landward of the outer limits of EEZs; where the species is fished beyond the EEZ, States concerned shall maintain consultations with a view to achieving agreement on terms and conditions of such fishing, giving due regard to the conservation requirements and the needs of the State of origin in respect of these stocks.[150]

Cape Verde,[151] São Tomé and Príncipe[152] and Uruguay[153] declared upon signature of the 1982 LOSC that states fishing straddling stocks in the adjacent area must reach agreement with the coastal State upon the necessary conservation measures. Some writers are supportive of those declarations, arguing that high seas fishing upon straddling species is subject to the sovereign rights of the coastal State by combining Articles 116 (b), 63 (2) and 56.[154] Nonetheless, the validity

---

148 Attard, above note 97, p. 184.

149 Churchill and Lowe, above note 98, p. 305.

150 Article 66 (3) (a). Similarly, with respect to catadromous species, a coastal State in whose waters these species spend the greater part of their life cycle shall have responsibility for the management of these species and shall ensure the ingress and egress of migrating fish. Harvesting of catadromous species shall be conducted only in waters landward of the outer limits of EEZs. In cases where catadromous fish migrate through the EEZ of another State, the management, including harvesting, of such fish shall be regulated by agreement between the coastal State and the other State concerned.

151 UNDOALOS, *The Law of the Sea: Declarations and Statements with Respect to the United Nations Convention on the Law of the Sea and to the Agreement Relating to the Implementation of Part XI of the United Nations Convention on the Law of the Sea of 10 December 1982* (New York, United Nations, 1997) p. 6.

152 *Ibid.*, p. 15.

153 *Ibid.*, p. 45.

154 For example, Burke argued: 'Because article 56 establishes the sovereign rights of the coastal state over the living resources of the EEZ, article 116 means that the right to fish on the high seas is subject to the sovereign rights, as well as the interests, of coastal states as provided in the articles of Part V of the 1982 Convention. Accordingly, the 1982 Convention might be interpreted as providing that high seas fishing upon stocks that also occur within a coastal state's EEZ is subject to the sovereign right of that coastal State.' Burke, above note 73, p. 133. See also B. Applebaum, 'The Straddling Stocks Problem: The Northwest Atlantic Situation, International Law, and Options for Coastal State Action', in A.H.A. Soons (ed.), *Implementation of the Law of the Sea Convention Through International Institutions, Proceedings of the 23rd Annual Conference of the Law of the Sea Institute 1989* (Honolulu, The Law of the Sea Institute, University of Hawaii, 1990) p. 302.

of this interpretation remains a matter of discussion since such an interpretation will lead to the extension of the coastal State's jurisdiction toward the high seas. It would seem that the *travaux préparatoires* of the 1982 LOSC do not support the interpretation of Article 63 (2) favouring the coastal State's interests. In the negotiations, proposals were made for recognition of the special interest of the coastal State with respect to straddling fish stocks in 1980. At the ninth session in 1980, Argentina and Canada made informal proposals for amendment of Article 63 in order to reflect the special interest of the coastal State in this matter. Nonetheless, the proposed amendment was not incorporated in the text of Article 63 owing to opposition to any recognition of a special interest of coastal States in straddling fish stocks from traditional distant water fishing States.[155] Thus there is no explicit reference to 'special interests' of the coastal State concerning straddling fish stocks in Article 63 (2). Article 63 (2) provides no requirement of compatibility of measures between the EEZ and the high seas.[156] It should also be noted that 'rights, duties and interests' provided in Article 116 create no jurisdiction of the coastal State in the adjacent area.[157] In summary, it should be interpreted that Article 63 (2) does not provide 'special interests' of the coastal State on the high seas resources beyond 200 miles.[158]

Finally, in relation to highly migratory species, Article 64 provides that:

1. The coastal State and other States whose nationals fish in the region for the highly migratory species listed in Annex I shall cooperate directly or through appropriate international organisations with a view to ensuring conservation and promoting the objective of optimum utilisation of such species throughout the region, both within and beyond the exclusive economic zone. In regions for which no appropriate international organisation exists, the coastal State and other States whose nationals harvest these species in the region shall cooperate to establish such an organisation and participate in its work.

2. The provisions of paragraph 1 apply in addition to the other provisions of this Part.[159]

---

155 Davies and Redgwell, above note 99, pp. 238–9; UNDOALOS, above note 119, pp. 23–4, paras 68–9. Concerning the summary of negotiation of this provision, see *Virginia Commentary*, above note 134, pp. 641–6.

156 Davies and Redgwell, above note 99, p. 239.

157 Lagoni, above note 134, p. 272. Furthermore, those elements are not clearly defined.

158 This interpretation is supported by writers, including Davies and Redgwell, above note 99, p. 239; Kwiatkowska, above note 97, p. 80; Meseguer, above note 143, pp. 898–9; R.C. Raigón, 'La pêche en haute mer', in Vignes *et al.*, above note 7, p. 212.

159 Although there is no definition of highly migratory fish stocks in the LOSC, these species are listed in Annex I. The list includes various species of tuna, marlin, sailfish, swordfish, dolphin, shark and cetacean.

This provision represents a compromise between Latin American countries, in particular those of the Pacific coast where tuna is abundant, and the distant-water tuna-fishing countries.[160] It is notable that unlike Article 63 (2) concerning straddling fish stocks, this provision places a clear obligation upon States to co-operate.[161] It is also noteworthy that Article 64 clearly provides for conservation and promoting the objective of optimum utilisation of these species in the EEZ as well as on the high seas.[162] On the other hand, like Article 63, Article 64 contains no specific mechanism ensuring co-operation in this matter. It remains unclear how it is possible to resolve problems when no co-operation can be achieved. Furthermore, Article 64 provides no guidance with respect to the question of how catches for highly migratory species can be allocated between the coastal State and States fishing on the high seas. Overall it may be an inescapable conclusion that Article 64 merely provides for guidelines reconciling the interests of the coastal States and those of fisheries States on the high seas.[163]

Conclusion

The results of the preceding study can be summarised in four points:

(i)   As shown in the case law relating to fishery disputes, the reconciliation of the national interest of the coastal State controlling offshore resources and that of the distant fishing State ensuring the freedom of fisheries is a question at the heart of international law relating to conservation of marine living resources. A primary function of the traditional zonal management approach was to reconcile those opposing interests. Thus it may be said that the zonal management approach is in essence an exploitation-oriented approach.

(ii)   In fact, State practice has shown that the safeguard of national interest of coastal States has been the moving force to promote the zonal management approach.[164] Consequently, it is not surprising that the obligation to conserve marine living resources in marine spaces under and beyond the national jurisdiction remains weak in the 1982 LOSC. Furthermore, it is argued that the implementation of the obligations to conserve marine living resources in the LOSC will face difficulties in

---

160 Caflisch, above note 97, p. 165.

161 Lucchini and Vœlckel, above note 74, p. 503; Raigón, above note 158, p. 216.

162 F. Orrego Vicuña, above note 21, p. 28.

163 Lucchini and Vœlckel, above note 74, p. 502; Carroz, above note 97, p. 193. See also H. Takabayashi, *A Study of the UN Convention on the Law of the Sea* (in Japanese) (Tokyo, Toshindo, 1996) p. 120.

164 *Cf.* W.T. Burke, 'U.S. Fishery Management and the New Law of the Sea' (1982) 76 *AJIL*, p. 53.

practice. In particular, the obligations relating to the allowable catch as well as MSY are difficult to implement owing to the paucity of marine scientific data. It is also difficult and costly for States to obtain the marine scientific data necessary to determine conservation measures.

(iii) As typically demonstrated in the *Bering Sea Fur-Seals* dispute, the conservation of migratory species relates to an inherent problem with the zonal management approach. Yet neither the 1958 High Seas Fishing Convention nor the 1982 LOSC adequately address this issue.

(iv) Concerning the mechanisms ensuring compliance with and enforcement of rules of international law concerning the conservation of marine species, the High Seas Fishing Convention and the LOSC are based on the traditional principle of exclusive jurisdiction of the flag State. Nonetheless, the factual situation shows that this principle alone is inadequate for ensuring compliance with and enforcement of rules of international law in this field. Thus, in addition to the traditional mechanism, there is a need to develop other mechanisms in this matter. It follows from the above discussions that the traditional zonal management approach is inadequate in order to properly conserve marine living resources.

Chapter 3

The Quest for an Integrated Management Approach to the Conservation of Marine Living Resources

Introduction

On the basis of the consideration of Chapter 2, Chapter 3 will address the question whether and to what extent novel concepts and approaches can be identified with a view to offsetting weaknesses of the zonal management approach after 1982. Special attention should be focused on four issues which are more or less related to the integrated management approach.

A first issue pertains to the concept of sustainable development. This concept seeks in essence to reconcile the requirements of environmental protection and those of development. In light of the over-exploitation of marine living resources, the reconciliation of these two requirements is a central issue underlying international law concerning conservation of those resources. Thus it is arguable that sustainable development becomes a cardinal concept in this field.

A second issue which needs to be discussed in this chapter relates to two novel approaches in this field: the ecosystem approach and the precautionary approach. As explained in Chapter 1, the ecosystem approach is a backbone of the integrated management approach at the ecological level. Furthermore, the precautionary approach, which was originally developed in the context of environmental protection, is increasingly seen in the context of the conservation of marine species. In light of the close linkage between the ecosystem and precautionary approaches, it will be advisable to examine these approaches at the same time.

A third issue concerns procedures ensuring compliance with rules of international law relating to conservation of marine living resources. In highly centralised domestic legal systems, compliance with relevant rules is secured eventually by central State authority. Hence, usually, securing compliance with relevant rules will not create a serious question in domestic legal systems. In the international legal system, however, there is no centralised machinery securing compliance with rules of international law. Thus compliance procedures securing relevant rules become an important question underlying international law, and law of the sea is no exception. In the context of the conservation of marine species, of particular importance will be the flag State's responsibility as well as international supervision through international institutions.

Finally, consideration should be given to the enforcement of rules of international law in this field. It is acknowledged that Illegal, Unreported and Unregulated Fishing (IUU Fishing) has an adverse impact on conservation of marine living resources.[1] In response to this problem, there is a need to enforce relevant rules in an integrated manner. In fact, the 2001 International Plan of Action to Prevent, Deter and Eliminate IUU Fishing encouraged States to take a comprehensive and integrated approach.[2] In relation to this, non-flag State enforcement at sea as well as in ports will invite serious consideration.

The Concept of Sustainable Development in Conservation of Marine Living Resources

The Concept of Sustainable Development

In international law relating to conservation of marine living resources, an important question arises concerning the reconciliation between the conservation of marine living resources and the need to develop the exploitation of these resources. Considering this question, of particular importance is the concept of sustainable development.[3] It is acknowledged that the concept of sustainable development was given currency by the Report of the World Commission on Environment

---

1 The 2005 Rome Declaration on Illegal, Unreported and Unregulated Fishing, paragraph 9 of the Preamble.

2 FAO, *International Plan of Action to Prevent, Deter and Eliminate Illegal, Unreported and Unregulated Fishing*, 2001, para. 9.3. This document is available at the homepage of FAO <http://www.fao.org>.

3 With respect to the development of the concept of sustainable development, see in particular Y. Matsui, 'The Road to Sustainable Development: Evolution of the Concept of Development in the UN', in K. Ginther, H. Denters and P.J.I.M. de Waart (eds), *Sustainable Development and Good Governance* (Dordrecht, Kluwer, 1995) pp. 53–71. The concept of sustainable development in international law has been discussed by many writers. See, for instance, M. Sanwal, 'Sustainable Development, the Rio Declaration and Multilateral Cooperation' (1993) 4 *Colorado Journal of International Environmental Law and Policy*, pp. 45–68; P. Sands, 'International Law in the Field of Sustainable Development' (1994) 65 *BYIL*, pp. 303–81; W. Lang (ed.), *Sustainable Development and International Law* (Dordrecht, Nijhoff, 1995); A.E. Boyle and D. Freestone (eds), *International Law and Sustainable Development: Past Achievements and Future Challenges* (Oxford, Oxford University Press, 1999); P. Sands, 'International Courts and the Application of the Concept of "Sustainable Development"' (1999) 3 *Max Planck Yearbook of United Nations Law*, pp. 389–405; T. Takashima, 'Sustainable Development and International Law' (in Japanese) (2002) 75 *Hogaku Kenkyu* (*Journal of Law, Politics and Sociology*), pp. 223–47; P. Schwarz, 'Sustainable Development in International Law' (2005) 5 *Non-State Actors and International Law*, pp. 127–52. Furthermore, the concept of sustainable development is one of the subjects for discussion in the International Law Association. So far the ILA Committee on the International Law on Sustainable Development has made two reports on

and Development, 'Our Common Future'.[4] In its report, the World Commission on Environment and Development (hereafter WCED) defined this concept as: 'development that meets the needs of the present without compromising the ability of future generations to meet their own needs.'[5] This concept seeks in essence to reconcile the need for development with environmental protection.[6] The WCED stated that: 'Environment and development are not separate challenges; they are inexorably linked. Development cannot subsist upon a deteriorating environmental resource base; the environment cannot be protected when growth leaves out of account the costs of the environmental destruction.'[7]

The basic idea is echoed by the ICJ in the *Gabčíkovo-Nagymaros Project* case[8] as well as the Arbitral Tribunal in the *Arbitration regarding the Iron Rhine Railway* of 2005.[9] Furthermore, the WCED stated that: 'Sustainable development seeks to meet the needs and aspirations of the present without compromising the ability to meet those of the future.'[10] In 1987, the UN General Assembly also agreed that an equitable sharing of the environmental costs and benefits of economic development between countries and between present and future generations was a key to achieving sustainable development.[11] It would follow that the concept of sustainable development reflects 'inter-generational equity'.[12]

Currently the concept of sustainable development is increasingly reflected in various documents concerning conservation of marine species. With respect to non-binding documents, for example, Chapter 17 of Agenda 21 of 1992 sets out that: 'States commit themselves to the conservation and sustainable use of marine living resources on the high seas.'[13] A similar commitment is stated with respect

---

this issue, in 2004 and 2006 respectively. These reports are available at the website of ILA <http://www.ila-hq.org/>.

4 The World Commission on Environment and Development, *Our Common Future* (Oxford, Oxford University Press, 1987).

5 *Ibid.*, p. 43.

6 Sands has argued that the principle of integration between environment and development is the most important in the concept of sustainable development. P. Sands, *Principles of International Environmental Law*, 2nd edn (Cambridge, Cambridge University Press, 2003) p. 263.

7 WCED, above note 4, p. 37.

8 ICJ Reports 1997, p. 78, para. 140.

9 The *Arbitration regarding the Iron Rhine Railway* case (Belgium and the Netherlands), pp. 28–9, para. 59. This award is available at:<http://www.pca-cpa.org/upload/files/BE-NL %20Award%20corrected%20200905.pdf>.

10 WCED, above note 4, p. 40.

11 UN General Assembly Resolution, *Report of the World Commission on Environment and Development*, A/RES/42/187, 11 December 1987, para. 4 of the operative part; para. 8 of the operative part; para. 2 of the Preamble.

12 Matsui, above note 3, p. 69.

13 Agenda 21, para. 17.46.

to marine living resources in marine spaces under national jurisdiction.[14] It is not unreasonable to argue that 'sustainable use' is regarded as a variant of the concept of sustainable development. The notion of sustainable development or sustainable use can also be seen in the Code of Conduct for Responsible Fisheries (hereafter the FAO Code of Conduct),[15] the 1999 Rome Declaration on the Implementation of the Code of Conduct for Responsible Fisheries,[16] and the 2001 Reykjavik Declaration on Responsible Fisheries in the Marine Ecosystem.[17]

At the treaty level, Article 2 of the 2001 Convention on the Conservation and Management of Fishery Resources in the South-East Atlantic Ocean stipulates that '[t]he objective of this Convention is to ensure the long-term conservation and sustainable use of the fishery resources in the Convention Area through the effective implementation of this Convention'.[18] A similar provision can be detected in the 2000 Convention on the Conservation and Management of Highly Migratory Fish Stocks in the Western and Central Pacific Ocean.[19] The 1992 Convention on Biological Diversity – which is applicable to marine biological diversity – also makes clear that one of its objectives is the sustainable use of components of biological diversity.[20] Furthermore, it is notable that the 1995 UN Fish Stocks Agreement contains provisions ensuring sustainable use in more detail.[21] Article

---

14 *Ibid.*, para. 17.75.

15 Article 7.2.1. This document was unanimously adopted on 31 October 1995 by the FAO Conference. For the text, see <http://www.fao.org/fi/agreem/codecond/ficonde.asp>. The Code is global in scope, and is directed toward members and non-members of FAO, fishing entities, subregional, regional and global organisations, whether governmental or non-governmental, and all persons concerned with the conservation of fishery resources and management and development of fisheries (Article 1.2). While the Code is a voluntary instrument relating to fisheries, certain parts of it are based on relevant rules of international law, including those reflected in the LOSC. The Code is to be interpreted and applied in conformity with the relevant rules of international law, as reflected in the 1982 LOSC. Nothing in this Code prejudices the rights, jurisdiction and duties of States under international law as reflected in the Convention. The Code is also to be interpreted and applied in conformity with the 1995 UN Fish Stocks Agreement (Article 3). With respect to the Code of Conduct, see, for instance, G. Moore, 'The Code of Conduct for Responsible Fisheries', in E. Hey (ed.), *Developments in International Fisheries Law* (The Hague, Kluwer, 1999) pp. 85–105.

16 The text of the Rome Declaration is available at the homepage of FAO <http://www/fao.org/>.

17 The text of the Reykjavik Declaration is available at the homepage of FAO <http://www/fao.org/>.

18 For the text of the Convention, see (2002) 41 *ILM*, p. 257.

19 Article 2. For the text of the Convention, see (2001) 40 *ILM*, p. 278.

20 Article 1. For the text of the Convention, see 1760 *UNTS*, 79.

21 The full title of this agreement is: Agreement for the Implementation of the Provisions of the United Nations Convention on the Law of the Sea of 10 December 1982 Relating to the Conservation and Management of Straddling Fish Stocks and Highly Migratory Fish Stocks. For the text of the agreement (1995) 34 *ILM*, p. 1547. F. Orrego Vicuña, 'The

2 of the Agreement makes explicit that: 'The objective of this Agreement is to ensure the long-term conservation and sustainable use of straddling fish stocks and highly migratory fish stocks through effective implementation of the relevant provisions of the Convention.'

More specifically Article 5 (a) requires coastal States and States fishing on the high seas to 'adopt measures to ensure long-term sustainability of straddling fish stocks and highly migratory fish stocks and promote the objective of their optimum utilisation'. Article 5 (h) further imposes upon coastal States and States fishing on the high seas the duty to 'take measures to prevent or eliminate over-fishing and excess fishing capacity and to ensure that levels of fishing effort do not exceed those commensurate with the sustainable use of fishery resources'.

Normativity of the Concept of Sustainable Development

This cursory survey shows that the importance of sustainable development is increasingly stressed in non-binding documents as well as treaties concerning the conservation of marine living resources. Given that marine species are renewable resources, there is little doubt that sustainable use of these resources is of central importance. Thus it is arguable that sustainable development is becoming a guiding principle in international law in this field. Furthermore, in light of its open-textured nature, it may be argued that the notion of sustainable development could be a catalyst stimulating intra-treaty, inter-discipline or intra-discipline integrations.[22] On the other hand, it should be noted that the notion of sustainable development contains some issues which need further reflection with respect to its normativity.

A first issue concerns specific contents of the concept of sustainable development. In order to specify its contents, some writers attempt to enumerate relevant components of the concept. For instance, Sands identified two categories of principles on the basis of the instruments of the UNCED. The first comprises core principles of sustainable development, which contain: (i) integration of environment and development; (ii) application of equity between States; (iii) consideration of the needs of future generations; and (iv) non-exhaustion of renewable natural resources.[23] A second category of principles purports to provide assistance in achieving sustainable development. These principles include: (i) that States have sovereignty over natural resources and the responsibility not to cause environmental damage; (ii) good neighbourliness and international co-operation; (iii) common but differentiated responsibility; (iv) precaution; and (v) the polluter-

---

International Law of High Seas Fisheries: From Freedom of Fishing to Sustainable Use', in O.S. Stokke (ed.), *Governing High Seas Fisheries: The Interplay of Global and Regional Regimes* (Oxford, Oxford University Press, 2001) pp. 32–3.

22 On this issue, see International Law Association, *The Second Report of the Committee on International Law on Sustainable Development*, ILA Toronto Conference (2006), pp. 14–18. This report is available at <http://www.ila-hq.org/>.

23 *Ibid.*, p. 338.

pays principle.[24] It would appear that this catalogue broadly includes basic elements of international environmental law. Later on, Sands selected, more succinctly, four recurring elements of the concept of sustainable development:

(i)   the need to preserve natural resources for the benefit of future generations (the principle of intergenerational equity);
(ii)   the aim of exploiting natural resources in a manner which is 'sustainable', or 'prudent', or 'wise' or 'appropriate' (the principle of sustainable use);
(iii) the 'equitable' use of natural resources, which implies that use by one State must take account of the needs of other States (the principle of equitable use); and
(iv)   the need to ensure that environmental considerations are integrated into economic and other development plans, programmes and projects, and that development needs are taken into account in allying environmental objectives (the principle of integration).[25]

Boyle and Freestone extrapolated substantive and procedural elements of the concept of sustainable development on the basis of the Rio Declaration. The substantive elements, which are mainly reflected in Principles 3–8 of the Rio Declaration, comprise:

(i)   the sustainable utilisation of natural resources;
(ii)   the integration of environmental protection and economic development;
(iii) the right to development; and
(iv)   the pursuit of equity in the allocation of resources both within the present generation and between present and future generations (intra- and inter-generational equity).

The procedural elements, which are set out in Principles 10–17, include public participation in decision-making and environmental impact assessment.[26]

On the other hand, P-M. Dupuy considered that the concept of sustainable development would include the following 'principles':

---

24 *Ibid.*

25 Sands, above note 6, p. 253.

26 Boyle and Freestone, above note 3, pp. 8–16. Furthermore, Fitzmaurice enumerates access to information, access to environmental justice, and transparency as the procedural elements of the concept of sustainable development. M.A. Fitzmaurice, 'International Protection of the Environment' (2001) 293 *RCADI*, p. 53.

(i)   Principle of integration between the environment and development;

(ii)   Precautionary principle;

(iii)   Principle of common concern of humanity;

(iv)   Principle of State sovereignty with State responsibility;

(v)   Principle of common but differentiated responsibility;

(vi)   Principle of global partnership and co-operation;

(vii)   Polluter-pays principle;

(viii)   Principle of participatory and informed decision-making.[27]

Although some common elements may be identified in the opinions of these writers, it appears that overall there is no uniform understanding with respect to the specific contents of the concept of sustainable development. The normativity of each component is also a matter of discussion.[28] Furthermore, the interrelationship between elements of this concept remains obscure. Thus, it appears to be an inescapable conclusion that there remains a considerable uncertainty as to the specific contents and the scope of this concept.[29] In summary, it would seem that the concept of sustainable development is no more than a label for a set of various components of international environmental law at a high level of abstraction. Nonetheless, it must be pointed out that the label itself is not a norm.[30] Hence it appears questionable that the concept of sustainable development itself can be regarded a norm purporting to constrain behaviour of States.[31]

A second issue to be addressed relates to the justiciability of this concept. It is important to note that the concept of sustainable development ultimately requires a change in the quality and patterns of life. In fact, the WCED Report explicitly stated that:

> In essence, sustainable development is a process of change in which the exploitation of resources, the direction of investments, the orientation of technological development, and institutional change are all in harmony and enhance both current and future potential to meet human needs and aspirations.[32]

---

27 P-M. Dupuy, 'Où en est le droit international de l'environnement à la fin du siècle' (1997) 101 *RGDIP*, pp. 888–91.

28 For instance, Lowe questioned the normative status of inter-generational equity. V. Lowe, 'Sustainable Development and Unsustainable Arguments', in Boyle and Freestone, above note 3, pp. 26–30.

29 This is accepted by many writers. See, for instance, Boyle and Freestone, above note 3, p 7; Sands, above note 3 (*MPYUN*), p. 396; Sands, above note 3 (*BYIL*) pp. 304–5; Fitzmaurice, above note 26, p. 49; P. Malanczuk, 'Sustainable Development: Some Critical Thoughts in the Light of the Rio Conference', in Ginther *et al.*, above note 3, p. 25.

30 Lowe, above note 28, p. 26.

31 *Ibid.*, pp. 23–5.

32 WCED, above note 4, p. 46.

According to WCED, sustainable development required 'a change in the content of growth, to make it less material- and energy-intensive and more equitable in its impact'.[33] Similarly, Principle 8 of the Rio Declaration sets out that: '[t]o achieve sustainable development and a higher quality of life for all people, States should reduce and eliminate unsustainable patterns of production and consumption and promote appropriate demographic policies.' Considering that sustainable development is closely interlinked to national policy of a State, however, it appears difficult to *a priori* determine specific measures to achieve sustainable development in international law. If this is the case, it will be difficult for international courts and tribunals to review the validity of national action by applying the concept of sustainable development.[34] In fact, arguably the majority opinion of the ICJ in the *Gabčíkovo-Nagymaros Project* case regarded sustainable development as only a 'concept', not a principle or a rule.[35] Thus it is debatable whether the concept of sustainable development itself can be an independent rule of adjudication.[36] Furthermore, without authoritative third-party decision-making, it would be hard to elaborate the content of the concept of sustainable development.[37] In summary, it may be argued that the normativity of the concept of sustainable development remains modest as a rule of conduct as well as a rule of adjudication.

It is not suggested, however, that the concept of sustainable development has no legal effect. Theoretically at least, the concept of sustainable development may provide a parameter guiding the direction of interpretation of rules of international law. For instance, faced with competing norms, it appears possible that international courts and tribunals may take this concept into account in making a judicial choice to lead to the preferred outcome. To this extent, the concept of sustainable development can be used as a factor to be taken into account with a view to

---

33 *Ibid.*, p. 52.

34 Boyle and Freestone, above note 3, p. 16; A.E. Boyle, 'The *Gabčíkovo-Nagymaros* Case: New Law in Old Bottles' (1997) 8 *Yearbook of Environmental Law*, p. 18. On this point, Birnie and Boyle argued that: 'Given the social, political, and economic value judgments involved in deciding on what is sustainable, and the necessity of weighting conflicting factors, of which environmental protection is only one, it is difficult to see an international court reviewing national action and concluding that it falls short of a standard of "sustainable development".' P. Birnie and A. Boyle, *International Law and the Environment*, 2nd edn (Oxford, Oxford University Press, 2002) p. 95.

35 Sands, above note 3 (*MPYUN*), p. 393.

36 Boyle and Freestone, above note 3, p. 16; Lowe, above note 28, pp. 24–5. For the same reason, it is debatable whether the concept of sustainable development can be regarded as a customary rule of international law. In fact, one should note that despite the frequent reference to sustainable development, it is highly difficult to find evidence of *opinio juris* in this matter. *Ibid.*, p. 24.

37 G. Handl, 'Environmental Security and Global Change: The Challenge to International Law' 1990 (1) *Yearbook of International Environmental Law*, p. 25; Malanczuk, above note 29, p. 50.

ensuring a preferable interpretation.[38] In the *Gabčíkovo-Nagymaros Project* case, for instance, the ICJ ruled that new norms and standards, including the concept of sustainable development, had been developed in the field of environmental protection; and that such new norms had to be taken into consideration, and such new standards given proper weight.[39] Thus the Court held that considering the concept of sustainable development, the Parties together should look afresh at the effects on the environment of the operation of the Gabčíkovo power plant.[40] In so stating, it would seem that the Court regarded this concept as a factor which should be taken into account in the process of decision-making by the Parties.[41] In conclusion, it may be argued that the concept of sustainable development can have a normative force as a judicial factor which may be taken into consideration in a judicial process.[42]

New Approaches to Conservation of Marine Living Resources

The Ecosystem Approach

Development of the Ecosystem Approach   As indicated in Chapter 1, it is becoming apparent that the intricate relationship of marine ecosystems and the environments that support them are important elements in establishing an effective ocean management regarding marine living resources as well as marine biological diversity; and that an approach focusing on ecological interaction, that is to say, the ecosystem approach, is of central importance in the conservation of marine species.[43] The ecosystem approach focuses on biological interactions between all

---

38 Lowe, above note 28, p. 31.

39 ICJ Reports 1997, p. 78, para. 140. The Arbitral Tribunal, in the *Iron Rhine Railway* case, echoed this view. Above note 9, p. 29, para. 59.

40 ICJ Reports 1997, p. 78, para. 140.

41 Boyle, above note 34, p. 18.

42 Lowe, above note 28, p. 31 and pp. 34–5. In a sense, it would appear that this concept plays a similar role to the concept of proportionality in the law of maritime delimitation. In fact, there are only a few State practices relating to proportionality in the law. Consequently, one cannot regard proportionality as customary international law. In addition, there is no treaty which requires international courts and tribunals to apply the concept of proportionality in maritime delimitations. Nevertheless, the concept of proportionality has been taken into account by almost all international decisions relating to maritime delimitations. To this extent, the concept has a certain degree of normative force. With respect to the concept of proportionality in the law of maritime delimitation, see Y. Tanaka, *Predictability and Flexibility in the Law of Maritime Delimitation* (Oxford, Hart Publishing, 2006) pp. 161–83; pp. 325–7.

43 E.J. Molenaar, 'Ecosystem-Based Fisheries Management, Commercial Fisheries, Marine Mammals and the 2001 Reykjavik Declaration in the Context of International

marine species in the same as well as in neighbouring zones, and the ecological conditions of the physical surroundings.[44]

In this respect, it is notable that the Report of the UN Secretary-General of 2004 highlighted the importance of the ecosystem approach with a view to promoting integrated ocean management:

> The ecosystem approach is the backbone of sustainable development. It is a strategy for the integrated management of all elements of the environment and all components of its resources in order to promote their conservation and sustainable use. Together with the precautionary approach, the ecosystem approach has been one of the most important concepts of environmental and natural resource management of the past two decades.[45]

The Report of the Secretary-General of 2006 amplified this view:

> [T]he development of ecosystem approaches in the marine context builds on the concept of integrated management, already widely used for the management of marine and coastal areas. Integrated management involves comprehensive planning and regulation of human activities towards a complex set of interacting objectives and aims at minimizing user conflicts while ensuring long-term sustainability. It recognizes the need to protect the ecosystem taking into account the effects of multiple uses and acknowledges the limitations of the sectoral approaches and the linkages between inland, coastal and ocean uses. *The ecosystem approach can be considered as an evolution of integrated management, with a greater emphasis on ecosystem implications.*[46]

The linkage between the ecosystem and the integrated management approach is also stressed by some writers. For instance, Freestone stated that: 'If the goal is to preserve marine biodiversity, it requires a holistic/comprehensive approach which can address the whole range of threats to marine species or ecosystems, including ecological processes and functions: in other words, an ecosystem approach.'[47]

Law' (2002) 17 *IJMCL*, pp. 561–95; L. Juda, 'Rio Plus Ten: The Evolution of International Marine Fisheries Governance' (2002) 33 *ODIL*, pp. 109–44 (in particular, pp. 131–2).

44 N. Matz, 'The Interaction between the Convention on Biological Diversity and the UN Convention on the Law of the Sea', in P. Ehlers, E. Mann-Borgese and R. Wolfrum (eds), *Marine Issues: From a Scientific, Political and Legal Perspective* (The Hague, Kluwer, 2002) p. 208.

45 United Nations, *Report of the Secretary-General, Oceans and the Law of the Sea*, A/59/62/Add.1, 18 August 2004, p. 63, para. 244.

46 Emphasis added. *Report of the Secretary-General, Oceans and the Law of the Sea*, A/61/63, 9 March 2006, p. 33, para. 117. See also p. 38, para. 136.

47 D. Freestone, 'The Conservation of Marine Ecosystems under International Law', in C. Redgwell and M. Bowman (eds), *International Law and the Conservation of Biological Diversity* (The Hague, Kluwer, 1996) pp. 105–6.

Similarly, Bliss argued that the ecosystem approach would provide an organising principle for integrated ocean management.[48]

In reality, the ecosystem approach is increasingly enshrined in various binding and non-binding documents relating to conservation of marine living resources. As for non-binding documents, Article 6.1 of the FAO Code of Conduct explicitly requires States to conserve marine ecosystems, by stating that: 'States and users of living aquatic resources should conserve aquatic ecosystems. The right to fish carries with it the obligation to do so in a responsible manner so as to ensure effective conservation and management of the living aquatic resources.' To this end, Article 6.2 makes clear that '[m]anagement measures should not only ensure the conservation of target species but also of species belonging to the same ecosystem or associated with or dependent upon the target species'. Article 10.1.1 further requires States to ensure that an appropriate policy, legal and institutional framework is adopted to achieve the sustainable and integrated use of the resources, taking into account the fragility of coastal ecosystems and the finite nature of their natural resources, and the needs of coastal communities. Similarly the 1999 Rome Declaration on the Implementation of the Code of Conduct for Responsible Fisheries noted that 'greater consideration should be given to the development of more appropriate eco-system approaches to fisheries development and management'.[49] Thus the Rome Declaration accorded highest priority to achieving sustainability of both capture fisheries and aquaculture within the framework of the ecosystem approach.[50] The ecosystem approach is also echoed by the 2001 Reykjavik Declaration on Responsible Fisheries in the Marine Ecosystem,[51] as well as the UN General Assembly Resolution 57/142.[52]

At the treaty level, it is of particular interest that the ecosystem approach is increasingly enshrined as part of the sustainable use of straddling and highly migratory fish stocks.[53] Examples may include:

---

48 M. Bliss, 'The Emerging Concepts for Developing and Strengthening the Legal Regime of the Oceans: Integrated Ocean Management, the Ecosystem-Based Approach and Marine Protected Areas', *Commemoration of the Twentieth Anniversary of the Adoption of the United Nations Convention on the Law of the Sea*, 9 December 2002, pp. 1 and 6.

49 Paragraph 6 of the Rome Declaration. This document is available at the homepage of FAO <http://www.fao.org/>.

50 *Ibid.*, c) of the operative part.

51 Paragraph 16 of the Preamble.

52 United Nations General Assembly, *Large-Scale Pelagic Drift-net Fishing, Unauthorized Fishing in Zones of National Jurisdiction and on the High Seas/Illegal, Unreported and Unregulated Fishing, Fisheries By-catch and Discards, and Other Developments*, A/RES/57/142. 26 February 2003, para. 4.

53 Fransisco Orrego Vicuña indicated that the biological unity of the stocks concerned was the starting point of the approach that sought to manage fisheries in an integrated manner in respect to both the high seas and the EEZ. F. Orrego Vicuña, *The Changing International Law of High Seas Fisheries* (Cambridge, Cambridge University Press, 1999) p. 177.

– the 1995 UN Fish Stocks Agreement;[54]
– the 1998 Agreement on the International Dolphin Conservation Program;[55]
– the 1999 Agreement between Iceland, Norway and Russia concerning Certain Aspects of Cooperation in the Area of Fisheries;[56]
– the 2000 Convention on the Conservation and Management of Highly Migratory Fish Stocks in the Western and Central Pacific Ocean;[57]
– the 2000 Framework Agreement for the Conservation of Living Marine Resources on the High Seas of the South-eastern Pacific;[58] and
– the 2001 Convention on the Conservation and Management of Fishery Resources in the South-East Atlantic Ocean.[59]

Take the 1995 UN Fish Stocks Agreement as an example. Article 5 of the UN Fish Stocks Agreement sets out general principles which explicitly take the marine ecosystem into account. Specifically Article 5 (d) obliges coastal States and States fishing on the high seas to 'assess the impacts of fishing, other human activities and environmental factors on target stocks and species belonging to the same ecosystem or dependent upon or associated with the target stocks'. In accordance with Article 5 (e), coastal States and States fishing on the high seas are obliged to 'adopt, where necessary, conservation and management measures for species belonging to the same ecosystem or dependent on or associated with the target stocks, with a view to maintaining or restoring populations of such species above levels at which their reproduction may become seriously threatened'. Article 5 (g) places a further obligation upon coastal States and States fishing on the high seas to protect biodiversity in the marine environment. It may be said that the 1995 UN Fish Stocks Agreement strongly reflects the ecosystem approach in the conservation and management of straddling and highly migratory species.

Limits of the Ecosystem Approach   The above survey reveals that the ecosystem approach is increasingly reflected in non-binding documents as well as treaties relating to the conservation of marine living resources. It can be observed that since the 1992 UNCED, in particular, international law relating to the conservation of marine species has acquired a stronger environmental dimension with the emergence of the ecosystem approach.[60] It may be argued that the backbone of the integrated management approach is being formulated in positive international

---

54 Article 5.
55 Article II (3), Article IV (1).
56 Article 2.
57 Preamble and Article 5 (f).
58 Article 5 (1) (c) (d).
59 Article 3 (f).
60 Birnie and Boyle, above note 34, p. 671.

law. On the other hand, it should be noted that the ecosystem approach gives rise to questions concerning its practical implementation.

A first difficulty pertains to scientific uncertainty over marine ecosystems. Ecosystem processes and functions are complex and variable, and the whole mechanism of an ecosystem is difficult to understand. Owing to the variability of marine species in space and time, delineation of ecosystem boundaries and determination of the appropriate scale is often difficult to determine.[61] Accordingly, it appears that the ecosystem approach will encounter scientific uncertainty as to its effective implementation.[62] In response to this question, considerable marine scientific research will be needed.[63]

A second difficulty is that the capability of implementing the ecosystem approach is not widespread. It is submitted that the implementation of the ecosystem approach may still be a difficult task even for the developed States with substantial resources for ocean management.[64] Thus, it appears more unlikely that developing States could implement the ecosystem approach owing to their limited capabilities of marine scientific research.

A third difficulty relates to the lack of specificity of this approach. Currently there is no universally agreed definition of an ecosystem approach. This approach is interpreted differently in different contexts.[65] Consequently, the adoption of the ecosystem approach does not directly specify any conservation measures. If this is the case, it appears difficult to judge the violation of the ecosystem approach when the application of this approach has been disputed between States. Thus it is debatable whether and to what extent the ecosystem approach can *legally* direct the conduct of States.

To those difficulties, another one must be added: the lack of congruence between jurisdictional zones and marine ecosystems.[66] In this respect, of particular importance is compatibility of conservation measures on the basis of the ecosystem approach between marine spaces under and beyond national jurisdiction. This

---

61 In this respect, Haeuber stated that: 'Ecosystems are dynamic, constantly changing, and vary continuously along gradients in space and time.' R. Haeuber, 'Setting the Environmental Policy Agenda: The Case of Ecosystem Management' (1996) 36 *Natural Resources Journal*, p. 6. See also L. Juda, 'Considerations in Developing a Functional Approach to the Governance of Large Marine Ecosystems' (1999) 30 *ODIL*, p. 92.

62 H. Wang, 'Ecosystem Management and Its Application to Large Marine Ecosystems: Science, Law, and Politics' (2004) 35 *ODIL*, p. 56; W.T. Burke, 'UNCED and the Oceans' (1993) 17 *Marine Policy*, p. 532.

63 This issue will be addressed in Chapter 6.

64 W.T. Burke, 'Evolution in the Fisheries Provisions of UNCLOS', in N. Ando, E. McWhinney and R. Wolfrum (eds), *Liber Amicorum Judge Shigeru Oda* (The Hague, Kluwer, 2002) p. 1362.

65 United Nations, *Report on the Work of the United Nations Open-ended Informal Consultative Process on Oceans and the Law of the Sea at its Seventh Meeting*, A/61/156, 17 July 2006, para. 6.

66 Juda, above note 61, p. 93. See also Chapter 1 of this study.

question is particularly at issue in conservation and management of straddling and highly migratory species. In this respect, Article 7 (1) of the UN Fish Stocks Agreement provides that with respect to straddling fish stocks, the relevant coastal States and the States whose nationals fish for such stocks in the adjacent high seas area shall *seek* to agree upon the measures necessary for the conservation of these stocks in the adjacent high seas areas; and that with respect to highly migratory fish stocks, the relevant coastal States and other States whose nationals fish for such stocks in the region shall co-operate with a view to ensuring conservation and promoting the objective of optimum utilisation of such stocks throughout the region, both within and beyond the areas under national jurisdiction. An issue arising is how it is possible to maintain the compatibility between measures which are taken by the coastal States and those taken by other fishing States. On this issue, Article 7 (2) of the UN Fish Stocks Agreement stipulates that:

> Conservation and management measures established for the high seas and those adopted for areas under national jurisdiction shall be compatible in order to ensure conservation and management of the straddling fish stocks and highly migratory fish stocks in their entirety. To this end, coastal States and States fishing on the high seas have a duty to cooperate for the purpose of achieving compatible measures in respect of such stocks.[67]

Thus States shall make every effort to agree on compatible conservation and management measures within a reasonable period of time in accordance with Article 7 (3) of the UN Fish Stocks Agreement. In relation to this, factors to be taken into account in determining compatible conservation and management measures are set out in Article 7 (2) in some detail.[68] Nevertheless, the UN Fish Stocks

---

67 The provision maintaining the compatibility of conservation and management measures is also contained in other conventions, such as: the Convention on the Conservation and Management of Fishery Resources in the South-East Atlantic Ocean (Article 19); the Convention on the Conservation and Management of Highly Migratory Fish Stocks in the Western and Central Pacific Ocean (Article 10); the Convention on Future Multilateral Cooperation in the North-west Atlantic Fisheries (Article 11 (3)).

68 Such criteria comprise: (a) the conservation and management measures adopted and applied in accordance with Article 61 of the LOSC; (b) previously agreed measures established and applied for the high seas in accordance with the LOSC by relevant coastal States and fishing States fishing on the high seas; (c) previously agreed measures established and applied in accordance with the LOSC by subregional or regional fisheries management organisations or arrangements; (d) the biological unity and other biological characteristics of the stocks and the relationships between the distribution of the stocks; (e) the respective dependence of the coastal States and the States fishing on the high seas on the stocks concerned; and (f) ensuring that such measures do not result in harmful impact on the living marine resources as a whole.

Agreement remains silent on the criterion for balancing these factors.[69] Some argue that Article 7 (2) (a), which requires States to ensure that measures established in respect of such stocks for the high seas do not undermine the effectiveness of such measures, will lead to a result in favour of coastal States.[70] However, such an interpretation will considerably limit the scope of the negotiation concerning conservation measures since the validity of conservation measures in marine spaces under national jurisdiction is already presumed; and the issue remaining is whether or not fishing States on the high seas accept these measures. Should these States accept conservation measures taken by the coastal States, an agreement will be concluded. If not, no agreement will be concluded. But the result remains the same since fishing States on the high seas are obliged to co-operate to achieve compatible measures on the basis of conservation measures in marine spaces under national jurisdiction. If this is the case, the negotiation will be pointless.[71] Hence, arguably Article 7 (2) should be construed in such a way that conservation and management measures established for the high seas and those adopted areas under national jurisdiction shall be mutually compatible, not that measures adopted for the high seas have to be compatible with measures adopted for areas under national jurisdiction.[72] In any case, with respect to the conservation of straddling and highly migratory species, it appears that the ecosystem approach cannot easily overcome the difficulty arising from the zonal management approach.[73] In light

---

69 Alex G. Oude Elferink, 'The Impact of Article 7 (2) of the Fish Stocks Agreement on the Formulation of Conservation and Management Measures for Straddling Highly Migratory Fish Stocks', *FAO Legal Papers Online #4*, August 1999, pp. 13–18. On this issue, see also by the same author, 'The Determination of Compatible Conservation and Management Measures for Straddling and Highly Migratory Fish Stocks' (2001) 5 *Max Planck Yearbook of United Nations Law*, pp. 551–607.

70 See, for instance, H. Gherari, 'L'accord du 4 août 1995 sur les stocks chevauchants et les stocks de poissons grands migrateurs' (1996) 100 *RGDIP*, p. 377; L. Lucchini and M. Vœlckel, *Droit de la mer, Tome 2 Délimitation, Navigation et Pêche Volume 2 Navigation et Pêche* (Paris, Pedone, 1996) p. 681; P.G.G. Davies and C. Redgwell, 'The International Legal Regulation of Straddling Fish Stocks' (1996) 67 *BYIL*, pp. 263–4; F. Orrego Vicuña, above note 53, p. 190.

71 R.C. Raigón, 'La pêche en haute mer', in D. Vignes, G. Cataldi and R.C. Raigón (eds), *Le droit international de la pêche maritime* (Bruxelles, Bruylant, 2000) p. 212.

72 Alex G. Oude Elferink, above note 69, p. 4 and p. 7. A. Tahindro, 'Conservation and Management of Transboundary Fish Stocks: Comments in Light of the Adoption of the 1995 Agreement for the Conservation and Management of Straddling Fish Stocks and Highly Migratory Fish Stocks' (1997) 28 *ODIL*, p. 17; M. Hayashi, 'High Seas Fisheries' (in Japanese), in C. Mizukami (ed.), *The Contemporary Law of the Sea* (Tokyo, Yushindo, 2003) p. 25.

73 The Review Conference of the UN Fish Stocks Agreement, which was held in New York, 22–26 May 2006, did not elaborate on this subject. The Review Conference merely called for improving co-operation between flag States and coastal States so as to ensure the achievement of compatibility of measures in accordance with Article 7 of the UN Fish Stocks Agreement. United Nations, *Report of the Review Conference on the Agreement for*

of the above difficulties, it remains to be seen whether and to what extent the ecosystem approach will legally bind States' behaviour.

The Precautionary Approach

Inter-linkage between the Ecosystem and Precautionary Approaches Another important approach in this field is the precautionary approach, which is increasingly enshrined in international instruments in this field.[74] Although the definition of the precautionary approach or principle varies depending on the instruments, it is generally understood that the essence of the precautionary approach is that once a risk has been identified, the lack of scientific proof of cause and effect shall not be used as a reason for not taking action to protect the environment.[75]

On the international plane, the precautionary approach was originally adopted in the context of the protection of the marine environment.[76] As shown in Table 3.1,

---

the Implementation of the Provisions of the United Nations Convention on the Law of the Sea of 10 December 1982 relating to the Conservation and Management of Straddling Fish Stocks and Highly Migratory Fish Stocks, A/CONF.210/2006/15, 5 July 2006, p. 33, para. 18 (b). For an overview of the Review Conference, see Y. Takei, 'Unfinished Business: Review Conference on the 1995 UN Fish Stocks Agreement' (2006) 21 *IJMCL*, pp. 551–68.

74 There are many articles addressing the precautionary approach or principle. For a relatively recent study of the precautionary approach along with bibliography in some detail, see A. Trouwborst, *Evolution and Status of the Precautionary Principle in International Law* (The Hague, Kluwer, 2002).

75 D. Freestone and E. Hey, 'Origin and Development of the Precautionary Principle', in D. Freestone and E. Hey (eds), *The Precautionary Principle and International Law: The Challenge of Implementation* (The Hague, Kluwer, 1996) p. 13. According to James Cameron and Juli Abouchar, the precautionary approach is composed of three elements: (i) regulatory inaction threatens non-negligible harm; (ii) there exists a lack of scientific certainty on the cause and effect relationship; and (iii) under these circumstances, regulatory inaction is unjustified. J. Cameron and J. Abouchar, 'The Status of the Precautionary Principle in International Law', in *ibid.*, p. 45.

76 In 1987, the participants to the Second International Conference on the Protection of the North Sea (Belgium, Denmark, France, Federal Republic of Germany, the Netherlands, Norway, Sweden, the UK and the Commission of the European Communities) acknowledged that: 'in order to protect the North Sea from possibly damaging effects of the most dangerous substances, a precautionary approach is necessary which may require action to control inputs of such substances even before a causal link has been established by absolutely clear scientific evidence.' *Ministerial Declaration of the Second International Conference on the Protection of the North Sea*, London, 24–25 November 1987, paragraph VII of the Preamble. This document is available at <http://www.sweden.gov.se/content/1/c6/05/78/43/4ffaa7cc.pdf>. Further to this, the Ministerial Declaration of the Third International Conference on the Protection of the North Sea stated that the participants to the Conference: 'will continue to apply the precautionary principle, that is to take action to avoid potentially damaging impacts of substances that are persistent, toxic and liable to bioaccumulate even where there is no scientific evidence to prove a causal link between

currently the precautionary approach is increasingly invoked in conventions and instruments concerning the conservation of marine living resources. In this relation, it is important to note that the precautionary approach is closely inter-linked to the concept of sustainable development as well as the ecosystem approach. Indeed, there seems to be a general sense that the precautionary approach is required in order to ensure sustainable use of marine living resources. In this respect, UN General Assembly Resolution 61/105 stresses that there is 'the urgent need for action at all levels to ensure the long-term sustainable use and management of fisheries resources through the wide application of the precautionary approach'.[77]

Furthermore, it is worth noting that legal instruments adopting the ecosystem approach tend to refer to the precautionary approach at the same time. For example, the linkage between the ecosystem and precautionary approaches may be found in the FAO Code of Conduct for Responsible Fisheries. The Code of Conduct stresses the ecosystem approach as one general principle, by stating that: 'management measures should not only ensure the conservation of target species but also of species belonging to the same ecosystem or associated with or dependent upon the target species.'[78] At the same time, the Code of Conduct clearly provides that:

> States should apply the precautionary approach widely to conservation, management and exploitation of living aquatic resources in order to protect them and preserve the aquatic environment. The absence of adequate scientific information should not be used as a reason for postponing or failing to take conservation and management measures.[79]

---

emissions and effects.' *Ministerial Declaration of the Third International Conference on the Protection of the North Sea*, The Hague, 8 March 1990. This document is available at <http://www.seas-at-risk.org/1mages/1990%20Hague%20Declaration.pdf>. For studies of the precautionary approach in law of the sea, see S. Marr, *The Precautionary Principles in the Law of the Sea: Modern Decision Making in International Law* (The Hague, Nijhoff, 2003); D. Vanderzwaag, 'The Precautionary Principle and Marine Environmental Protection: Slippery Shores, Rough Seas, and Rising Normative Tide' (2002) 33 *ODIL*, pp. 165–88; P-M. Dupuy, 'Le principe de précaution et le droit international de la mer', in *La mer et son droit, Mélanges offerts à Laurent Lucchini et Jean Pierre Quéneudec* (Paris, Pedone, 2003) pp. 205–20. With respect to a thorough examination of State practice relating to the precautionary approach, see Trouwborst, above note 74. See also Pascale Martin-Bidou, 'Le principe de précaution en droit international de l'environnement' (1999) 103 *RGDIP*, pp. 631–66 (in particular, pp. 634–45); O. McIntyre and T. Mosedale, 'The Precautionary Principle as a Norm of Customary International Law' (1997) 9 *Journal of Environmental Law*, pp. 223–35. For analysis of municipal laws concerning the precautionary approach, see P.H. Sand, 'The Precautionary Principle: Coping with Risk' (2000) 40 *Indian Journal of International Law*, pp. 1–13.

77 UN General Assembly Resolution A/RES/61/105, paragraph 8 of the Preamble.

78 Para. 6.2. In addition, the Code of Conduct refers to marine ecosystems in many paragraphs.

79 Para. 7.5.1. See also paras 7.5.2 and 6.5.

Table 3.1   Treaties which adopted both the ecosystem and precautionary approaches

Year	Title	Ecosystem Approach	Precautionary Approach	Entered into force
1980	Convention on the Conservation of Antarctic Marine Living Resources (CCAMLR)	Art. 2 (3)	Article 2[1]	1982
1980	Convention on Future Multilateral Co-operation in North-East Atlantic Fisheries[2]	Art. 4 (c) (d)	Art.4 (b)	1982
1992	Convention for the Protection of the Marine Environment of the North-East Atlantic (OSPAR)	Art. 2 (1) (a) Annex V	Art. 2 (2) (a)	1998
1992	Convention on Biological Diversity	Art. 8	Preamble	1993
1992	Convention on the Protection of the Marine Environment of the Baltic Sea Area	Preamble and Art. 3 (1), 15	Art. 3 (2)	2000
1995	Straddling and Highly Migratory Fish Stocks Agreement	Art. 5, 7 (2)	Art. 5 (c), 6	2001
1995	Protocol Concerning Specially Protected Areas and Biological Diversity in the Mediterranean	Parts I, II, III and IV	Preamble	1999
1995	†Code of Conduct for Responsible Fisheries	Art. 2 (i), 6, 7, and 9, 10, 12	Art. 7.5, 6.5	
1995	Convention for the Protection of the Marine Environment and the Coastal Region of the Mediterranean	Art. 10	Art. 4 (3) (a)	*
1996	Protocol to the Convention on the Prevention of Marine Pollution by Dumping of Wastes and Other Matter	Preamble and Art. 1 (10)	Art. 3 (1)	*

1998	Agreement on the International Dolphin Conservation Program	Preamble and Art 2 (3), 4, 6	Art. 4 (1)	1999
1999	Agreement Concerning the Creation of a Marine Mammal Sanctuary in the Mediterranean	Art. 2 (1)	Declaration to the Agreement	2002
2000	Framework Agreement for the Conservation of Living Marine Resources on the High Seas of the South-eastern Pacific	Preamble Art. 5 (1) (c) (d)	Art. 5 (1) (b)	*
2000	Convention on the Conservation and Management of Highly Migratory Fish Stocks in the Western and Central Pacific Ocean	Preamble and Art. 5 (f), 8	Preamble Art. 5 (c), 6	2004
2001	Convention on the Conservation and Management of Fishery Resources in the South-East Atlantic Ocean	Art. 3 (f)	Art. 3 (b), 6 (g), 7 and Preamble	2003

*: not yet into force

†: the Code is a voluntary instrument

This list is not exhaustive.

1   There is no explicit reference to the precautionary approach in Article 2. Nevertheless, the document 'Understanding CCAMLR's Approach to Management' elaborated by the Scientific Committee in 2000 is of the view that Article 2 embodies the precautionary approach. The document is available at: <http://www.ccamlr.org/pu/e/e_pubs/am/text.pdf>. Wang is also supportive of this view, above note 62, p. 47.

2   Amended in 2004 and 2006, respectively.

The UN General Assembly Resolution 60/31 also calls upon all States to 'apply, in accordance with international law, the precautionary approach and an ecosystem approach widely to the conservation, management and exploitation of fish stocks, including straddling fish stocks and highly migratory fish stocks'.[80]

The linkage between the ecosystem approach and the precautionary approach is also reflected in the Common Fisheries Policy in the European Community. Article 2 (1) of the Council Regulation No 2371/2002 stipulates that:

> The Common Fisheries Policy shall ensure exploitation of living aquatic resources that provides sustainable economic, environmental and social conditions.
>
> For this purpose, the Community shall apply the precautionary approach in taking measures designed to protect and conserve living aquatic resources, to provide for their sustainable exploitation and to minimise the impact of fishing activities on marine ecosystems. It shall aim at a progressive implementation of an ecosystem-based approach to fisheries management.[81]

As shown in Table 3.1, the linkage between the two approaches can also be seen at the treaty level. It appears that this phenomenon is not merely a coincidence. Considering the scientific uncertainty relating to the mechanisms of marine ecosystems, it appears logical that the ecosystem approach should be connected to the precautionary approach.[82] Hence it is conceivable that the ecosystem

---

80 UN General Assembly Resolution, *Sustainable Fisheries, including through the 1995 Agreement for the Implementation of the Provisions of the United Nations Convention on the Law of the Sea of 10 December 1982 relating to the Conservation and Management of Straddling Fish Stocks and Highly Migratory Fish Stocks, and Related Instruments*, A/RES/60/31, 10 March 2006, p. 5, para. 4.

81 The Council Regulation No 2371/2002 of 20 December 2002 on the Conservation and Sustainable Exploitation of Fisheries Resources under the Common Fisheries Policy.

82 On this point, Kaye clearly indicated the linkage between the precautionary principle and the ecosystem approach. S.B. Kaye, *International Fisheries Management* (The Hague, Kluwer, 2001) pp. 273–4. Juda also echoed this view, by saying that: 'Consideration of marine ecosystems may well lend strength to the emergence of the proactive concept of precautions.' L. Juda, *International Law and Ocean Use Management: The Evolution of Ocean Governance* (London and New York, Routledge, 1996) p. 289. Furthermore, the Statement on the Ecosystem Approach to the Management of Human Activities, which was adopted in the First Joint Meeting of the Helsinki and OSPAR Commission, states that the application of the precautionary principle is equally a central part of the ecosystem approach. *First Joint Ministerial Meeting of the Helsinki and OSPAR Commissions, Statement on the Ecosystem Approach to the Management of Human Activities*, , Record of the Meeting, Annex 5 (Ref. §6.1), Bremen, 25–26 June 2003, p. 2, para. 5. The Report of the Secretary-General also stated that since scientific understanding of ocean ecosystems was still very limited, the application of the precautionary approach in the face of uncertainty

and precautionary approaches could be principal elements in implementing the integrated management approach at the ecological level on a treaty basis.[83]

Case Law Relating to the Precautionary Approach   On the other hand, a question is raised where the application of the precautionary approach has been disputed between States and the dispute has been submitted before international courts.

In practice, it appears that international courts and tribunals have been wary about applying this approach in disputes relating to fisheries as well as environmental protection.[84] Take the *Southern Bluefin Tuna* case between Australia, New Zealand and Japan as an example. This case concerned a dispute over the Japanese unilateral experimental fishing programme for southern bluefin tuna, as well as total allowable catch (TAC). From 1995 onwards, Japan sought an increase of TAC on the ground that the southern bluefin tuna had begun to recover, although Australia and New Zealand consistently opposed such proposals. In this connection, Japan proposed that there be a joint experimental fishing programme in order to assess the recovery of the stock.[85] Although the Parties had discussed the experimental fishing programme for several years, agreement was not reached on this matter. Thus Japan unilaterally conducted a pilot experimental fishing programme in the southern Indian Ocean from 10 July 1998 to 31 August 1998, despite opposition from Australia and New Zealand. Furthermore, Japan unilaterally initiated a

---

was essential. *Report of the Secretary-General, Oceans and the Law of the Sea*, A/61/63, 9 March 2006, p. 39, para. 138.

83 On the other hand, opinion remains divided over the status in customary law of the precautionary approach. In this respect, the Commission of the European Communities argues that the precautionary principle has been progressively consolidated in international environmental law, and so it has since become a full-fledged and general principle of international law. Commission of the European Communities, *Communication from the Commission on the Precautionary Principle*, COM (2001) 1, p. 11, section 4. Some also argue that the precautionary approach is now a customary law. See, for instance, Cameron and Abouchar, above note 75, pp. 29–52; Trouwborst, above note 74, p. 286; Sands, above note 6, p. 279; McIntyre and Mosedale, above note 76, p. 235. By contrast, other writers are more cautious about accepting the customary law character of the precautionary approach. See, for example, Martin-Bidou, above note 76, pp. 658–65; Birnie and Boyle, above note 34, pp. 118–21; D. Bodansky, 'Remarks', in *The American Society of International Law, Proceedings of the 85ᵗʰ Annual Meeting*, Washington, DC, 17–20 April 1991, pp. 413–17; T. Iwama, 'On the Precautionary Principle in International Environmental Law' (in Japanese) (2004) 1264 *Jurist*, p. 57; Y. Takamura, 'The Precautionary Principle in International Environmental Law: Its Current Status and Functions' (in Japanese) (2005) 104 *The Journal of International Law and Diplomacy*, p. 250; X. Zhang, 'Issues Concerning Precautionary Principle in Environmental Protection: A Chinese Perspective' (in Japanese) (2007) 26 *Yearbook of World Law*, pp. 69–81.

84 Dupuy, above note 76, pp. 215–20.

85 Response of the Government of Japan to Request for Provisional Measures and Counter-Request for Provisional Measures (hereafter Response of Japan), pp. 6–8, paras 13–17. The written pleadings in this case were provided by ITLOS.

second year of experimental fishing in June 1999.[86] Against this background, on 15 July 1999, Australia and New Zealand requested the establishment of an Arbitral Tribunal under Annex VII of the LOSC for determination of the merits of the dispute.

Furthermore, Australia and New Zealand sought provisional measures in ITLOS with a view to bringing about immediate cessation of the unilateral experimental fishing of the southern bluefin tuna. The applicants claimed that Japan's actions amounted to a failure to conserve and to co-operate in the conservation of the southern bluefin tuna stock; that Japan, by initiating a unilateral experimental fishing programme for southern bluefin tuna in 1998 and 1999, threatened serious or irreversible damage to the southern bluefin tuna population.[87] By contrast, Japan denied the allegations by applicants, and requested that ITLOS grant Japan provisional relief that Australia and New Zealand urgently and in good faith recommence negotiations with Japan.[88]

There appears to be little doubt that the divergence of opinion concerning fish stock data, which prompted Japan's unilateral fisheries investigation, was at the heart of this dispute. According to ITLOS, there was no disagreement between the Parties that the stock of southern bluefin tuna was at its historically lowest level.[89] Nevertheless, the Parties differed as to whether the scientific data available showed an upward trend from the current level and whether Japan's experimental fishing programme (EFP) would have a negative impact upon the southern bluefin tuna stock.[90] On the one hand, Japan considered that the southern bluefin tuna stock was on the road to recovery.[91] Furthermore, Japan contended that the implementation of its EFP would cause no further threat to the southern bluefin tuna stock; and that the EFP remained necessary to reach a more reliable assessment of the potential of the stock to recover.[92] On the other hand, Australia and New Zealand maintained that the amount of southern bluefin tuna taken under the EFP could endanger the existence of the stock.[93] Thus, Professor Crawford, Counsel of Australia, referred to the precautionary approach, saying that with the precautionary principle or approach, the conservation of southern bluefin tuna was decisively required.[94] Nonetheless,

---

86 Statement of Claim and Grounds on which it is Based, Submitted by Australia, p. 8, paras 13–14. See also Written Pleadings of Australia, pp. 3–5, paras 9–15.

87 Southern bluefin tuna (*Thunnus maccoyii*) is a highly migratory fish species, which traverses the exclusive economic zone and territorial sea of several countries and the high seas, including the Southern Ocean.

88 Order by ITLOS on 27 August 1999, (1999) 38 *ILM*, p. 1630, para. 33.

89 *Ibid.*, p. 1634, para. 71. See also Annex 4 of Australia's Request for Provisional Measures: A Scientific Overview of the Status of the Southern Bluefin Tuna Stock.

90 Request for Provisional Measures by Australia, p. 3, para. 11; Request for Provisional Measures by New Zealand, p. 5, para. 11.

91 Response of the Government of Japan, above note 85, p. 6, para. 13.

92 Order by ITLOS, above note 88, p. 1634, para. 73.

93 *Ibid.*, p. 1634, para. 74.

94 Public Sitting of 18 August 1999, ITLOS/PV.99/21/Rev.1, p. 20.

the ITLOS did not examine this approach, and held that: 'the parties should in the circumstances act with prudence and caution to ensure that effective conservation measures are taken to prevent serious harm to the stock of southern bluefin tuna.'[95] Although Judge Laing interpreted this phrase as the Tribunal having adopted the precautionary approach,[96] majority opinion has never used the term 'precautionary approach'. Nor did it touch on the legal status of this approach.[97]

A similar judicial hesitation may be seen in the *MOX Plant* case between Ireland and the UK of 2001.[98] In this case, Ireland argued that the manufacture of MOX fuel at Sellafield involved significant risks for the Irish Sea, since such manufacture would inevitably lead to some discharges of radioactive substances into the marine environment, via direct discharges and through the atmosphere;[99] and that the precautionary principle was to be applicable as a rule of customary international law.[100] Nonetheless, the ITLOS did not prescribe the provisional measures requested by Ireland, on the ground that there was no urgency of the situation in the short period before the constitution of the Annex VII Arbitral Tribunal.[101] It is true that the ITLOS considered that prudence and caution required that Ireland and the United Kingdom co-operate in exchanging information concerning risks or effects of the operation of the MOX plant and in devising ways to deal with them.[102] Nonetheless, no explicit mention was made of the precautionary approach in this case.[103]

---

95 Order by ITLOS, above note 88, p. 1634, para. 77.

96 Separate Opinion by Judge Laing, *ibid.*, p. 1642, para. 19.

97 Dupuy, above note 76, p. 216.

98 With respect to the activities of the MOX plant located in Sellafield, a series of litigations were submitted to international courts and tribunals. Concerning the studies on this dispute, see C. Brown, 'Provisional Measures before the ITLOS: The MOX Plant Case' (2002) 17 *IJMCL*, pp. 267–88; R. Churchill and V. Lowe, 'The International Tribunal for the Law of the Sea: Survey for 2001' (2002) 17 *IJMCL*, pp. 477–84; Ch. Nouzha, 'L'affaire de l'usine MOX (Irlande c. Royaume-Uni) devant le Tribunal international du droit de la mer: quelles mesures conservatoires pour la protection de l'environnement?' [PDF version] (2002) mars *Actualité et Droit International* <http://www.ridi.org/adi>, pp. 1–12; B. Kwiatkowska, 'The Ireland v United Kingdom (MOX Plant) Case: Applying the Doctrine of Treaty Parallelism' (2003) 18 *IJMCL*, pp. 1–58; R. Churchill and J. Scott, 'The MOX Plant Litigation: The First Half-Life' (2004) 53 *ICLQ*, pp. 643–76; V. Röben, 'The Order of the UNCLOS Annex VII Arbitral Tribunal to Suspend Proceedings in the Case of the MOX Plant at Sellafield: How Much Jurisdictional Subsidiarity?' (2004) 73 *Nordic Journal of International Law*, pp. 223–45.

99 Request for Provisional Measures and Statement of Case of Ireland, 9 November 2001, p. 15, para. 28; 49, paras 109–10. The written pleadings in this case were provided by ITLOS.

100 *Ibid.*, pp. 44–5, paras 97–101 (in particular, para. 101).

101 (2002) 41 *ILM*, 2002, p. 415, para. 81.

102 *Ibid.*, para. 84.

103 Judge Wolfrum stated that: '[i]t is still a matter of discussion whether the precautionary principle or the precautionary approach in international environmental law

The judicial hesitation was echoed by the ICJ. In the *Request for an Examination of the Situation in Accordance with Paragraph 63 of the Court's Judgment of 20 December 1974 in the Nuclear Tests Case* of 1995, New Zealand contended that France was under an obligation to provide evidence that its new underground nuclear tests would not result in the introduction of such material to the environment in accordance with the 'precautionary principle'.[104] New Zealand further claimed that by virtue of the adoption into environmental law of the 'precautionary principle', the burden of proof fell on a State wishing to engage in potentially damaging environmental conduct to show in advance that its activities would not cause contamination.[105] However, the ICJ discarded New Zealand's request on the ground that its Judgement of 1974 dealt exclusively with atmospheric nuclear tests; and that it was impossible for the Court to take into consideration questions relating to underground nuclear tests.[106] In so deciding, the Court did not touch on the applicability of the 'precautionary principle' in this case.[107]

Similarly, in the *Gabčíkovo-Nagymaros Project* case of 1997, Hungary argued that the previously existing obligation not to cause substantive damage to the territory of another State had evolved into an *erga omnes* obligation of prevention of damage pursuant to the 'precautionary principle'.[108] Furthermore, Hungary justified its conduct of suspending or abandoning certain works required in the 1977 Treaty on the basis of a 'state of ecological necessity'.[109] In this respect, the

---

has become part of international customary law.' Separate Opinion of Judge Wolfrum, *ibid.*, pp. 428–9. See also Separate Opinion of Judge Treves, *ibid.*, 431.

104 ICJ Reports 1995, p. 290, para. 5.

105 *Ibid.*, p. 298, para. 34. See also Written Pleadings by New Zealand, pp. 53–7, paras 105–10.

106 ICJ Reports 1995, p. 306, para. 63.

107 On the other hand, Judge *ad hoc* Palmer stated that: 'the norm involved in the precautionary principle has developed rapidly and may now be a principle of customary international law relating to the environment.' Dissenting Opinion of Judge *ad hoc* Palmer, ICJ Reports (1995), p. 412, para. 91.

108 In its pleadings, Hungary alleged that: 'States shall take precautionary measures to anticipate, prevent or minimise damage to their transboundary resources and mitigate adverse effects. Where there are threats of serious or irreversible damage, lack of full scientific certainty shall not be used as a reason for postponing such measures. Art. 2, paragraph 5 (a) of the Convention on the Protection and Use of Transboundary Watercourses and International Lakes, adopted in Helsinki on 17 March 1992, as well as the IUCN Draft Art. 6 and the Brundtland Report, Art. 10, provide support for the obligation in general international environmental law to apply the precautionary principle to protect a transboundary resource. This duty has extreme importance in this dispute where the damage threatening Hungary is irreparable and enormous.' Application of the Republic of Hungary *v.* The Czech and Slovak Federal Republic on the Diversion of the Danube River, reproduced in P. Sands, R. Tarasofsky and M. Weiss (eds), *Documents in International Environmental Law: Principles of International Environmental law IIA* (Manchester, Manchester University Press, 1994) pp. 693–8 (at 696–7).

109 ICJ Reports 1997, pp. 35–7, paras 40–42.

ICJ held that the Hungarian argument on the state of necessity could not convince the Court unless it was at least proven that a real, 'grave' and 'imminent' 'peril' existed in 1989 and that the measures taken by Hungary were the only possible response to it.[110] In relation to this, the ICJ stated that 'a state of necessity could not exist without a "peril" duly established at the relevant point in time; the mere apprehension of a possible "peril" could not suffice in that respect'.[111] Moreover, in the Court's view, the concept of 'imminence' goes far beyond the concept of 'possibility'.[112] In conclusion, the ICJ held that the peril alleged by Hungary was not sufficiently certain and imminent; and that Hungary could have resorted to other means in order to respond to the dangers that it apprehended.[113] In so deciding, the ICJ did not touch on the precautionary principle at all. It is unclear whether the Court in this case considered that the environmental risks were sufficiently certain to require no reliance on the precautionary principle, or whether the Court did not regard the principle as having any legal status.[114] Considering that the Court interpreted the notion of risk in a restrictive manner, however, it may not be absurd to presume that the ICJ was still prudent to apply the precautionary approach.[115]

It would appear that there are good reasons for this judicial hesitation.[116] Indeed, it is foreseeable that the application of the precautionary approach will encounter difficulties in practice.

First, a question may be raised how it is possible to determine the existence of serious or irreversible risks which may trigger the application of the precautionary approach. Due to its nature, a need for the application of the precautionary approach is to be determined on the basis of *potential* risks. Yet the assessment of serious risk is often difficult to make since such risk may not be well known or discoverable through present-day science.[117] This is so because the scientific knowledge of the oceans as well as of marine ecosystems is still inadequate.[118] It must also be noted that the results of the assessment of possible serious harm may change in accordance with the development of scientific technology.[119] More difficulties arise where there are scientific uncertainties relating to techniques

---

110 *Ibid.*, p. 42, para. 54.

111 *Ibid.*

112 *Ibid.*

113 *Ibid.*, pp. 44–5, para. 56.

114 Boyle, above note 34, p. 17.

115 J. Sohnle, 'Irruption du droit de l'environnement dans la jurisprudence de la C.I.J.: l'affaire *Gabčíkovo-Nagymaros*' (1998) 102 *RGDIP*, pp. 110–11.

116 Birnie and Boyle, above note 34, p. 119; E. Fisher, 'Is the Precautionary Principle Justiciable?' (2001) 13 *Journal of Environmental Law*, pp. 315–34. See also M. Feintuck, 'Precautionary Maybe, but What's the Principle? The Precautionary Principle, the Regulation of Risk, and the Public Domain' (2005) 32 *Journal of Law and Society*, p. 385.

117 Martin-Bidou, above note 76, p. 647.

118 *Cf.* D.M. Dzidzornu, 'Four Principles in Marine Environment Protection: A Comparative Analysis' (1998) 29 *ODIL*, p. 99.

119 Martin-Bidou, above note 76, p. 651.

or approaches to the assessment of species to be harvested. In reality, it appears difficult if not impossible for a judicial organ to evaluate opposing scientific evidence. In the *Southern Bluefin Tuna* case, for instance, there were two principal approaches, which produced very different results: a variable square approach which assumes the absence of fish in areas not currently being fished, and a constant square approach which assumes the same number of fish in those areas as in the areas being fished.[120] Japan argued that the variable square approach indicated stability or continued decline in the 1990s, while the constant square approach indicated stability or increases in the same period.[121] The situation was more complex since there was another uncertainty about the age at which the fish mature, with estimates varying between eight and twelve years.[122] Thus the ITLOS in the *Southern Bluefin Tuna* case had to state that it could not conclusively assess the scientific evidence presented by the Parties.[123]

Secondly and more fundamentally, it must be noted that the application of the precautionary approach may restrict economic and industrial activities by States. This is particularly true of fisheries. Considering the importance of the fisheries industry in fishing States, it is essential to reconcile environmental protection with economic interests. To this end, there is a great need to consider not only scientific factors but also economic, social and political factors in the application of the precautionary approach. The cost-effectiveness of the implementation of the precautionary approach is of particular importance.[124] But the evaluation of those factors concerns in essence a policy of relevant States which can be best answered by politicians, rather than jurists or scientists.[125] Here it would appear that there is an inherent limit to the applicability of the precautionary approach before international courts and tribunals.

This does not mean, however, that this approach has no normative force in international adjudication. It is arguable that, like the concept of sustainable development, the precautionary approach can be regarded as a judicial factor to be taken into account in ensuring a preferable interpretation where there are

---

120 C.E. Foster, 'The "Real Dispute" in the Southern Bluefin Tuna Case: a Science Dispute?' (2001) 16 *IJMCL*, p. 588. Butterworth has explained that the constant square approach makes the 'overly optimistic' assumption, while the variable square approach is 'overly pessimistic'. Response of the Government of Japan, above note 85, Annex 2, Statement of D.S. Butterworth, pp. 5–6.

121 Response of the Government of Japan, above note 85, Annex I, Southern Bluefin Tuna: Panel Statement on Experimental Fishery Program, p. 2.

122 Foster, above note 120, p. 577.

123 Order by ITLOS, above note 88, p. 1634, para. 80.

124 The importance of cost-effectiveness is highlighted, for instance, by Lucchini. L. Lucchini, 'Le principe de précaution en droit international de l'environnement: ombres plus que lumières' (1999) 45 *AFDI*, pp. 727–9.

125 A. Kiss, 'The Rights and Interests of Future Generations and the Precautionary Principle', in Freestone and Hey, above note 75, p. 27. See also Birnie and Boyle, above note 34, p. 119.

competing interpretations.[126] In practice, it is desirable that the application of the precautionary approach should be decided by an international forum. Accordingly, the institutionalisation of the decision-making process concerning the application of the precautionary approach should be underscored.[127]

Compliance Procedures in Treaties Relating to Conservation of Marine Living Resources

The third issue to be discussed concerns procedures ensuring compliance with rules of international law relating to conservation of marine living resources. While the definition of compliance in international law varies according to writers,[128] for the purpose of this study, the concept of compliance may broadly be defined as the behaviour of a State which conforms to international obligations.[129] For the purpose of

---

126 *Cf.* Takamura, above note 83, p. 251.

127 A. Kanehara, 'A Critical Analysis of Changes and Recent Developments in the Concept of Conservation of Fishery Resources on the High Seas' (1998) 41 *The Japanese Annual of International Law*, p. 14.

128 It appears that international documents do not provide definite guidance in this matter. On this point, see R. Wolfrum, 'Means of Ensuring Compliance with and Enforcement of International Environmental Law' (1998) 272 *RCADI*, pp. 28–9.

129 Distinction should be made between compliance and enforcement; it is understood that enforcement is an action to compel States to achieve compliance. Should compliance not be forthcoming, enforcement may come into play. On this point, see Wolfrum, *ibid.*, pp. 28–30; R. Rayfuse, 'To Our Children's Children's Children: From Promoting to Achieving Compliance in High Seas Fisheries' (2005) 20 *IJMCL*, pp. 511–12; L.F. Damrosch, 'Enforcing International Law Through Non-Forcible Measures' (1997) 269 *RCADI*, pp. 22–4. On the other hand, one will note that international instruments often refer to 'implementation' of measures and obligations. Although international documents do not provide a clear definition of implementation, it may be said that implementation is an action to give practical effect to international obligations or the fulfilment of those obligations. In any case, there appears to be little doubt that compliance cannot be ensured without implementation of relevant obligations. In this sense, it may be argued that the concepts of compliance and implementation are closely inter-linked. On this issue, cf. Wolfrum, above note 128, p. 29. With respect to the concept of compliance or compliance control, see also P. Sands, 'Compliance with International Environmental Obligations: Existing International Legal Arrangements', in J. Cameron, J. Werksman and P. Roderick (eds), *Improving Compliance with International Environmental Law* (London, Earthscan Publications Ltd, 1996) pp. 48–81; R.B. Mitchell, 'Compliance Theory: An Overview', in J. Cameron *et al.*, *ibid.*, pp. 3–28; W. Lang, 'Compliance Control in International Environmental Law: Institutional Necessities' (1996) 56 *ZaöRV*, pp. 685–95; T. Marauhn, 'Towards a Procedural Law of Compliance Control in International Environmental Relations', *ibid.*, pp. 696–731; B. Kingsbury, 'The Concept of Compliance as a Function of Competing Conceptions of International Law' (1998) 19 *Michigan Journal of International Law*, pp. 345–72; U. Beyerlin, P-T. Stoll and R. Wolfrum (eds), *Ensuring Compliance with Multilateral*

this study, two procedures are particularly important: enhancement of the flag State's responsibility and international supervision through international institutions.

Flag State Responsibility

Flag State Responsibility in Non-Binding Documents   It is well established under customary law that with a few exceptions,[130] the flag State has exclusive jurisdiction over vessels flying its flag.[131] This is called the principle of the exclusive jurisdiction of the flag State. In this respect, Article 94 (1) of the 1982 LOSC obliges every State to effectively exercise its jurisdiction and control in administrative, technical and social matters over ships flying its flag, while Article 91 (1) of the LOSC requires States to establish a genuine link between the State and the ship. Nonetheless, experience shows that the principle of the exclusive jurisdiction of the flag State is inadequate to effectively control activities of vessels in the oceans. This is particularly true of the conservation of marine living resources. In accordance with the principle *pacta tertiis nec nocent nec prosunt*, conservation measures established by treaties are binding only on the Parties to the treaties. In reality, the owners of fishing vessels often re-register their vessels in States that are not Parties to relevant fisheries treaties in order to evade treaty obligations. It is acknowledged that the practice of 'reflagging' causes a serious problem in eroding conservation measures for marine species.[132] In addition to this, concern is voiced that a growing number of newly built fishing vessels are directly registered in the flag of convenience.[133]

In response to these problems, various non-binding documents called for States to take effective measures controlling fishing activities of vessels flying their flags. For instance, the 1992 Declaration of the International Conference on Responsible Fishing (the Cancun Declaration) calls for States to 'take effective action, consistent with international law, to deter reflagging of vessels as a means of avoiding compliance with applicable conservation and management rules

---

Environmental Agreement: A Dialogue between Practitioners and Academia (Leiden and Boston, Nijhoff, 2006); G. Ulfstein (ed.), *Making Treaties Work: Human Rights, Environment and Arms Control* (Cambridge, Cambridge University Press, 2007).

130 Exceptions provided for in Article 110 of the LOSC are: piracy, transporting slaves, unauthorised broadcasting, Stateless vessels and disguised vessels of the interfering State.

131 With respect to an analysis of the right of the flag State to give its nationality to vessels, see P. Gautier, 'L'Etat du pavillon et la protection des intérêts liés au navire', in M.G. Kohen (ed.), *Promoting Justice, Human Rights and Conflict Resolution through International Law, Liber Amicorum Lucius Caflisch* (Leiden, Nijhoff, 2007) pp. 717–45.

132 With respect to the practice of reflagging, see, for instance, D.A. Balton, 'The Compliance Agreement', in E. Hey (ed.), *Developments in International Fisheries Law* (The Hague, Kluwer, 1999) pp. 34–5; P. Birnie, 'Reflagging of Fishing Vessels on the High Seas' (1993) 2 *RECIEL*, pp. 270–76.

133 Balton, above note 132, p. 40.

for fishing activities on the high seas'.[134] Article 8.2.2 of the Code of Conduct requires the flag States to ensure that no fishing vessels entitled to fly their flag fish on the high seas or in waters under the jurisdiction of other States unless such vessels have been issued with a Certificate of Registry and have been authorised to fish by the competent authority. Article 8.2.3 further ensures that fishing vessels authorised to fish on the high seas or in waters under the jurisdiction of a State other than the flag State should be marked in accordance with uniform and internationally recognisable vessel marking systems. The flag States are also required to take enforcement measures in respect of fishing vessels entitled to fly their flag which have been found by them to have contravened applicable conservation and management measures. Sanctions applicable in respect of violations should be adequate in severity to be effective in securing compliance and to discourage violations wherever they occur, and should deprive offenders of the benefits accruing from their illegal activities.[135] The call to action on flag State responsibility is also echoed by Chapter 17 of Agenda 21.[136]

Flag State Responsibility at the Treaty Level   At the global treaty level, reinforced flag State responsibility was enshrined in two Agreements: the 1993 Agreement to Promote Compliance with International Conservation and Management Measures by Fishing Vessels on the High Seas (hereafter the FAO Compliance Agreement),[137] and the 1995 UN Fish Stocks Agreement.

The FAO Compliance Agreement clearly states that the practice of reflagging as well as the failure of flag States to fulfil their responsibility are factors which seriously undermine the effectiveness of conservation of marine living resources.[138] Thus the FAO Compliance Agreement sets out two primary objectives: (i) to specify flag States' responsibility in respect of fishing vessels entitled to fly their flags and operate on the high seas, including the authorisation by the flag State of

---

134 Paragraph 13 of the operative part of the declaration.

135 Article 8.2.7.

136 Paragraph 17.52.

137 The FAO Compliance Agreement entered into force on 24 April 2003. For text, see the Compliance Agreement (1994) 33 *ILM*, pp. 968ff. With respect to this Agreement, see G. Moore, 'The FAO Compliance Agreement', in M.H. Nordquist and J.N. Moore (eds), *Current Fisheries Issues and the Food and Agriculture Organisation of the United Nations* (The Hague, Kluwer, 2000) pp. 77–91; by the same writer, 'The Food and Agriculture Organisation of the United Nations Compliance Agreement' (1995) 10 *IJMCL*, pp. 412–16; E. Hey, 'Global Fisheries Regulations in the First Half of the 1990s' (1996) 11 *IJMCL*, pp. 469–71; P. Birnie, 'New Approaches to Ensuring Compliance at Sea: The FAO Agreement to Promote Compliance with International Conservation and Management Measures by Fishing Vessels on the High Seas' (1999) 8 *RECIEL*, pp. 48–55; Balton, above note 132, pp. 31–53.

138 Paragraph 9 of the Preamble. It is common knowledge that the FAO Compliance Agreement was originally designed to address the problem of reflagging. Moore, above note 137, ('The FAO Compliance Agreement'), p. 78.

such operations; and (ii) to strengthen international co-operation and increased transparency through the exchange of information on high seas fishing.[139]

With respect to the first objective, Article III (1) (a) places a clear obligation upon each Party to 'take such measures as may be necessary to ensure that fishing vessels entitled to fly its flag do not engage in any activity that undermines the effectiveness of international conservation and management measures'.[140] Article III (2) further provides that: 'no Party shall allow any fishing vessel entitled to fly its flag to be used for fishing on the high seas unless it has been authorized to be so used by the appropriate authority or authorities of that Party.' Article III (3) prohibits a Party to authorise any fishing vessel entitled to fly its flag to be used for fishing on the high seas unless the Party is satisfied that it is able to exercise effectively its responsibilities under this Agreement in respect of that fishing vessel. In relation to this, Article III (5) prohibits a Party from authorising any fishing vessel previously registered in the territory of another Party that has undermined the effectiveness of international conservation and management measures to be used for fishing on the high seas. Article III (8) also requires each Party to take enforcement measures in respect of fishing vessels entitled to fly its flag which act in contravention of the provisions of this Agreement. Sanctions applicable in respect of such contraventions shall be of sufficient gravity as to be effective in securing compliance with the requirement of this Agreement. Article II (2) allows a Party to exempt fishing vessels of less than 24 metres in length entitled to fly its flag from the application of this Agreement. Nevertheless, such Parties are obliged to take effective measures in respect of any such fishing vessel that undermines the effectiveness of international conservation and management measures in accordance with Article III (1) (b).

With respect to international co-operation, Article V (1) places an explicit obligation upon the Parties to co-operate as appropriate in the implementation of this Agreement, in particular, in the exchange of information. Thus each Party is under the obligation to make readily available to FAO the relevant information in accordance with Article VI.[141] In particular, it is notable that each Party is obliged to

---

139 Paragraph 10 of the Preamble. In the FAO Compliance Agreement, the term 'fishing vessel' is broadly defined to cover 'any vessel used or intended for use for the purposes of the commercial exploitation of living marine resources' in Article I (1). It would seem to follow that vessels that support fishing activities in indirect ways, for example, cargo vessels that merely deliver fuel, would be excluded. Balton, above note 132, p. 47.

140 'International conservation and management measures' are defined as: 'measures to conserve or manage one or more species of living marine resources that are adopted and applied in accordance with the relevant rules of international law as reflected in the 1982 United Nations Convention on the Law of the Sea. Such measures may be adopted either by global, regional or subregional fisheries organizations, subject to the rights and obligations of their members, or by treaties or other international agreements.'

141 For instance, in accordance with Article VI (1), such information includes: (a) name of fishing vessel, registration number, previous names (if known), and port of registry; (b) previous flag (if any); (c) International Radio Call Sign (if any); (d) name and address of

report promptly to FAO all relevant information regarding any activities of fishing vessels flying its flag that undermine the effectiveness of international conservation and management measures under Article VI (8) (a). In this case, FAO is to circulate this information promptly to all Parties and, on request, individually to any Party as well as to any global, regional or subregional fisheries organisation by virtue of Article VI (10). Where it has reasonable grounds to believe that a fishing vessel not entitled to fly its flag has engaged in any activity that undermines the effectiveness of international convention and management measures, each Party is required to draw this to the attention of the flag State concerned and may, as appropriate, draw it to the attention of FAO in conformity with Article VI (8) (b). In this case, FAO shall also circulate this information to all Parties as well as to any global, regional or subregional fisheries organisation, provided that the flag State has had an opportunity to comment on the allegation and evidence submitted, or to object as the case may be.[142] It would appear that the circulation of information will provide a useful tool to enhance the effectiveness of flag State responsibility.[143]

Equally, the 1995 UN Fish Stocks Agreement sets out the dual objective, that is to say, 'the effective control' by the flag State as well as international co-operation in this matter.[144] With respect to the former, Article 18 (1) imposes upon the flag State to take such measures as may be necessary to ensure that vessels flying its flag comply with subregional and regional conservation and management measures and that such vessels do not engage in any activity which undermines the effectiveness of such measures. To this end, Article 18 (2) calls upon a State to 'authorise the use of vessels flying its flag for fishing on the high seas only where it is able to exercise effectively its responsibilities in respect of such vessels under the Convention [1982 LOSC] and this Agreement'. In relation to this, the UN Fish Stocks Agreement enumerates a series of measures to be taken by the flag States in some detail.[145] A State is also required to ensure compliance by

owner or owners; (e) where and when built; (f) type of vessel; (g) length. See also Article VI (2) (3) (5) (6) (7) (8) and (9).

142 Article VI (8) (b) and (10).

143 Moore, above note 137 (*IJMCL*), p. 415.

144 The 2006 Report of the Review Conference recorded that many delegations stressed the important role of flag States for the effective implementation of the Agreement. The Conference Report, above note 73, p. 21, para. 100; Outcome, *ibid.*, p. 38, para. 36.

145 These measures include: control by means of fishing licences, authorisations or permits in accordance with regionally or globally agreed procedures, establishment of regulations on their fishing activities on the high seas, establishment of a national record of authorised fishing vessels on the high seas, requirements for marking of fishing vessels and fishing gear for identification in accordance with uniform and internationally recognisable vessel and gear marking systems, requirements for recording and timely reporting of vessel position, catch of target and non-target species, fishing efforts and other relevant fishing data, monitoring, control and surveillance of such vessels, their operations and related activities, regulation of transhipment on the high seas, and regulation of activities to ensure compliance with regional or global measures (Article 18 (3)).

vessels flying its flag with subregional and regional conservation and management measures for straddling fish stocks and highly migratory fish stocks in accordance with Article 19 (1). In relation to this, all investigations and judicial proceedings shall be carried out expeditiously. Furthermore, sanctions applicable in respect of violations shall be adequate in severity to be effective in securing compliance and to discourage violations wherever they occur, and shall deprive offenders of the benefits accruing from their illegal activities.[146]

Concerning co-operation among States Parties, Article 20 (1) imposes upon States to co-operate, either directly or through subregional or regional fisheries management organisations or arrangements, to ensure compliance with and enforcement of subregional and regional conservation and management measures for straddling fish stocks and highly migratory fish stocks. In particular, the flag State shall co-operate with the coastal State in taking appropriate enforcement action where there are reasonable grounds for believing that a vessel on the high seas has been engaged in unauthorised fishing within an area under the jurisdiction of a coastal State, and may authorise the relevant authorities of the coastal State to board and inspect the vessel on the high seas. It may be said that overall the 1995 UN Fish Stocks Agreement may be viewed as a sister instrument of the FAO Compliance Agreement enhancing flag State responsibility and international co-operation in this field.[147]

It is welcome that the FAO Compliance Agreement as well as the UN Fish Stocks Agreement elaborate the flag States' responsibility in some detail. On the other hand, it appears that these instruments are not free from difficulty as to their effective implementation.

First, the FAO Compliance Agreement as well as the UN Fish Stocks Agreement purport to ensure the effectiveness of '(international) conservation and management measures'. Thus the existence of these measures is a prerequisite to give the practical effect of these instruments. Nonetheless, it is debatable whether or not such measures are adequately set out in each and every region in reality. Furthermore, despite the definition of the term '(international) conservation and management measures',[148] it would seem that the contents of those measures need further specification.[149]

Secondly, attention should be drawn to the fact that developing coastal States lack the capacity of flag States to properly ensure compliance by vessels flying their flag with the rules of relevant treaties in this field. Accordingly, further assistance is needed with a view to building the capacity of developing States.[150]

---

146 Article 19 (2).

147 Moore, above note 137 ('The FAO Compliance Agreement'), p. 85.

148 Article 1 (b) of the FAO Compliance Agreement; Article 1 (1) (b) of the UN Fish Stocks Agreement.

149 Hey, above note 137, p. 471 and pp. 481–2.

150 This issue was highlighted in the 2006 Review Conference of the UN Fish Stocks Agreement. The Outcome of the Review Conference, above note 73, pp. 41–3, paras 44–57.

Thirdly, it must be pointed out that the number of States Parties to these Agreements remains limited. In May 2007, only 35 States had become Parties to the FAO Compliance Agreement, and 66 States ratified the UN Fish Stocks Agreement.[151] It appears doubtful whether States often involved with IUU fisheries as well as flags of convenience will ratify the FAO Compliance Agreement as well as the UN Fish Stocks Agreement in the near future. For these reasons, it appears that these Agreements are of limited effectiveness in deterring the practice of reflagging or the flag of convenience.

International Supervision through International Institutions

Reporting from States Parties   Another mode of securing compliance with treaties may be international supervision or control through international institutions.[152] While international supervision or control is a concept with more than one meaning, for the purpose of this study, the concept may be defined as procedures for supervising compliance with a treaty through multilateral international institutions.[153] International supervision seeks to supervise compliance with treaties by various procedures, such as reporting from States Parties, inter-State complaints, which examine complaints by a contracting State against another Party, individual petitions, verification, and decisions as well as recommendations through the Conference of the Parties, and so on. It is acknowledged that international supervision has a valuable role to play, particularly in international human rights law, environmental protection, and disarmament and arms control.[154]

The efficacy of international supervision ensuring compliance with a treaty relies on the quality and the quantity of information reported from the Contracting

---

151   The number of the Parties to the LOSC is 153 in 2007. For data on the 1982 LOSC as well as the UN Fish Stocks Agreement, see 'Multilateral Treaties Deposited with the Secretary-General of the UN' <http://untreaty.un.org/ENGLISH/bible/englishinternetbible/bible.asp>. Concerning the States Parties to the FAO Compliance Agreement, see <http://www.fao.org/Legal/treaties/012s-e.htm>.

152   Birnie and Boyle stressed the importance of supervision by international institutions. Birnie and Boyle, above note 34, pp. 201–2.

153   The present study uses the term 'international institutions' in a broad sense, including inter-governmental organisations as well as a committee established by a Conference of the Parties of a convention. With respect to the analysis of the concept of international supervision or international control in detail, see A. Morita, *Le contrôle international: théorie et pratique* (in Japanese) (Tokyo, Tokyo Daigaku Shuppan Kai, 2000) (in particular, pp. 12 and 54). See also L. Kopelmanas, 'Le contrôle international' (1950-II) 77 *RCADI*, pp. 57–147; H.J. Hahn, 'International Control', in R. Bernhardt (ed.), *Encyclopedia of Public International Law*, Vol. 2 (Amsterdam, North-Holland, 1995) pp. 1079–84; P-M. Dupuy, *Droit international public*, 8th edn (Paris, Dalloz, 2006) pp. 529–38.

154   T. Sato, 'International Supervision by International Organizations with Regard to States' (in Japanese) (1995) 114 *The Hitotsubashi Review*, pp. 99–115; Birnie and Boyle, above note 34, 200–20.

Parties to the treaties. Thus there appears to be little doubt that among various compliance procedures, the reporting system, which obliges States Parties to treaties to make periodic reports on matters affecting the treaty, can provide an appropriate means to supervise compliance with a convention by the Parties.[155] In fact, it is acknowledged that reporting can play an important role in ensuring compliance with treaties with respect to the protection of human rights as well as protection of the environment.[156] The same applies to law of the sea.

It is of particular interest that the reporting system is increasingly enshrined in various treaties relating to the conservation of marine living resources (see Table 3.2). It is especially noteworthy that the 1946 International Convention for the Regulation of Whaling (hereafter the 1946 International Whaling Convention) already provided for a reporting system from the Contracting Parties.[157] Article 8 (3) of this Convention places an obligation upon each Contracting Government to transmit to such bodies as may be designated by the International Whaling Commission scientific information with respect to whales and whaling, including the result of research conducted pursuant to Articles 8 (1) and 4, at intervals of not more than one year. Furthermore, Article 9 (4) imposes upon each Contracting Government to transmit to the International Whaling Commission 'full details of each infraction of the provisions of this Convention by persons or vessels under the jurisdiction of that Government as reported by its inspectors'. The Contracting Governments are also required to ensure prompt transmission to the International Bureau of Whaling Statistics at Sandefjord in Norway, or to such other bodies as the International Whaling Commission may designate, of notifications and statistical and other information required by this Convention in accordance with Article 7. In relation to this, the International Whaling Commission may amend the provisions of the Schedule considering relevant factors, including scientific findings by virtue of Article 5.

---

155 D.M. Dzidzornu, 'Marine Environment Protection under Regional Conventions: Limits to the Contribution of Procedural Norms' (2002) 33 *ODIL*, pp. 291–8; Birnie and Boyle, above note 34, 205–6; Sato, above note 154, p. 104. With respect to reporting systems in general, see K.J. Partsch, 'Reporting Systems in International Relations', in R. Bernhardt, *Encyclopaedia of Public International Law* (Amsterdam, North-Holland Elsevier, 2000) pp. 191–5.

156 Sato, above note 154, pp. 102–3; 106–7.

157 For the text of the Convention, see 161 *UNTS* 72; P.W. Birnie and A. Boyle, *Basic Documents on International Law and the Environment* (Oxford, Oxford University Press, 1995) pp. 586–611. With respect to the recent studies of the practice under this Convention, see P.W. Birnie, 'Marine Mammals: Exploiting the Ambiguities of Article 65 of the Convention on the Law of the Sea and Related Provisions: Practice under the International Convention for the Regulation of Whaling', in D. Freestone, R. Barnes and D. Ong (eds), *The Law of the Sea: Progress and Prospects* (Oxford, Oxford University Press, 2006) pp. 261–80; by the same writer, 'Comment on the Compliance Control Mechanism within the Framework of the International Whaling Convention', in Beyerlin *et al.*, above note 129, pp. 175–200.

Later on, the reporting system was increasingly embodied in treaties relating to the conservation of marine species, particularly after 1980. It is to be noted that these treaties commonly require the Contracting Parties to submit information to committees established by treaties with respect to: (i) statistical and biological data; (ii) fishing activities in the relevant Convention Area; and (iii) relevant conservation measures. As a typical example, Article 23 (2) of the 2000 Convention on the Conservation and Management of Highly Migratory Fish Stocks in the Western and Central Pacific Ocean sets out that each member of the Commission for the Conservation and Management of Highly Migratory Fish Stocks in the Western and Central Pacific Ocean shall:

(a) provide annually to the Commission statistical, biological and other information in accordance with Annex I of the Agreement and, in addition, such data and information as the Commission may require;

(b) provide to the Commission in the manner and at such intervals as may be required by the Commission, information concerning its fishing activities in the Convention Area, including fishing areas and fishing vessels in order to facilitate the compilation of reliable catch and effort statistics; and

(c) provide to the Commission at such intervals as may be required information on steps taken to implement the conservation and management measures adopted by the Commission.

It is arguable that the reporting system can play an important role in enhancing compliance with treaties relating to the conservation of marine living resources for at least three reasons.

First, it is arguable that the collection of reliable scientific data is a prerequisite in the conservation and management of marine living resources.[158] Thus, the regular submission of biological data from States Parties will be a useful tool to collect information necessary to enhance the effectiveness of conservation measures in this field.

Secondly, the reporting system can play a valuable role in ensuring the continuous observation of the performance of States. Indeed, the reports from the Contracting Parties are the only formal source of information on compliance with relevant treaties. These reports will allow treaty commissions to identify problems associated with compliance with treaties. At the same time, reporting will provide States Parties with a good opportunity to review the State's conduct concerning compliance with relevant treaties.

Thirdly, the reports will provide valuable information reviewing the validity of conservation measures adopted by relevant treaty commissions. As the ecological conditions in the oceans may be changeable, there is a need to flexibly adopt

---

158 This issue will be discussed in Chapter 6.

Table 3.2   Examples of the reporting systems in treaties relating to the conservation of marine living resources*

Year	Title	Relevant Provisions
1946	International Convention for the Regulation of Whaling	Articles 8 and 9
1966	International Convention for the Conservation of Atlantic Tunas	Article 9
1978	Convention on Future Multilateral Cooperation in the North-west Atlantic Fisheries	Article 6 (3)
1979	South Pacific Forum Fisheries Agency Convention	Article 9
1980	Convention on Future Multilateral Co-operation in North-East Atlantic Fisheries	Article 16
1980	Convention on the Conservation of Antarctic Marine Living Resources (CCAMLR)	Articles 20, 21
1992	Convention for the Conservation of Anadromous Stocks in the North Pacific Ocean	Article 7 (3)(6)
1993	Convention for the Conservation of Southern Bluefin Tuna	Article 5 (2)
1994	Convention on the Conservation and Management of Pollock Resources Central Bering Sea	Article 10 (2)
1996	Agreement on the Conservation of Cetaceans of the Black Sea, Mediterranean Sea and Contiguous Atlantic Area	Article 8
1999	Treaty between the Government of Canada and the Government of the United States of America Concerning Pacific Salmon	Article 4 (3)
2000	Convention on the Conservation and Management of Highly Migratory Fish Stocks in the Western and Central Pacific Ocean	Article 23 (2) (3) (4)
2001	Convention on the Conservation and Management of Fishery Resources in the South-East Atlantic Ocean	Article 13 (1) (2) (5)

*This list is not exhaustive.

appropriate measures necessary for the conservation of marine species on the basis of the most recent data. To this end, it appears that the reporting system can play an essential role in enhancing the effectiveness of conservation measures.

Effectiveness of the Reporting System   On the other hand, it appears that the reporting system raises some issues which need further reflection. First, it should be noted that the effectiveness of the reporting system depends on the diligence of the reporting authorities.[159] In this respect, concern is voiced that many States, including both developed and developing countries, fail to fulfil the reporting obligation.[160] In reality, the regular submission of reports depends on the capability of a Contracting Party. The facts show that developing countries frequently lack sufficient financial and technical facilities to collect relevant data.[161] Where a Contracting Party encounters problems complying with the obligation to report, it is advisable to provide financial and technical assistance.[162] In fact, the 1992 Convention on Biological Diversity as well as the 1992 Framework Convention on Climate Change oblige the developed country Party to provide new and additional financial resources to enable developing country Parties to meet the agreed full incremental costs to them of implementing measures which fulfil the obligations of the Conventions.[163] There seems to be a general sense that financial and technical assistance act as an incentive for Contracting Parties to comply with the obligation to report.[164]

Secondly, it must be stressed that the effectiveness of the reporting system also relies on the accuracy of data. In this respect, there are growing concerns that many States submit merely superficial reports to the relevant international institutions. In order to enhance the accuracy of data, one may point to at least three solutions.

A first solution is to place an explicit obligation upon States Parties to collect data in some detail. For example, Article 13 (1) (b) of the 2001 Convention on the

---

159 Birnie and Boyle, above note 34, p. 206.

160 With respect to this problem, see, for instance, Sands, above note 6, pp. 181–2; Dzidzornu, above note 155, p. 297; Laurence Boisson de Chazournes, 'Technical and Financial Assistance and Compliance: the Interplay', in Beyerlin *et al.*, above note 129, p. 283.

161 United States General Accounting Office, 'International Environment: Strengthening the Implementation of Environmental Agreements', Report to Congressional Requesters, GAO/RCED-92-188 August (1992), p. 4.

162 A. Kiss, 'Reporting Obligations and Assessment of Reports', in Beyerlin *et al.*, above note 129, p. 245. With respect to the role of technical and financial assistance for promoting compliance with treaty obligations, see in particular Laurence Boisson de Chazournes, above note 160, pp. 273–300.

163 Article 20 (2) and (4) of the Convention on Biological Diversity; Article 4 (3) of the Framework Convention on Climate Change. See also Article 5 (5) of the Montreal Protocol of the Vienna Convention for the Protection of the Ozone Layer.

164 Kiss, above note 162, p. 245; Laurence Boisson de Chazournes, above note 160, p. 283.

Conservation and Management of Fishery Resources in the South-East Atlantic Ocean places an obligation upon each Contracting Party to ensure that data are collected in sufficient detail to facilitate effective stock assessment and are provided in a timely manner to fulfil the requirements of the South-East Atlantic Fisheries Commission. Article 13 (1) (c) clearly requires each Contracting Party to take appropriate measures to verify the accuracy of data.

A second solution is that a third body, such as treaty commissions or the Conference of the Parties, has the power to verify the accuracy of data.[165] In this respect, it is worth noting that the International Whaling Commission possesses the jurisdiction to independently collect and analyse relevant information concerning the current condition of the whale stocks.[166] Similarly the Commission for the Conservation of Antarctic Marine Living Resources is required to compile data on the status of, and changes in the population of, Antarctic marine living resources.[167] Furthermore, the Scientific Committee for the Conservation of Antarctic Marine Living Resources is empowered to regularly assess the status and trends of the populations of Antarctic marine living resources.[168] It is also notable that the Commission for the Conservation and Management of Highly Migratory Fish Stocks in the Western and Central Pacific Ocean may engage the services of scientific experts to provide information and advice on the fishery resources covered by the Convention.[169]

---

165 In international human rights law, a typical example of an inquiry by a committee established in a treaty may be furnished by the 1984 Convention Against Torture and Other Cruel, Inhuman or Degrading Treatment or Punishment. Article 20 (2) of the Convention stipulates that: 'Taking into account any observations which may have been submitted by the State Party concerned, as well as any other relevant information available to it, the Committee may, if it decides that this is warranted, designate one or more of its members to make a confidential inquiry and to report to the Committee urgently.'

166 Article 4 (1) of the 1946 International Convention for the Regulation of Whaling.

167 Article 9 (1) (b) of the CCAMLR. For the text of the Convention, see 1329 *UNTS* 47.

168 Article 15 (2) (b) of the CCAMLR.

169 The scientific expert may, as directed by the Commission, conduct scientific research in conformity with Article 13 (2) (a). Furthermore, under Article 13 (3), the scientific expert is entrusted with the function to undertake various research activities, such as:

(a) undertake the collection, compilation and dissemination of fisheries data;

(b) conduct assessment of highly migratory fish stocks, non-target species, and species belonging to the same ecosystem or associated with or dependent upon such stocks, within the Convention Area;

(c) assess the impacts of fishing, other human activities and environmental factors on target stocks and species belonging to the same ecosystem or dependent upon or associated with the target stocks;

(d) assess the potential effects of proposed changes in the methods or levels of fishing and of proposed conservation and management measures; and investigate such other scientific matters as may be referred to them by the Commission.

A third solution is to use information from an independent scientific organisation, such as the International Council for the Exploration of the Sea (ICES). In this regard, it is to be noted that Article 14 (1) of the 1980 Convention on Future Multilateral Co-operation in North-East Atlantic Fisheries (hereafter the 1980 North-East Atlantic Fisheries Convention) requires the North-East Atlantic Fisheries Commission (NEAFC) to seek information and advice from the ICES. In accordance with the same provision, this includes information and advice on the biology and population dynamics of the fish species concerned, the state of the fish stocks, the effect of fishing on those stocks, and measures for their conservation and management. The information and advice from the third body, that is to say, ICES, is useful for collecting reliable data concerning the environmental conditions in the region in a holistic manner. It would seem that independent information given by NGOs can also contribute to verifying the accuracy of the reports submitted by States Parties.[170]

Thirdly, transparency of the examination process of relevant information is an important factor in enhancing the effectiveness of international supervision. It is arguable that access to information is particularly important. In relation to this, the participation of NGOs in the review process will be useful to improve the transparency of information reported from each Contracting Party. Thus the NEAFC accepts the participation of NGOs in its meeting without vote as an observer. Chapter 8 of the Rules of Procedure of the NEAFC provides that:

> 34. All non-governmental organisations (NGOs) which support the objectives of the Convention, have a demonstrated interest in the species under the purview of NEAFC and are in good standing should be eligible to participate as an observer in all plenary meetings of the Commission, except meetings held in executive sessions or meetings of Heads of Delegations.

In accordance with paragraph 37 of Chapter 8, any NGO admitted to a meeting of the Commission may make an oral statement, distribute documents through the Secretary, and engage in other activities as appropriate and as approved by the Chairman.

Finally, there is a need to ensure the comparability of the reports with a view to obtaining a relatively objective picture of the conservation of marine species.[171] Thus, it will be advisable to formulate common guidelines specifying information which should be contained in the reports.

---

170 A. Epiney, 'The Role of NGO in the Process of Ensuring Compliance with MEAs', in Beyerlin *et al.*, above note 129, p. 328. Concerning the role of NGOs in the implementation of international law in general, see R. Ranjeva, 'Les organisations non gouvernementales et la mise en oeuvre du droit international' (1997) 270 *RCADI*, pp. 9–106.

171 Dzidzornu, above note 155, p. 292.

Non-Flag Enforcement

The last issue which needs to be discussed in this chapter relates to the enforcement of rules of international law relating to conservation of marine living resources. It is evident that the flag State must undertake the primary responsibility to enforce relevant rules on vessels flying its flag. As explained earlier, however, it is argued that the flag State responsibility alone is inadequate to deter IUU fisheries. Accordingly, currently growing attention is focused on non-flag enforcement. Non-flag enforcement may be divided into two categories: inspections at sea and port State control. Each category is further divided into two sub-categories: non-flag enforcement on vessels of the Contracting Parties and non-flag enforcement on vessels of non-Contracting Parties.[172]

Inspections at Sea

At-Sea Inspections of Vessels of the Contracting Parties	At the global level, it is notable that the 1995 UN Fish Stocks Agreement establishes, for the first time, a procedure allowing non-flag States to board and inspect fishing vessels of another State on the high seas.[173] Article 21 (1) of the Agreement provides that:

> In any high seas area covered by a subregional or regional fisheries management organisation or arrangement, a state Party which is a member of, or a participant in, such organisation or arrangement may, through its duly authorised inspectors, board and inspect, in accordance with paragraph 2, fishing vessels flying the flag of another State Party to this Agreement, whether or not such State Party is also a member of, or a participant in, the organisation or arrangement, for the purpose of ensuring compliance with conservation and management measures for straddling fish stocks and highly migratory fish stocks established by that organisation or arrangement.

To this end, States, through subregional or regional fisheries management organisations or arrangements, are required to establish procedures for boarding and inspection.[174] If any organisation or arrangement has not established such procedures within two years of the adoption of this Agreement, however, boarding and inspection as well as any subsequent enforcement actions shall be conducted in accordance with Articles

---

172 With respect to the analysis of this issue in detail, see R.G. Rayfuse, *Non-Flag State Enforcement in High Seas Fisheries* (Leiden, Nijhoff, 2004). Concerning modes of exercising non-flag enforcement, see, in particular, *ibid.*, pp. 61–70.

173 M. Hayashi, 'Enforcement by Non-Flag States on the High Seas Under the 1995 Agreement on Straddling and Highly Migratory Fish Stocks' (1996) 9 *The Georgetown International Environmental Law Review*, p. 27. At the regional level, however, there are bilateral and multilateral fisheries agreements which permit a non-flag State to board and inspect a vessel flying the flag of another State Party. *Ibid.*, pp. 9–10.

174 Article 21 (2) of the UN Fish Stocks Agreement.

21 and 22.[175] It follows that pending the establishment of such procedures, boarding and inspection of fishing vessels on the high seas is conducted by inspecting States, including coastal States on the basis of their national laws.

Where there are clear grounds for believing that a vessel has engaged in any activity contrary to the conservation and management measures referred to in Article 21 (1), the inspecting State shall promptly notify the flag State of the alleged violation.[176] In response to the notification, the flag State shall either fulfil its obligations under Article 19 to investigate and, if evidence so warrants, take enforcement action with respect to the vessel, or authorise the inspecting State to investigate. The response should be made within three working days in accordance with Article 21 (6). Where the flag State authorises the inspecting State to investigate an alleged violation, the inspecting State is to communicate the results of that investigation to the flag State. The flag State shall, if evidence so warrants, fulfil its obligations to take enforcement action with respect to the vessel. Alternatively the flag State may authorise the inspecting State to take such enforcement action as the flag State may specify with respect to the vessel.[177] Where there are clear grounds for believing that a vessel has committed a serious violation, and the flag State has either failed to respond or to take relevant action, the inspectors may remain on board and secure evidence and may require the master to assist in further investigation including by bringing the vessel without delay to the nearest appropriate port. In this case, the inspecting State shall immediately inform the flag State of the name of the port to which the vessel is to proceed pursuant to Article 21 (8). Where the master of a vessel refuses to accept boarding and inspection, the flag State shall direct the master of the vessel to submit immediately to boarding and inspection and, if the master does not comply with such direction, shall suspend the vessel's authorisation to fish and order the vessel to return immediately to port.[178]

The procedure for inspection in the UN Fish Stocks Agreement is innovative in the sense that a Member State of a regional fisheries organisation is allowed to board and inspect vessels of another State on the high seas which fall within the regulatory area of the regional organisation, provided that both States are Parties to the UN Fish Stocks Agreement. To this extent, this procedure constitutes an important exception to the traditional principle of the exclusive jurisdiction of the flag State. At the same time, it should also be noted that the UN Fish Stocks Agreement contains several provisions aimed at safeguarding the rights of the flag States. For instance, in accordance with Article 21 (12), the flag State may, at any time, take action to fulfil its obligations under Article 19 with respect to an alleged violation. Where the vessel is under the direction of the inspecting State, the inspecting State shall, at the request of the flag State, release the vessel to the flag State along with

---

175 Article 21 (3) of the UN Fish Stocks Agreement.
176 Article 21 (5) of the UN Fish Stocks Agreement.
177 Article 21 (7) of the UN Fish Stocks Agreement.
178 Article 22 (4) of the UN Fish Stocks Agreement.

full information on the progress and outcome of its investigation.[179] Action taken by States other than the flag State in respect of vessels having engaged in activities contrary to subregional or regional conservation and management measures shall be proportionate to the seriousness of the violation.[180] States shall also be liable for damage or loss attributable to them arising from action taken pursuant to this Article when such action is unlawful or exceeds that reasonably required in the light of available information to implement the provisions of Article 21.[181] It is arguable that these provisions are particularly important to prevent the abuse of rights by States other than the flag State.

Furthermore, the inspections of vessels of the Contracting Parties at sea are echoed by some regional fisheries organisations, such as the North Pacific Anadromous Fish Commission (NPAFC),[182] CCAMLR,[183] NAFO,[184] NEAFC,[185] and in the Central Bering Sea.[186] Take NEAFC as an example. The inspection scheme of NEAFC can be divided into two stages.

The first stage relates to inspections at sea. Article 15 (1) of the Scheme of Control and Enforcement (hereafter the NEAFC Control Scheme) ensures that control and surveillance of NEAFC are to be carried out by inspectors of the fishery control service of the Contracting Parties, that is to say, NEAFC inspectors. In accordance with Article 15 (2) of the Scheme, each Contracting Party is required to ensure that NEAFC inspectors from another Contracting Party shall be allowed to carry out inspections on board those of its fishing vessels to which the Control and Enforcement Scheme applies. In this respect, each Contracting Party is under the duty to ensure that inspections carried out by that Party shall be carried out in a non-discriminatory manner and in accordance with the Scheme. The number of inspections shall be based upon fleet size, taking into account the time spent in the Regulatory Area pursuant to Article 15 (3). With respect to specific inspection, no boarding shall be conducted without prior notice by radio being sent to the fishing vessel or without the fishing vessel being given the appropriate signal using the International Code of Signals under Article 18 (1). An inspector is given

---

179 Article 21 (12) of the UN Fish Stocks Agreement.

180 Article 21 (16) of the UN Fish Stocks Agreement.

181 Article 21 (18) of the UN Fish Stocks Agreement.

182 Article V of the 1992 Convention for the Conservation of Anadromous Stocks in the North Pacific Ocean. The text of the convention is available at <http://www.oceanlaw.net/texts/npas.htm>.

183 The CCAMLR System of Inspection.

184 Chapter IV of the North-west Atlantic Fisheries Organisation Conservation and Enforcement Measures, NAFO/FC Doc. 07/1 (Revised). With respect to the practice of the NAFO in this matter, see Rayfuse, above note 172, pp. 243–50.

185 Chapter IV of the NEAFC Scheme of Control and Enforcement, Entered into Force on 1 May 2007.

186 Article X of the 1994 Convention on the Conservation and Management of Pollock Resources Central Bering Sea. The text of the Convention is available at <http://www.oceanlaw.net/texts/bering.htm>.

the authority to examine all relevant areas of the fishing vessels, catch and relevant facilities by virtue of Article 18 (2). After the inspection, a copy of each inspection report is to be transmitted without delay to the Contracting Party of the inspected vessel and to the Secretary in accordance with Article 18 (11).

The second stage pertains to follow up in the case of serious infringements. If an inspector considers that there are clear grounds for believing that the master of a fishing vessel has committed a serious infringement, he shall promptly notify the Secretary, the flag Contracting Party of the vessel, and the flag Contracting Party or Parties of donor vessels where transhipment operations are involved in conformity with Article 30 (1). The flag Contracting Party is required to ensure that the fishing vessel concerned is inspected within 72 hours by an inspector duly authorised by that Contracting Party in accordance with Article 30 (2). Under Article 30 (5), the flag Contracting Party shall, if evidence so warrants, require the fishing vessel to proceed immediately to a port designated by that Contracting Party for a thorough inspection. Each Contracting Party is obliged to report any serious infringement to the Secretary. The report shall indicate the current status of the case as well as any sanctions or penalties imposed in accordance with Article 32.

It would appear that non-flag State inspection at sea has a valuable role in enhancing the effectiveness of regulatory measures of regional fisheries organisations. At the same time, the following points should be noted.

First, the inspection schemes do not purport to establish a general regime applicable to high seas fisheries in general. For instance, the UN Fish Stocks Agreement regulates solely straddling and highly migratory fish stocks. Similarly the scope of jurisdiction of regional fisheries organisations is limited to certain regions and specific species. It would seem to follow that the inspection schemes do not change the principle of the exclusive jurisdiction of the flag State in the high seas in a general manner.

Secondly, it must be noted that the ultimate discretion concerning prosecution and sanction are always left to the flag State.[187] To this extent, the primacy of flag State jurisdiction is maintained in the inspection scheme.

---

187 For instance, Article XI (7) (c) of the 1994 Convention on the Conservation and Management of Pollock Resources Central Bering Sea makes clear that: 'Only the authorities of the flag-State Party may try the offence and impose penalties therefor.' Similarly Article XI of the CCAMLR System of Inspection provides that: 'If, as a result of inspection activities carried out in accordance with these provisions, there is evidence of violation of measures adopted under the Convention, the Flag State shall take steps to prosecute and, if necessary, impose sanctions.' See also Article V (2) (d) of the 1992 Convention for the Conservation of Anadromous Stocks in the North Pacific Ocean; Article 36 of the North-west Atlantic Fisheries Organisation, *Conservation and Enforcement Measures*, NAFO/FC Doc. 07/1 (Revised); Article 30 of the NEAFC Scheme of Control and Enforcement. Furthermore, in the 2006 Review Conference of the UN Fish Stocks Agreement, it was noted that flag States possessed the primary jurisdiction to impose sanctions effectively. The Conference Report, above note 73, p. 23, para. 105.

Thirdly, the scheme is costly, and may give rise to disputes relating to participation, cost recovery, objectivity of inspections, interference with fishing activity, economic loss, and evidentiary value of surveillance information as well as inspection reports.[188] Furthermore, co-operation between national enforcement agencies is required in order to make the scheme truly effective. It would appear, however, that this is still inadequate in most regional fisheries organisations.[189]

Fourthly, an obvious weakness of this scheme is that it is not applicable to vessels of non-Contracting Parties. In response to this question, as will be seen, inspections of vessels of non-Contracting Parties at sea are currently receiving close attention.

At-Sea Inspections of Vessels of Non-Contracting Parties It can be observed that inspection of vessels of non-Contracting Parties is adopted by regional fisheries organisations, including North-West Atlantic Fisheries Organisation (NAFO)[190] as well as NEAFC.[191] Again take NEAFC as an example.[192] The inspections of vessels of non-Contracting Parties at sea in the NEAFC scheme can be summarised as follows.

First, Contracting Parties are required to transmit to the Secretary without delay any information regarding non-Contracting Party vessels sighted or by other means identified as engaging in fishing activities in the Convention Area in accordance with Article 37 (1). Under this provision, the Secretary is to transmit this information to all Contracting Parties within one business day of receiving this information according to the same procedure, and to the flag State of the sighted vessel as soon as possible. Under Article 37 (2), the Contracting Party which sighted the non-Contracting Party vessel is obliged to attempt to inform such a vessel without delay that it has been sighted or by other means identified as engaging in fishing activities in the Convention Area.

Secondly, the non-Contracting Party vessels which have been sighted by Contracting Parties or by other means identified as engaging in fishing activities in the Conventional Area are presumed to be undermining the effectiveness of Recommendations established under the NEAFC Convention in accordance with Article 37 (2) as well as Article 44 (1). In the case of a non-Contracting Party vessel sighted or by other means identified as engaging in transhipment activities,

---

188 Rayfuse, above note 172, p. 520.

189 *Ibid.*

190 North-west Atlantic Fisheries Organisation, *Conservation and Enforcement Measures*, NAFO/FC Doc. 07/1 (Revised).

191 NEAFC, Scheme of Control and Enforcement, Entered into Force on 1 May 2007.

192 The members are: Denmark (in respect of the Faroe Islands and Greenland), the European Union, Iceland, Norway and Russia. With respect to an outline of the institutional aspects of the NEAFC, see T. Henriksen, G. Hønneland and A. Sydnes (eds), Law and Politics in Ocean Governance: The UN Fish Stocks Agreement and Regional Fisheries Management Regimes (Leiden and Boston, Nijhoff, 2006) pp. 99–130.

the presumption of undermining conservation and enforcement measures applies to any other non-Contracting Party vessel that has been identified as having engaged in such activities with that vessel by virtue of Article 37 (3). This presumption is provided in regulatory measures of other fisheries organisations,[193] such as the Indian Ocean Tuna Commission (IOTC),[194] the International Commission for the Conservation of Atlantic Tunas (ICCAT),[195] CCAMLR,[196] and NAFO.[197] In particular, in light of the existence of stocks that straddle the boundary between regulatory areas of NAFO and NEAFC as well as the global nature of IUU vessel activities, a non-Contracting Party vessel that has been placed on the NEAFC IUU list is presumed to be undermining the effectiveness of Conservation and Enforcement Measures of NAFO.[198]

Thirdly, NEAFC inspectors are to request permission to board and inspect non-Contracting vessels sighted or by other means identified by a Contracting Party in conformity with Article 38 (1).[199] In light of the principle of the exclusive jurisdiction of the flag State, arguably the consent of the flag State is an essential condition. The consent of the flag State is also important with a view to preventing the abuse of rights by inspectors.[200] If the vessel consents to be boarded the inspection shall be documented by completing an inspection report as set out in Annex XIII. Where evidence so warrants, a Contracting Party may take such action as may be appropriate in accordance with international law.[201] On the other hand, if the master does not consent for his vessel to be boarded and inspected or does not

---

193 R. Rayfuse, 'Regulation and Enforcement in the Law of the Sea: Emerging Assertions of a Right to Non-Flag State Enforcement in the High Seas Fisheries and Disarmament Contexts' (2005) 24 *Australian Yearbook of International Law*, p. 188.

194 Paragraph 2 of Resolution 01/03 Establishing a Scheme to Promote Compliance by Non-Contracting Party Vessels with Resolutions Established by IOTC, 2001. The resolution is available at the homepage of IOTC, <http://www/iotc/org/>.

195 Recommendation by ICCAT Concerning the Ban on Landings and Transshipments of Vessels from Non-Contracting Parties Identified as Having Committed a Serious Infringement, Entered into Force 21 June 1999. This recommendation is available at the homepage of ICCAT, <http://www.iccat.es/>.

196 Conservation Measure 118/XX Scheme to Promote Compliance by Non-Contracting Party Vessels with CCAMLR Conservation Measures. This document is available at the homepage of CCAMLR, <http://www.ccamlr.org>.

197 Article 44 of the North-west Atlantic Fisheries Organization, Conservation and Enforcement Measures.

198 Article 44 (2) of the North-west Atlantic Fisheries Organisation, Conservation and Enforcement Measures.

199 A similar provision may be seen in Article 45 (1) of the North-west Atlantic Fisheries Organisation, Conservation and Enforcement Measures.

200 In the Review Conference on the UN Fish Stocks Agreement, several States expressed their misgivings that boarding and inspection could result in the use of force and be carried out contrary to international law. Conference Report, above note 73, p. 22, para. 102.

201 Article 38 (1).

fulfil any one of the obligations laid down in Articles 19 (a) to (e), the vessel is to be presumed to have engaged in IUU activities by virtue of Article 38 (2).

Fourthly, the Secretary of NEAFC shall place such vessels on a provisional list of IUU vessels ('A' list) in accordance with Article 44 (1). Vessels appearing on the IUU 'A' list that enter ports are not authorised to land or tranship therein but are inspected in accordance with the provisions of Article 40.[202] Furthermore, each year the Permanent Committee for Control and Enforcement (PECCOE) is to consider the 'A' list and as appropriate recommend to the Commission that the vessels be removed or transferred to a confirmed IUU list ('B' list) pursuant to Article 44 (3). Contracting Parties are required to take all necessary measures in order that fishing vessels, support vessels, refuel vessels, the mother-ships and cargo vessels flying their flag do not in any way assist IUU vessels or participate in any transhipment or joint fishing operations with vessels registered on the IUU lists; and that the supply of provisions, fuel or other services to vessels registered on the IUU lists is prohibited.[203] In addition to this, Contracting Parties are obliged to take the following measures with respect to vessels on the 'B' list: (a) prohibit the entry into their ports of such vessels; (b) prohibit the authorisation of such vessels to fish in waters under their national jurisdiction; (c) prohibit the chartering of such vessels; (d) refuse the granting of their flag to such vessels; (e) prohibit the imports of fish coming from such vessels; (f) encourage importers, transporters and other sectors concerned, to refrain from negotiating and from transhipping of fish caught by such vessels; (g) collect and exchange any appropriate information with other Contracting Parties or co-operating non-Contracting Parties with the aim of detecting, controlling and preventing false import/export certificates regarding fish from such vessels.[204] On the other hand, these measures cannot, by themselves, deter reflagging to other non-Contracting Parties.[205]

Fifthly, the Secretariat shall transmit the IUU 'B' list and any relevant information regarding the list to the Executive Secretary of the NAFO with a request to circulate this to all NAFO Contracting Parties. The Secretary shall also circulate the IUU 'B' list to other regional fisheries management organisations in accordance with Article 44 (5). At the same time, vessels that have been placed on the IUU list established by NAFO shall be placed on the NEAFC 'B' list under Article 44 (6). Equally the Secretariat of NAFO is to transmit its IUU list and any relevant information regarding the list to the Secretariat of NEAFC with a request to circulate this to all NEAFC Contracting Parties.[206] In this sense, it may be said that regulatory measures of NAFO and NEAFC are interlinked.

---

202 Article 45 (1) (a).

203 Article 45 (1) (b) (c).

204 Article 45 (2).

205 Rayfuse, above note 172, p. 524.

206 Article 49 (6) of the North-west Atlantic Fisheries Organisation, Conservation and Enforcement Measures.

It would appear that the inspections of vessels of non-Contracting Parties at sea with their consent, making of IUU lists and the circulation of relevant information will not give rise to questions in international law. On the other hand, the presumption of undermining the effectiveness of the regulatory areas is not free from controversy.

First, it appears that this presumption shifts the burden of proving innocence to vessels of non-Contracting Parties. Nonetheless, there is scope to consider the question whether the reversal of the burden of proof is not contrary to the principle of freedom of fisheries. It is true that all States are under the duty to co-operate with other States in taking the conservation measures concerning the living resources of the high seas in accordance with Article 117 of the 1982 LOSC. Furthermore, Article 118 of the LOSC requires States to co-operate with each other in the conservation and management of living resources in the areas of the high seas. Yet it is questionable whether the duty to co-operate will automatically lead to the reversal of the burden of proof.[207]

Secondly, the presumption of undermining the effectiveness of regulatory measures relies on the validity of these measures in the relevant regulatory area. Given that the regulatory measures are qualified by economic, political and social needs of the coastal State(s),[208] however, opinions may be divided with respect to the validity of regulatory measures between the Contracting Parties. Thus some fisheries organisations affirm that a State Party which is opposed to a regulatory measure adopted by a fisheries organisation is exempted from the application of the measure.[209] It appears absurd that vessels of third States are automatically bound to the regulatory measures of the regional fisheries organisations, while Member States may be released from such regulations by opposition.

Thirdly, it must be remembered that in accordance with the principle *pacta tertiis nec nocent nec prosunt*, the regional treaty is not binding upon non-Contracting Parties unless rules of the treaty become part of customary law. Thus, in positive international law, there is no obligation upon the non-Contracting Parties to *automatically* accept measures of regional fisheries organisations. Overall it would appear that the presumption of undermining the effectiveness of regulations runs a risk of unilaterally imposing regulatory measures on third States without their consent. It may be argued that such a presumption is beyond the scope of the 1982 LOSC.

---

207 M. Hayashi, 'New Developments in International Fisheries Law and the Freedom of High Seas Fishing' (in Japanese) (2003) 102 *The Journal of International Law and Diplomacy*, p. 173.

208 See Chapter 2.

209 For instance, Article 12 (2) (b) (c) of the NEAFC Convention; Article XII (1) and (3) of the 1978 Convention on Future Multilateral Cooperation in the North-west Atlantic Fisheries; Article VIII (3) (c) and (e) of the 1966 International Convention for the Conservation of Atlantic Tunas.

Inspections in Port

Port Inspections of Vessels of the Contracting Parties Although the 1982 LOSC provides for investigation by port States with respect to the regulation of vessel-source pollution,[210] it does not provide for similar procedures in relation to fishing vessels. Nonetheless, some post-LOSC documents call for States to carry out port inspection. For instance, Article 8.3.1 of the Code of Conduct requires that port States should take such measures as are necessary to achieve and to assist other States in achieving the objectives of this Code, and should make known to other States details of regulations and measures they have established for this purpose. When taking such measures a port State should not discriminate in form or in fact against the vessels of any other State. Port States are also required to provide such assistance to flag States when a fishing vessel is voluntarily in a port or at an offshore terminal of the port State and the flag State of the vessel requests the port State for assistance in respect of non-compliance with subregional, regional or global conservation and management measures or with internationally agreed minimum standards for the prevention of pollution and for safety, health and conditions of work on board fishing vessels. In 2003, FAO also approved the Model Scheme on Port State Measures to Combat Illegal, Unreported and Unregulated Fishing with a view to facilitating the implementation of effective action by port States to prevent IUU fishing.[211]

At the treaty level, port inspection is enshrined in Article V (2) of the FAO Compliance Agreement:

> When a fishing vessel is voluntarily in the port of a Party other than its flag State, that Party, where it has reasonable grounds for believing that the fishing vessel has been used for an activity that undermines the effectiveness of international conservation and management measures, shall promptly notify the flag State accordingly. Parties may make arrangements regarding the undertaking by port States of such investigatory measures as may be considered necessary to establish whether the fishing vessel has indeed been used contrary to the provisions of this Agreement.

This port inspection is echoed by Article 23 of the UN Fish Stocks Agreement:

> 1. A port State has the right and the duty to take measures, in accordance with international law, to promote the effectiveness of subregional, regional and global conservation and management measures. When taking such measures a port State shall not discriminate in form or in fact against the vessels of any State.

---

210 Article 218.

211 FAO, *Model Scheme on Port State Measures to Combat Illegal, Unreported and Unregulated Fishing.* The document is available at the homepage of FAO <http://www.fao.org>.

2. A port State may, *inter alia*, inspect documents, fishing gear and catch on board fishing vessels, when such vessels are voluntarily in its ports or at its offshore terminals.[212]

Whereas the words '*inter alia*' appear to suggest that the above list of actions may not be exhaustive, it remains obscure what other actions are allowed.[213] With respect to action after inspection, Article 23 (3) specifies that the port State may prohibit landings and transhipment where it has been established that the catch has been taken in a manner which undermines the effectiveness of subregional, regional or global conservation and management measures on the high seas. By applying the concept of port State control to fisheries, it would appear that the UN Fish Stocks Agreement marks an innovation expanding the scope of the concept.[214] On the other hand, unlike in the regulation of vessel-source pollution, there are no 'applicable international rules and standards established through the competent international organisation or general diplomatic conference' in the field of fisheries. Hence it is conceivable that subregional or regional agreements will have a primordial role to play.[215]

Furthermore, it can be observed that port State inspection of vessels of the Contracting Parties is also undertaken by regional fisheries organisations, such as IOTC,[216] NAFO[217] and NEAFC.[218] Where the Contracting Parties have agreed to the port inspection of their vessels by becoming a Party to the relevant global or regional agreements or arrangements, it appears that port inspection will not produce legal questions. On the other hand, the port State inspection of vessels of non-Contracting Parties may need further reflection.

Port Inspections of Non-Contracting Party Vessels   Some regional fisheries organisations apply port inspections to vessels of non-Contracting Parties. For

---

212 In the Review Conference of 2006, delegations emphasised the importance of the role of port States in inspecting incoming fishing vessels to ensure that they were not in violation of conservation measures. The Conference Report, above note 73, p. 23, para. 107.

213 M. Hayashi, 'The 1995 UN Fish Stocks Agreement and the Law of the Sea', in D. Vidas and W. Østreng (eds), *Order for the Oceans at the Turn of the Century* (The Hague, Kluwer, 1999) p. 46.

214 *Ibid.*, p. 46.

215 M. Hayashi, 'The Straddling and Highly Migratory Fish Stocks Agreement', in E Hey (ed.), *Developments in International Fisheries Law* (The Hague, Kluwer, 1999) p. 72.

216 Resolution 02/01 Relating to the Establishment of an IOTC Programme of Inspection in Port.

217 Articles 41 and 42 of the North-west Atlantic Fisheries Organisation, *Conservation and Enforcement Measures*, NAFO/FC Doc. 07/1 (Revised).

218 Chapter V of the NEAFC Scheme of Control and Enforcement, Entered into Force on 1 May 2007.

instance, Article 40 (1) of the NEAFC Scheme of Control and Enforcement provides that:

> When a non-Contracting Party vessel enters a port of any Contracting Party, it shall be inspected by authorised Contracting Party officials knowledgeable of Recommendations established under the Convention and shall not be allowed to land or tranship any fish until this inspection has taken place. Each inspection shall be documented by completing an inspection report as provided for in Article 27.

Where the master of the vessel has failed to fulfil any one of the obligations set down in Article 19 (a) to (e), the vessel is to be presumed to have engaged in IUU activities in accordance with Article 40 (2). In this case, landings and transhipments are to be prohibited pursuant to Article 41. Article 41 sets out that where the inspection reveals that the vessel has species onboard which are subject to Recommendations established in the NEAFC Convention, landings and transhipments of all fish from a non-Contracting Party vessel shall be prohibited in the ports and waters of all Contracting Parties. The vessel shall not be authorised to land or engage in a transhipment operation if the flag State of the vessel, or the flag State or States of donor vessels, does not provide the confirmation under Article 23. Article 43 also requires each Contracting Party to report to the Secretary by 15 September each year for the period 1 July to 30 June 'the number of inspections of non-Contracting Party vessels it conducted under this Scheme at sea or in its ports, the names of the vessels inspected and their respective flag state, the date and as appropriate, the ports where the inspection was conducted, and the results of such inspections'.

Similarly paragraph 3 of a Scheme to Promote Compliance of non-Contracting Party Vessels of IOTC explicitly sets out that when a vessel of a Non-Contracting Party enters voluntarily a port of any Contracting Party, it shall be inspected by authorised Contracting Party officials knowledgeable of IOTC measures and shall not be allowed to land or tranship any fish until this inspection has taken place.[219] Furthermore, landings and transhipments of all fish from vessels of a non-Contracting Party which have been inspected pursuant to paragraph 3 are to be prohibited in all Contracting Party ports if such inspection reveals that the vessel has on board species subject to IOTC conservation or management measures, unless the vessel establishes that the fish were caught outside the IOTC area or in compliance with the relevant IOTC conservation measures and requirements under the Agreement creating the IOTC in accordance with paragraph 4 of the Scheme.[220] Similar measures may be seen in a Scheme to Promote Compliance by

---

219 Paragraph 3 of Resolution 01/03 Establishing a Scheme to Promote Compliance by Non-Contracting Party Vessels with Resolutions Established by IOTC, 2001.

220 *Ibid.*, paragraph 4.

Non-Contracting Party Vessels with CCAMLR Conservation Measures[221] as well as NAFO Conservation and Enforcement Measures.[222] Given that the port is part of internal waters which are under the territorial sovereignty of the coastal State, there is no doubt that the State is entitled to regulate access to its ports as well as landings and transhipments there.[223]

On the other hand, it is foreseeable that the prohibition of access, landing and transhipments in the port runs a risk of producing a dispute between the port State and the fishing State. The *EU-Chile Swordfish* dispute will furnish a clear example in this matter.[224] By Decree 598 of 1999, which was enacted pursuant to Article 165 of the 1991 Fisheries Law, Chile extended the application of its conservation measures concerning swordfish to the high seas. Under the Chilean legislation, the European Communities' fishing vessels operating in the South-East Pacific were not allowed to unload their swordfish in Chilean ports either to land them for warehousing or to tranship them onto other vessels. Consequently Chile made transit through its ports impossible for swordfish. This prohibition also rendered impossible the importation of the affected catches into Chile. The EU refused to admit the application of Chile's conservation measures beyond the limit of the EEZ.[225] Thus, on 6 November 2000, the European Community (EC) requested the establishment of a panel to determine the validity of the prohibition on unloading of swordfish in Chilean ports.[226] Later on, in December 2000, the Government of Chile and the European Community requested the ITLOS to form a special Chamber which was composed of five judges to deal with the dispute.[227] On the one hand, Chile asked the Chamber to adjudicate whether the European Community had complied with obligations under the LOSC, especially Article

---

221 Paragraphs 4 and 5 of the Conservation Measure 118/XX Scheme to Promote Compliance by Non-Contracting Party Vessels with CCAMLR Conservation Measures.

222 Article 46 of the North-west Atlantic Fisheries Organisation, *Conservation and Enforcement Measures*, NAFO/FC Doc. 07/1 (Revised). Furthermore, it is suggested that several States, such as the USA, Canada, Norway and Russia, deny access to their ports to foreign vessels fishing on certain areas of the high seas. Rayfuse, above note 172, p. 350.

223 In fact, the ICJ, in the *Nicaragua* case, clearly stated that: 'It is also by virtue of its sovereignty that the coastal State may regulate access to its port.' ICJ Reports 1986, p. 111, para. 212.

224 With respect to the *EU-Chile Swordfish* dispute, see M.A. Orellana, 'The Swordfish Dispute between the EU and Chile at the ITLOS and the WTO' (2002) 71 *Nordic Journal of International Law*, pp. 55–81; Rayfuse, above note 172, pp. 320–23.

225 For the background to this dispute, see Orellana, above note 224, pp. 60–61; Rayfuse, above note 172, pp. 320–21.

226 World Trade Organisation, Chile – Measures Affecting the Transit and Importation of Swordfish, Request for the Establishment of a Panel by the European Communities, WT/DS193/2, 7 November 2000.

227 ITLOS, Case Concerning the Conservation and Sustainable Exploitation of Swordfish Stocks in the South-Eastern Pacific Ocean, 20 December 2000. This order is available at <http://www.itlos.org/>.

64, as well as Articles 116–119. On the other hand, the EC requested the Chamber to determine whether the Chilean Decree 598, which purported to apply Chile's unilateral conservation measures relating to swordfish on the high seas, was in breach of, *inter alia*, Articles 87, 89 and 116 to 119 of the Convention.[228] It would follow that the scope of obligations concerning Articles 116–119 of the LOSC, which concerned conservation and management of the living resources of the high seas, was a core issue in this dispute. As both cases were suspended in March 2001,[229] the validity of Chile's measures remains a matter of speculation. As a tentative evaluation, the coastal State should be cautious about unilaterally applying its conservation measures to vessels of third States fishing on the high seas, since this runs a risk of extending *de facto* national jurisdiction of the coastal State to the high seas and producing abuse of rights.[230]

Further to this, it should be noted that vessels of non-Contracting Parties can avoid the port State inspection simply by using ports in non-Contracting Party States which will accept their landings.[231] Consequently, port State inspections cannot totally prevent IUU fishing. Thus it becomes important to prevent the emergence of 'ports of convenience', undermining the effectiveness of port State inspections.[232]

Conclusion

The analysis of the preceding study yields the following conclusions:

(i) It is argued that sustainable development is a holistic concept encompassing various elements which should be taken into account in determining environmental and development policy.[233] In light of its general and flexible nature, sustainable development can provide a cardinal concept reconciling the exploitation and the conservation of marine living resources. Owing to the vagueness of its contents, however, it is questionable that this concept itself is a norm purporting to constrain the behaviour of States. Considering that sustainable development relates in essence to national policy, it appears difficult if not impossible for international courts and tribunals to determine whether or not the conduct of a State is contrary to sustainable development. Hence it must be pointed out that the normativity of

---

228 *Ibid.*, para. 2.

229 WTO, Chile – Measures Affecting the Transit and Importation of Swordfish, Arrangement between the European Communities and Chile, Communication from the European Communities, WT/DS193/3, 6 April 2001 (01-1770); ITLOS, Case Concerning the Conservation and Sustainable Exploitation of Swordfish Stocks in the South-Eastern Pacific Ocean, 15 March 2001.

230 *Cf.* Hayashi, above note 207, pp. 172–3.

231 Rayfuse, above note 172, p. 223.

232 The Report of the Review Conference of the UN Fish Stocks Agreement recorded that a number of delegations called for the development of international standards and guidelines to prevent the emergence of 'ports of convenience'. Above note 73, p. 24, para. 108.

233 Sands, above note 3 (*BYIL*), p. 379.

the concept of sustainable development is weak as a rule of conduct as well as a rule of adjudication. Thus, arguably this concept should be regarded as a relevant factor which is to be considered in the judicial process.

(ii) Reflecting the importance of marine ecosystems, the ecosystem approach is increasingly enshrined in various instruments concerning the conservation of marine living resources. This approach is of central importance in stimulating the integrated management approach at the ecological level. On the other hand, it is argued that the ecosystem approach will encounter difficulties as to its implementation in practice. Such difficulties include:

 – limited understanding of marine ecosystems as well as their variability,
 – technological incapability particularly of developing States,
 – obscurity of specific meaning of this approach,
 – compatibility between conservation measures in marine spaces under and beyond national jurisdiction.

Consequently, it remains to be seen to what extent this approach may direct the behaviour of States in practice.

(iii) Owing to the scientific uncertainty over marine ecosystems, it appears inevitable that the ecosystem approach should be linked to the precautionary approach. In fact, treaty practice shows that the ecosystem and precautionary approaches are intimately intertwined. Nonetheless, it has to be stressed that the application of the precautionary approach is largely qualified by economic, social and political factors. In other words, the decision-making process of the precautionary approach can be in essence political in its nature, not legal or scientific. Thus, it remains to be seen whether and to what extent the precautionary approach constrains the behaviour of States. For the same reason, it appears difficult, if not impossible, for international courts to judge the violation of the precautionary approach when a dispute concerning the application of those approaches is submitted before the courts. Hence it is desirable that the mode of application of the ecosystem and precautionary approaches be determined through an international forum. Arguably the institutionalisation of the decision-making process will become particularly important in the implementation of the ecosystem and precautionary approaches.

(iv) With a view to ensuring compliance with relevant rules of international law in the conservation of marine living resources, it is evident that the flag State has a primary responsibility to secure compliance with relevant rules by vessels flying its flag. Thus there seems to be a general sense that flag State responsibility should be ensured in an effective manner. In this respect, it is welcome that the FAO Compliance Agreement as well as the UN Fish Stocks Agreement elaborate the flag States' responsibility in some detail. Considering that the number of States Parties to these Agreements remains highly limited, however, the effect of these Agreements in deterring the practice of reflagging or the flag of convenience remains to be seen. Alternatively, it is of particular interest that international supervision through reporting systems is increasingly enshrined in various treaties relating to the conservation of marine living resources. It is argued that the reporting system can play a valuable role in obtaining scientific data and ensuring the continuous observation of the performance of States.

(v) State practice shows that non-flag enforcement is increasingly introduced in regional fisheries organisations. It appears that non-flag enforcement of vessels at sea is useful with a view to securing the enforcement of relevant rules in an integrated manner. At the same time, it must be stressed that the consent of the flag State is required in order to board and inspect vessels of non-Contracting Parties at sea. Similarly the port inspection of vessels of non-Contracting Parties can be seen as an appropriate means of ensuring the integrated enforcement of relevant rules in this field. On the other hand, the validity of the presumption of undermining the effectiveness of measures taken in the regulatory areas appears to remain a matter of discussion.

The above conclusions appear to reveal that some basic elements stimulating the integrated management approach, that is to say, the concept of sustainable development, the ecosystem and precautionary approaches, international supervision through international institutions, and non-flag enforcement, are developing in treaties as well as in various non-binding documents relating to the conservation of marine living resources. It is of particular interest that procedures ensuring compliance with and enforcement of rules of international law relating to conservation of marine living resources are being increasingly tightened. On the other hand, it should be noted that the normative level of substantive elements – the concept of sustainable development, the ecosystem and precautionary approaches – remains modest. Thus it remains to be seen whether and to what extent the emergence of these elements will constrain the behaviour of States in practice.

At the same time, it must be noted that the decline of marine living resources cannot be attributed solely to the deficiencies of international law in this field. It is argued that a more fundamental problem concerns the over-capacity of the fishing industry, that is to say, the situation where there are far more vessels than are economically justified or necessary to catch the fish available.[234] The over-capacity enhances demand to increase total allowable catch above the level recommended by scientists, and prompts fishermen to disregard conservation measures.[235] Hence there are good reasons to argue that the over-capacity is the root cause of the over-exploitation. In fact, the UN General Assembly Resolution 61/105 calls upon States 'to commit to urgently reducing the capacity of the world's fishing fleets to

---

234 R. Churchill and V. Lowe, *The Law of the Sea*, 3rd edn (Manchester, Manchester University Press, 1999) p. 321. Churchill and Lowe suggest that in the EC, for instance, over-capacity is estimated to be of the order of 40 per cent. See also R. Churchill, '10 Years of the UN Convention on the Law of the Sea: Towards a Global Ocean Regime? A General Appraisal' (2005) 48 *GYIL*, p. 107.

235 Churchill and Lowe, above note 234, p. 321.

levels commensurate with the sustainability of fish stocks'.[236] In reality, however, it is highly difficult if not impossible to address the problem of over-capacity since it may create unemployment for fishermen.[237]

---

236 UN General Assembly Resolution 61/105, *Sustainable Fisheries, including through the 1995 Agreement for the Implementation of the Provisions of the United Nations Convention on the Law of the Sea of 10 December 1982 relating to the Conservation and Management of Straddling Fish Stocks and Highly Migratory Fish Stocks, and Related Instruments*. A/RES/61/105, 6 March 2007, para. 57 of the operative part. Thus this resolution urges States to eliminate subsidies that contribute to illegal, unreported and unregulated fishing and to fishing overcapacity. *Ibid.*, para. 58.

237 Churchill and Lowe point to the fact that the EC has spent a decade trying to reduce over-capacity with no appreciable success so far. Above note 234, p. 322.

PART II
The Dual Approach to Conservation of Marine Biological Diversity

Conservation of Marine Biological Diversity in International Law: A General Appraisal

Introduction

Nature of the Problem

Conservation of marine biological diversity provides another field where interaction between the zonal and integrated management approaches is vividly at issue in international law. Article 2 of the 1992 Convention on Biological Diversity (hereafter the Rio Convention) defines 'biological diversity' as: 'the variability among living organisms from all sources including, *inter alia*, terrestrial, marine and other aquatic ecosystems and the ecological complexes of which they are part; this includes diversity within species, between species and of ecosystems.'[1] Arguably, conservation of biological diversity is of central importance to human life for at least four reasons.

First, it is acknowledged that biological diversity provides essential services for the maintenance of the biosphere in a condition which supports human and other life.[2] For instance, it is suggested that marine biological diversity produces a

---

1 The text of the Rio Convention and the material associated with it are accessible at <http://www.cbd.int/default.shtml>. According to Gaston and Spicer, most straightforwardly, biological diversity means 'the variety of life', and refers collectively to variation at all levels of biological organisation. Biological diversity can be divided into three groups: (i) genetic diversity, which encompasses the components of the genetic coding that structures organisms and variation in the genetic make-up between individuals within a population and between populations; (ii) organismal diversity, which encompasses the taxonomic hierarchy and its components, from individuals upwards to species, genera and beyond; and (iii) ecological diversity, which encompasses the scales of ecological differences from populations, through niches and habitats, on up to biomes. K.J. Gaston and J.I. Spicer, *Biodiversity: An Introduction*, 2nd edn (Oxford, Blackwell Publishing, 2004) p. 5. With respect to the definition of biological diversity, see also P. Sands, *Principles of International Environmental Law*, 2nd edn (Cambridge, Cambridge University Press, 2003) p. 499; P. Birnie and A. Boyle, *International Law and the Environment* (Oxford, Oxford University Press, 2002) p. 549.

2 P. Sands, 'International Law in the Field of Sustainable Development' (1994) 65 *BYIL*, p. 333; E.O. Wilson, *The Diversity of Life*, new edition (London, Penguin Group, 2001) p. 331.

third of the oxygen and moderates global climate.[3] It would be no exaggeration to say that sound biological diversity is a prerequisite to maintain the biosphere in a condition supporting human and other life.

Secondly, biological diversity is of critical importance for meeting the food, health and other needs of the growing world population.[4] In fact, biological diversity is an important source of biological resources.[5] It can also be assumed that a vast array of beneficent but still unknown species exists.[6] It may be argued that biological diversity has a great potential for producing new resources, such as food, pharmaceutical and other material values.[7]

Thirdly, as confirmed by the preambles of many environmental treaties,[8] biological diversity has a considerable scientific value. All living species are genetic libraries which record evolutionary events on the earth.[9] Scientific research concerning biological diversity will contribute to better understanding the mechanisms of ecosystems in the biosphere supporting human and other life.

Finally, it may be argued that biological diversity should be maintained for its ethical and aesthetic values, independent of its utility for humans.[10] In this respect, the 1982 World Charter for Nature stated that: 'Every form of life is unique, warranting respect regardless of its worth to man, and, to accord other organisms such recognition, man must be guided by a moral code of action.'[11] At the treaty level, the 1979 Convention on the Conservation of European Wildlife and Natural Habitats recognises in its Preamble that wild flora and fauna constitute a natural heritage of aesthetic and intrinsic value that needs to be preserved and handed on

---

3 United Nations, *Report of the Secretary-General, Oceans and the Law of the Sea*, A/58/65, 3 March 2003, p. 45, para. 143.

4 Preamble of the Convention on Biological Diversity. See also Gaston and Spicer, above note 1, pp. 92–8.

5 Sands, above note 2, p. 333.

6 Wilson, above note 2, p. 269. He has argued that: 'Biodiversity is our most valuable but least appreciated resource.' *Ibid.*

7 *Ibid.*, p. 297. For instance, currently, the genetic resources of deep-sea organisms are attracting special attention. This issue will be discussed later in this chapter.

8 Examples include: the 1940 Convention on Nature Protection and Wild-Life Preservation in the Western Hemisphere; the 1973 Convention on International Trade in Endangered Species of Wild Flora and Fauna; the 1979 Convention on the Conservation of Migratory Species of Wild Animals; the 1979 Convention on the Conservation of European Wildlife and Natural Habitats; and the 1992 Convention on Biological Diversity.

9 Wilson, above note 2, p. 329.

10 Sands, above note 2, p. 333; M. Bowman, 'The Nature, Development and Philosophical Foundations of the Biodiversity Concept in International Law', in C. Redgwell and M. Bowman (eds), *International Law and the Conservation of Biological Diversity* (The Hague, Kluwer, 1996) pp. 15–21.

11 Preamble. This document is reproduced in P.W. Birnie and A. Boyle (eds), *Basic Documents on International Law and Environment* (Oxford, Oxford University Press, 1995) p. 15ff.

to future generations.[12] Similarly the Rio Convention acknowledges the intrinsic and aesthetic values of biological diversity.[13]

In reality, however, biological diversity is rapidly declining in the world.[14] In particular, there are growing concerns that marine biological diversity is declining or being lost at global, regional and national levels owing to various human activities.[15] In this respect, the UN General Assembly Resolution 60/30 of 2006 reiterated its concern:

> at the adverse impacts on the marine environment and biodiversity, in particular on vulnerable marine ecosystems, including corals, of human activities, such as overutilization of living marine resources, the use of destructive practices, physical impacts by ships, the introduction of alien invasive species and marine pollution from all sources, including from land-based sources and vessels, in particular through the illegal discharge of oil and other harmful substances, the loss or release of fishing gear and the dumping of hazardous waste such as radioactive materials, nuclear waste and dangerous chemicals.[16]

---

12 For the text of the Convention, see *ibid.*, pp. 455ff.

13 Preamble. Furthermore, many treaties concerning biological diversity confirm in their Preambles the aesthetic value, along with economic and scientific values. Examples include: the 1940 Convention on Nature Protection and Wild-Life Preservation in the Western Hemisphere; the 1973 Convention on International Trade in Endangered Species of Wild Flora and Fauna; the 1979 Convention on the Conservation of Migratory Species of Wild Animals; and the 1979 Convention on the Conservation of European Wildlife and Natural Habitats.

14 IUCN indicates that current extinction rates of threatened species are 50 to 500 times higher than extinction rates in the fossil record. J.E.M. Baillie, C. Hilton-Taylor and S.N. Stuart (eds), *2004 IUCN Red List of Threatened Species. A Global Species Assessment* (Gland, IUCN, 2004) p. xxi. This document is available at <http://www.iucn.org/themes/ ssc/red_list_2004/GSA_book/Red_List_2004_book. pdf>.

15 The *Ad Hoc* Technical Expert Group on Protected Areas of the Convention on Biological Diversity suggested that the following human activities have a negative impact on marine biological diversity: over-exploitation of biological diversity; impacts of extraction methods, such as bottom trawling, long-lining, mining and dredging, and seismic surveys; sedimentation arising from activities on adjacent land; infilling of estuaries, alteration of sediment movement by groynes, and other physical changes to the marine environment; water pollution; impacts of tourists and divers; climate change; alien species invasions; subdivision and development on the coast; and fragmentation of habitats. The Convention on Biological Diversity, *Ad Hoc* Technical Expert Group on Protected Areas, *Report of the Ad Hoc Technical Expert Group on Marine and Coastal Protected Area*, UNEP/CBD/ AHTEG-PA/1/INF/5, 6 June 2003, pp. 8–9, paras 11–12. See also United Nations, *Report of the Secretary-General, Oceans and the Law of the Sea*, A/59/62/Add.1, 18 August 2004, pp. 54–61, paras 205–36.

16 UN General Assembly Resolution 60/30, *Ocean and the Law of the Sea*, A/ RES/60/30, 8 March 2006, para. 10 of the Preamble.

Thus conservation of marine biological diversity is becoming an important subject in international law.[17]

As will be seen, it is arguable that the zonal management approach provides the principal legal framework for conservation of marine biological diversity in the law. In light of the cross-sectoral nature of marine ecosystems, however, concern is increasingly voiced that the traditional zonal management approach is inadequate to protect marine biological diversity.[18] In fact, the Report of the UN Secretary-General of 2003 emphasised that:

> The most effective approach to ensure the protection of vulnerable ecosystems is through the adoption of *an integrated, multidisciplinary and multizonal coastal and ocean management* at the national level, as recommended in chapter 17 of Agenda 21 and by the Plan of Implementation of the World Summit for Social Development, as well as by the Consultative Process. It is also necessary to adopt an ecosystem-based management, providing *a more holistic approach*, which would focus on managing marine ecosystems as a whole rather than specific individual elements within them and to enable the development of a longer-term sustainable strategy.[19]

It follows that efforts to preserve marine biological diversity should arguably be made on the basis of the dual approach, that is to say, the zonal and integrated management approaches. Against this background, Part Two will consider the dual approach to conservation of marine biological diversity in international law. To this end, the present chapter will analyse existing legal frameworks for conservation of marine biological diversity at the global and regional levels. After briefly examining principal approaches to conserving marine biological diversity

---

17 Studies on this issue include: S. Iudicello and M. Lytle, 'Marine Biodiversity and International Law: Instruments and Institutions that can be Used to Conserve Marine Biological Diversity Internationally' (1994) 8 *Tulane Environmental Law Journal*, pp. 123–61; C.C. Joyner, 'Biodiversity in the Marine Environment: Resource Implications for the Law of the Sea' (1995) 28 *Vanderbilt Journal of Transnational Law*, pp. 635–87; D. Freestone, 'The Conservation of Marine Ecosystems under International Law', in Redgwell and Bowman, above note 10, pp. 91–107; D.K. Anton, 'Law for the Sea's Biological Diversity', in J.I. Charney, D.K. Anton and M.E. O'Connell (eds), *Politics, Values and Functions: International Law in the 21ˢᵗ Century. Essays in Honour of Professor Louis Henkin* (The Hague, Nijhoff, 1997) pp. 325–52; A.C. de Fontaubert, D.R. Downes and T.S. Agardy, 'Biodiversity in the Seas: Implementing the Convention on Biological Diversity in Marine and Coastal Habitats' (1998) 10 *Georgetown International Environmental Law Review*, pp. 753–854.

18 Freestone, above note 17, p. 94; Anton, above note 17, p. 330.

19 Emphasis added. United Nations, *Report of the Secretary-General, Oceans and the Law of the Sea*, A/58/65, 3 March 2003, p. 64, para. 219. In 2004, UN General Assembly Resolution 58/240 also reiterated its call for 'urgent consideration of ways to integrate and improve, on a scientific basis, the management of risks to the marine biodiversity of seamounts, cold water coral reefs and certain other underwater features'. A/RES/58/240, *Oceans and the Law of the Sea*, 5 March 2004, para. 51.

prior to 1982, the next section will analyse global legal frameworks in this matter. Focus will be on the 1982 LOSC as well as the 1992 Rio Convention. Next, the conservation of marine biological diversity in the North-East Atlantic will be examined as a regional case study. Finally, conclusions will be added.

Conservation of Marine Biological Diversity in Treaties Prior to 1982

Although conservation of specific species has been discussed since the nineteenth century,[20] conservation of marine biological diversity has until recently attracted little attention in international law. An explanation might be that the importance of marine biological diversity was little known in the international community. It would seem, however, that a more fundamental reason should be sought in the nature of international law governing the oceans. As discussed in Chapter 2, the fundamental function of the traditional zonal management approach is to reconcile two opposing interests, that is to say, the national interests of the maritime States, which is secured by the principle of freedom of the high seas, and the national interest of the coastal States on the basis of the principle of sovereignty. After the Second World War, in particular, control of offshore natural resources by the coastal State became the moving force to promote the zonal management approach. Owing to the exploitation-oriented nature of this approach, it was not surprising that States drew little attention to conservation of marine biological diversity. In light of the paucity of State practice, customary international law contains few rules in this matter. Hence it becomes necessary that substantive rules concerning conservation of marine biological diversity should be sought primarily in treaties.

It appears that the 1972 Stockholm Declaration marked an important step toward the development of treaties in this field.[21] Principle 2 of the Declaration stated that: '[t]he natural resources of the earth including the air, water, land, flora and fauna and especially representative samples of natural ecosystems must be safeguarded for the benefit of present and future generations through careful planning or management, as appropriate.' Principle 4 made clear that: 'Man has a special responsibility to safeguard and wisely manage the heritage of wildlife and its habitat which are now gravely imperilled by a combination of adverse factors. Nature conservation including wildlife must therefore receive importance in planning for economic development.' Later on, growing attention was devoted

---

20 For instance, the regulation of whaling has been discussed under the auspices of the League of Nations. The Convention for the Regulation of Whaling and International Convention for the Regulation of Whaling were concluded in 1931 and 1946, respectively. The Protocol to the 1946 Convention was further adopted in 1956. Nevertheless, these conventions aimed to preserve solely the whale, and the idea of the conservation of marine biological diversity was not clearly seen. L. Juda, *International Law and Ocean Use Management: The Evolution of Ocean Governance* (London and New York, Routledge, 1996) pp. 67–71.

21 For the text of the Declaration, see Birnie and Boyle, above note 11, p. 1ff.

Table 4.1   Examples of biological diversity-related treaties and declarations

Year	Title
1902	Convention for the Protection of Birds Useful to Agriculture
1911	Convention respecting Measures for the Preservation and Protection of Fur Seals in the North Pacific Ocean
1931	Convention for the Regulation of Whaling
1933	Convention Relative to the Preservation of Fauna and Flora in their Natural State
1940	Convention on Nature Protection and Wild-Life Preservation in the Western Hemisphere
1946	International Convention for the Regulation of Whaling
1957	Interim Convention of the Conservation of North Pacific Fur Seals
1958	Convention on Fishing and Conservation of the Living Resources of the High Seas
1968	African Convention of Nature and Natural Resources
1970	Benelux Convention Concerning Hunting and the Protection of Birds
1971	Convention on Wetlands of International Importance, Especially as Waterfowl Habitat
1972	Stockholm Declaration on the Human Environment
1972	UNESCO Convention concerning the Protection of World Cultural and Natural Heritage
1972	Convention for the Conservation of Antarctic Seals
1973	Convention on International Trade in Endangered Species of Wild Fauna and Flora
1973	Agreement on the Conservation of Polar Bears
1976	Convention on Conservation of North Pacific Fur Seals (amended in 1980 and 1984)
1976	Convention concerning Conservation of Flora in North America
1977	Protocol amending the Benelux Convention on the Hunting and Protection of Birds
1977	Agreement on Joint Regulations on Fauna and Flora
1979	Convention on the Conservation of Migratory Species of Wild Animals
1979	Convention on the Conservation of European Wildlife and Natural Habitats
1980	Convention on the Conservation of Antarctic Marine Living Resources
1982	United Nations Convention on the Law of the Sea
1982	World Charter for Nature
1985	ASEAN Agreement on the Conservation of Nature and Natural Resources
1992	Rio Declaration
1992	Convention on Biological Diversity
1992	Convention for the Protection of the Marine Environment of the North-East Atlantic
1993	Conjoint Declaration relating to the Institution of the Mediterranean Sanctuary for Marine Mammals
1995	Protocol Concerning Specially Protected Areas and Biological Diversity in the Mediterranean
1996	Inter-American Convention for the Protection and Conservation of Sea Turtles
2000	Cartagena Protocol on Biosafety to the Convention on Biological Diversity
2002	World Summit on Sustainable Development: Plan of Implementation

to conservation of biological diversity at the treaty level.[22] In examining these treaties, three principal approaches can be identified.[23]

The first approach is the species-specific approach which seeks to conserve a certain category of species. An example of the traditional approach may be provided by the 1979 Convention on the Conservation of Migratory Species of Wild Animals (CMS/Bonn Convention).[24] The Bonn Convention purports to protect migratory species of wild animals that live within or pass through one or more national jurisdictional boundaries. Appendix I lists migratory species which are endangered, while Appendix II lists migratory species which have an unfavourable conservation status and which would significantly benefit from international co-operation.[25] More than ten cetacean species are included in Appendix I, and approximately 40 cetaceans are listed in Appendix II.[26] With several exceptions, Parties that are Range States of a migratory species listed in Appendix I shall prohibit the taking of animals belonging to such species by virtue of Article III (5). With respect to species listed in Appendix II, the Bonn Convention provides for two kinds of agreement, that is, AGREEMENTS (Article IV (3)) and agreements (Article IV (4)). Under Article IV (3), Parties that are Range States of migratory species listed in Appendix II shall endeavour to conclude AGREEMENTS where these would benefit the species. These Parties are also encouraged to conclude agreements for any population or any geographically separate part of the population of any species or lower taxon of wild animals, members of which periodically cross one or more national jurisdictional boundaries by virtue of Article IV (4). Examples of agreements under this provision include the 1996 Agreement on the Conservation of Cetaceans of the Black Sea, Mediterranean Sea and Contiguous Atlantic Area (ACCOBAMS), the 1992 Agreement on the Conservation of Small Cetaceans of the Baltic and North Seas (ASCOBANS) and the 1990 Agreement on the Conservation of Seals in the Wadden Sea.[27]

The second approach purports to regulate certain activities threatening the survival of endangered species. A typical example of the activity-specific approach may be furnished by the 1973 Convention on International Trade in Endangered

---

22 See Table 4.1. This list is not exhaustive.

23 *Cf.* Sands, above note 1, p. 502.

24 For the text of the Agreement, see (1980) 19 *ILM*, p. 15; Birnie and Boyle, above note 11, pp. 433ff. Entered into force on 1 November 1983.

25 Articles III and IV of the Bonn Convention. Appendix I and II are available at <http://www.cms.int/documents/appendix/Appendices_COP8_E.pdf.>.

26 M. Prideaux, *Conserving Cetaceans: The Convention on Migratory Species and its Relevant Agreements for Cetacean Conservation* (Munich, WDCS, 2003) p. 5. This document is available at <http://www.cms.int/publications/publications_on_cms.htm>.

27 CMS, 'How to Become a Member of CMS and CMS-related Agreements', CMS Accession Guidelines (2006), pp. 3–4. This document is available at <http://www.cms.int/about/cmsMembership_howTo.pdf>.

Species of Wild Flora and Fauna (CITES/1973 Washington Convention).[28] The Washington Convention seeks to control international commercial trade in endangered species or their products. The Convention recognised, in its Preamble, that wild fauna and flora are an irreplaceable part of the natural systems of the earth which must be protected for this generation and the generations to come. Under Article III of the Washington Convention, trade in specimens of species listed in Appendix I is subject to particularly strict regulation in order not to endanger further their survival.[29] Appendix I includes marine species, such as Minke Whales and Monk Seal, in its list.[30] It should be noted, however, that the Washington Convention is not designed directly to conserve biological diversity.[31]

The third approach seeks to conserve marine ecosystems in a certain ocean space or a habitat. The regional approach is typically seen in the 1980 Convention on the Conservation of Antarctic Marine Living Resources (CCAMLR).[32] The Preamble of the CCAMLR recognises the importance of safeguarding the environment and protecting the integrity of the ecosystem of the seas surrounding Antarctica.[33] Thus Article 2 (3) (b) requires the maintenance of the ecological relationships between harvested, dependent and related populations of Antarctic marine living resources. Article 2 (3) (c) places a clear obligation to prevent changes or minimise the risk of changes in the marine ecosystem which are not potentially reversible over two or three decades. The CCAMLR is innovative in the sense that it clearly focuses on conservation of marine ecosystems. Overall, however, it must be pointed out that prior to the adoption of the 1982 LOSC, there were few treaties which directly addressed conservation of marine biological diversity.

Global Legal Frameworks for Conservation of Marine Biological Diversity

The 1982 UN Convention on the Law of the Sea

General Obligations   There is little doubt that the 1982 LOSC provides a global framework governing the use of the oceans. Nonetheless, conservation of marine

---

28 Entered into force on 1 July 1975. For the text of the Agreement, see 993 *UNTS* 243. Concerning comments on this Convention, see Birnie and Boyle, above note 1, pp. 625–31; Sands, above note 1, pp. 505–15.

29 Appendices are available at <http://www.cites.org/eng/app/appendices.pdf>.

30 A proposal to transfer most populations of Minke and Bryde's whales from Appendix I to Appendix II, which allows for the resumption of trade, was rejected. United Nations, above note 3, p. 47, para. 151.

31 Birnie and Boyle, above note 1, p. 625.

32 Entered into force on 7 April 1982. For the text of the Agreement, see 1329 *UNTS* 47.

33 In accordance with Article I (3), '[t]he Antarctic marine ecosystem means the complex of relationships of Antarctic marine living resources with each other and with their physical environment'.

biological diversity attracts little attention in the LOSC. In fact, the Convention contains only two general provisions relating directly to this issue.

First, Article 194 (5) requires the protection of rare or fragile ecosystems, by providing that: 'The measures taken in accordance with this Part [XII] shall include those necessary to protect and preserve rare or fragile ecosystems as well as the habitat of depleted, threatened or endangered species and other forms of marine life.' Arguably the 'marine environment' includes the ocean as a whole including the high seas. It follows that States are under obligation to protect and preserve rare or fragile ecosystems in marine spaces under and beyond national jurisdiction. Nonetheless, it appears that this obligation is too general to be very useful.

Secondly, Article 196 (1) places an obligation upon the States to take all measures necessary to prevent, reduce and control pollution of the marine environment resulting from the use of technologies under their jurisdiction or control, or the intentional or accidental introduction of species, alien or new, to a particular part of the marine environment, which may cause significant and harmful changes thereto.[34] Later on, Article 196 was amplified in the 2004 International Convention for the Control and Management of Ships' Ballast Water and Sediments.[35] Apart from these provisions, however, little mention was made in relation to the conservation of marine biological diversity in the LOSC. Thus one may be forced to conclude that under the Convention, conservation of marine biological diversity is to be undertaken within the framework of the traditional zonal management approach.

Conservation of Marine Biological Diversity in Spaces under the National Jurisdiction   The sovereignty of the coastal State extends to the internal waters as well as the territorial sea in accordance with Article 2 (1) of the 1982 LOSC as well as customary law. In light of the comprehensive nature of sovereignty, there is little doubt that in internal waters and territorial seas, the coastal State has jurisdiction relating to conservation of marine biological diversity in accordance with international law. Equally it is arguable that the coastal State can exercise jurisdiction over conservation of marine biological diversity in archipelagic waters since these waters are under the territorial sovereignty of the archipelagic States. On the other hand, under the LOSC, there is no distinct obligation to conserve

---

34 The definition of 'pollution' adopted by the 1982 UN Convention does not make explicit reference to impacts on marine ecosystems, while this definition refers to 'deleterious effects as harm to living resources and marine life'. Freestone, above note 17, p. 103.

35 The text of the Convention is reproduced in (2004) 19 *IJMCL*, pp. 446–82. With respect to this convention, see M. Tsimplis, 'Alien Species Stay Home: The International Convention for the Control and Management of Ships' Ballast Water and Sediments 2004', *ibid.*, pp. 411–45.

marine biological diversity in these zones. It would follow that the coastal State is subject only to general obligations in Articles 192, 194 (5) and 196 of the LOSC.

In the EEZ, the coastal State has sovereign rights for the purpose of exploring and exploiting, conserving and managing the natural resources in accordance with Article 56 (1) (a). At the same time, the coastal State has the duty to take conservation measures concerning the living resources in the EEZ pursuant to Article 61. While, under the LOSC, there is no explicit provision concerning conservation of marine biological diversity in the EEZ, it may not be far-fetched to argue that marine biological diversity can be included in the scope of the 'natural resources' in Article 56 (1) (a) as well as the 'living resources' in Article 61, since such diversity concerns the variability among marine living organisms. It must also be remembered that the coastal State is under the general obligation to protect and preserve rare or fragile ecosystems, as well as the habitat of depleted, threatened or endangered species and other forms of marine life in its EEZ by virtue of Articles 194 and 196. Further to this, the coastal State has the general obligation to protect and preserve the marine environment under Article 192. In this respect, Article 56 (b) (iii) confers on the coastal State jurisdiction with regard to the protection and preservation of the marine environment. It is also notable that Article 234 provides coastal States with the right to adopt and enforce non-discriminatory laws and regulations for the prevention, reduction and control of marine pollution from vessels in ice-covered areas within the limits of the EEZ, where pollution of the marine environment could cause major harm to or irreversible disturbance of the ecological balance. Arguably, the cumulative effect of these provisions is that the coastal State can exercise jurisdiction over conservation of marine biological diversity in its EEZ.[36]

One issue arising relates to the reconciliation between the conservation of marine biological diversity and other legitimate uses of the ocean, such as navigation and laying submarine cables and pipelines, in the EEZ. In the EEZ, all States enjoy the freedom of navigation and overflight in accordance with Article 58 (1) of the LOSC. In relation to this, Article 211 (1) of the LOSC requires States to promote the adoption of routeing systems designed to minimise the threat of accidents which might cause pollution of the marine environment. Articles 211 (5) and 220 confer on the coastal States powers to prevent vessel-source pollution. It would follow that the coastal State may regulate navigation in the form of routeing measures in order to protect the environment of its EEZ, including its biological diversity. Concerning submarine cables, all States enjoy the freedom of the laying of such cables and pipelines in the EEZ.[37] Under Article 79 (3) of the LOSC, however, the delineation of the course for the laying of such pipelines on the

---

36 *Cf.* R. Long and A. Grehan, 'Marine Habitat Protection in Sea Areas under the Jurisdiction of a Coastal Member State of the European Union: The Case of Deep-Water Coral Conservation in Ireland' (2002) 17 *IJMCL*, p. 242.

37 Article 58 (1) of the LOSC.

continental shelf is subject to the consent of the coastal State.[38] Thus it is arguable that the coastal State can regulate the course for laying cables and pipelines with a view to protecting marine biological diversity in the EEZ.

The legal status of marine biological diversity on the continental shelf is more controversial. This is particularly at issue with respect to conservation of cold-water coral reefs on the continental shelf.[39] Cold-water coral systems can be found in fjords, along the edge of the continental shelf, and around offshore submarine banks and seamounts. Scientific findings demonstrate that cold-water coral ecosystems are hotspots of important biodiversity and a biological resource with intrinsic and socio-economic value; and that these ecosystems are slow growing and vulnerable to physical damage.[40] Evidence suggests that these vulnerable ecosystems are already being damaged by human activities, in particular, the increasing intensity of deep-water trawling.[41] Thus there is a special need to protect cold-water coral reefs on the continental shelf.

There is no doubt that the coastal State has sovereign rights for the purpose of exploring and exploiting 'natural resources' on the continental shelf by virtue of Article 77 (1) of the LOSC as well as customary law. Nonetheless, the natural resources on the continental shelf concern only 'mineral and other non-living resources of the sea-bed and subsoil'. In accordance with Article 77 (4) of the LOSC, the only living components of natural resources falling within the continental shelf regime are sedentary species, which include oysters, clams and abalone.[42] It would seem that, literally interpreted, the coastal State does not possess jurisdiction in relation to marine organisms other than sedentary species on its continental shelf. If this is the case, it appears that cold-water coral reefs are beyond the scope of the natural resources on the continental shelf. Furthermore, unlike the EEZ, there is no duty under the LOSC to conserve natural resources on the continental shelf. Hence the scope of the duty of the coastal State is limited as

---

38 It should be noted that the concept of EEZ includes the seabed and its subsoil as well. Thus once the coastal State has claimed the EEZ, the continental shelf becomes part of the seabed of the EEZ. Yet when a coastal State does not yet claim an EEZ, or where the continental shelf extends beyond 200 nautical miles, the continental shelf regime *per se* is at issue.

39 Concerning this issue, see in particular, Long and Grehan, above note 36, pp. 235–61.

40 A. Freiwald, J.H. Fosså, A. Grehan, T. Koslow and J.M. Roberts, *Cold-Water Coral Reefs* (Cambridge, UNEP World Conservation Monitoring Centre, 2004) p. 6.

41 *Ibid.*, p. 10. See also Long and Grehan, above note 36, pp. 237–40.

42 R.R. Churchill and R.V. Lowe, *The Law of the Sea*, 3rd edn (Manchester, Manchester University Press, 1999), p. 151. But the scope of 'sedentary species' remains a matter of discussion. M.H. Nordquist, S.N. Nandan and S. Rosenne (eds), *United Nations Convention on the Law of the Sea 1982: A Commentary*, Vol. II, Centre for Oceans Law and Policy, University of Virginia School of Law (The Hague, Nijhoff, 1993) p. 898; J. Mossop, 'Protecting Marine Biodiversity on the Continental Shelf Beyond 200 Nautical Miles' (2007) 38 *ODIL*, p. 292. See also S.V. Scott, 'The Inclusion of Sedentary Fisheries within the Continental Shelf Doctrine' (1992) 41 *ICLQ*, pp. 788–807.

compared to the EEZ.[43] It should be noted, however, that the coastal State is under the general obligation to protect and preserve 'rare or fragile ecosystems' pursuant to Article 194 (5). As there is no geographical limit in this provision, it may be argued that Article 194 (5) also covers the continental shelf. In order to implement this obligation, it appears inevitable that the coastal State exercises jurisdiction over marine biological diversity on its continental shelf. In addition to this, Article 81 of the LOSC stipulates that the coastal State shall have the exclusive right to authorise and regulate drilling on the continental shelf 'for all purposes'.[44] It would seem to follow that the coastal State may regulate drilling on the continental shelf with a view to preventing adverse impact on ecosystems there.

Conservation of Marine Biological Diversity in Spaces beyond the Limits of National Jurisdiction Under the LOSC, there is no explicit provision relating to conservation of marine biological diversity on the high seas. Rather, the Convention places merely general obligations to preserve living resources in conformity with Articles 117, 118 and 119. Nonetheless, these provisions pertain in essence to the regulation of fisheries, not conservation of marine biological diversity. Furthermore, there is no provision concerning conservation of marine biological diversity straddling the EEZ/EFZ (exclusive fishing zone) and the high seas in the LOSC. It may be argued that this is an inherent weakness of the application of the zonal management approach to this issue.

With respect to marine spaces beyond the limits of national jurisdiction, an important issue arising is the conservation of marine biological diversity in the Area.[45] Due to the unique and extreme environment where the organisms have

---

43 Long and Grehan, above note 36, p. 243.

44 According to Oda, this provision implies that jurisdiction of the coastal State is not limited to the exploration and exploitation of natural resources on the continental shelf. S. Oda, *Chukai Kokuren Kaiyoho Jyoyaku* (Commentary on the UN Convention on the Law of the Sea, in Japanese) (Tokyo, Yuhikaku, 1985) p. 268.

45 This issue attracts growing attention from writers. See, for instance, L. Glowka, 'The Deepest of Ironies: Genetic Resources, Marine Scientific Research, and the Area' (1996) 12 *Ocean Yearbook*, pp. 154–78; by the same author, 'Genetic Resources, Marine Scientific Research and the International Seabed Area' (1999) 8 *RECIEL*, pp. 56–66; by the same author, 'Beyond the Deepest of Ironies: Genetic Resources, Marine Scientific Research and International Seabed Area', in J-P. Beurier, A. Kiss and S. Mahmoudi (eds), *New Technologies and Law of the Marine Environment* (The Hague, Kluwer, 2000) pp. 75–93; C.H. Allen, 'Protecting the Oceanic Gardens of Eden: International Law Issues in Deep-Sea Vent Resource Conservation and Management' (2000–2001) 13 *The Georgetown International Environmental Law Review*, pp. 565–660; N. Matz, 'Marine Biological Resources: Some Reflections on Concepts for the Protection and Sustainable Use of Biological Resources in the Deep Seabed' (2002) 2 *Non-State Actors and International Law*, pp. 279–300; T. Scovazzi, 'Mining, Protection of the Environment, Scientific Research and Bioprospecting: Some Considerations on the Role of the International Sea-Bed Authority' (2004) 19 *IJMCL*, pp. 383–409; by the same author, 'Bioprospecting on the Deep Seabed:

been living, it is expected that species living in the deep seabed can provide important information about the evolution of life and the earth.[46] It is believed that these species, in particular micro-organisms, present great interest for marine biotechnological industry. For instance, hydrothermal organisms may yield useful medicines, enzymes, nutritional additives, and improved chemical, energy and agricultural products.[47] On the other hand, concern is voiced that the increased demand for genetic resources in the deep seabed may result in their unsustainable collection or even in the extinction of species.[48] In fact, it is becoming apparent that marine ecosystems in the deep ocean floors are threatened by various human activities, such as marine scientific research, bioprospecting, deep seabed mining and fishing activities. Thus, in 2004, UN General Assembly Resolution 58/240 required the relevant global and regional bodies to 'investigate urgently how to better address, on a scientific basis, including the application of precaution, the threats and risks to vulnerable and threatened marine ecosystems and biodiversity

---

A Legal Gap Requiring to be Filled', in F. Francioni and T. Scovazzi (eds), *Biotechnology and International Law* (Oxford and Portland, Oregon, Hart Publishing, 2006) pp. 81–97; by the same author, 'Biodiversity in the Deep Seabed' (1996) 7 *Yearbook of International Environmental Law*, pp. 481–7; D.K. Leary, *International Law and the Genetic Resources of the Deep Sea* (Leiden and Boston, Nijhoff, 2007); Y. Tanaka, 'Reflections on the Conservation and Sustainable Use of Genetic Resources in the Deep Seabed Beyond the Limits of National Jurisdiction' (2008) 38 *ODIL*, pp. 129–149.

46 Glowka, above note 45 (*Ocean Yearbook*), p. 159. W.T. Burke, 'State Practice, New Ocean Uses, and Ocean Governance under UNCLOS', in T.A. Mensah (ed.), *Ocean Governance: Strategies and Approaches for the 21st Century: Proceedings of The Law of the Sea Institute Twenty-eighth Annual Conference, Honolulu, Hawaii, July 11–14* (Honolulu, The Law of the Sea Institute, University of Hawaii 1996) p. 229. See also International Seabed Authority, *Summary Presentations on Polymetallic Massive Sulphide Deposit and Cobalt-Rich Ferromanganese Crusts*, Doc. ISBA/8/A/1, 9 May 2002, p. 5, para. 19. This document is available at the homepage of the Authority <http://www.isa.org.jm>.

47 Glowka, above note 45 (*Ocean Yearbook*), pp. 159–61; Allen, above note 45, pp. 584–5; Leary, above note 45, pp. 158–64; I. Mgbeoji, '(Under) Mining the Seabed? Between the International Seabed Authority Mining Code and Sustainable Bioprospecting of Hydrothermal Vent Ecosystems in the Seabed Area: Taking Precaution Seriously' (2004) 18 *Ocean Yearbook*, pp. 423–4. Marine genetic resources already have a huge commercial value. It is estimated that worldwide sales of all marine biotechnology-related products was US$ 100 billion for the year 2000. UNEP/CBD/SBSTTA/11/11, *Marine and Coastal Biological Diversity: Status and Trends of, and Threats to, Deep Seabed Genetic Resources Beyond National Jurisdiction, and Identification of Technical Options for Their Conservation and Sustainable Use*, 22 July 2005, p. 8, para. 22. This document is available at the homepage of the Convention on Biological Diversity <http://www/biodiv.org/>. Concerning marine biotechnology, see B. Cicin-Sain, R.W. Knedht, L.D. Bowman and G.W. Fisk, 'Emerging Policy Issues in the Development of Marine Biotechnology' (1996) 12 *Ocean Yearbook*, pp. 179–206.

48 Such concern is voiced by SBSTTA of the Convention of Biological Diversity. UNEP/CBD/SBSTTA/11/11, above note 47, p. 9, para. 27.

in areas beyond national jurisdiction'.[49] Nonetheless, the 1982 LOSC contains no provision in this matter since biological resources in the Area were little known when the Convention was drafted.[50] Hence there is an urgent need to develop rules relating to conservation of biological diversity in the Area. Considering this issue, of particular importance is jurisdiction of the International Seabed Authority (hereafter the Authority) over the Area.[51] Two points should be highlighted here.

First, it should be noted that the Authority has prescriptive jurisdiction concerning environmental protection in the Area. Article 17 (1) (b) (ix) and (xii) of Annex III of the LOSC call for the Authority to adopt and uniformly apply rules, regulations and procedures for the prevention of interference with other activities in the marine environment as well as mining standards and practices, including those relating to operational safety, the conservation of the resources and the protection of the marine environment. The prescriptive jurisdiction of the Authority is further amplified in Article 145 of the LOSC, which provides that:

> Necessary measures shall be taken in accordance with this Convention with respect to activities in the Area to ensure effective protection for the marine environment from harmful effects which may arise from such activities. To this end the Authority shall adopt appropriate rules, regulations and procedures for *inter alia:*
>
> (a) the prevention, reduction and control of pollution and other hazards to the marine environment, including the coastline, and of interference with the ecological balance of the marine environment, particular attention being paid to the need for protection from harmful effects of such activities as drilling, dredging, excavation, disposal of waste, construction and operation or maintenance of installations, pipelines and other devices related to such activities;
>
> (b) the protection and conservation of the natural resources of the Area and the prevention of damage to the flora and fauna of the marine environment.

It is of particular interest that Article 145 (b) explicitly refers to 'the ecological balance of the marine environment' as well as 'the flora and fauna of the marine environment'. Those phrases appear to suggest that the Authority's prescriptive jurisdiction covers the protection of the flora and fauna of the Area.[52] In this respect, the Secretary-General of the Authority stated that: 'the Authority also has a broader regulatory role with respect to the protection and preservation of the marine environment (including its biodiversity) as well as with respect to marine scientific research in the Area generally.'[53] The Secretary-General also argued

---

49 UN General Assembly, above note 19, p. 10, para. 52.

50 J-P. Lévy, 'La première decennie de l'autorité internationale des fonds marins' (2005) 109 *RGDIP*, p. 119.

51 Scovazzi, above note 45 (*IJMCL*), pp. 392–6.

52 *Ibid.*, p. 393.

53 International Seabed Authority, *Report of the Secretary-General of the International Seabed Authority under Article 166, paragraph 4, of the United Nations Convention on the*

that it was clearly within the responsibility of the Authority to take measures to protect extreme biological communities associated with polymetallic sulphides and cobalt-rich crusts in the Area.[54]

The prescriptive jurisdiction of the Authority is confirmed by the 1994 Agreement relating to the Implementation of Part XI of the United Nations Convention on the Law of the Sea of 10 December 1982 (hereafter the 1994 Agreement). Section 1 of paragraph 5 (g) of the Annex of the 1994 Agreement stipulates that between the entry into force of the LOSC and the approval of the first plan of work of exploitation, the Authority shall concentrate on '[a]dopting of rules, regulations and procedures incorporating applicable standards for the protection and preservation of the marine environment'. Section 1 (7) of the Annex of the 1994 Agreement further requires that '[a]n application for approval of a plan of work shall be accompanied by an assessment of the potential environmental impacts of the proposed activities and by a description of a programme for oceanographic and baseline environmental studies in accordance with the rules, regulations and procedures adopted by the Authority'.[55] It follows that the Authority is empowered to legislate rules and procedures with respect to environmental impact assessment as well as oceanographic and environmental programmes.[56] It is also notable that Regulation 31 of the 2000 Mining Code calls upon the Authority, in accordance with the Convention and the Agreement, to establish and keep under periodic review environmental rules, regulations and procedures to ensure effective protection for the marine environment from harmful effects which may arise from activities in the Area.

Secondly, the Authority is empowered to exercise enforcement jurisdiction with a view to protecting the environment of the Area. The Council of the Authority has

---

Law of the Sea, ISBA/8/A/5, 7 June 2002, p. 12, para. 52. See also United Nations General Assembly, *Report on the Work of the United Nations Open-ended Informal Consultative Process on Oceans and the Law of the Sea at its Fifth Meeting*, A/59/122, 1 July 2004, p. 17, para. 66.

54 International Seabed Authority, *Report of the Secretary-General of the International Seabed Authority under Article 166, paragraph 4, of the United Nations Convention on the Law of the Sea*, ISBA/10/A/3, 31 March 2004, p. 43, para. 133.

55 See also section 1 (5) (k) of the Annex. In addition, it should be noted that Article 206 of the LOSC provides an obligation concerning assessment of potential effects of activities upon the marine environment in a general manner.

56 It is noteworthy that Regulation 31 (7) of the 2000 Mining Code requires the Contractor to propose areas to be set aside and used exclusively as impact reference zones and preservation reference zones. 'Impact reference zones' means areas to be used for assessing the effect of each contractor's activities in the Area on the marine environment and which are representative of the environmental characteristics of the Area. 'Preservation reference zones' means areas in which no mining shall occur to ensure representative and stable biota of the seabed in order to assess any changes in the flora and fauna of the marine environment. Arguably the creation of those zones can be an important tool to assess the environmental consequences of the exploration and exploitation in the Area.

a jurisdiction to 'supervise and co-ordinate the implementation of the provisions of this Part [XI] on *all questions and matters within the competence of the Authority* and invite the attention of the Assembly to cases of non-compliance'.[57] Accordingly the environmental protection of the Area is supervised by the Council of the Authority. In relation to this, it is notable that the Authority also has a power to suspend the exercise of the rights and privileges of membership of a State Party which has grossly and persistently violated the provisions of Part XI of the LOSC by virtue of Article 185 (1). Article 162 (2) (w) of the 1982 LOSC further obliges the Council of the Authority to 'issue emergency orders, which may include orders for the suspension or adjustment of operations, to prevent serious harm to the marine environment arising out of activities in the Area'.[58] This obligation is confirmed by Regulation 32 (5) of the 2000 Mining Code. It should also be noted that the Council of the Authority is to disapprove areas for exploitation by contractors or the Enterprise in cases where substantial evidence indicates the risk of serious harm to the marine environment in accordance with Article 162 (2) (x) of the LOSC. It is true that rules and regulations prescribed by the Authority relate in essence to the prevention of pollution from the 'activities in the Area', that is to say, 'all activities of exploration for, and exploitation of, the resources of the Area'.[59] Considering that those activities may have adverse impacts upon the marine environment of the Area, however, it is arguable that these rules and regulations can serve for the protection of marine biological diversity in the Area.

The 1992 Convention on Biological Diversity

Scope of the Convention on Biological Diversity   A decade after the adoption of the LOSC, the first global treaty was concluded in the field of conservation of biological diversity: the 1992 Convention on Biological Diversity (the Rio Convention).[60] The Rio Convention seeks three objectives: (i) the conservation of biological diversity; (ii) the sustainable use of its components; and (iii) the fair and equitable sharing of the benefits arising out of the utilisation of genetic resources.[61] The definition of biological diversity in Article 2 covers terrestrial, marine and other aquatic ecosystems and the ecological complexes of which they are part. It follows that the Convention is also applicable to the conservation of marine biological diversity.[62] In fact, Article 22 places a clear obligation upon Contracting Parties to

---

57   Emphasis added. Article 162 (2) (a).

58   See also Article 18 of Annex III of the LOSC.

59   Article 1, para. 1 (3) of the 1982 LOSC.

60   Entered into force on 29 December 1993.

61   Article 1.

62   Joyner, above note 17, p. 645. See also M-A. Hermitte, 'La convention sur la diversité biologique' (1992) 38 *AFDI*, p. 861; M. Chandler, 'The Biodiversity Convention: Selected Issues of Interest to the International Lawyer' (1993) 4 *Colorado Journal of International Environmental Law and Policy*, pp. 151–2.

implement this Convention with respect to the marine environment consistently with the rights and obligations of States under the law of the sea. In addition to this, the term 'sovereign rights', not 'sovereignty', used in Article 3 appears to suggest that the Rio Convention may be applicable to the EEZ as well as the continental shelf. This interpretation is supported by the practice of the Conference of the Parties (COP) of the Rio Convention. In particular, the Jakarta Ministerial Statement reaffirmed the critical need for the COP to address the conservation and sustainable use of marine and coastal biological diversity, and referred to the new global consensus on the importance of marine and coastal biological diversity as the 'Jakarta Mandate on Marine and Coastal Biological Diversity'.[63] Overall, it may be argued that the Rio Convention provides a global legal framework for the conservation of marine biological diversity. Thus it becomes necessary to examine principal provisions applicable to this matter.[64]

Rules Applicable to Conservation of Marine Biological Diversity under the Rio Convention   It appears that relevant rules of the Rio Convention applicable to conservation of marine biological diversity may be divided into four categories.

---

63 Jakarta Ministerial Statement on the Implementation of the Convention on Biological Diversity, para. 14. This document is available at <http://www.oceanlaw.net/texts/jakarta.htm>. See also M.M. Goote, 'Convention on Biological Diversity: The Jakarta Mandate on Marine and Coastal Biological Diversity' (1997) 12 *IJMCL*, pp. 377–95.

64 The comprehensive analysis of the Rio Convention is beyond the scope of this study. With respect to this Convention, there are already many articles. See, for instance, Hermitte, above note 62, pp. 844–70; Françoise Burhenne-Guilmin and Susan Casey-Lefkowitz, 'The Convention on Biological Diversity: A Hard Won Global Achievement' (1992) 3 *Yearbook of International Environmental Law*, pp. 43–59; Cyrille de Klemm, *Biological Diversity Convention and the Law: Legal Mechanisms for Conserving Species and Ecosystems* (Gland, IUCN-The World Conservation Union, 1993); Chandler, above note 62, pp. 141–75; A.E. Boyle, 'The Rio Convention on Biological Diversity', in Redgwell and Bowman, above note 10, pp. 33–49; by the same author, 'The Convention on Biological Diversity', in L. Campiglio, L. Pineschi, D. Siniscalco, T. Treves and F.E.E. Mattei (eds), *The Environment After Rio: International Law and Economics* (London, Graham & Trotman and Nijhoff, 1994) pp. 111–27; A.A. Yusuf, 'International Law and Sustainable Development: The Convention on Biological Diversity' (1994) 2 *African Yearbook of International Law*, pp. 109–37; C. Wold, 'The Futility, Utility, and Future of the Biodiversity Convention' (1998) 9 *Colorado Journal of International Environmental Law and Policy*, pp. 1–41: G. Henne and S. Fakir, 'The Regime Building of the Convention on Biological Diversity on the Road to Nairobi' (1999) 3 *Max Planck Yearbook of United Nations Law*, pp. 315–61; R. Wolfrum, 'The Protection and Management of Biological Diversity', in F.L. Morrision and R. Wolfrum (eds), *International, Regional and National Environmental Law* (The Hague, Kluwer, 2000), pp. 355–72; Secretariat of the Convention on Biological Diversity, *Handbook of the Convention on Biological Diversity* (London and Sterling, Earthscan, 2001); A.H. Ansari and P. Jamal, 'The Convention on Biological Diversity: A Critical Appraisal with Special Reference to Malaysia' (2000) 40 *Indian Journal of International Law*, pp. 137–77; Birnie and Boyle, above note 1, pp. 568–98; Sands, above note 1, pp. 515–23. With respect to the

A first category concerns general rules of international environmental law. Article 3 confirms that States have the sovereign right to exploit their own resources pursuant to their own environmental policies. It follows that the authority to determine access to genetic resources rests with the national governments and is subject to national legislation in conformity with Article 15 (1).[65] However, the sovereign rights are balanced by the general duty to ensure that activities within their jurisdiction or control do not cause damage to the environment of other States or areas beyond the limits of national jurisdiction. There appears to be little doubt that the rule of *sic utere tuo ut alienum non laedas* is a basic principle in international environmental law;[66] and that this rule is also applicable to conservation of marine biological diversity. In this respect, it should be noted that the Rio Convention regards the conservation of biological diversity as 'a common concern of humankind'.[67] The concept of the 'common concern of humankind' appears to suggest that the management of biological diversity under a State's jurisdiction is no longer the internal matter of a State but is a matter of concern for the international community as a whole.[68] Further to this, the Rio Convention imposes on each Contracting Party to promote sustainable use of components of biological diversity.[69] Thus, Article 6 (b) also requires each Contracting Party to integrate, as far as possible and as appropriate, the conservation and sustainable use of biological diversity into relevant sectoral or cross-sectoral plans, programmes and policies. Article 10 (a) requires each Contracting Party to integrate consideration of the conservation and sustainable use of biological resources into national decision-making. Each Contracting Party is also obliged to encourage co-operation between its governmental authorities and its private sector in developing methods for sustainable use of biological resources.[70] It may be said that the concept of sustainable development is reflected here. Yet it remains to be

---

legislative history of the Rio Convention, see F. McConnell, *The Biodiversity Convention: A Negotiating History* (London, Kluwer, 1996).

65 See also Article 15 (4) of the Rio Convention.

66 See Principle 21 of the Stockholm Declaration of 1972, Principle 21 of the Rio Declaration of 1992. The customary law character of this rule was confirmed by the International Court of Justice in the *Advisory Opinion concerning Legality of the Threat or Use of Nuclear Weapons*. ICJ Reports 1996, pp. 241–2, para. 29. This view was echoed by the *Gabčíkovo-Nagymaros Project* case of 1997. ICJ Reports 1997, p. 41, para. 53.

67 Preamble of the Rio Convention.

68 Wolfrum, above note 64, pp. 362–3; F. Burhenne-Guilmin and S. Casey-Lefkowitz, above note 64, p. 48; Boyle, above note 64 ('The Convention on Biological Diversity'), pp. 117–18.

69 In accordance with Article 2, 'sustainable use' means 'the use of components of biological diversity in a way and at a rate that does not lead to the long-term decline of biological diversity, thereby maintaining its potential to meet the needs and aspirations of present and future generations'.

70 Article 10 (b)–(e) of the Rio Convention.

seen how one can reconcile the conservation and sustainable use of biological diversity at the same time.[71]

A second category relates to rules concerning conservation measures. The Rio Convention provides two types of conservation: *in-situ* conservation and *ex-situ* conservation. In accordance with Article 2, '*in-situ* conservation' means 'the conservation of ecosystems and natural habitats and the maintenance and recovery of viable populations of species in their natural surroundings and, in the case of domesticated or cultivated species, in the surroundings where they have developed their distinctive properties'. The *in-situ* conservation is of central importance in conservation of biological diversity. Thus, each Contracting Party is, *inter alia*, obliged to adopt measures concerning the following matters: regulation of important biological resources; promotion of environmentally sound and sustainable development in areas adjacent to protected areas; rehabilitation of degraded ecosystems and promotion of the recovery of threatened species; establishment of means to regulate the risks associated with the use and release of living modified organisms; prevention of the introduction of those alien species which threaten ecosystems, habitats or species; providing the conditions needed for compatibility between present uses and the conservation of biological diversity; preservation of knowledge, innovations and practices of indigenous and local communities; development of necessary legislation; regulation of the relevant processes and categories of activities; and co-operation in providing financial and other support particularly to developing countries.[72] Although the Rio Convention does not explicitly refer to the term 'the ecosystem approach', it would seem that these measures reflect this approach.[73] In light of the paucity of our knowledge of biological diversity,[74] however, it would appear that the application of the ecosystem approach encounters considerable difficulty in practice.

Under Article 2, '*ex-situ* conservation' means the conservation of components of biological diversity outside their natural habitats. In this respect, each Contracting Party is obliged to take the following measures in accordance with Article 9: adoption of measures for the *ex-situ* conservation of components of biological diversity; establishment and maintenance of facilities for such a conservation; adoption of measures for the recovery and rehabilitation of threatened species; regulation and management of the collection of biological resources; co-operation in providing financial and other support for *ex-situ* conservation. It is argued

---

71 Hermitte, above note 62, p. 863.

72 Article 8.

73 The application of the ecosystem approach has been discussed in the COP of the Rio Convention. For instance, Decision V/6 stated that the application of the ecosystem approach would help to reach a balance of the three objectives of the Convention. COP, Annex of Decision V/6, *Ecosystem Approach*, UNEP/CBD/COP/5/23, 2000, para. 1. This Decision is reproduced in Secretariat of the Convention on Biological Diversity, *Handbook of the Convention on Biological Diversity* (London, Earthscan, 2001) pp. 565–71.

74 Wilson, above note 2, p. 299.

that the techniques of *ex situ* conservation differ for animals, plants and micro-organisms. For animals, usually the conservation response is to collect them from the wild for captive breeding. For plants, *ex situ* conservation measures are more diverse, including gene banks for seeds, tissues or pollen. *Ex situ* conservation of micro-organisms also includes the establishment and maintenance of cultures.[75] In relation to this, it should be remembered that, historically, most *ex-situ* conservation has been undertaken in developed countries; and that most collections of genetic materials were carried out without the approval of the country of origin, which was often a developing country. Thus, it is not surprising that developing countries were against the argument emphasising *ex-situ* conservation as a principal measure. As a result, Article 9 makes clear that *ex-situ* conservation should serve as a complement to *in-situ* measures.[76]

In relation to this, particularly for the purpose of *in-situ* and *ex-situ* conservation and sustainable use of components of biological diversity, Article 7 (a) and (b) calls for States to identify and monitor components of biological diversity. Article 7 (c) obliges each Contracting Party to identify processes and categories of activities which have or are likely to have significant adverse impacts on the conservation and sustainable use of biological diversity, and to monitor their effects through sampling and other techniques. Where a significant adverse effect on biological diversity has been determined pursuant to Article 7, each Contracting Party shall regulate or manage the relevant processes and categories of activities in accordance with Article 8 (l). While there is no specific standard to evaluate the degree of 'significant adverse impacts',[77] it may be argued that the precautionary approach should be taken into account since risks to marine ecosystems remain uncertain. Although the precautionary approach is not enshrined in the provisions of the Rio Convention,[78] the application of this approach was set out as guidance for all activities affecting marine biological diversity in Decision IV/5 of the COP.[79] Decision VII/5 of 2004 also stressed the need for rapid action to address these threats on the basis of the precautionary approach and the ecosystem approach

---

75 L.M. Warren, 'The Role of *Ex Situ* Measures in the Conservation of Biodiversity', in Redgwell and Bowman, above note 10, p. 135. See also Yusuf, above note 64, p. 124.

76 *Ibid.* From the scientific viewpoint, it is also argued that *ex situ* conservation is not and never will be enough, although this method will save a few species otherwise beyond hope. Wilson, above note 2, p. 319.

77 The Convention on Biological Diversity, SBSTTA, *Marine and Coastal Biodiversity: Review, Further Elaboration and Refinement of the Programme of Work*, UNEP/CBD/ SBSTTA/8/INF/3/Rev.1, 22 February 2003, pp. 21–2, para. 82.

78 In the Rio Convention, the reference to the precautionary approach is made in its Preamble, which notes that 'where there is a threat of significant reduction or loss of biological diversity, lack of full scientific certainty should not be used as a reason for postponing measures to avoid or minimise such a threat'.

79 The Convention on Biological Diversity, COP Decision IV/5, *Conservation and Sustainable Use of Marine and Coastal Biological Diversity, including a Programme of Work*, Annex, Section B-2, para. 4.

in marine areas beyond the limits of national jurisdiction, in particular areas with seamounts, hydrothermal vents, and cold-water corals, other vulnerable ecosystems and certain other underwater features, resulting from processes and activities in such areas.[80]

A third category pertains to procedural rules purporting to minimise adverse impacts upon biological diversity. In order to prevent such impacts, it is important to examine the impact of planned activities. Thus Article 14 (1) (a) imposes on each Contracting Party to introduce, 'as far as possible and as appropriate', procedures requiring environmental impact assessment of its proposed projects that are likely to have significant adverse effects on biological diversity, with a view to avoiding or minimising such effects. In light of the transboundary nature of (marine) biological diversity, it is arguable that international co-operation becomes particularly important in this matter. In this respect, Article 14 (1) (c) requires each Contracting Party, 'as far as possible and as appropriate', to 'promote, on the basis of reciprocity, notification, exchange of information and consultation on activities under their jurisdiction or control which are likely to significantly affect adversely the biological diversity of other States or areas beyond the limits of national jurisdiction, by encouraging the conclusion of bilateral, regional or multilateral arrangements, as appropriate'. In the case of imminent or great danger or damage, originating under its jurisdiction or control, to biological diversity within the area under jurisdiction of other States or in areas beyond the limits of national jurisdiction, each Contracting Party is required to notify immediately the potentially affected States of such danger or damage, as well as initiate action to prevent or minimise such danger or damage pursuant to Article 14 (1) (d). To this end, Article 14 (1) (e) provides an obligation to promote national arrangements for emergency responses to activities or events.

A fourth category concerns rules relating to financial, technological and scientific co-operation with developing States. In general, States situated in the lower latitudes have more abundant biological diversity than those of higher latitude. Consequently, conservation of biological diversity is in essence characterised by a North–South axis.[81] As many habitats to be protected are located in the territories of developing States, financial and technological assistance to these States becomes particularly important in ensuring the effective implementation of the Convention. Thus, for the first time in a global treaty concerning environmental protection, Article 20 (2) places an explicit obligation upon the developed country to provide 'new and additional financial resources to enable developing country Parties to meet the agreed full incremental costs to them of implementing measures'. Further to this, Article 16 (1) calls for each Contracting Party to provide and/or facilitate access for and transfer to other Contracting Parties of technologies that are relevant

---

80 The Convention on Biological Diversity, COP Decision VII/5, *Marine and Coastal Biological Diversity: Review of the Programme of Work on Marine and Coastal Biodiversity*, UNEP/CBD/COP/7/21, February 2004, para. 60.

81 Yusuf, above note 64, p. 112.

to the conservation and sustainable use of biological diversity. Such access to and transfer of technology is to be provided under fair and most favourable terms in accordance with Article 16 (2). It should be noted, however, that the transfer of technology under Article 16 is not mandatory in its nature.[82] It should also be noted that the deterioration of biological diversity is closely linked to the widespread poverty in developing countries. In this respect, importantly, Article 20 (4) of the Rio Convention recognises the fact that 'economic and social development and eradication of poverty are the first and overriding priorities of the developing country Parties'.[83] Overall it would appear that the effectiveness of conservation of biological diversity relies in essence on the allocation of economic benefits and transfer of technology to developing countries.[84]

Limits of the Rio Convention   Concerning the conservation of marine biological diversity, one must point to the following limitations of the Rio Convention.

First, it must be noted that, as with the LOSC, the Rio Convention relies in essence on the traditional zonal management approach distinguishing the spaces under and beyond national jurisdiction. Article 4 distinguishes the components of biological diversity, and processes and activities in relation to biological diversity. In the case of *processes and activities*, the provisions of the Rio Convention apply, regardless of where their effects occur, when carried out under national jurisdiction or control, within the area of its national jurisdiction or beyond the limits of national jurisdiction. In the case of *components* of biological diversity, however, the rules of the Rio Convention apply in areas only within the limits of a State's national jurisdiction. In areas beyond national jurisdiction, any obligation under the Convention is limited to co-operation between States.[85] Hence the provisions of the Rio Convention relating to conservation apply solely to components of biological diversity in areas within the limits of a State's national jurisdiction. In areas beyond the limits of national jurisdiction, the provisions of the Convention pertain only to activities and processes carried out under a Contracting Party's jurisdiction or control which may have an adverse impact on biological diversity. It would seem to follow that Contracting Parties have no direct obligation relating

---

82 Wolfrum, above note 64, p. 367.

83 This is also confirmed in the Preamble of the Rio Convention.

84 Boyle, above note 64 ('The Convention on Biological Diversity'), pp. 126–7. The responsibilities of developed States are confirmed by Article 20 (4), which states that '[t]he extent to which developing country Parties will effectively implement their commitments under this Convention will depend on the effective implementation by developed country Parties of their commitments under this Convention related to financial resources and transfer of technology'.

85 Article 5.

to the conservation of specific components of biological diversity in marine spaces beyond the limits of national jurisdiction.[86]

Secondly, like the LOSC, the Rio Convention draws little attention to the transboundary nature of biological diversity. With respect to transboundary damage on biological diversity, the Rio Convention merely places on Contracting Parties the obligation to exchange information and the obligation to consult each other.[87] It would seem that the Rio Convention did not advance existing international law on this matter.

Thirdly, another weakness of the Rio Convention is that the wording of the principal articles is heavily qualified by the words 'as far as possible' and 'as appropriate'.[88] This will leave much discretion to the Contracting Parties. Hence it remains to be seen to what extent rules of this Convention constrain the behaviour of the Contracting Parties in practice.

Fourthly, attention should be focused on geographical and ecological divergences in the oceans. The ocean environment is not homogeneous, and there is a wide variety of different ecosystems in the oceans. It appears that the need for conservation of marine biological diversity varies depending on the marine area. Accordingly, it seems difficult if not impossible to establish uniform and detailed rules relating to conservation of marine biological diversity at the global level. Furthermore, in light of economic and technological difficulties in developing countries, it will be difficult to place the same obligations upon them to conserve marine biological diversity.[89] Thus it will be necessary to tailor any rules in this field to the particular needs and circumstances of the States and regions. It is arguable that the conservation of marine biological diversity is to be regionalised in practice. As will be seen in the next section, this view is to some extent supported by the fact that a regional legal framework is being progressively developed in this field.

---

86 Glowka, above note 45 (*Ocean Yearbook*), p. 168. SBSTTA of the Rio Convention also takes the same interpretation. Above note 77, p. 19, para. 70.

87 Boyle, above note 64 ('The Convention on Biological Diversity'), p. 119.

88 *Ibid.*, p. 126; Birnie and Boyle, above note 1, p. 572.

89 It may be argued that the principle of common but differentiated responsibility may come into play. In accordance with this principle, developing countries have different and more diminished obligations. This is clearly reflected in Principle 7 of the Rio Declaration, as well as various environment-related treaties. In the context of marine environmental protection, it is noteworthy that Article 207 (4) of the 1982 LOSC requires States to take into account 'characteristic regional features, the economic capacity of developing States and their need for economic development'. It would seem that the principle of common but different responsibility is worth considering for conservation of marine biological diversity at the global level. With respect to this principle, see D. French, 'Developing States and International Environmental Law: The Importance of Differentiated Responsibilities' (2000) 49 *ICLQ*, pp. 35–60; Y. Matsui, 'The Principle of "Common But Differentiated Responsibilities"', in N. Schrijver and F. Weiss (eds), *International Law and Sustainable Development, Principles and Practice* (The Hague, Brill, 2004) pp. 73–96.

A Regional Legal Framework for Conservation of Marine Biological Diversity – A Case Study of the North-East Atlantic

Expansion of the Scope of the 1992 Convention for the Protection of the Marine Environment of the North-East Atlantic

General Observations   It is acknowledged that the North-East Atlantic is rich in biological diversity, and some important habitats exist in this region.[90] In particular, one will note with interest that some of the largest coral structures (*lophelia*) in the world are found in the cold waters of the North-East Atlantic.[91] Nonetheless, there are growing concerns that biological diversity in the North-East Atlantic is threatened by various human activities, including fishing activities. In particular, 30–50 per cent of the *lophelia* reefs in Norwegian waters have already been damaged or impacted by trawling.[92] Land-based marine pollution also poses a threat to marine biological diversity in this region. In the North-East Atlantic, many major industrial centres are located along estuaries of the coastal States. As a result, several estuaries are under considerable pressure from industrial pollution as a result of paper milling, petroleum refining, production of chlorine, titanium dioxide and surface coatings, iron and steel working, metal fabrication and other heavy industries. It has also been argued that some nuclear power plants and the French and UK reprocessing plants could be discharging heat and radioactive substances into the marine environment.[93] In addition to this, the introduction of alien species is becoming a matter of concern in this region.[94] Overall it is arguable

---

90   International Council for the Exploration of the Sea (ICES), *Environmental Status of the European Seas*, 2003, pp. 20–22. With respect to biology in the North-East Atlantic in some detail, see OSPAR Commission, *The Quality Status Report 2000* (hereafter QSR 2000) (London, OSPAR Commission, 2000) pp. 65–83.

91   With respect to the distribution of hard cold-water corals tentatively identified as *Lophelia pertusa*, see ICES, *Cooperative Research Report No. 262, Report of the ICES Advisory Committee on Ecosystems*, 2003, pp. 121–7. See also Freiwald *et al.*, above note 40, pp. 12–39; Long and Grehan, above note 36, pp. 237–8.

92   J.H. Fosså, P.B. Mortensen and D.M. Furevik, 'The Deep-Water Coral *Lophelia Pertusa* in Norwegian Waters: Distribution and Fishery Impacts' (2002) 471 *Hydrobiologa*, p. 11. See also ICES, *Environmental Status of the European Seas*, 2003, p. 42; WWF, 'The Gift to the Earth: Norwegian Coldwater Coral Protection, Setting an International Example in Marine Conservation', 11 June 2003. This document is available at <http://assets.panda. org/downloads/norwayfinallr.pdf>.

93   QSR 2000, above note 90, p. 32, para. 3.12.

94   To date, over 100 non-indigenous species representing a large spectrum of taxonomic and ecological groups of organisms (plankton, macroalgae and benthos) have been recorded in this region. QSR 2000, p. 72. These alien species may have adverse impacts on marine ecosystems by upsetting predator–prey relationships and introducing previously unknown diseases.

that conservation of marine biological diversity in this region requires a holistic regulation of sources and activities producing these threats.

Conservation of Marine Biological Diversity in the OSPAR Convention Of particular importance for the conservation of biological diversity in this region is the 1992 Convention for the Protection of the Marine Environment of the North-East Atlantic (hereafter the OSPAR Convention).[95] Concerning the Convention, it is important to note that there were two kinds of development. A first development concerns the expansion of the scope of the Convention. A second development relates to the inter-linkage between the OSPAR Convention and other relevant treaties and institutions. In this section, we will address the first development.

Originally the principal purpose of the OSPAR Convention was to create a quasi-comprehensive regime in a single legal instrument for the protection of the marine environment of the North-East Atlantic. Thus the Convention provides regulation of land-based pollution (Article 3/Annex I), dumping or incineration (Article 4/Annex II), pollution from offshore sources (Article 5/Annex III), and pollution from other sources (Article 7).[96] While Article 2 (1) (a) referred to conservation of marine ecosystems in a general manner,[97] the original text of the OSPAR Convention did not make for further precision on this issue.

However, it should be noted that the move towards the conservation of marine biological diversity in the North-East Atlantic had already begun in various international fora. Of particular importance was the International North Sea Conference (hereafter INSC). The INSC is a political forum ensuring more efficient implementation of the existing international rules related to the marine environment in all North Sea States.[98] The participant States to the INSC largely

---

95 The OSPAR Convention was adopted on 22 September 1992 and entered into force on 25 March 1998, replacing the two preceding conventions of 1972 (Oslo Convention) and 1974 (Paris Convention). States Parties of the OSPAR Convention are those of the Oslo and Paris Conventions (Belgium, Denmark, the Commission of the European Communities, Finland, France, Germany, Iceland, Ireland, the Netherlands, Norway, Portugal, Spain, Sweden and the United Kingdom) as well as Luxembourg and Switzerland. Regarding an analysis of this Convention in general, see J. Hilf, 'The Convention for the Protection of the Marine Environment of the North-East Atlantic: New Approaches to an Old Problem?' (1995) 55 *ZaöRV*, pp. 580–603; L. De La Fayette, 'The OSPAR Convention Comes into Force: Continuity and Progress' (1999) 14 *IJMCL*, pp. 247–97.

96 The OSPAR Convention does not address vessel-source pollution, which is regulated by MARPOL 73/78.

97 R. Lagoni, 'Monitoring Compliance and Enforcement of Compliance Through the OSPAR Commission', in P. Ehlers, E. Mann-Borgese and R. Wolfrum (eds), *Marine Issues: From a Scientific, Political and Legal Perspective* (The Hague, Kluwer, 2002) pp. 157–8.

98 Background of the North Sea Conferences. This document is available at the home page of the INSC, <http://odin.dep.no/md/engelsk/>.

overlap with the Contracting Parties to the OSPAR Convention.[99] In the 1990 International North Sea Conference, ministers had already agreed to give further protection to marine wildlife in the North Sea.[100] In the 1995 North Sea Conference at Esbjerg, ministers invited OSPAR to assess by 1997 the co-ordinated work and other work necessary to improve the protection of marine species and their habitats outside territorial waters, and the action needed to co-ordinate that work with the corresponding work within territorial waters. They further invited OSPAR to consider by the year 2000 the machinery for organising such harmonisation.[101] In response to this invitation, the Ministerial Meeting of the OSPAR Commission adopted a new Annex V on the Protection and Conservation of the Ecosystems and Biological Diversity of the Maritime Area and a new Appendix 3, 'Criteria for Identifying Human Activities for the Purpose of Annex V'.[102] It may be said that the INSC gave Contracting Parties to the OSPAR Convention an impetus to promote conservation of marine biological diversity in the North-East Atlantic.[103]

The obligation to conserve marine biological diversity was much amplified by Annex V as well as Appendix 3. Article 2 of Annex V stipulates that:

> In fulfilling their obligation under the Convention to take, individually and jointly, the necessary measures to protect the maritime area against the adverse effects of human activities so as to safeguard human health and to conserve marine ecosystems and, when practicable, restore marine areas which have been adversely affected, as well as their obligation under the Convention on Biological Diversity of 5 June 1992 to develop strategies, plans or programmes for the conservation and sustainable use of biological diversity, Contracting Parties shall:
>
> a. take the necessary measures to protect and conserve the ecosystems and the biological diversity of the maritime area, and to restore, where applicable, marine areas which have been adversely affected: and
>
> b. cooperate in adopting programmes and measures for those purposes for the control of the human activities identified by the application of the criteria in Appendix 3.

---

99 The participants in the North Sea Conferences are Belgium, Denmark, France, Germany, the Netherlands, Norway, Sweden, the United Kingdom and the European Commission. Furthermore, the Swiss Confederation attended for the first time in the third Conference held at The Hague in 1990.

100 Ministerial Declaration of the Third International Conference on the Protection of the North Sea, 8 March 1990, para. 39.

101 Esbjerg Declaration, para. 9.

102 In accordance with Article 15.5 of the Convention, Annex V has entered into force: on 30 August 2000 for Finland, Spain, Switzerland, Luxembourg, the European Community, the United Kingdom and Denmark; on 5 October 2000 for Sweden. See also W. Heintschel von Heinegg, 'The Development of Environmental Standards for the North-East Atlantic, including the North Sea', in Ehlers *et al.*, above note 97, pp. 141–3.

103 De La Fayette, above note 95, pp. 265–6.

The human activities for the purposes of Annex V are identified on the basis of a list of criteria enumerated in Appendix 3, which include: (a) the extent, intensity and duration of the human activity under consideration; (b) actual and potential adverse effects of the human activity on specific species, communities and habitats; (c) actual and potential adverse effects of the human activity on specific ecological processes; (d) irreversibility or durability of these effects.[104] These criteria are not necessarily exhaustive or of equal importance for the consideration of a particular activity.[105]

The implementation of Annex V is designed to be secured by the OSPAR Commission, which is made up of representatives of each of the Contracting Parties.[106] The OSPAR Commission is *inter alia* under the duty to draw up programmes and measures for the control of the human activities identified by the application of the criteria in Appendix 3. In so doing, the Commission is required:

(i)   to collect and review information on such activities and their effects on ecosystems and biological diversity;

(ii)   to develop means, consistent with international law, for instituting protective, conservation, restorative or *precautionary measures* related to specific areas or sites or related to particular species or habitats;

(iii)   subject to Article 4 of this Annex, to consider aspects of national strategies and guidelines on the sustainable use of components of biological diversity of the maritime area as they affect the various regions and sub-regions of that area;

(iv)   subject to Article 4 of this Annex, to aim for the application of *an integrated ecosystem approach.*[107]

Later on, the 2003 OSPAR Strategy on the Protection and Conservation of the Ecosystems and Biological Diversity of the Maritime Area required the Commission to further develop the programmes and measures needed for the protection and conservation of the ecosystems and biological diversity of the maritime area.[108] To this end, the OSPAR Commission was required to assess which species and habitats need to be protected and those human activities that are likely to have an actual or potential adverse effect on these species and habitats or on ecological processes.[109] On the basis of the assessment, the OSPAR Commission is to continue to draw up programmes and measures in accordance with Annex V of the

---

104 Appendix 3 (1).

105 Appendix 3 (2).

106 Article 10 (1).

107 Emphasis added. Article 2 (1) (b) of Annex V. It is to be noted that the ecosystem approach and the precautionary approach are set out at the same time.

108 The 2003 OSPAR Strategy, para. 2.1.

109 *Ibid.*, para. 2.2.

OSPAR Convention. Such programmes and measures could include guidance for the selection and the establishment of a system of specific areas and sites which need to be protected and the management of human activities there. In so doing, account will be taken of the need to develop integrated coastal zone management and to ensure the proper spatial planning of the maritime area.[110] In addition to this, the OSPAR Commission will undertake actions to complement those of the Contracting Parties in developing the OSPAR Network of Marine Protected Areas.[111]

It is of particular interest that the OSPAR Convention contains a relatively strong mechanism for ensuring compliance with its provisions. Article 22 obliges the Contracting Parties to report to the Commission at regular intervals on:

(a) the legal, regulatory, or other measures taken by them for the implementation of the provisions of the Convention and of decisions and recommendations adopted thereunder, including in particular measures taken to prevent and punish conduct in contravention of those provisions;

(b) the effectiveness of the measures referred to in subparagraph (a) of this Article;

(c) problems encountered in the implementation of the provisions referred to in subparagraph (a) of this Article.

It is arguable that the detailed reporting system is useful in precluding States Parties from failing to fulfil the reporting obligation or from reporting superficially to the relevant international institutions. Furthermore, Article 10 stipulates that the OSPAR Commission has duties (a) to supervise the implementation of the Convention, and (b) generally to review the condition of the maritime area, the effectiveness of the measures being adopted, the priorities and the need for any additional or different measures. To this end, Article 23 provides that:

The Commission shall:

(a) on the basis of the periodical reports referred to in Article 22 and any other report submitted by the Contracting Parties, *assess* their compliance with the Convention and the decisions and recommendations adopted thereunder;

(b) when appropriate, *decide upon and call for steps to bring about full compliance with the Convention*, and decisions adopted thereunder, and promote the implementation of recommendations, including measures to assist a Contracting Party to carry out its obligations.[112]

It is arguable that this provision further reinforces the supervision and control power of the Commission. It should also be noted that Article 23 refers to measures 'to assist a Contracting Party'. Although the meaning of the 'measures'

---

110 *Ibid.*, para. 2.3.

111 *Ibid.*, para. 4.4. The marine protected areas will be discussed in Chapter 5.

112 Emphasis added.

remains obscure, it would seem that they could include administrative, technical or scientific help.[113] On the basis of those mechanisms, the compliance of the OSPAR Convention is to be supervised and controlled by the OSPAR Commission.

It is not suggested, however, that the OSPAR Commission possesses enforcement jurisdiction against a Contracting Party.[114] In this respect, Article 13 (1) makes it clear that decisions and recommendations shall be adopted by unanimous vote of the Contracting Parties. In reality, it is inconceivable that the Contracting Party whose action was alleged to be contrary to the Convention would vote in favour of such a decision against its own interests. Furthermore, while the Commission may adopt decisions or recommendations by a three-quarters majority vote, the decisions become binding 200 days after their adoption for the Contracting Parties that have voted for it and not withdrawn their vote, provided that these constitute three-quarters of the Contracting Parties.[115] It would seem to follow that a Contracting Party which has voted against a decision is not bound by it. In spite of this limitation, it is worth noting that an international body possessing supervisory and control power has appeared in the field of marine environmental protection and conservation of marine biological diversity.

Inter-linkage between the OSPAR Convention and Relevant Treaties and Institutions

In response to multiple threats to marine biological diversity in this region, the establishment of a network of relevant instruments and institutions becomes of central importance. In this respect, it is worth noting that in the North-East Atlantic, the inter-linkages between relevant treaties and institutions are being formulated on the basis of the OSPAR Convention. It may be argued that the development of the inter-linkages has a valuable role in stimulating an integrated management approach at the normative and implementation levels. These inter-linkages may be divided into two rubrics: the inter-linkage between the OSPAR Convention and other relevant conventions, and the inter-linkage between the OSPAR Convention and international institutions.

Inter-treaty Linkage between the OSPAR Convention and Other Conventions   Recalling the provisions of the LOSC as well as other global and regional agreements on the conservation of marine biological diversity, the Preamble of Annex V of the OSPAR Convention underlines the importance of co-ordination and harmonisation of work in different forums for the protection of marine species and their habitats. Thus the Contracting Parties to the OSPAR Convention decided to consider two themes: (i) the need to avoid duplication with action which is already prescribed by other international conventions and the subject of appropriate

---

113 Lagoni, above note 97, 161.
114 *Ibid.*, pp. 161–2. See also Hilf, above note 95, p. 593.
115 Article 13 (2) of the OSPAR Convention.

measures agreed by other international organisations; and (ii) the need to consider whether action could be taken more appropriately under some other international convention or arrangement.[116] With respect to inter-treaty linkages, in particular, two examples should be highlighted.

A first inter-treaty linkage concerns the interrelationship between the OSPAR and the Rio Conventions. All Contracting Parties to the OSPAR Convention are also Parties to the Rio Convention. Thus they are required to implement obligations to conserve marine biological diversity under the OSPAR and Rio Conventions at the same time. At the normative level, the inter-linkage between these two conventions is demonstrated by the fact that Article 1 of Annex V of the OSPAR Convention refers to the definitions in the Rio Convention of 'biological diversity', 'ecosystem' and 'habitat'.[117] Furthermore, Article 2 of Annex V explicitly refers to the obligation of Parties to the Rio Convention to develop strategies, plans or programmes for the conservation and sustainable use of biological diversity. It may be argued that the OSPAR Convention is closely linked to the Rio Convention in the field of conservation of marine biological diversity.[118]

A second inter-treaty linkage pertains to the interrelationship between the OSPAR Convention and the 1992 Convention on the Protection of the Marine Environment of the Baltic Sea Area (hereafter the Helsinki Convention). It is of particular interest that the co-operation between the OSPAR Commission and Helsinki Commission (HELCOM) is being enhanced in relation to the protection of marine biological diversity. In 2003, the first joint Ministerial Meeting of the Helsinki and OSPAR Commissions adopted a 'Statement on the Ecosystem Approach to the Management of Human Activities: "Towards an Ecosystem Approach to the Management of Human Activities"'.[119] The Statement confirmed the application of the ecosystem approach in the HELCOM and OSPAR frameworks. The Statement suggested that the Helsinki and OSPAR Commissions would focus particularly on promoting understanding and acceptance by all stakeholders of the ecosystem approach to the management of human activities, monitoring the ecosystems of the marine environment, setting objectives for environmental quality and assessing the impact of human activities upon biota and humans.[120] Co-operation between the Helsinki and OSPAR Commissions on this subject is also confirmed in the Statement on the European Marine Strategy.[121]

---

116 Preamble of Annex V of the OSPAR Convention.

117 De La Fayette, above note 95, p. 267.

118 *Ibid.*

119 *Joint Meeting of the Helsinki and OSPAR Commissions, Statement on the Ecosystem Approach to the Management of Human Activities*, Bremen, 25–26 June 2003, Record of the Meeting, Annex 5 (Ref. §6.1).

120 *Ibid.*, para. 15.

121 *Statement on the European Marine Strategy, 'What HELCOM and OSPAR can Bring to the Development of the European Marine Strategy'*, First Joint Meeting of the

Inter-linkage   between   the   OSPAR   Convention   and   International Institutions   Concerning the inter-linkage between the OSPAR Convention and other international institutions,[122] in particular, four examples should be highlighted.

A first instance relates to the interaction between the OSPAR Convention and North-East Atlantic Fisheries Commission. Article 4 of Annex V of the 1992 OSPAR Convention makes clear that no programme or measure concerning a question relating to the management of fisheries shall be adopted under this Annex. However, this provision continues that:

> [W]here the Commission considers that action is desirable in relation to such a question, it shall draw that question to the attention of the authority or international body competent for that question. Where action within the competence of the Commission is desirable to complement or support action by those authorities or bodies, the Commission shall endeavour to cooperate with them.

On the basis of this provision, the Chairperson of the OSPAR Commission wrote a letter to all fisheries authorities in the convention area. This letter states that the OSPAR Commission has concluded that action is desirable on a number of issues relating to the state of commercial fish stocks and of deep-sea fish species in the North-East Atlantic in light of its QSR 2000.[123] Thus, this letter clarifies that the OSPAR Commission strongly supports the integration of environmental policies and fisheries policies, and that measures should be taken that integrate environmental policies and fisheries policies.[124] This letter is of particular interest in that it appears to mark a step forward in linking the marine protection regime with that of fisheries.[125] Furthermore, the OSPAR Commission required co-operation with the North-East Atlantic Fisheries Commission with a view to protecting deep-water coral reefs. Indeed, a letter was drafted to the North-East Atlantic Fisheries Commission (NEAFC) in 2004. In this letter, the OSPAR Commission suggested that cold-water coral reefs created by *Lophelia pertusa* are threatened by bottom-trawling. In light of the importance of the cold-water coral reefs, the OSPAR Commission required that the NEAFC draw attention to

---

Helsinki and OSPAR Commissions, Bremen, 25–26 June 2003, Record of the Meeting, Annex 6 (Ref. §6.1), paras 6–7.

122 Concerning interaction between the OSPAR, the INSC and the EU in environmental protection of the North-East Atlantic, see, for instance, J.B. Skjærseth, 'Protecting the North-East Atlantic: Enhancing Synergies by Institutional Interplay' (2006) 30 *Marine Policy*, pp. 157–66.

123 OSPAR Commission, *Draft Letter to Fisheries Authorities*, Summary Record OSPAR 2001, OSPAR 01/18/1, Annex 12 (Ref. § 6.25), Valencia, 25–29 June 2001, para. 4.

124 *Ibid.*, para. 8.

125 E. Hey, 'The International Regime for the Protection of the North Sea: From Functional Approaches to a More Integrated Approach' (2002) 17 *IJMCL*, pp. 347–8.

this issue.[126] In relation to this, it is noteworthy that the NEAFC agreed to close five seamounts and a section of Reykjanes Ridge on the high seas in the NEAFC Regulatory Area for three years to bottom-trawling and static gear, so as to protect vulnerable deep-water habitats. Furthermore, the NEAFC agreed to reduce fishing pressure in deep waters for a number of vulnerable fish species by 30 per cent in 2005.[127] In 2003, the NEAFC also agreed on temporary measures to freeze efforts in fisheries for fish species inhabiting deep waters in the Regulatory Area from 1 January 2004.[128] Given that fishing activities are one of the major threats to marine biological diversity, collaboration with fisheries organs will arguably be increasingly important in this field.

Secondly, the OSPAR Convention contains no provision concerning maritime transport. Given that navigation of vessels may affect marine ecosystems, however, co-operation between the Parties to the OSPAR Convention and the IMO is of particular importance in conservation of marine biological diversity. In this respect, Article 4 of Annex V highlights the need to co-operate with the IMO. In accordance with this Article, where the OSPAR Commission considers that action under this Annex is desirable in relation to a question concerning maritime transport, it shall draw that question to the attention of the IMO. This provision also requires the Contracting Parties who are members of the IMO to co-operate within that organisation in order to achieve an appropriate response including, in relevant cases, that organisation's agreement to regional or local action, taking account of any guidelines developed by that organisation on the designation of special areas, the identification of particularly sensitive areas or other matters.

Thirdly, consideration should be given to the inter-linkage between the OSPAR Convention and the European Community (EC). Apart from Switzerland, Contracting Parties to the OSPAR Convention are, at the same time, Member States of the EC. It follows that Contracting Parties to the Convention, which are Member States of the EC at the same time, are required to comply with relevant rules and directives of the EC. With respect to the conservation of biological diversity in the North-East Atlantic, of particular importance is the Council Directive 92/43/EEC of 21 May 1992 on the Conservation of Natural Habitats and of Wild Fauna and Flora (the Habitats Directive).[129] The Habitats Directive seeks to protect both

---

126 OSPAR Commission, *Draft Letter to NEAFC*, Summary Record OSPAR 2004, OSPAR 04/23/1-E, Annex 6 (Ref. § 5.14a), Reykjavik, 18 June–1 July 2004.

127 Convention on Future Multilateral Cooperation in North-East Atlantic Fisheries, Press Release, 15 November 2004, p. 1.

128 *Ibid.*, p. 3.

129 OJ No. L206, 22.7.92, pp. 0007–0050; last amended by Council Directive 97/62/EC of 27 October 1997, OJ No. L305, 8.11.97, pp. 0042–0065. See also L. Krämer, *EC Environmental Law*, 4th edn (London, Sweet and Maxwell, 2000), pp. 135–40. This section examines only the Habitat Directive, and the full examination of the role of the EC in the conservation of biological diversity in general is beyond the scope of this study. With respect to this issue, the following studies are of particular interest: P. Birnie, 'The European Community and Preservation of Biological Diversity', in Redgwell and Bowman, note 10,

habitat and species in a region, introducing the concept of restoring or maintaining habitats or species of 'community interest' at 'a favourable conservation status'.[130] The Habitats Directive seeks to contribute towards ensuring biodiversity through the conservation of natural habitats and of wild fauna and flora in the European territory of the Member States to which the Treaty establishing the European Economic Community applies.[131] To this end, the Habitats Directive provides a comprehensive framework for the conservation of habitats as well as species in the territory of Member States.

While the Habitat Directive refers to the term 'territory' in several provisions, its spatial scope is not clearly specified. On this issue, the European Commission is of the opinion that the Habitats Directive may be applicable not only to the territorial seas but also to the 200-mile EEZ. In its words:

> The provisions of the 'Habitats' Directive automatically apply to the marine habitats and marine species located in territorial waters (maximum 12 miles). However, if a Member State exerts its sovereign rights in an exclusive economic zone of 200 nautical miles (for example, the granting of an operating license for a drilling platform), it thereby considers itself competent to enforce national laws in that area, and consequently the Commission considers in this case that the 'Habitats' Directive also applies, in that Community legislation is an integral part of national legislation.[132]

pp. 211–34; A. Kiss and D. Shelton, *Manual of European Environmental Law*, 2nd edn (Cambridge, Cambridge University Press, 1997) pp. 181–249.

130 Birnie, above note 129, p. 226. 'Species of Community interest' means species which are endangered, vulnerable, rare, endemic and requiring particular attention by reason of the specific nature of their habitat and/or the potential impact of their exploitation on their habitat and/or the potential impact of their exploitation on their conservation status (Article 1 (g)). In accordance with Article 1 (i), the conservation status will be taken as 'favourable' when population dynamic data on the species concerned indicate that it is maintaining itself on a long-term basis as a viable component of its natural habitats, and the natural range of the species is neither being reduced nor is likely to be reduced for the foreseeable future, and there is, and will probably continue to be, a sufficiently large habitat to maintain its populations on a long-term basis.

131 Article 2 (1). 'Natural habitats' means terrestrial or aquatic areas distinguished by geographic, abiotic and biotic features, whether entirely natural or semi-natural (Article 1 (b)). In addition, 'conservation' in the Directive means a series of measures required to maintain or restore the natural habitats and the populations of species of wild fauna and flora at a favourable status (Article 1 (a)).

132 Commission of the European Communities, *Communication from the Commission to the Council and the European Parliament, Fisheries Management and Nature Conservation in the Marine Environment*, COM (1999) 363 final, 14 July 1999, p. 10., 5.2.2. See also C. Bury and J. Sack, 'The European Union', in E. Franckx and P. Gautier (eds), *La zone économique exclusive et la Convention des Nations unies sur le droit de la mer, 1982–2000: un premier bilan de la pratique des Etats* (Bruxelles, Bruylant, 2003) p. 75.

Later on, this interpretation was supported by the High Court of the United Kingdom in *Queen v. Secretary of State for Trade and Industry, ex parte Greenpeace Limited.*[133] It follows that Member States are required to apply the Habitats Directive in their terrestrial territory as well as in marine space under national jurisdiction.[134]

Specifically Article 3 of the Habitats Directive obliges Member States to establish a coherent European ecological network of special areas where the necessary conservation measures shall be established under the title Natura 2000.[135] In accordance with Article 3 (2), each Member State is obliged to contribute to the creation of Natura 2000 in proportion to the representation within its territory of the natural habitat types and the habitats of species referred to in Article 3 (1). Each Member State is also under obligation to undertake surveillance of the conservation status of the natural habitats and species referred to in Article 2 with particular regard to priority natural habitat types and priority species in accordance with Article 11. Further to this, Member States are obliged to bring into force the laws, regulations and administrative provisions necessary to comply with this Directive within two years of its notification.[136] In summary, in so far as Contracting Parties to the OSPAR Convention are Member States of the EC, the dual regime of the OSPAR and the Habitat Directive is to be applicable to the conservation of biological diversity in the North-East Atlantic. On the one hand, it is arguable that the inter-linkage between the OSPAR Convention and the EC will enhance the effectiveness of the conservation of marine biological diversity in the region. On the other hand, it would seem that the large overlap in membership produces a question relating to duplication of effort between the OSPAR Convention regime and the EC legislations. In this regard, the Commission

---

133 High Court of Justice Queen's Bench Division, 5 November 1999 (2002) 120 *ILR*, pp. 617–56. In this case, the applicability of the Habitats Directive in the United Kingdom's exclusive fisheries zone was at issue. The United Kingdom argued that the geographical scope of the Habitats Directive was limited to the territorial sea of 12 nautical miles. By contrast, Greenpeace contended that this Directive was applicable to the continental shelf of the United Kingdom and its adjacent waters. On this issue, the High Court partly based its decision on the consistency with the object and purpose of the Habitats Directive. The High Court focused on the fact that *Lophelia pertusa* and cetaceans, which the Directive *inter alia* aimed to protect, were to be found beyond territorial waters. *Ibid.*, p. 626. On the basis of the purposive or teleological interpretation, the High Court considered that the purpose of the Directive in relation to them was more likely to be achieved if the geographical scope was liberally construed. *Ibid.*, pp. 625–6; p. 636. Furthermore, in the High Court's view, such an interpretation has been supported by practice under community law. *Ibid.*, pp. 627–30. In conclusion, the High Court ruled that this Directive covered all marine spaces where the Member States exercised sovereign rights beyond the limit of the territorial sea.

134 Long and Grehan, above note 36, pp. 249; 253–4.

135 Special areas under the Habitats Directive will be addressed in the context of marine protected areas.

136 Article 23.

of the European Communities indicated that while the strategies were broadly comparable and consistent with EC legislation, there was a degree of duplication of effort, given that these issues were also addressed in the EC.[137] Thus, careful co-ordination between the OSPAR Convention and the EC legislations will be required in order to avoid unnecessary duplication.

Finally, some mention should be made of the inter-linkage between the OSPAR Convention and the INSC. The INSC has been held at irregular intervals since the 1984 Bremen Conference in order to intensify the protection of the marine environment in all the North Sea. Declarations adopted in each conference have often referred to the activities of the Paris and Oslo Commissions, later the OSPAR Commission and EEC/EC concerning the regulation of marine pollution.[138] The political goals and measures adopted in the INSC were to be reflected in the OSPAR Convention regime. At the same time, the OSPAR Convention can also adjust to external demands for more action. Here one may find an interesting interplay between the political body, that is, the INSC, and the OSPAR Convention in the protection of the marine environment as well as marine biological diversity.[139]

Conclusion

The above discussions appear to yield the following conclusions:

(i) The 1982 LOSC and the 1992 Rio Convention maintain the zonal management approach. Thus, one may be forced to accept that despite some writers' criticisms of the approach, conservation of marine biological diversity is in essence undertaken on the basis of the traditional approach. However, this approach inevitably makes arbitrary divisions in marine ecosystems. In this respect, neither the LOSC nor the Rio Convention contains an effective mechanism for conserving marine ecosystems straddling man-made limits and delimitation lines in the oceans. Furthermore, it appears that obligations to conserve marine biological diversity remain weak, particularly in marine spaces beyond the limits of national jurisdiction. Arguably this is due to the exploitation-oriented nature of the zonal management approach.

---

137 Commission of the European Communities, *Communication from the Commission to the Council and the European Parliament, Towards a Strategy to Protect and Conserve the Marine Environment*, COM (2002) 539 final, 2 October 2002, p. 46, para. 2.3.

138 See Bremen Declaration of the International Conference on the Protection of the North Sea of 1984, London Declaration of 1987 and The Hague Declaration of 1990. These Declarations are reproduced in D. Freestone and T. Ijlstra (eds), *The North Sea: Basic Legal Documents on Regional Environmental Co-operation* (Dordrecht, Graham & Trotman and Nijhoff, 1991) pp. 3–89.

139 Anderson stresses the importance of the dual approach, that is, combining a 'hard legal' regime with a 'soft political' regime. S. Anderson, 'The North Sea and Beyond: Lessons Learned', in M.J. Valencia (ed.), *Maritime Regime Building: Lessons Learned and Their Relevance for Northeast Asia* (The Hague, Nijhoff, 2001) pp. 63–4.

(ii) Further to this, it should be noted that there is an inherent difficulty in establishing a global legal framework for conservation of marine biological diversity. In light of economic, technological and ecological divergence in the world, it appears difficult if not impossible to formulate uniform and detailed rules concerning conservation of marine biological diversity. Accordingly, it appears that regional treaties which contain more specific rules will assume considerable importance in conserving marine biological diversity.

(iii) In fact, it can be observed that a relatively advanced legal framework for the conservation of marine biological diversity is developing in the North-East Atlantic. In particular, it is notable that there has been positive development on two levels: the expansion of the material scope of the OSPAR Convention, and the promotion of inter-linkage between the Convention and other relevant treaties and international institutions. Concerning the former, the scope of the OSPAR Convention was expanded to cover conservation of marine biological diversity in the North-East Atlantic. At the same time, conservation measures were further elaborated through the COP of the Convention. With respect to the latter, the OSPAR Convention is increasingly promoting inter-linkages with the Rio Convention, the Helsinki Convention, the NEAFC, the IMO, the EC and the INSC. It would appear that, to some extent, these developments are useful in stimulating an integrated management approach to conservation of marine biological diversity in this region.

(iv) On the other hand, it is foreseeable that the development of regional legal frameworks for conservation of marine biological diversity will not be uniform. It would appear that the development of treaties in this field relies essentially on the economic, social and political environment in a region. In the case of the OSPAR Convention, Contracting Parties are essentially developed States, sharing common political and economic systems. It should also be remembered that there have been political commitments through the INSC to intensify the protection of the marine environment in all the North Sea. It may be argued that those political and economic commitments stimulate a relatively advanced legal framework for the protection of the marine environment and the conservation of marine biological diversity in the North-East Atlantic. Currently, however, one cannot easily expect the same development in each and every region. It has to be stressed that conservation of (marine) biological diversity is essentially qualified by economic, technological and political elements in each State.

Chapter 5

Marine Protected Areas in Conservation of Marine Biological Diversity: In Search of an Integrated Management Approach

Introduction

Nature of the Problem

In search of an integrated management approach to the conservation of marine biological diversity, considerable attention is currently focused on marine protected areas (MPAs).[1] Although there is no uniform definition of MPAs in international law,[2] the Biodiversity Committee of the Convention for the Protection of the

---

1 There are many studies on MPAs. With respect to the general analysis of MPAs, see T.S. Agardy, *Marine Protected Areas and Ocean Conservation* (California and London, Academic Press, 1997); G. Kelleher (ed.), *Guidelines for Marine Protected Areas* (Gland, IUCN-The World Conservation Union, 1999); R.V. Salm, J. Clark and E. Siirila, *Marine and Coastal Protected Areas: A Guide for Planners and Managers*, 3rd edn (Gland, IUCN, 2000); Ange-Laurent Bindi, 'La création et la gestion des aires marines spécialement protégées (AMSP)' (2000) 5 *Annuaire du droit de la mer*, pp. 165–75; National Research Council, *Marine Protected Areas: Tools for Sustaining Ocean Ecosystems* (Washington, DC, National Academy Press, 2001). With respect to MPAs in international law, see in particular T. Scovazzi (ed.), *Marine Specially Protected Areas: The General Aspects and the Mediterranean Regional System* (The Hague, Kluwer, 1999); N. Tanaka (ed.), 'Kaiyo hogoku no kokusaiho teki kento' (Reflections on Marine Protected Areas in International Law) (in Japanese) (Tokyo, Ministry of Foreign Affairs, 2004) pp. 1–96; Y. Kagami, 'Developing MPAs under the UNCLOS Regime: Focusing on the Practice in the Exclusive Economic Zone' (in Japanese) (2005) 1 *Ocean Policy Studies*, pp. 153–220. Concerning regional State practice on MPAs, see, for instance, P. Salmona and D. Verardi, 'The Marine Protected Area of Portofino, Italy: A Difficult Balance' (2001) 44 *Ocean and Coastal Management*, pp. 39–60; S. Wolf, 'Neue Tendenzen zur Ausdehnung küstenstaatlicher Umweltkompetenzen auf See: Eine Untersuchung am Beispiel der französischen "zone de protection écologique" im Mittelmeer' (2006) 66 *ZaöRV*, pp. 73–141.

2 A frequently quoted definition is provided by IUCN: 'Any area of intertidal or subtidal terrain, together with its overlying water and associated flora, fauna, historical and cultural features, which has been reserved by law or other effective means to protect part or all of the enclosed environment.' Kelleher, above note 1, p. xviii. Similarly, the IMO defines MPAs as: 'Areas of intertidal or subtidal terrain together with their overlying waters and associated flora, fauna, historical and cultural features, which have been reserved to protect

Marine Environment of the North-East Atlantic (hereafter the OSPAR Convention) defines MPAs as: 'An area within the maritime area for which it is appropriate to institute, consistently with international law, protective, conservation, restorative or precautionary measures for the purpose of protecting and conserving species, habitats, ecosystems or ecological processes of the marine environment of the maritime area.'[3] Unlike the species-specific approach, MPAs seek to protect marine ecosystems of a certain area as a whole. In this sense, MPAs can be regarded as one of the tools to implement the ecosystem approach.

Although the establishment of MPAs is not a new phenomenon in municipal law,[4] it was not until recently that MPAs have received attention at the international level. In 1992, Chapter 17 of Agenda 21 stressed the need to establish MPAs, by stating that:

> Coastal States, with the support of international organizations, upon request, should undertake measures to maintain biological diversity and productivity of marine species and habitats under national jurisdiction. Inter alia, these measures might include: surveys of marine biodiversity, inventories of endangered species and critical coastal and marine habitats; *establishment and management of protected areas*; and support of scientific research and dissemination of its results.[5]

A decade later, the Plan of Implementation of the World Summit on Sustainable Development (Johannesburg, 2002) required States to:

> develop and facilitate the use of diverse approaches and tools, including the ecosystem approach, the elimination of destructive fishing practices, *the establishment of marine protected areas* consistent with international law and based on scientific information, including representative networks by 2012 and

---

part or all of the enclosed environment.' IMO Resolution A. 720 (17), *Guidelines for the Designation of Special Areas and the Identification of Particularly Sensitive Sea Areas*, 6 November 1991, para. 1.1.2. With respect to the definition of MPAs, see also Kagami, above note 1, pp. 163–4.

3 Meeting of the Biodiversity Committee, *Draft OSPAR Recommendation on a Network of Marine Protected Areas*, BDC/03/10/1-E Annex 10, 20–24 January 2003, Dublin, para. 1.3.

4 It is suggested that probably the first MPA dates back to 1935 when the Fort Jefferson National Monument in Florida, USA, was set up as a conservation area covering 18,850 ha. of sea along with 35 ha. of coastal land. IMO Resolution A. 720 (17), *Guidelines for the Designation of Special Areas and the Identification of Particularly Sensitive Sea Areas*, 6 November 1991 (Agenda item 12), 1.1.1. In accordance with the study by Kelleher *et al.*, 1,111 MPAs were identified in 1994. Quoted in S. Gubbay, 'Marine Protected Areas – Past, Present and Future', in S. Gubbay (ed.), *Marine Protected Areas: Principles and Techniques for Management* (London, Chapman and Hall, 1995) p. 5.

5 Emphasis added. Para. 17.7.

time/area closures for the protection of nursery grounds and periods, proper coastal land use.[6]

The UN General Assembly Resolution 57/141 of 2003 follows this wording and adds 'proper coastal and land use and watershed planning, and the integration of marine and coastal areas management into key sectors'.[7] In light of the growing international attention to MPAs at the international level, first there is a need to clarify the MPA-related concepts in international law.[8]

A second issue to be examined in this chapter relates to the interrelationship between MPAs and the integrated management approach. In this respect, the 2003 meeting of the United Nations Open-ended Informal Consultative Process on Oceans and the Law of the Sea recorded that 'many delegations expressed support for the establishment of MPAs *as a management tool for integrated ocean management* in areas within and beyond national jurisdiction'.[9] Thus it will be necessary to examine the question whether and to what extent the concept of MPAs may serve as an instrument for promoting the integrated management approach in conservation of marine biological diversity.

Furthermore, recently the need to establish MPAs is increasingly voiced in various fora with a view to protecting marine biological diversity in marine spaces beyond the limit of national jurisdiction. Arguably the establishment of MPAs in those areas will necessitate serious considerations concerning its legal ground as well as its practical implementation in positive international law. Thus, a third issue to be addressed in this chapter is whether or not MPAs may be established marine spaces beyond the limit of national jurisdiction in international law.

This chapter will be divided into six sections. After briefly reviewing the development of MPAs in international law, the second section will analyse MPA-related concepts in treaties as well as other legal documents at the global level. The next section will examine as a regional case study the MPAs in the North-East Atlantic area. On the basis of these considerations, the fourth section will focus on the inter-linkage between MPAs, environmental protection and the regulation of fisheries in order to consider the interrelationship between MPAs and the integrated

---

6 Emphasis added. Para. 31 (c).

7 UN General Assembly Resolution, 57/141 *Oceans and the Law of the Sea*, A/RES/57/141, 21 February 2003, p. 10, para. 53.

8 For the purpose of this study, this chapter will focus on MPAs in international law and, thus, the analysis of MPAs in municipal law is beyond its scope. With respect to an overview of municipal law in this matter, see T. Scovazzi, 'Marine Specially Protected Areas under Domestic Legislation', in Scovazzi, above note 1, pp. 3–16; Kagami, above note 1, pp. 167–84.

9 Emphasis added. United Nations, *Report on the Work of the United Nations Open-ended Informal Consultative Process on Oceans and the Law of the Sea*, A/58/95, 26 June 2003, p. 29, para. 104.

management approach. The fifth section will further address MPAs beyond the limits of national jurisdiction. Finally, conclusions will be given.

Development of the MPAs in International Law

Treaty Practice relating to MPAs   Arguably, treaties creating MPAs may date back to the 1940s. The 1940 Convention on Nature Protection and Wildlife Preservation in the Western Hemisphere calls for the Contracting Governments to explore the possibility of establishing in their territories national parks, national reserves, nature monuments and strict wilderness reserves in accordance with Article 2.[10] The term 'territories' appears to suggest that the geographical scope of this Convention covers the internal waters as well as the territorial seas. Under Article 3, the Contracting Governments agreed to prohibit hunting, killing and capturing of members of the fauna and destruction or collection of representatives of the flora in national parks, except by or under the direction or control of the park authorities, or for duly authorised scientific investigations. In 1946, the International Convention for the Regulation of Whaling was adopted with a view to ensuring proper and effective conservation and development of whale stocks.[11] Article V (1) of this Convention empowered the International Whaling Commission to adopt regulations with respect to the conservation and utilisation of whale resources, fixing '(c) open and closed waters, including the designation of sanctuary areas'.

Nonetheless, it was not until the 1970s that MPA-related concepts caught the attention of States.[12] In 1971, for instance, the Convention on Wetlands of International Importance (Ramsar Convention) was concluded.[13] Article 2 (1) of the Ramsar Convention requires each Contracting Party to designate suitable wetland within its territory for inclusion in a List of Wetlands of International Importance. The Contracting Parties are required to formulate and implement their planning so as to promote the conservation of the wetlands included in the list, and as far as possible the wise use of wetlands in their territory in accordance with Article 3 (1). Such wetlands may cover offshore areas pursuant to Article 1 (1) as well as Article 2 (1).[14] It is suggested that some 48 per cent of the designated Ramsar sites include the coast; and that these sites may contain marine components.[15]

---

10 Entry into force in 1942. For the text of the Convention, see 161 *UNTS* 193

11 For the text of the convention, see 161 *UNTS* 72; P.W. Birnie and A. Boyle, *Basic Documents on International Law and the Environment* (Oxford, Oxford University Press, 1995) pp. 586ff.

12 See Table 5.1.

13 For the text of the convention, see 161 *UNTS* 72; Birnie and Boyle, above note 11, pp. 447ff.

14 Article 1 (1) clearly provides that wetlands include areas of marine water the depth of which at low tide does not exceed six metres. Furthermore, Article 2 (2) provides that the boundaries of each wetland may incorporate bodies of marine water deeper than six metres at low tide lying within the wetlands.

15 Kelleher, above note 1, p. 4.

An MPA-related concept may also be seen in the 1972 Convention for the Protection of the World Cultural and Natural Heritage.[16] The 1972 World Heritage Convention aims to protect cultural and natural heritages, including habitats of 'threatened species of animals and plants of outstanding universal value from the point of view of science or conservation'.[17] In this regard, Articles 4 and 5 of the Convention provide for an explicit duty of conservation of cultural and natural heritage. Accordingly, there seems to be a general sense that the designation of 'natural heritage' can to some extent serve for the protection of marine species. In fact, the List of World Heritage so far covers the Belize Barrier Reef and the Great Barrier Reef (Australia). Moreover, several World Heritage sites – such as Tubbataha Reef (Philippines), Ujong Kulong (Indonesia), Shark Bay (Australia), Galapagos Islands (Ecuador) and Glacier Bay (Canada) – contain large marine components. Banc d'Arguin (Mauritania) as well as the Sunderbans (Bangladesh) also cover estuarine waters.[18]

It is also notable that UNESCO's Man and the Biosphere (MAB) programme was launched in 1972.[19] In accordance with Article 1 of the Statutory Framework of the World Network of Biosphere Reserves, biosphere reserves are defined as 'areas of terrestrial and coastal/marine ecosystems or a combination thereof, which are internationally recognized within the framework of UNESCO's programme on Man and the Biosphere (MAB)'.[20] Each biosphere reserve remains under the sovereignty of the State where it is situated and submitted to State legislation only.[21] The Biosphere Reserves network was launched in 1976. As of March 2005, the network had grown to 459 reserves in 97 countries.[22] Each biosphere reserve purports to fulfil the three functions under Article 3 of the Statutory Framework:

---

16 For the text of the convention, see H. Hohmann, *Basic Documents of International Environmental Law*, Vol. 3 (London, Nijhoff, 1992) pp. 1334–5; Birnie and Boyle, above note 11, pp. 375ff; (1972) 11 *ILM* p. 1358.

17 Article 2. For this convention, see, for instance, S. Lyster, *International Wildlife Law: Analysis of International Treaties Concerned with the Conservation of Wildlife* (Cambridge, Grotius Publications Limited, 1985) pp. 208–38.

18 Kelleher, above note 1, p. 5.

19 With respect to the outline of this programme, see J. Roberts, *Marine Environment Protection and Biodiversity Conservation: The Application and Future Development of the IMO's Particularly Sensitive Sea Area Concept* (Berlin, Springer, 2007) pp. 40–42; Kelleher, above note 1, pp. 5–6.

20 The text of the statutory framework is available at the homepage of UNESCO <http://www.unesco.org/mab/BRA/offDoc.shtml>.

21 Introduction, *ibid.* General criteria to designate a biosphere reserve are provided in Article 4 of the statutory framework.

22 Roberts, above note 19, p. 40.

Table 5.1   Examples of treaties which provide the establishment of MPAs

Year	Title	Relevant Provision
1940	Convention on Nature Protection and Wildlife Preservation in the Western Hemisphere	Article 2
1946	International Convention for the Regulation of Whaling	Article 5 (1)
1968	African Convention on the Conservation of Nature and Natural Resources	Articles 3 (4), 10 (1)
1971	Convention on Wetlands of International Importance Especially as Waterfowl Habitat	Article 2 (1)
1972	Convention Concerning the Protection of the World Cultural and Natural Heritage	Article 5 (d)
1973	International Convention for the Prevention of Pollution from Ships, as Modified by Protocol of 1978	Annexes I, II, V and VI
1976	Convention for the Protection of the Mediterranean Sea against Pollution	Article 10
1976	Convention on Conservation of Nature in the South Pacific	Article II
1980	Convention on the Conservation of Antarctic Marine Living Resources	Article 9 (2) (g)
1981	Convention for Co-operation in the Protection and Development of the Marine and Coastal Environment of the West and Central African Region	Article 11
1982	Protocol Concerning Mediterranean Specially Protected Areas	Articles 3 (1) and 6 (1)
1982	UN Convention on the Law of the Sea	Articles 211 (6) and 234
1983	Convention for the Protection and Development of the Marine Environment of the Wider Caribbean Region	Article 10
1985	Convention for the Protection, Management and Development of the Marine and Coastal Environment of the Eastern African Region	Article 10
1985	Protocol Concerning Protected Areas and Wild Fauna and Flora in the Eastern African Region	Article 8 (1)
1985	ASEAN Agreement on the Conservation of Nature and Natural Resources	Article 3 (3) (a)
1986	Convention for the Protection of the Natural Resources and Environment of the South Pacific Region	Article 14
1989	Protocol for the Conservation and Management of Protected Marine and Coastal Areas of the South-East Pacific	Articles 2 and 3

1990	Protocol Concerning Specially Protected Areas and Wildlife in the Wider Caribbean Region	Articles 1, 4 (1)
1990	Agreement on the Conservation of Seals in the Wadden Sea	Article VII
1991	Protocol on Environmental Protection to the Antarctic Treaty	Annex V
1992	Convention on Biological Diversity	Article 8 (a)
1992	Convention for the Protection of the Marine Environment of the North-East Atlantic (OSPAR Convention)	See note below
1992	Convention on the Protection of the Marine Environment of the Baltic Sea Area (Helsinki Convention)	See note below
1993	Conjoint Declaration Relating to the Institution of the Mediterranean Sanctuary for Marine Mammals	Articles 4, 6
1995	Protocol Concerning Specially Protected Areas and Biological Diversity in the Mediterranean	Articles 8, 9, Annex I
1996	Agreement on the Conservation of Cetaceans of the Black Sea, Mediterranean Sea and Contiguous Atlantic Area (ACCOBAMS)	Article II (1)
1996	Inter-American Convention for the Protection and Conservation of Sea Turtles	Article 4 (1) (d)

Note: The list is not exhaustive. Although there is no explicit provision relating to MPAs in the OSPAR Convention, as will be seen, the institution of MPAs is developing through the OSPAR Commission. Similarly, Baltic Sea Protected Areas (BSPAs) are developing through the Helsinki Commission, although the Helsinki Convention did not refer to BSPAs. With respect to the list of treaties in this matter, see note 1, pp. 85–96; T. Scovazzi, 'Marine Specially Protected Areas under International Law,' in Scovazzi, above note 1, pp. 121–6. As the concept of an MPA is not well established in international law, the selection of treaties relating to MPAs may vary according to writers. For instance, Scovazzi includes the 1979 Convention on the Conservation of Migratory Species of Wild Animals, as well as the 1979 Convention on the Conservation of European Wildlife and Natural Habitats, in the list of treaties creating MPAs. *Ibid.*, pp. 22–3.

(i)   conservation – contribute to the conservation of landscapes, ecosystems, species and genetic variation;

(ii)   development – foster economic and human development which is socio-culturally and ecologically sustainable;

(iii)   logistic support – support for demonstration projects, environmental education and training, research and monitoring related to local, regional, national and global issues of conservation and sustainable development.

By combining the three functions, the world network of biosphere reserves seeks to contribute to conservation and sustainable development on a regional scale.[23] Thus it appears that biosphere reserves are more than simply protected areas with respect to conservation of biological diversity.[24]

In the 1980s, MPAs were enshrined in various treaties. It is worth noting that the geographical scope of the MPAs expanded from coastal areas toward the high seas. While most MPAs were set in place in territorial seas near to coastal areas in the 1970s,[25] the geographical scope of MPAs tended to be extended to the EEZ in the 1980s and after.[26] Furthermore, as indicated earlier, the need to establish MPAs in marine spaces beyond the limits of national jurisdiction is increasingly voiced in various fora.[27] In 2003, for instance, the fifth IUCN World Parks Congress recommended utilising available mechanisms and authorities to establish and effectively manage by 2008 at least five ecologically significant

---

23 Article 3 of the Statutory Framework. In order to perform these three functions, a biosphere reserve is composed of three interrelated zones, that is to say, the core area, the buffer zone and the transition area. The core area is a legally constituted area devoted to long-term protection. The buffer zone is an area contiguous to the core area where only activities compatible with the conservation objectives can take place. The transition area is an area where sustainable resource management practices are promoted. Article 4 (5) of the Statutory Framework.

24 Roberts, above note 19, p. 40. See also UNESCO, 'The Seville Strategy for Biosphere Reserves'.

25 Kagami, above note 1, p. 160.

26 Tanaka, above note 1, p. 32. See, for instance, the 1985 Protocol Concerning Protected Areas and Wild Fauna and Flora in the Eastern African Region, the 1989 Protocol for the Convention and Management of Protected Marine and Coastal Areas of the South-East Pacific, the 1990 Protocol Concerning Specially Protected Areas and Wildlife in the Wider Caribbean Region, and the 1992 Convention on Biological Diversity.

27 An International Meeting on Wild Ocean Reserves, convened by the United States National Oceanic and Atmospheric Administration in October 1991, has already urged that a global network of high seas MPAs be established with a view to ensuring the future sustainability of critically sensitive marine ecosystems and ocean resources of unique scientific, cultural and aesthetic value. K.M. Gjerde, 'High Seas Marine Protected Areas' (2001) 16 *IJMCL*, pp. 515–16.

and globally representative high seas MPAs.[28] The COP of the Convention on Biological Diversity (hereafter the Rio Convention) echoed this idea, by stating that: 'marine protected areas are one of the essential tools to help achieve conservation and sustainable use of biodiversity in marine areas beyond the limits of national jurisdiction.'[29] It is also reported that a number of delegates in the UN *Ad Hoc* Open-ended Informal Working Group to study this issue recognised that 'multi-purpose marine protected areas would be a key tool in the future to manage biodiversity beyond areas of national jurisdiction'.[30] Thus, the establishment of MPAs in marine spaces beyond the limits of national jurisdiction is becoming a matter of important concern in international law.

Typology of MPAs in International Law   Although objectives and mechanisms of MPAs may vary, MPAs embodied in relevant treaties may be divided into two principal categories: MPAs concerning the protection of the marine environment, and MPAs relating directly to conservation of marine biological diversity. With respect to the former, at least five MPA-related concepts can be detected in treaties as well as non-binding documents at the global level:

(i)   'Clearly Defined Area' in Article 211 (6) of the 1982 LOSC;
(ii)   Ice-Covered Areas in Article 234 of the LOSC;
(iii)   Special Areas under MARPOL 73/78;
(iv)   Particularly Sensitive Sea Areas (PSSA) in IMO Guidelines;
(v)   Specially Protected Areas in the 1985 Montreal Guidelines.

While basically these concepts purport to regulate marine pollution from a specific source, it may be argued that the establishment of these areas can indirectly contribute to protecting marine biological diversity.

With respect to MPAs relating directly to the conservation of marine biological diversity, of particular importance is the 'protected area' established in the Rio Convention. Furthermore, there are various regional treaties creating MPAs. It would seem that MPAs in regional treaties may be divided into two sub-categories.

A first sub-category relates to MPAs which seek to protect and preserve rare or fragile ecosystems as well as the habitat of depleted or endangered species and other marine life in a particular region. Examples include:

(i)   the 1976 Convention on Conservation of Nature in the South Pacific

---

28 IUCN, *Recommendations of the 5th IUCN World Parks Congress*, 2003, WPC Rec 5.23. This document is available at the home page of IUCN <http://www.iucn.org/>.

29 Convention on Biological Diversity, COP Decision VIII/24, *Protected Area*, UNEP/CBD/COP/8/31, 2006, p. 8, para. 38.

30 United Nations, *Report of the Ad Hoc Open-ended Informal Working Group to Study Issues Relating to the Conservation and Sustainable Use of Marine Biological Diversity beyond Areas of National Jurisdiction*, A/61/65, 20 March 2006, p. 16, para. 61.

(Article II);[31]

(ii)   the 1980 Convention on the Conservation of Antarctic Marine Living Resources (Article 9 (2) (g));[32]

(iii)   the 1981 Convention for Cooperation in the Protection and Development of the Marine and Coastal Environment of the West and Central African Region (Article 11);[33]

(iv)   the 1985 Convention for the Protection, Management and Development of the Marine and Coastal Environment of the Eastern African Region (Article 10);[34]

(v)   the 1985 Protocol Concerning Protected Areas and Wild Fauna and Flora in the Eastern African Region (Article 8);[35]

(vi)   the 1985 ASEAN Agreement on the Conservation of Nature and Natural Resources (Article 3 (3) (a));[36]

(vii)   the 1986 Convention for the Protection of the Natural Resources and Environment of the South-Pacific Region (Article 14);[37]

(viii)   the 1989 Protocol for the Conservation and Management of Protected Marine and Coastal Areas of the South-East Pacific (Article 2);[38]

(ix)   the 1990 Protocol Concerning Specially Protected Areas and Wildlife to the Convention for the Protection and Development of the Marine Environment of the Wider Caribbean Region (Article 4);[39]

(x)   Annex V of the 1992 OSPAR Convention;[40]

(xi)   the 1992 Helsinki Convention;[41]

(xii)   the 1995 Protocol Concerning Specially Protected Areas and Biological Diversity in the Mediterranean.[42]

A second sub-category concerns a species-specific MPA which seeks to protect specific marine life, such as marine mammals. Examples will be furnished by:

---

31 For the text of the Convention, see <http://sedac.ciesin.org/entri/texts/nature.south. pacific.1976.html.>.

32 For the text of the Convention, see 1329 *UNTS* 47

33 For the text of the Convention, see (1981) 20 *ILM*, p. 746.

34 For the text of the convention, see <http://sedac.ciesin.org/entri/texts/marine. coastal.east.africa.1985. html>.

35 For the text of the protocol, see <http://sedac.ciesin.columbia.edu/etri/texts/ EastAfrPro.html>.

36 For the text of the agreement, see <http://www.aseansec.org/1490.htm>.

37 For the text of the convention, see (1987) 26 *ILM*, p. 38.

38 For the text of the convention, see <http://www.intfish.net/treaties/sepac 1989.htm>.

39 For the text of the convention, see <http://www.cep.unep.org/pubs/legislation/spaw. html>.

40 The text of the convention is available at the homepage of the OSPAR <http://www. ospar.org/>.

41 The text of the Convention is available at <http://www.helcom.fi>.

42 The text of the protocol is reproduced in Scovazzi, above note 1, pp. 163–77.

(i)   the 1990 Agreement on the Conservation of Seals in the Wadden Sea;[43]

(ii)   the 1993 Déclaration conjointe relative à l'institution d'un sanctuaire méditerranéen pour les mammifères marins;[44]

(iii) the 1996 Agreement on the Conservation of Cetaceans of the Black Sea, Mediterranean Sea and Contiguous Atlantic Area (ACCOBAMS);[45]

(iv)   the 1996 Inter-American Convention for the Protection and Conservation of Sea Turtles.[46]

(v)   the 1999 Agreement Establishing a Sanctuary for Marine Mammals;[47]

It appears, however, that MPAs in this sub-category are basically in line with the traditional species-specific approach.

MPAs in Global Legal Documents

MPAs relating to the Protection of the Marine Environment

'Clearly Defined Area' in Article 211 (6) of the LOSC   A first MPA-related concept to be addressed pertains to 'clearly defined area' in Article 211 (6) of the 1982 LOSC.[48] While the words 'Marine Protected Area' are not used, Article 211 (6) stipulates that coastal States 'may' take preventive measures in a 'particular, clearly defined area (or special area)' of their EEZ. The 'particular, clearly defined area' seeks to prevent vessel-source pollution in an area where the adoption of special mandatory measures to this matter is required for recognised technical reasons in relation to its oceanographical and ecological conditions, as well as its utilisation or the protection of its resources and the particular character of its traffic. At the same time, the phrase 'ecological conditions' appears to suggest that this concept may also relate to the conservation of marine ecosystems. Although

43 For the text of the Convention, see <http://cwss.www.de/management/SMP/Seals-Agreement.pdf>.

44 The text of the protocol is reproduced in Scovazzi, above note 1, pp. 243–5.

45 For the text of the convention, see <http://www.accobams.org/2006.php/documents/show/30>; (1997) 36 *ILM*, p. 777.

46 For the text of the convention, see <http://www.lclark.edu/org/ielp/objects/interamerican.pdf>.

47 With respect to the 1999 Sanctuary Agreement, see T. Scovazzi, 'The Mediterranean Marine Mammals Sanctuary' (2001) 16 *IJMCL*, pp. 132–41. The text of the Agreement is reproduced in *ibid.*, pp. 142–5.

48 With respect to this concept, see in particular E.J. Molenaar, *Coastal State Jurisdiction Over Vessel-Source Pollution* (The Hague, Kluwer, 1998) pp. 402–30. R. Lagoni, 'Marine Protected Areas in the Exclusive Economic Zone', in A. Kirchner (ed.), *International Maritime Environmental Law: Institutions, Implementation and Innovations* (The Hague, Kluwer, 2003) pp. 157–67.

the outer limit of 'a particular clearly defined area' is the limit of the EEZ of the coastal State, the inner limit of this area is not clearly defined in the 1982 LOSC. Hence, it remains obscure whether or not such special areas may include part of the territorial sea. Given that the coastal State has more extensive jurisdiction in its territorial sea than in its EEZ, there seems to be a general sense that the coastal State may create such areas in its territorial sea.[49]

Article 211 (6) places substantive and procedural conditions on creating a 'clearly defined area'. With respect to the substantive conditions, there must be a situation where the established international rules and standards to prevent vessel-source pollution are inadequate. Furthermore, there must be 'reasonable grounds for believing' that such an area is needed in light of 'recognised technical reasons' for adopting special mandatory measures for the prevention of pollution from vessels. In this case, the coastal States may adopt additional laws and regulations for the special areas. Such additional laws and regulations may relate to discharges or navigational practices, but shall not require foreign vessels to observe design, construction, manning or equipment standards other than generally accepted international rules and standards. In this respect, it should be noted that the coastal State is not free to adopt any laws and regulations as it considers appropriate; only laws and regulations implementing international rules and standards concerning vessel-source pollution may be adopted. It would seem that such international rules will be those embodied in MARPOL 73/78.[50] Considering that those rules and standards relate solely to discharges from vessels and to navigational practices accepted for special areas under MARPOL 73/78, arguably freedom of navigation as well as other internationally lawful uses of the sea cannot be excluded from a 'clearly defined area'.[51] In addition, those laws and regulations shall not become applicable to foreign vessels until 15 months after the submission of the communication to the organisation.[52]

In relation to the procedural conditions, the coastal State has to submit relevant information to the competent international organisation, that is, the IMO. Only when the organisation so determines, may the coastal States adopt laws and regulations for the prevention of pollution from vessels with a view to implementing such international rules and standards or navigational practices as are made applicable, through the organisation, for special areas. It would follow that the prescriptive jurisdiction of the coastal State is to be qualified by the IMO. At the same time, the coastal States shall publish the limits of any such particular, clearly defined area in accordance with Article 211 (6) (b). In reality, there is no clearly defined area designated under Article 211 (6).[53] Hence, the practical role of the 'clearly defined area' remains to be seen.

---

49 Molenaar, above note 48, p. 402.
50 *Ibid.*, p. 162.
51 *Ibid.*
52 Article 211 (6) (a).
53 Lagoni, above note 48, p. 162.

'Ice-Covered Areas' in Article 234 of the LOSC   Another MPA-related concept in the 1982 LOSC concerns 'ice-covered areas' enshrined in Article 234. This article seeks to balance the interests of the coastal State in ice-covered areas within the limits of its EEZ with the interests of international navigation.[54] While in ice-covered areas the coastal States remain bound by international rules or standards as a minimum, they may unilaterally impose more stringent requirements. At the same time, it should be noted that coastal States' power to adopt and enforce laws and regulations in ice-covered areas is subject to several conditions.[55]

First, with respect to the spatial scope of the 'ice-covered areas', the outer limit of these areas is the limit of the EEZ of the coastal State. Yet the inner limit of this area is not clearly defined in the 1982 LOSC. Given that the jurisdiction of the coastal State is presumed to be more extensive in the territorial sea than the EEZ, however, it appears that the ice-covered areas could also be situated in the territorial sea.[56] In any case, in light of the legislative process, it appears that the spatial scope of this article is limited to the Arctic in reality.[57] Accordingly, it would seem that the role of the 'ice-covered areas' is of limited value from geographical viewpoints.

Secondly, a marine area to which Article 234 is applicable must be a zone where particularly severe climatic conditions and the presence of ice covering such areas for most of the year create obstructions or exceptional hazards to navigation. The ice-covered area must be a zone where pollution of the marine environment could cause major harm to or irreversible disturbance of the ecological balance. The reference to the 'ecological balance' appears to show that this provision reflects the theme of Article 194 (5), which imposes on States to protect rare or fragile ecosystems.

Thirdly, laws and regulations must have due regard to navigation and the protection and preservation of the marine environment based on the best available scientific evidence. It would follow that navigation of foreign vessels is not excluded in ice-covered areas.[58] Such laws and regulations of the coastal State applicable to ice-covered areas must be non-discriminatory.

---

54 M.H. Nordquist, S.N. Nandan and S. Rosenne, *United Nations Convention on the Law of the Sea 1982: A Commentary* (hereafter *Virginia Commentary*) Vol. 4 (The Hague, Nijhoff, 1991) p. 393. Article 234 is one of the few provisions in the 1982 LOSC the terms of which were negotiated directly between States concerned, that is to say, Canada, the USSR and the USA. *Ibid.*

55 *Ibid.*, p. 397.

56 Molenaar, above note 48, p. 419.

57 International Law Association, *Final Report of the Committee on Coastal State Jurisdiction Relating to Marine Pollution* (International Law Association, London Conference, 2000). Reproduced in E. Franckx (ed.), *Vessel-source Pollution and Coastal State Jurisdiction: The Work of the ILA Committee on Coastal State Jurisdiction Relating to Marine Pollution (1991–2000)* (The Hague, Kluwer, 2001) p. 100.

58 T. Kuribayashi, *Chukai Kokuren Kaiyoho Jyoyaku* (in Japanese) (*Commentary on the United Nations Convention on the Law of the Sea*) (Tokyo, Yuhikaku, 1994) p. 146;

Finally, it should be noted that Article 234 comes within the scope of Part XV for the compulsory dispute settlement mechanism.[59] It would follow that disputes relating to the interpretation and application of Article 234 are under the control of the third-party dispute settlement mechanism in the LOSC.

Special Areas under MARPOL 73/78   A third concept which relates to MPAs is 'special areas' established in MARPOL 73/78. Annexes I, II and V of MARPOL 73/78 seek to protect certain marine areas by designating them as 'special areas'. A 'special area' means: 'a sea area where for recognised technical reasons in relation to its oceanographical and ecological condition and to the particular character of its traffic the adoption of special mandatory methods for the prevention of sea pollution by oil is required.'[60] The geographical scope of a 'special area' may include marine spaces beyond the limit of national jurisdiction.[61] Under MARPOL 73/78, these special areas are provided with a higher level of protection than other areas of the sea.

More specifically, Annex I of MARPOL 73/78 purports to prevent oil pollution from ships while operating in special areas. Such areas cover: the Mediterranean Sea area, the Baltic Sea area, the Black Sea area, the Red Sea area, the 'Gulfs area', the Gulf of Aden area, the Antarctic area, and the North-West European Waters.[62] Annex II seeks to prevent sea pollution by noxious liquid substances in special areas, which comprise: the Baltic Sea area, the Black Sea area, and the Antarctic area.[63] Furthermore, Annex V regulates disposal of garbage within special areas. In accordance with Regulation 5 (1), such areas are: the Mediterranean Sea area, the Baltic Sea area, the Black Sea area, the Red Sea area, the 'Gulfs area', the North Sea area, the Antarctic area, and the Wider Caribbean Region, including the Gulf of Mexico and the Caribbean Sea. On the other hand, Annex VI provides for sulphur oxides (SOx) emission control areas, which shall include: the Baltic Sea area as well as other areas designated by the organisation in accordance with criteria and procedures in Appendix III of this Annex.[64] Each Annex contains detailed rules protecting 'special areas' from vessel-source marine pollution.

Virginia Commentary, above note 54, p. 397.

59   *Ibid.*, p. 396.

60   Regulation 1 (10) of Annex I of MARPOL 73/78. For the text of the Convention, see International Maritime Organisation, *MARPOL 73/78 Consolidated Edition 2002* (London, IMO, 2002), 1340 *UNTS*, 184 and 61.

61   N. Oral, 'Protection of Vulnerable Marine Ecosystems in Areas Beyond National Jurisdiction: Can International Law Meet the Challenge?', in A. Strati, M. Gavouneli and N. Skourtos (eds), *Unresolved Issues and New Challenges to the Law of the Sea: Time Before and Time After* (Leiden and Boston, Nijhoff, 2006) p. 104.

62   Regulation 10 (1) of Annex I of MARPOL 73/78.

63   Regulation 1 (7) of Annex II of MARPOL 73/78.

64   Regulation 14 (3) of Annex VI of MARPOL 73/78.

On 29 November 2001, the Assembly of the IMO adopted new Guidelines for the Designation of Special Areas under MARPOL 73/78.[65] These Guidelines aim to provide guidance to Contracting Parties to MARPOL 73/78 in the formulation and submission of applications for the designation of special areas under Annexes I, II and V to the Convention.[66] In accordance with the 2001 Guidelines, a special area may encompass the maritime zones of several States, or even an entire enclosed or semi-enclosed area.[67] A proposal to designate a given sea area as a special area should be submitted to the IMO for consideration by its Marine Environment Protection Committee (MEPC).[68] Special area designation should be made on the basis of the oceanographic, and ecological conditions and vessel traffic characteristics. Ecological conditions should indicate that protection of the area from harmful substances is needed to preserve:

(i)   depleted, threatened or endangered marine species;
(ii)   areas of high natural productivity;
(iii)   spawning, breeding and nursery areas for important marine species and areas representing migratory routes for sea birds and marine mammals;
(iv)   rare or fragile ecosystems, such as coral reefs;
(v)   critical habitats for marine resources including fish stocks and/or areas of critical importance for the support of large marine ecosystems.[69]

It would seem to follow that, to a certain extent, the establishment of special areas under MARPOL 73/78 can serve for the conservation of marine biological diversity. Given that the purpose of MARPOL 73/78 concerns the regulation of vessel-source pollution, however, it is obvious that measures taken in the special area cannot be extended to other ocean use, such as fishing activities.

IMO Guidelines for the Identification of Particularly Sensitive Sea Areas   With respect to MPAs in non-binding instruments, of particular importance are the particularly sensitive sea areas (PSSAs).[70] The increasing shipping activities in global trade may cause adverse effects upon and damage to the marine

---

65 Annex 1 of IMO Resolution A. 927(22).

66 *Ibid.*, p. 3, para. 1.1.

67 *Ibid.*, para. 2.2.

68 *Ibid.*, p. 5, para. 3.1.

69 *Ibid.*, p. 4, para. 2.5.

70 With respect to PSSAs, see in particular J.A. Roach, 'Particularly Sensitive Sea Areas: Current Developments', in M.H. Nordquist, J.N. Moore and S. Mahmoudi (eds), *The Stockholm Declaration and Law of the Marine Environment* (The Hague, Nijhoff, 2003) pp. 311–50; Roberts, above note 19; (1994) 9 *IJMCL* (Special Issue). Principal documents of PSSAs are reproduced in International Maritime Organisation, *Particularly Sensitive Sea Areas: Compilation of Official Guidance Documents and PSSAs Adopted Since 1990* (London, IMO, 2007).

environment owing to operational discharges, accidental or intentional pollution, and physical damage to marine habitats or organisms.[71] In particular, sinking of oil tankers causes environmental disasters in the oceans. In light of a series of oil tanker disasters, marine security is becoming a matter of important concern in the international community.[72] In response to this concern, the MEPC of the IMO commenced its study concerning the concept of particularly sensitive sea areas,[73] and on 6 November 1991, the Guidelines for the Designation of Special Areas and the Identification of Particularly Sensitive Sea Areas were adopted in the Assembly of the IMO.[74] Later on, Revised Guidelines for the Identification and Designation of Particularly Sensitive Sea Areas (hereafter 2001 Revised Guidelines) were adopted on 29 November 2001.[75] On 1 December 2005, these Guidelines were revised again (the 2005 Revised Guidelines).[76]

In accordance with the 2005 Revised Guidelines, a PSSA is defined as: 'an area that needs special protection through action by IMO because of its significance for recognized ecological, socio-economic or scientific attributes where such attributes may be vulnerable to damage by international shipping activities.'[77] Thus, PSSAs seek to protect the marine environment from international shipping activities. As the term 'should' is used in the Guidelines, it is understood that the PSSA scheme is not mandatory.[78] The main features of the PSSA can be summarised as follows.

First, with respect to spatial scope, PSSAs may cover all marine spaces, including the high seas.[79] The spatial scope of PSSAs is wider than that of 'clearly

---

71 IMO Resolution A. 982 (24), *Revised Guidelines for the Identification and Designation of Particularly Sensitive Sea Areas* (hereafter the 2005 Revised Guidelines), adopted on 1 December 2005, A 24/Res. 982, 6 February 2006. This document is available at the home page of IMO <http://www.imo.org/>.

72 It is said that the *Prestige* sinking on 19 November 2002 is regarded as one of the worst environmental catastrophes in history. With respect to a re-evaluation of the existing legal framework concerning marine security, see in particular V. Frank, 'Consequences of the Prestige Sinking for European and International Law' (2005) 20 *IJMCL*, pp. 1–64.

73 With respect to the development of the PSSA concept, see G. Peet, 'Particularly Sensitive Sea Areas: A Documentary History' (1994) 9 *IJMCL*, pp. 469–506.

74 IMO Resolution A. 720 (17). *Guidelines for the Designation of Special Areas and the Identification of Particularly Sensitive Sea Areas.* With respect to PSSAs, see in particular articles included in (1994) 9 *IJMCL* (Special Issue).

75 IMO Resolution A.927 (22), Annex 2.

76 The 2005 Revised Guidelines, above note 71.

77 *Ibid.*, p. 3, para. 1.2.

78 On this point, the 2005 Revised Guidelines state that: '[m]ember Governments should take all appropriate steps to ensure that ships flying their flag comply with the associated protective measures adopted to protect the designated PSSA.' *Ibid.*, para. 9.3. This point is confirmed by writers. See T. Scovazzi, 'Marine Protected Areas on the High Seas: Some Legal and Policy Considerations' (2004) 19 *IJMCL*, p. 9; J. Roberts, M. Tsamenyi, T. Workman and L. Johnston, 'The Western European PSSA Proposal: A "Politically Sensitive Sea Area"' (2005) 29 *Marine Policy*, p. 432; Roberts, above note 19, p. 99.

79 Scovazzi, above note 78, p. 9. See also Lagoni, above note 48, p. 163.

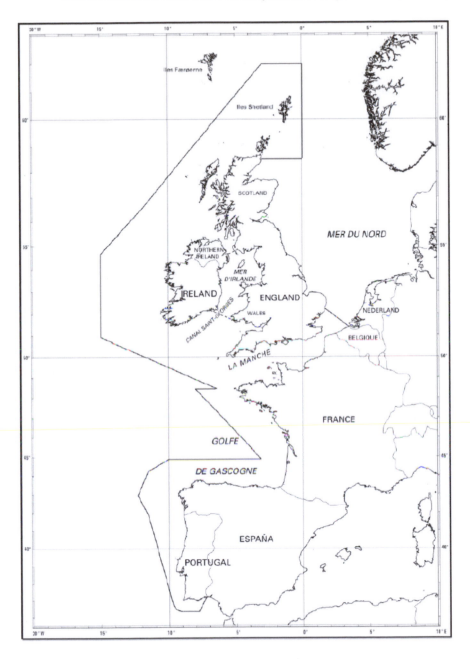

Figure 5.1   **The Western European Particularly Sensitive Sea Area**

Source: IMO Resolution MEPC.121(52), p. 3.

defined area' under Article 211 (6) (a) of the 1982 LOSC.[80] PSSAs may also include a buffer zone, that is to say, 'an area contiguous to the site-specific feature (core area) for which specific protection from shipping is sought'.[81] On the other hand, a series of Guidelines are silent with respect to the size of PSSAs. The issue of size became a subject of discussion indesignating the Western European PSSA.[82] The proposed area covered large geographical areas including the western coasts of the United Kingdom, Ireland, Belgium, France, Spain and Portugal. Although a number of delegations expressed concerns regarding the large size of the proposed area,[83] in the end, the Western European PSSA was approved with a small reduction in size. In this respect, it should be recalled that under the 2005 Revised Guidelines, in some cases, a PSSA may be identified within a special area under MARPOL 73/78 and vice versa.[84] Considering that special areas in MARPOL 73/78 may include entire regional seas, such as the Baltic Sea or the Mediterranean Sea, there seems to be a general sense that a PSSA may cover rather extended areas.[85]

Secondly, the IMO is the only international body responsible for designating areas as PSSAs and adopting associated protective measures. Hence, Member States wishing to have the IMO designate a PSSA should submit an application to the MEPC on the basis of the relevant criteria and proposed associated protective measures.[86] In this regard, the 2005 Revised Guidelines provide three criteria, that is to say, ecological criteria, social, cultural and economic criteria, and scientific and educational criteria.[87] In order to be identified as a PSSA, the area should meet at least one of the criteria, and information and supporting documentation should be provided to establish that at least one of the criteria exists throughout the entire proposed area, though the same criterion need not be present throughout the entire area.[88] These criteria apply to the identification of PSSAs only with respect to the adoption of measures to protect such areas against damage from international shipping activities. Thus, they do not apply to the identification of such areas for the purpose of establishing whether they should be protected from dumping

---

80   It has to be stressed that the concept of PSSAs differs from the concept of a 'clearly defined area' under Article 211 (6) (a) of the 1982 LOSC. On this point, see Roberts, above note 19, pp. 100–103.

81   The 2005 Revised Guidelines, above note 71, p. 8, para. 6.3.

82   Roberts *et al.*, above note 78.

83   *Ibid.* See also Frank, above note 72, p. 34.

84   The 2005 Revised Guidelines, above note 71, p. 7, para. 4.5.

85   Frank, above note 72, p. 35; Roberts *et al.*, above note 78, p. 439.

86   The 2005 Revised Guidelines, above note 71, p. 4, paras 3.1 and 3.2. Unlike Article 211 (6) (b) of LOSC, there is no time limit in the procedure of PSSAs.

87   *Ibid.*, p. 5, para. 4. In particular, ecological criteria contain the following factors: (i) uniqueness or rarity, (ii) critical habitat, (iii) dependency, (iv) representativeness, (v) diversity, (vi) productivity, (vii) spawning or breeding grounds, (viii) naturalness, (ix) integrity, (x) vulnerability, and (xi) bio-geographic importance. *Ibid.*, para. 4.4.ff.

88   *Ibid.*, para. 4.4.

Table 5.2   Particularly Sensitive Sea Areas in the world

Year	PSSA	Proposing Member Government(s)
1990	The Great Barrier Reef	Australia
1997	The Sabana-Camagüey Archipelago	Cuba
2002	Malpelo Island	Colombia
2002	The sea around the Florida Keys	USA
2002	The Wadden Sea	Denmark, Germany, Netherlands
2003	Paracas National Reserve	Peru
2004	Western European Waters	Belgium, France, Ireland, Portugal, Spain, UK
2005	Extension of the existing Great Barrier Reef PSSA to include the Torres Strait	Australia and Papua New Guinea
2005	Canary Islands	Spain
2005	The Galapagos Archipelago	Ecuador
2005	The Baltic Sea Area	Denmark, Estonia, Finland, Germany, Latvia, Lithuania, Poland, Sweden

activities, since that is implicitly covered by the London Dumping Convention of 1972, as well as the 1996 Protocol of that Convention.[89]

Thirdly, an application for PSSA designation should contain a proposal for an associated protective measure that the proposing Member Government intends to submit to the appropriate IMO body.[90] The associated protective measures for PSSAs are limited to actions that are to be, or have been, approved by the IMO.[91] If the measure is not already available under an IMO instrument, the proposing State is required to identify the legal basis for each measure in its application. The legal bases for such measures are:

(i)   any measure that is already available under an existing IMO instrument;

---

89 *Ibid.*, paras 4.1 and 4.2.

90 *Ibid.*, p. 9, para. 7.1.

91 Those measures include: (i) designation of an area as a special area under MARPOL Annexes I, II or V, or a SOx emission control area under MARPOL Annex VI, or application of special discharge restrictions to vessels operating in a PSSA; (ii) adopting of ships' routeing and reporting systems near or in the area, under the International Convention for the Safety of Life at Sea and in accordance with the General Provisions on Ships Routeing and the Guidelines and Criteria for Ship Reporting Systems; (iii) development and adoption of other measures aimed at protecting specific sea areas against environmental damage from ships, provided that they have an identified legal basis. *Ibid.*, p. 8, para. 6.1.

or
(ii)   any measure that does not yet exist but could become available through
         amendment of an IMO instrument or adoption of a new IMO instrument.
         The legal basis for any such measure would only be available after the
         IMO instrument was amended or adopted, as appropriate; or
(iii)   any measure proposed for adoption in the territorial sea, or pursuant
         to Article 211 (6) of the United Nations Convention on the Law of the
         Sea where existing measures or a generally applicable measure (as set
         forth in sub-paragraph (ii) above) would not adequately address the
         particularized need of the proposed area.[92]

The measures proposed for adoption in the territorial sea cannot derogate from
the rights and duties of the coastal State in the territorial sea as provided in the
1982 LOSC.[93] A proposing Member Government is also required to ensure that
any associated protective measure is implemented in accordance with the LOSC.[94]
It is conceivable that associated protective measures applying to PSSAs cannot be
extended to other fields such as fishing or mining.[95]

     When a PSSA is finally designated, all associated protective measures should be
identified on charts in accordance with the symbols and methods of the International
Hydrographic Organisation (IHO).[96] Member Governments are required to take all
appropriate steps to ensure that ships flying their flag comply with the associated
protective measures adopted to protect the designated PSSA.[97] Furthermore, those
Member Governments which have received information of an alleged violation
of an associated protective measure by a ship flying their flag should provide the
government which has reported the offence with the details of any appropriate
action taken.[98] In practice, the PSSA has not been widely established yet. As of
2005, there are only eleven designated PSSAs.[99] Instead, the application of ship's
routeing measures specifically for environmental protection purposes has become
a more widespread practice.[100] An explanation may be that the mandatory routeing
measures for ships in the territorial sea pursuant to Articles 21 and 22 of the 1982
LOSC may provide the same level of protection as PSSA designation. By applying
such measures, the coastal State can also avoid the lengthy process of creating

---

92 *Ibid.*, p. 10, para. 7.5.2.3.
93 *Ibid.*, para. 7.5.2.3 (iii), footnote.
94 *Ibid.*, p. 13, para. 9.2.
95 Scovazzi, above note 78, p. 9; Oral, above note 61, p. 105.
96 The 2005 Revised Guidelines, above note 71, p. 13, para. 9.1.
97 *Ibid.*, para. 9.3.
98 *Ibid.*, para. 9.3.
99 See Table 5.2. The information is available at the homepage of IMO <http://www.
imo.org/>. With respect to State practice on PSSA in some detail, see Roberts, above note
19, pp. 141–93.
100 J. Roberts, 'Protecting Sensitive Marine Environments: The Role and Application
of Ships' Routeing Measures' (2005) 20 *IJMCL*, pp. 152–3.

a PSSA through the IMO.[101] Furthermore, most of the PSSAs are set out in the territorial seas or internal waters. As those marine spaces are under the territorial sovereignty of the coastal State, the latter is entitled to take measures necessary to protect the marine environment in conformity with international law, regardless of the establishment of a PSSA. In this sense, it would appear that the practical role of the PSSA remains modest.

Specially Protected Areas in the Montreal Guidelines (1985)   Finally, the 1985 Montreal Guidelines for the Protection of the Marine Environment against Pollution from Land-Based Sources also introduced the concept of specially protected areas with a view to protecting fragile ecosystems from land-based pollution.[102] In these areas, States should take all appropriate measures, such as the establishment of marine sanctuaries and reserves, to protect certain areas to the fullest possible extent from pollution, including that from land-based sources, taking into account the relevant provisions of Annex I.[103] Furthermore, States are required, as far as is practicable, to undertake to develop environmental quality objectives for specially protected areas, conforming with the intended uses, and strive to maintain or ameliorate existing conditions by comprehensive environmental management practices.[104] On this point, Annex I states that the strategy on specially protected areas involves the identification of unique or pristine areas, rare or fragile ecosystems, critical habitats and the habitat of depleted, threatened or endangered species and other forms of marine life. Those areas to be protected or preserved from pollution, including that from land-based sources, are selected on the basis of a comprehensive evaluation of factors, including conservational, ecological, recreational, aesthetic and scientific values. To this end, States are required to notify an appropriate international organisation of the establishment of any modification to such areas, with a view to the inclusion of such information in an inventory of specially protected areas.[105]

It should be noted that activities which may cause land-based pollution are in essence within the territorial sovereignty of each State; and such activities are closely bound up with crucial national programmes for economic, industrial and social development of those countries. Hence, States are often reluctant to approve any attempts at restricting their economic developments by legally binding instruments in this field. In fact, attempts to address land-based marine pollution

---

101 In fact, Roberts suggests that those are the reasons that New Zealand applied the mandatory routeing measures without using PSSA. *Ibid.*, p. 151.

102 1985 Montreal Guidelines, para. 7 and para. 1.3.2.3 of Annex I. These Guidelines are of a voluntary nature. See Introduction to the Montreal Guidelines. These Guidelines are available in Hohmann, above note 16, Vol. 1, pp. 130–47.

103 Montreal Guidelines, para. 7 (a).

104 Montreal Guidelines, para. 7 (b).

105 Para. 1.3.2.3 of Annex I.

at the global level have been made only in the form of less formal instruments.[106] Thus, the effectiveness of specially protected areas under the 1985 Montreal Guidelines remains to be seen.

MPAs Concerning the Conservation of Marine Biological Diversity: 'Protected Area' in the Convention on Biological Diversity

With respect to MPAs for the conservation of marine biological diversity, of particular importance is 'protected area' in the Rio Convention. The 'protected area' means 'a geographically defined area which is designated or regulated and managed to achieve specific conservation objectives'.[107] Given that the geographical scope of the Rio Convention includes marine spaces, 'protected areas' can be created in marine spaces. In fact, the establishment of MPAs has been discussed in the Conference of the Parties (COP) as well as the Subsidiary Body on Scientific, Technical and Technological Advice (SBSTTA).[108] In particular, in its decision VII/5, the COP to the Rio Convention agreed that MPAs were one of the essential tools and approaches in the conservation and sustainable use of marine and coastal biological diversity.[109]

The *Ad Hoc* Technical Expert Group on Marine and Coastal Protected Areas, which was established within the framework of the Rio Convention, adopted the following definition of 'Marine and Coastal Protected Area':

[A]ny defined area within or adjacent to the marine environment, together with its overlying waters and associated flora, fauna, and historical and cultural features, which has been reserved by legislation or other effective means, including custom, with the effect that its marine and/or coastal biodiversity enjoys a higher level of protection than its surroundings.[110]

With respect to the function of the 'Marine and Coastal Protected Area', the COP stated:

---

106 Y. Tanaka, 'Regulation of Land-Based Marine Pollution in International Law: A Comparative Analysis between Global and Regional Legal Frameworks' (2006) 66 *ZaöRV*, pp. 547–8.

107 Article 2 of the Rio Convention.

108 The SBSTTA is the advisory body to the COP.

109 The Convention on Biological Diversity, Conference of the Parties, Decision VII/5, *Marine and Coastal Biological Diversity*, UNEP/CBD/COP/7/21, 2004, para. 16.

110 Secretariat of the Convention on Biological Diversity, *Ad Hoc* Technical Expert Group on Marine and Coastal Protected Areas (AHTEG), *Technical Advice on the Establishment and Management of a National System of Marine and Coastal Protected Areas* (CBD Technical Series No. 13, 2004) p. 7. AHTEG used the term 'Marine and Coastal Protected Area' in order to make it clear that its advice to the parties to the Rio Convention applies to coastal areas as well as the sea. *Ibid.*

Within the context of national and regional efforts to promote integrated marine and coastal area management, networks of marine and coastal protected areas, other conservation areas, and biosphere reserves, provide useful and important management tools for different levels of conservation, management and sustainable use of marine and coastal biological diversity and resources, consistent with customary international law.[111]

It is interesting to note that in this language, MPAs are regarded as a tool for integrated ocean management. Such a linkage between MPAs and integrated ocean management is also highlighted in the Jakarta Mandate of 1995.[112]

Specifically, Article 8 (a) of the Rio Convention provides that each Contracting Party shall, 'as far as possible and as appropriate', establish a system of protected areas or areas where special measures need to be taken to conserve biological diversity. This qualification by the words 'as far as possible and as appropriate' shows that in practice the Contracting Parties have a large discretion relating to the establishment of protected areas. It should also be noted that the Marine and Coastal Protected Area in the Rio Convention can be established only within the marine spaces under coastal State jurisdiction.[113] Article 8 (b) of the Rio Convention requires each Contracting Party to develop 'where necessary, guidelines for the selection, establishment and management of protected areas or areas where special measures need to be taken to conserve biological diversity'. Article 8 (c) imposes on each Contracting Party to 'regulate or manage biological resources important for the conservation of biological diversity whether within or outside protected areas, with a view to ensuring their conservation and sustainable use'. Similarly each Contracting Party is obliged to 'promote environmentally sound and sustainable development in areas adjacent to protected areas with a view to furthering protection of these areas' in conformity with Article 8 (e). It is interesting to note that the Rio Convention sets out an obligation to conserve biological diversity both within and outside protected areas.

---

111 COP of the Convention on Biological Diversity, *Annex to Recommendation I/8 of the Convention on Biological Diversity*, UNEP/CBD/COP/2/5, 1995, para. 9.

112 Para. 10 (a) and (b) of Recommendation 1/8. The Jakarta Mandate consists of the recommendations formulated by the first SBSTTA meeting in September 1995 and the subsequent decision taken by the Second Meeting of the Conference of the Parties in November 1995. For the Jakarta Mandate, see M.M. Goote, 'Convention on Biological Diversity: The Jakarta Mandate on Marine and Coastal Biological Diversity' (1997) 12 *IJMCL*, pp. 377–95.

113 D.K. Anton, 'Law for the Sea's Biological Diversity', in J.I. Charney, D.K. Anton and M.E. O'Connell (eds), *Politics, Values and Functions: International Law in the 21st Century. Essays in Honour of Professor Louis Henkin* (The Hague, Nijhoff, 1997) p. 341; R. Warner, 'Marine Protected Areas Beyond National Jurisdiction – Existing Legal Principles and Future Legal Frameworks', paper presented at the *Expert Workshop on Managing Risks to Biodiversity and the Environment on High Seas, including Tools such as MPAs, Scientific Requirement and Legal Aspects* (Federal Agency for Nature Conservation, Isle of Vilm, Germany, February 2001) p. 158.

On the other hand, a question arising is the compatibility between the creation of MPAs and other legitimate use of the oceans. Article 22 (2) of the Rio Convention requires Contracting Parties to 'implement this Convention with respect to the marine environment consistently with the rights and obligations of States under the law of the sea'. In this respect, of particular importance is the interrelationship between MPAs and the freedom of navigation. Given that navigation concerns highly important economic and military activities, the 1982 LOSC carefully safeguards the right of navigation in each jurisdictional zone. Thus, ships of all States have the right of innocent passage in the territorial sea.[114] The coastal State shall not hamper the innocent passage of foreign ships through the territorial sea in conformity with Article 24 (1) of the LOSC. The coastal State may suspend innocent passage only temporarily.[115] Furthermore, all ships and aircraft enjoy the right of transit passage in international straits where Part III of the LOSC is applied.[116] There shall be no suspension of transit passage.[117] Moreover, all ships and aircraft enjoy the right of archipelagic sea lanes passage in archipelagic waters under Article 53 (2) of the LOSC. Article 52 (2) of the LOSC sets out that the archipelagic State may suspend only 'temporarily' the innocent passage of foreign ships if such suspension is essential for the protection of its security. In the EEZ, all States enjoy the freedoms of navigation and overflight by virtue of Article 58 (1) of the LOSC. In light of these provisions, it is arguable that the establishment of MPAs which totally exclude vessels would be contrary to the LOSC.[118] Accordingly, it could well be said that MPAs in the Rio Convention must be balanced with the freedom of navigation in accordance with the LOSC as well as customary law.[119]

MPAs in Regional Legal Instruments – A Case Study of the North-East Atlantic

Considering that the marine environment and its biological diversity are not homogeneous, it is conceivable that threats to marine biological diversity may vary depending on the regions. For instance, the threats against the deep-water coral reefs will not be the same as those against marine ecosystems in the enclosed

---

114 Article 17 of the LOSC.

115 Article 25 (3) of the LOSC.

116 Article 38 of the LOSC.

117 Article 44 of the LOSC.

118 R. Wolfrum and N. Matz, 'The Interplay of the United Nations Convention on the Law of the Sea and the Convention on Biological Diversity' (2000) 4 *Max Planck Yearbook of United Nations Law*, p. 467.

119 M. Chandler, 'The Biodiversity Convention: Selected Issues of Interest to the International Lawyer' (1993) 4 *Colorado Journal of International Environmental Law and Policy*, pp. 152–3.

or semi-enclosed seas.[120] Indeed, while the primary threats to the deep-water coral reefs which are found on the seabed of certain regions concern fishing activities, including deep-sea bottom trawling, arguably the major threats against marine ecosystems in the enclosed or semi-enclosed seas relate mainly to land-based marine pollution. Accordingly, there will be a need to tailor any rules protecting marine biological diversity to take the particular circumstances of each region into account.

In fact, State practice has shown that regional treaties creating MPAs concerning the conservation of marine living resources as well as the protection of the marine environment have been concluded particularly since the 1980s. Those regional treaties cover: the Antarctic, the West and Central African Region, the Wider Caribbean Region, the Eastern African Region, the South Pacific Region, the South-East Pacific Region, the Mediterranean Sea, the Baltic Sea, and the North-East Atlantic.[121] Apart from the Mediterranean Sea, basically the creation of MPAs is limited to marine spaces under national jurisdiction. As the examination of each and every regional treaty falls outside of this study because of the limitation of space, this section will address as an example MPAs in the North-East Atlantic area.

Development of MPAs in the North-East Atlantic

In the North-East Atlantic area, the 1992 OSPAR Convention provides a principal legal framework for the protection of the marine environment. As discussed earlier, a remarkable feature of the Convention is its evolutionary approach.[122] Although there is no explicit provision concerning MPAs in the original text of the OSPAR Convention, the concept of MPAs was formulated through the OSPAR Commission. In 1998, the Sintra Statement called for the OSPAR Commission to 'promote the establishment of a network of marine protected areas to ensure the sustainable use and protection and conservation of marine biological diversity and its ecosystems'.[123] In 2003, a series of documents relating to MPAs was adopted under the auspices of the OSPAR Commission:[124]

---

120 Oral, above note 61, p. 107.

121 See Table 5.1.

122 See Chapter 4.

123 This Statement is available at the home page of the OSPAR Commission <http://www.ospar.org/>.

124 Those documents are available at the home page of the OSPAR Commission. *Ibid.*

(i)   OSPAR Recommendation 2003/3 on a Network of Marine Protected Areas (hereafter OSPAR Recommendation);[125]

(ii)   Guidelines for the Identification and Selection of Marine Protected Areas in the OSPAR Maritime Area (hereafter the Identification Guidelines);[126]

(iii)   Guidelines for the Management of Marine Protected Areas in the OSPAR

(iv)   Maritime Area (hereafter the Management Guidelines);[127]

(v)   Strategies of the OSPAR Commission for the Protection of the Marine Environment of the North-East Atlantic (hereafter the 2003 OSPAR Strategies).[128]

A common purpose of those documents is the establishment of the OSPAR Network of Marine Protected Areas.[129] The OSPAR Recommendation makes explicit that it seeks to ensure that by 2010 there is an ecologically coherent network of well-managed MPAs.[130] In relation to this, the OSPAR Recommendation provides three purposes of the OSPAR MPAs:

> a. protect, conserve and restore species, habitats and ecological processes which are adversely affected as a result of human activities;
> b. prevent degradation of and damage to species, habitats and ecological processes, following the precautionary approach;
> c. protect and conserve areas that best represent the range of species, habitats and ecological processes in the maritime area.[131]

---

125 *Summary Record OSPAR 2003*, OSPAR 03/17/1-E, Annex 9 (Ref. § A-4.44a), Bremen, 23–27 June 2003.

126 *Summary Record OSPAR 2003*, Reference number: 2003-17, OSPAR 03/17/1-E, Annex 10 (Ref. § A-4.44b (i)), Bremen, 23–27 June 2003.

127 *Summary Record OSPAR 2003*, Reference number: 2003-18, OSPAR 03/17/1-E, Annex 11 (Ref. §A-4.44b (ii)), Bremen, 23–27 June 2003.

128 This document is available at <http://www.ospar.org/eng/html/welcome.html>.

129 OSPAR Recommendation, above note 125, p. 2, para. 2.1; the Identification Guidelines, above note 126, p. 1, para. 2; the Management Guidelines, above note 127, p.1, para. 2; the 2003 OSPAR Strategies, above note 128, para. 4.3.c. and 4.4.

130 OSPAR Recommendation, above note 125, p. 2, para. 2.1. According to the Recommendation, 'the OSPAR Network of Marine Protected Areas' means 'those areas which have been, and remain, reported by a Contracting Party under paragraph 3.1, paragraph 3.2 or paragraph 3.4 below, together with any other area in the maritime area outside the jurisdiction of the Contracting Parties which has been included as a component of the network by the OSPAR Commission'. *Ibid.*, para. 1.1.

131 *Ibid.*, p. 2, para. 2.1. These aims were confirmed in para. 4 of the Identification Guidelines as well as the Management Guidelines.

In accordance with the Management Guidelines, the OSPAR Network should take into account the linkages between marine ecosystems and the dependence of some species and habitats on processes that occur outside the MPA most directly concerned.[132] In order to establish the OSPAR Network of MPAs, the OSPAR Recommendation requires each Contracting Party to report to the Commission the areas that it has selected as components of the OSPAR Network of Marine Protected Areas.[133] Specifically, criteria for the identification and selection of MPAs are provided by the Identification Guidelines. In accordance with these Guidelines, the process of identification and selection of MPAs is divided into two stages.

The first stage concerns the identification of possible sites. For this stage, the ecological criteria/considerations listed in Appendix 1 are to be applied.[134] These criteria/considerations include: (i) threatened or declining species and habitats/biotopes; (ii) important species and habitats/biotopes; (iii) ecological significance; (iv) high natural biological diversity; (v) representativity; (vi) sensitivity; and (vii) naturalness.[135]

The second stage relates to the prioritisation of sites for designation. In this stage, the ecological criteria/considerations in Appendix 1 should be reapplied in order to help prioritise the identified sites. Furthermore, the practical criteria/considerations in Appendix 2 should be taken into account with a view to developing a prioritised list of sites.[136] These criteria/considerations comprise: (i) size; (ii) potential for restoration; (iii) degree of acceptance; (iv) potential for success of management measures; (v) potential damage to the area by human activities; and (vi) scientific value.[137] The Identification Guidelines stress that OSPAR MPAs should form an ecologically coherent network of well-managed MPAs. This is particularly important for highly mobile species, such as certain birds, mammals and fish, to safeguard the critical stages and areas of their life cycle.[138] It is worth noting that the institution of MPAs is developing through the OSPAR Commission. Thus, the OSPAR Convention will provide an interesting example of the 'evolution' of a multilateral treaty.[139]

---

132 The Identification Guidelines, above note 126, p. 1, para. 5; the Management Guidelines, above note 127, p. 1, para. 5.

133 *Ibid.*, para. 3.1.b.

134 The Identification Guidelines, above note 126, p. 2, para. 7.

135 *Ibid.*, p. 3, Appendix 1.

136 *Ibid.*, p. 2, para. 9.

137 *Ibid.*, p. 4, Appendix 2.

138 *Ibid.*, p. 1, paras 5–6.

139 On this issue, see, for instance, A. Boyle, 'Further Development of the Law of the Sea Convention: Mechanisms for Change' (2005) 54 *ICLQ*, pp. 563–84.

Network of MPAs in the North-East Atlantic

It is of particular interest that a network of MPAs is developing in the North-East Atlantic region. In this respect, the OSPAR Management Guidelines consider that the establishment of OSPAR MPAs will contribute to and take account of Contracting Parties' obligations under other international Conventions and Directives, which include: EC Directives, the Bern, Bonn and Ramsar Conventions, the Convention on Biological Diversity, the Helsinki Convention, the Barcelona Convention, the Trilateral Wadden Sea Co-operation and the North Sea Conference.[140] The 2003 OSPAR Strategy also requires the OSPAR Commission to contribute to the development of the Natura 2000 network and the implementation of the EC's Council Directive 92/43/EEC on the Conservation of Natural Habitats and Wild Flora and Fauna (hereafter the Habitats Directive),[141] and the Council Directive 79/409/EEC on the Conservation of Birds.[142] In this respect, of particular importance will be the inter-linkage between the MPAs in the OSPAR Convention and the Habitats Directive.

The Habitats Directive requires each Member State to create 'special areas of conservation'. In the wording of Article 3 (2) of the Directive:

> Each Member State shall contribute to the creation of Natura 2000 in proportion to the representation within its territory of the natural habitat types and the habitats of species referred to in paragraph 1. To that effect each Member State shall designate, in accordance with Article 4, sites as *special areas of conservation* taking account of the objectives set out in paragraph 1.[143]

Furthermore, according to Article 1 (l) of this Directive:

> *special area of conservation* means a site of Community importance designated by the Member States through a statutory, administrative and/or contractual act where the

---

140 The Management Guidelines, above note 127, p. 1, para. 2.

141 OJ No. L206, 22.7.92, pp. 0007–0050; last amended by Council Directive 97/62/EC of 27 October 1997, OJ No. L305, 8.11.97, pp. 0042–0065. See also L. Krämer, *EC Environmental Law*, 4th edn, (London, Sweet and Maxwell, 2000) pp. 135–40. The full examination of the role of the EC in the conservation of biological diversity in general is beyond the scope of this study. With respect to this issue, the following studies are of particular interest: P. Birnie, 'The European Community and Preservation of Biological Diversity', in C. Redgwell and M. Bowman (eds), *International Law and the Conservation of Biological Diversity* (The Hague, Kluwer, 1996) pp. 211–34; A. Kiss and D. Shelton, *Manual of European Environmental Law*, 2nd edn (Cambridge, Cambridge University Press, 1997) pp. 181–249; A. Nollkaemper, 'Habitat Protection in European Community Law: Evolving Conceptions of a Balance of Interests' (1997) 9 *Journal of Environmental Law*, pp. 271–86.

142 2003 OSPAR Strategies, above note 128, para. 3.1.

143 Emphasis added.

necessary conservation measures are applied for the maintenance or restoration, at a favourable conservation status, of the natural habitats and/or the populations of the species for which the site is designated.[144]

As the Habitats Directive is applicable to marine spaces under national jurisdiction, it is conceivable that special areas of conservation can be created in these spaces.[145] In special areas of conservation, Member States are obliged to establish the necessary conservation measures involving, if need be, appropriate management plans specifically designated for the sites or integrated into other development plans, and appropriate statutory, administrative or contractual measures which correspond to the ecological requirements of the natural habitat types in Annex I and the species in Annex II present on sites in conformity with Article 6 (1). Under Article 6 (2), Member States are also required to take appropriate steps to avoid the deterioration of natural habitats and the habitats of species, as well as disturbance of the species for which the areas have been designated, in so far as such disturbance could be significant in relation to the objectives of this Directive. If a plan or project must nevertheless be carried out for imperative reasons of overriding public interest, including those of a social or economic nature, the Member State is required to take all compensatory measures necessary to ensure that the overall coherence of Natura 2000 is protected. At the same time, it shall inform the Commission of the compensatory measures adopted.[146]

The OSPAR Convention attempts to ensure the inter-linkage between MPAs under the Convention and 'Specially Protected Areas' under the Habitats Directive. Indeed, the network of MPAs may include areas in the OSPAR maritime area which the Contracting Parties which are EU Member States are required to designate as Special Areas of Conservation or Specially Protected Areas under the EC Habitats and Birds Directives.[147] Specifically where a Contracting Party is required, under the EC Birds Directive or the EC Habitats Directive, to designate any area in the maritime area as a Special Protection Area or a Special Area of Conservation, the Contracting Party may report that area to the OSPAR Commission as a component of the OSPAR Network of MPAs, as if the Contracting Party had selected it as such.[148] In this case, the Contracting Party is required to send to the OSPAR

---

144 In addition, Article 1 (j) states that: 'site means a geographically defined area whose extent is clearly delineated'.

145 There is a view that the scope of the Directive could be extended to the outer limits of the continental shelf. R. Long and A. Grehan, 'Marine Habitat Protection in Sea Areas under the Jurisdiction of a Coastal Member State of the European Union: The Case of Deep-Water Coral Conservation in Ireland' (2002) 17 *IJMCL*, pp. 248–50; 253–5.

146 Article 6 (4) of the Habitats Directive.

147 2003 OSPAR Strategies, above note 128, para. 4.3 (c). The 2003 OSPAR Strategies require that by 2010, the areas forming part of this network will be formally designated and management plans will have been adopted for them. *Ibid.* See also para. 4.4.

148 The OSPAR Recommendation, above note 125, p. 3, para. 3.5.a.

Commission copies of any reports which it makes to the European Commission about that area.[149] On the other hand, the Contracting Party should be under no obligations under the 2003 OSPAR Recommendation to take any action in respect of that area.[150]

In practice, it can be observed that various MPAs are being formulated in the North-East Atlantic area. For instance, in 2004, a Western European PSSA was established in the North-East Atlantic.[151] The application of the PSSA encompasses the western coasts of the United Kingdom, Ireland, Belgium, France, Spain and Portugal, from the Shetland Isles in the north to Cape Vicente in the South, including the English Channel and its approaches.[152] In this area, in 1996, Belgium designated a Special Area of Conservation in that environment under the Habitats Directive. Part of the sandbanks of the coastal zone of Belgium was designated as wetlands of international importance under the Ramsar Convention. Belgium is also in the process of establishing three Special Protection Areas for seabirds in the area.[153] Similarly, in the North-East Atlantic and the Bay of Biscay coasts, Spain established various protected areas, such as the Atlantic Islands National Park, Ramsar areas, special areas for the protection of birds and areas of common European interest, included within the Natura 2000, under European Directives on birds and habitats, and biosphere reserves under the UNESCO programme on man and biosphere.[154] Arguably, the network of MPAs in the same region will enhance the effectiveness of the protection of biological diversity. Considering that legal bases as well as conservation measures may vary according to the MPA, however, further consideration should be given to positive co-ordination among different MPAs in order to ensure a consistency of protective measures.[155]

---

149 *Ibid.*, para. 3.5.c.

150 *Ibid.*, para. 3.5.b.

151 IMO Resolution MEPC. 121 (52), *Designation of the Western European Waters as a Particularly Sensitive Sea Area*, 15 October 2004. With respect to the Western European PSSA, see M. Detjen, 'The Western European PSSA – Testing a Unique International Concept to Protect Imperilled Marine Ecosystems' (2006) 30 *Marine Policy*, pp. 442–53. Roberts, above note 19, pp. 143–50; Frank, above note 72, pp. 30–37; Roberts *et al.*, above note 78, pp. 431–40.

152 IMO Resolution MEPC. 121 (52), above note 151, p. 2, para. 1.1.

153 *Ibid.*, p. 4, para. 2.1.9.

154 *Ibid.*, pp. 5–6, paras 2.1.13–2.1.15. These regions have a remarkable cultural, scientific and touristic value to Spain.

155 In this respect, the 2003 OSPAR Strategies require that: 'To promote consistency, other relevant measures which have been agreed or are being negotiated by some or all Contracting Parties in other forums shall be taken into account in the light of their applicability to different geographical areas.' Above note 128, para. 3.2.

Analysis – Need for Inter-Linkage between MPAs, Environmental Protection and the Regulation of Fisheries

The above survey demonstrates that the establishment of MPAs is increasingly reflected in binding and non-binding instruments at global as well as regional levels. On the other hand, concern is voiced that, in many cases, MPAs have not been effective in meeting their objectives because of problems related to their management, size and habitat coverage.[156] Thus, further consideration should be given to the effectiveness of MPAs for the conservation of marine biological diversity.[157] Obviously this question invites a multi-disciplinary consideration. From the viewpoint of international law, special emphasis should be placed on the inter-linkage between MPAs and environmental protection as well as the regulation of fisheries.

---

156 The Convention on Biological Diversity, Conference of the Parties, Decision VII/5, *Review of the Programme of Work on Marine and Coastal Biodiversity*, 2004, para. 13. The *Ad Hoc* Technical Expert Group pointed to eleven commonly recurring themes for the failure of marine protected areas to achieve their objectives. Those problems include:

(a) Insufficient financial and technical resources to develop and implement management plans or lack of trained staff;

(b) Lack of scientific data and information for management decisions, including information on the impacts of resource use and on the status of biological resources;

(c) Lack of public support and unwillingness of users to follow management rules, often because users have not been involved in establishing such rules;

(d) Inadequate commitment to enforcing management rules and regulations;

(e) Unsustainable use of resources occurring within Marine and Coastal Protected Areas (MCPAs);

(f) Impacts from activities in land and sea areas outside the boundaries of MCPAs, including pollution and overexploitation;

(g) Lack of clear organisational responsibilities for management and absence of co-ordination between agencies with responsibilities relevant to MCPAs;

(h) Problems related to the size and habitat coverage of MCPAs;

(i) Conflicting objectives of the MCPA;

(j) Lack of national or regional networks of MCPAs; and

(k) Lack of understanding and integration of social and economic issues into the establishment and management of MCPAs.

Convention on Biological Diversity *Ad Hoc* Technical Expert Group on Protected Areas, *Report of the Ad Hoc Technical Expert Group on Marine and Coastal Protected Areas*, UNEP/CBD/AHTEG-PA/1/INF/5, 6 June 2003, p. 10.

157 On this issue, see, for instance, S.C. Jameson, M.H. Tupper and J.M. Ridley, 'The Three Screen Doors: Can Marine "Protected" Areas be Effective?' (2002) 44 *Marine Pollution Bulletin*, pp. 1177–83.

Need for Inter-Linkage between MPAs and Environmental Protection

MPAs and the Protection of the Marine Environment   The first issue which needs some reflection pertains to the need for inter-linkage between the MPAs for the conservation of marine biological diversity and the protection of the marine environment. Given that marine species cannot be separated from the marine environment, the protection of the environment is of vital importance in the conservation of marine biological diversity. While sources of marine pollution may vary, the 1982 LOSC specifies six sources: (i) pollution from land-based sources; (ii) pollution from sea-bed activities subject to national jurisdiction; (iii) pollution from activities in the Area; (iv) pollution by dumping; (v) pollution from vessels; (vi) pollution from or through the atmosphere. Among those sources, land-based pollution represents the single most important cause of marine pollution.[158] In reality, the threat of land-based marine pollution is a serious one since it mainly affects coastal waters, which are sites of high biological diversity.[159] Adverse impacts from land-based marine pollution are more serious in shallow enclosed or semi-enclosed coastal sea areas than in open oceanic areas.[160] Nevertheless, MPAs relating directly to the conservation of marine biological diversity, such as protected areas in the Rio Convention, cannot, on their own, protect marine biological diversity from marine pollution since usually the regulation of marine

---

158   It is suggested that land-based sources contribute approximately 80 per cent of marine pollution. UN General Assembly, *Report of the Secretary-General, Oceans and the Law of the Sea*, 18 August 2004, A/59/62/Add.1, p. 29, para. 97. In accordance with the report, sewage remains the largest source of contamination. *Ibid.* To date, there is no global agreement relating to the regulation of land-based marine pollution, and such pollution is regulated primarily by a limited number of regional agreements. Currently conventions and protocols on land-based marine pollution have been concluded in the following regions: the Baltic Sea, the Black Sea, the Mediterranean Sea, the North-East Atlantic, the Kuwait Region, the South-East Pacific, and the Wider Caribbean Sea. On the other hand, no specific protocol in this field has been developed in the East Asian Seas, Red Sea and Gulf of Aden, South Pacific, West and Central Africa, East Africa, the North-East Pacific, the North-West Pacific, the South Asian Seas, the South-West Atlantic, and Arctic. With respect to recent studies on the regulation of land-based marine pollution, see for instance D. Hassan, *Protecting the Marine Environment from Land-Based Sources of Pollution: Towards Effective International Cooperation* (Hampshire, Ashgate, 2006); Tanaka, above note 106, pp. 535–74.

159   S. Kuwabara, *The Legal Regime of Protection of the Mediterranean Against Pollution from Land-Based Sources* (Dublin, Tycooly International Publishing Ltd, 1984) xvii; A. Nollkaemper, 'Balancing the Protection of Marine Ecosystems with Economic Benefits from Land-Based Activities: the Quest for International Legal Barriers' (1996) 27 *ODIL*, p. 154.

160   P. Birnie and A. Boyle, *International Law and Environment*, 2nd edn (Oxford, Oxford University Press, 2002) pp. 410–11. This does not, however, deny a possibility that certain persistent materials may contaminate the open oceanic areas. A.L. Dahl, 'Land-Based Pollution and Integrated Coastal Management' (1993) 17 *Marine Policy*, pp. 561–2.

pollution is beyond the scope of the MPAs.[161] Similarly MPAs relating to the prevention of pollution from shipping activities – such as 'clearly defined areas' in Article 211 (6) of the LOSC, ice-covered areas in Article 234 of the LOSC, special areas under MARPOL 73/78, and PSSA in IMO Guidelines – are unable to protect vulnerable marine ecosystems from marine pollution other than vessel-source pollution. Hence, there are good reasons to argue that MPAs for the conservation of marine biological diversity must be combined with the regulation of marine pollution in an integrated manner.

In this respect, it is worth noting that regional agreements creating MPAs seek to enhance the linkage between the conservation of vulnerable marine ecosystems and marine environmental protection in a (quasi-)comprehensive manner.[162] An interesting example may be furnished by the so-called 'Barcelona system' in the Mediterranean Sea. The 'Barcelona system' is composed of several treaties relating to the protection of the marine environment of the Mediterranean Sea as well as the conservation of marine biological diversity.[163] Apart from vessel-source pollution, marine pollution is to be regulated in a quasi-comprehensive manner by combining these treaties within the Barcelona system.[164] In the Mediterranean Sea, the creation of MPAs is explicitly provided for in two treaties: the 1995 Protocol Concerning Specially Protected Areas and Biological Diversity (hereafter the 1995 Specially Protected Areas Protocol) and the 1999 Agreement on the Creation in the Mediterranean Sea of a Sanctuary for Marine Mammals between France, Italy

---

161 D. Freestone, 'The Conservation of Marine Ecosystems under International Law', in Redgwell and Bowman, above note 141, p. 94.

162 See the list in Table 5.1.

163 At present, the Barcelona system contains the following treaties: (i) the 1995 Convention for the Protection of the Marine Environment and the Coastal Region of the Mediterranean; (ii) the 1976 Protocol for the Prevention of the Pollution of the Mediterranean Sea by Dumping from Ships and Aircraft, as amended in Barcelona on 10 June 1995; (iii) the 2002 Protocol Concerning Co-operation in Combating Pollution of the Mediterranean Sea by Oil and Other Harmful Substances in Cases of Emergency; (iv) the 1980 Protocol for the Protection of the Mediterranean Sea against Pollution from Land-Based Sources, as amended in Syracuse on 7 March 1996; (v) the 1995 Protocol Concerning Specially Protected Areas and Biological Diversity, which replaced the 1982 Protocol Concerning Mediterranean Specially Protected Areas; (vi) the 1994 Protocol for the Protection of the Mediterranean Sea Against Pollution Resulting from Exploration and Exploitation of the Continental Shelf and the Seabed and its Subsoil; (vii) the 1996 Protocol on the Prevention of Pollution of the Mediterranean Sea by Transboundary Movements of Hazardous Wastes and their Disposal; (viii) the 2008 Protocol on Integrated Coastal Zone Management in the Mediterranean. I am obliged to Professor Scovazzi for information on the Balcerona system. With respect to the Barcelona system, see T. Scovazzi, 'New International Instruments for Marine Protected Areas in the Mediterranean Sea', in Strati, Gavouneli and Skourtos, above note 61, pp. 111–12.

164 Yet it should be noted that some conventions have not yet entered into effect.

and Monaco (hereafter the 1999 Sanctuary Agreement).[165] Those MPAs in the Mediterranean Sea will be placed within the Barcelona system. Thus it is possible that the linkage between the MPAs and the Barcelona system will enhance the effectiveness of MPAs in the Mediterranean Sea.

MPAs and Climate Change Furthermore, special attention should be drawn to adverse impacts of climate change on marine biological diversity. It is acknowledged that the role of terrestrial and marine ecosystems as sinks and reservoirs of greenhouse gases is particularly important.[166] At the same time, it should be noted that the marine environment is sensitive to climate and atmospheric changes.[167] In fact, the Report of the *Ad Hoc* Technical Expert Group (AHTEG) on Biodiversity and Climate Change of 2003, established by the SBSTTA of the Rio Convention, suggests that climate change can affect marine ecosystems in many ways, modifying ecosystem structure and functioning.[168] According to the report, changes in the physical and chemical characteristics of the ocean and seas (for instance, currents or circulation patterns, nutrient availability, pH, salinity, and the temperature of the ocean waters) will affect marine ecosystems.[169] For instance, some ecosystems, including coral reefs, are particularly vulnerable to climate change. In fact, the AHTEG suggested that coral reefs would be impacted detrimentally if sea surface temperatures increase by more than 1°C above the seasonal maximum temperature.[170] It is also reported that climate change could affect food chains, particularly those that include marine mammals.[171] There are also growing concerns that global warming will accelerate sea-level rise and cause significant damage to small islands and low-lying coasts.[172] Thus, the UN General Assembly urged 'the international community to provide effective and timely support to countries affected by sea-level rise, particularly developing countries, in their efforts to develop and implement strategies to protect themselves and their

---

165 These documents will be discussed later in this chapter.

166 In its Preamble, the United Nations Framework Convention on Climate Change acknowledges the role and importance in terrestrial and marine ecosystems of sinks and reservoirs of greenhouse gases.

167 Agenda 21, para. 17.96. See also J. van Ettinger, 'Oceans, Climate Change, and Energy' (1993) 10 *Ocean Yearbook*, pp. 132–46.

168 Convention on Biological Diversity, SBSTTA, *Biological Diversity and Climate Change, Report of the Ad Hoc Technical Expert Group on Biodiversity and Climate Change*, UNEP/CBD/SBSTTA/9/INF12, 30 September 2003, pp. 27–43, paras 37–72.

169 *Ibid.*, p. 38, para. 64.

170 *Ibid.*, p. 37, para. 63. The same concern was voiced by UNESCO. See, for instance, UNESCO, *Case Studies on Climate Change and World Heritage* (Paris, UNESCO World Heritage Centre, 2007) pp. 30–35.

171 SBSTTA, above note 168, p. 38, para. 67.

172 J. van Ettinger, above note 167, p. 136. Agenda 21, para. 17.97. See also D. Freestone, 'International Law and Sea Level Rise', in R. Churchill and D. Freestone (eds), *International Law and Global Climate Change* (London, Nijhoff, 1991) pp. 109–25.

vulnerable natural marine ecosystems from the particular threats of sea-level rise caused by climate change'.[173]

Nonetheless, MPAs cannot, in themselves, prevent adverse impacts upon marine biological diversity by climate change. In this respect, it is notable that the COP of the Rio Convention is increasing its co-operation with the United Nations Framework Convention on Climate Change (hereafter the Climate Change Framework Convention).[174] The COP of the Rio Convention, at its fifth meeting, noted that there was significant evidence that climate change is a primary cause of the recent and severe extensive coral bleaching, and this evidence is sufficient to warrant remedial measures being taken in line with the precautionary approach. Thus, the COP of the Rio Convention urged the Climate Change Framework Convention 'to take all possible actions to reduce the effect of climate change on water temperatures and to address the socio-economic impacts on the countries and communities most affected by coral bleaching'.[175] Furthermore, the COP of the Rio Convention called for collaboration with the Climate Change Framework Convention in the development and implementation of a specific work plan on coral bleaching. These actions include the initiation of efforts to develop joint actions among the Rio Convention, the Climate Change Framework Convention and the Ramsar Convention in order to: (i) develop approaches for assessing the vulnerability of coral-reef species to global warming; (ii) build capacity for predicting and monitoring the impacts of coral bleaching; (iii) identify approaches for developing response measures to coral bleaching; and (iv) provide guidance to financial institutions, including the Global Environment Facility, to support such activities.[176] Considering that terrestrial and oceanic ecosystems can make a significant contribution to reducing the build up of greenhouse gases in the

---

173 UN General Assembly Resolution, *Possible Adverse Effects of Sea-Level Rise on Islands and Coastal Areas, Particularly Low-lying Coastal Areas*, A/RES/44/206, 22 December 1989.

174 Convention on Biological Diversity, *Climate Change and Biological Diversity: Cooperation between the Convention on Biological Diversity and the United Nations Framework Convention on Climate Change, Note by the Executive Secretary of the Convention on Biological Diversity submitted to the Conference of the Parties to the United Nations Framework Convention on Climate Change (UNFCCC) at its Sixth Session and the UNFCCC Subsidiary Body on Scientific and Technological Advice at the Second Part of its Thirteenth Session, The Hague, 13–24 November 2000*. This document is available on the homepage of the Convention on Biological Diversity <http://www.cbd.int/default.shtml>.

175 Above note 168 (*Biological Diversity and Climate Change*), p. 2, para. 4.

176 *Ibid.*, para. 5.

atmosphere,[177] it appears that the objectives of the two Conventions are interacting, and to a large extent mutually supportive.[178]

Need for Inter-Linkage between MPAs and the Regulation of Fisheries

A second issue to be addressed in this section relates to the need for a positive co-ordination between fisheries and MPAs. There is little doubt that fishing activities are one of the major threats to marine biological diversity. Nevertheless, one may observe a general trend that fisheries treaties and biodiversity-related treaties are usually concluded as distinct legal instruments. With few exceptions,[179] the regulation of fisheries is not addressed in treaties with respect to the conservation of marine biological diversity; conversely, treaties regulating fisheries do not directly address the conservation of marine biological diversity. Consequently, there is an interruption between two legal fields.[180] Furthermore, given that the conservation of marine living resources in the EEZ has been ineffective, it appears questionable whether MPAs can effectively protect marine biological diversity in the EEZ. Hence, there appears to be a strong need to promote a positive co-ordination between the MPAs and the regulation of fisheries with a view to enhancing the effectiveness of MPAs. In this respect, it is worth noting that Article 7 (b) of the 1999 Sanctuary Agreement requires Parties to comply with international regulations and those of the EC regarding the use and the keeping of fishing

---

177 Convention on Biological Diversity, *Ad Hoc* Technical Expert Group on Biodiversity and Climate Change, *Interlinkages between Biological Diversity and Climate Change and Advice on the Integration of Biodiversity Considerations into the Implementation of the United Nations Framework Convention on Climate Change and its Kyoto Protocol, Draft Executive Summary* (CBD Technical Series 10) (Montreal, Secretary of the Convention on Biological Diversity, 2003) p. 4, para. 13.

178 In light of negative impacts on natural and cultural world heritage, the collaboration between the World Heritage Convention and the UNFCCC is also becoming a subject of consideration. On this issue, see 'Predicting and Managing the Effects of Climate Change on World Heritage: A Joint Report from the World Heritage Centre, Its Advisory Bodies, and a Broad Group of Experts to the 30th Session of the World Heritage Committee (Vilnius, 2006)', WHC-06/30.COM/7.1, p. 37, para. 61.

179 Exceptionally, the 1990 Protocol Concerning Specially Protected Areas and Wildlife to the Convention for the Protection and Development of the Marine Environment of the Wider Caribbean Region requires each Party to take measures concerning the regulation or prohibition of fishing, hunting, taking or harvesting of endangered or threatened species of fauna and flora and their parts or products within the protected area (Article 5 (2.4.)). Similarly, the 1985 Protocol Concerning Protected Areas and Wild Fauna and Flora in the Eastern African Region obliges the Contracting Parties to regulate fishing and hunting and the capture of animals and harvesting of plants within the protected area (Article 10 (d)).

180 Convention on Biological Diversity, *Ad Hoc* Open-Ended Working Group on Protected Areas, *Options for Cooperation for the Establishment of Marine Protected Areas in Marine Areas Beyond the Limits of National Jurisdiction*, UNEP/CBD/WG-PA/1/2, 20 April 2005, p. 13, para. 33.

equipment known as 'driftnet'. The Parties are also required to exchange views to promote the adoption of regulations relating to the use of new fishing equipment that could result in the indirect capture of marine mammals or that could endanger their sources of prey in conformity with Article 7 (c). Considering that fisheries may, directly or indirectly, have adverse impacts on marine mammals, the linkage between the protection of marine mammals and the regulation of fisheries in the Sanctuary Agreement is worth noting.

At the same time, attention should be drawn to the fact that MPAs could be ineffective or even counter-productive for fisheries if designed with lack of attention to the needs of fisheries. For instance, it is likely that the establishment of an MPA could displace fishers from traditional fishing areas, forcing them to more remote fishing areas, increasing operational costs and possibly risks to crew life. Consequently, fishers may simply concentrate fishing effort in other areas. Furthermore, MPAs may disrupt traditional arrangements and exploitation patterns on migratory species, increasing sources of conflict. Similarly, MPAs may disrupt coastal livelihoods, potentially depriving them of their traditional processing and trade activities. Thus, it is not surprising that there is still commonly a strong resistance from the fishing community to the concept of excluding fishing from traditional fishing grounds.[181] Overall it would appear that the effectiveness of MPAs relies essentially on the sound balance between the requirement of the conservation of marine biological diversity and the need for economic, social and political development of each State.

The above considerations appear to reveal that as marine issues are interrelated, an integrated management approach co-ordinating the regulations of various marine issues is indispensable in order to enhance the effectiveness of MPAs. Thus, it may be concluded that MPAs are not a tool for integrated ocean management, but the integrated management approach is needed for the proper management of MPAs.

MPAs in Marine Spaces beyond the Limits of National Jurisdiction

The last issue to be addressed in this chapter is MPAs beyond the limits of national jurisdiction.[182] A fundamental question arising here concerns the legal ground

---

181 FAO, Committee of Fisheries, Twenty-Sixth Session, *Marine Protected Areas (MPAs) and Fisheries*, COFI/2005/8, 7–11 March 2005, p. 4, para. 8.

182 With respect to the analysis of this issue, see Gjerde, above note 27, pp. 515–28; T.R. Young, 'Developing a Legal Strategy for High Seas Marine Protected Areas', Legal Document in IUCN, WCPA and WWF High Seas Marine Protected Areas Workshop, Malaga, 15–17 January 2003, pp. 1–36; S. Gubbay, 'Protecting the Natural Resources of the High Seas', Scientific Document in *ibid.*, pp. 1–29; R. Warner, 'Marine Protected Areas Beyond National Jurisdiction: Existing Legal Principles and Future Legal Frameworks', in Workshop on Managing Risks to Biodiversity and the Environment on the High Seas, Including Tools Such as Marine Protected Areas – Scientific Requirements and Legal

for creating MPAs in marine spaces beyond the limit of national jurisdiction in positive international law. Despite pioneer studies on MPAs, it would seem that the legal ground of such MPAs is still in a state of flux. Considering this issue, distinction should be made between the high seas which are located within the potential EEZ of the coastal State (the high seas in a broad sense) and the high seas beyond 200 nautical miles (the high seas in a strict sense), because the legal status of those areas is not the same. Furthermore, there is a need to conceptually distinguish MPAs in the Area and those in superjacent waters to the Area, namely the high seas.[183] The former concerns the protection of marine biological diversity in the seabed and its subsoil, while the latter relates to the protection of such diversity in the waters. Given that there are seamounts, cold-water coral reefs and hydrothermal vents located in the seabed beyond the limit of national jurisdiction, that is to say, the Area, strictly speaking, MPAs protecting those sites and species should be called MPAs in the Area. On the other hand, threats to those deep seabed ecosystems are often caused by activities from superjacent waters to the Area, namely the high seas. Accordingly, it may be argued that high seas MPAs will also serve for the conservation of biological diversity in the Area. In this sense, it may be said that MPAs on the high seas and MPAs in the Areas are closely interrelated.

MPAs on the High Seas

MPAs on the High Seas in a Broad Sense   A typical example of the high seas in a broad sense may be provided by the Mediterranean Sea.[184] In this region, large extents of waters located beyond the 12-mile limit remain the high seas, as most Mediterranean States have not yet established 200-mile EEZs. Should coastal States establish their EEZs in the Mediterranean Sea, however, the whole area will fall into the EEZs of these States. In this sense, high seas areas in the Mediterranean Sea can be regarded as a *potential* EEZ of the coastal State. In the

---

Aspects; H. Thiel, 'Approaches to the Establishment of Protected Areas on the High Seas', in A. Kirchner (ed.), *International Marine Environmental Law: Institutions, Implementation and Innovations* (The Hague, Kluwer, 2003) pp. 169–92; Scovazzi, above note 78, pp. 1–17.

183   Under the 1982 LOSC, superjacent waters to the Area are the high seas. Yet the seabed of the high seas is not always the Area. The seabed of the high seas may be the continental shelf beyond the 200 nautical miles.

184   Concerning the situation of the Mediterranean Sea, see T. Scovazzi, 'Les zones côtières en Méditerranée: evolution et confusion' (2001) 4 *Annuaire du droit de la mer*, pp. 95–108; M. Vœlckel, 'Comment vit la zone économique exclusive?' *ibid.*, pp. 111–14; B. Vukas, 'State Practice in the Aftermath of the UN Convention on the Law of the Sea: The Exclusive Economic Zone and the Mediterranean Sea,' in Strati *et al.*, above note 61, pp. 251–8.

Mediterranean Sea, two treaties provide for the establishment of MPAs on the high seas in the broad sense.[185]

The first treaty which needs to be discussed in this context is the 1995 Specially Protected Area Protocol (hereafter the 1995 Protocol).[186] The 1995 Protocol is applicable to all the marine waters of the Mediterranean Sea, the seabed and its subsoil, as well as the terrestrial coastal areas designated by each of the Parties, including wetlands.[187] The 1995 Protocol establishes two types of MPAs in the Mediterranean Sea: 'Specially Protected Areas' (SPAs) and 'Specially Protected Areas of Mediterranean Importance' (SPAMIs). SPAs may be established in the marine and coastal zones subject to its sovereignty or jurisdiction in accordance with Article 5 (1) of the 1995 Protocol. On the other hand, under Article 9 (1) of the Protocol, SPAMIs may be established in: '(a) the marine and coastal zones subject to the sovereignty or jurisdiction of the Parties; (b) *zones partly or wholly on the high seas*' (emphasis added). It follows that SPAMIs are to be established on the high seas in the broad sense.

With respect to SPAMIs, the Parties agree to recognise the particular importance of these areas for the Mediterranean; and to comply with the measures applicable to the SPAMIs and not to authorise nor undertake any activities that might be contrary to the objectives for which the SPAMIs were established.[188] In this regard, the Parties are required to draw up a List of Specially Protected Areas of Mediterranean Importance (SPAMI List) in order to promote co-operation in the management and conservation of natural areas, as well as in the protection of threatened species and their habitats.[189] The SPAMI List may include sites which:

– are of importance for conserving the components of biological diversity in the Mediterranean;
– contain ecosystems specific to the Mediterranean area or the habitats of endangered species;
– are of special interest at the scientific, aesthetic, cultural or educational levels.[190]

---

185 With respect to MPAs in the Mediterranean Sea, see Scovazzi, above note 163, pp. 109–20.

186 The text of the 1995 Protocol is reproduced in Scovazzi, above note 1, pp. 163 ff. With respect to an analysis of this Protocol, see Scovazzi, above note 163, pp. 112–15.

187 Article 2 (1) of the 1995 Protocol. Geographical scope is determined by Article 1 (1) of the Convention for the Protection of the Mediterranean Sea against Pollution, adopted in 1976 and amended in 1995.

188 Article 8 (3) of the 1995 Protocol.

189 Article 8 (1) of the 1995 Protocol.

190 Article 8 (2) of the 1995 Protocol. Section B (2) of Annex I of the 1995 Protocol enumerates general features of the areas that could be included in the SPAMI List. Those requirements include: uniqueness, natural representativeness, diversity, naturalness, presence of habitats that are critical to endangered, threatened or endemic species, cultural representativeness.

Procedures for the establishment and listing of SPAMIs are provided in Article 9 of the 1995 Specially Protected Area Protocol in some detail. If the area is situated in a zone already delimited, over which it exercises sovereignty or jurisdiction, proposals for inclusion in the List may be submitted only by the Party concerned in conformity with Article 9 (2) (a). Should SPAMIs be situated, partly or wholly, on the high seas, proposals for inclusion in the List may be submitted by two or more neighbouring Parties by virtue of Article 9 (2) (b). Where the limits of sovereignty or jurisdiction have not yet been defined, proposals for inclusion in the List may be submitted by the neighbouring Parties concerned in areas under Article 9 (2) (c). Parties making proposals for inclusion in the SPAMI List shall provide the Regional Activity Centre for Specially Protected Areas with an introductory report containing information on the area's geographical location, its physical and ecological characteristics, its legal status, its management plans and the means for their implementation, as well as a statement justifying its Mediterranean importance.[191] Furthermore, proposals made under Article 9 (2) shall indicate the protection and management measures applicable to the area as well as the means of their implementation.[192] In the case of areas situated, partly or wholly, on the high seas or in a zone where the limits of national sovereignty or jurisdiction have not yet been defined, the legal status, the management plan, the applicable measures and the other elements provided for in Article 9 (3) of the Protocol will be provided by the neighbouring Parties concerned in the proposal for inclusion in the SPAMI List.[193] With respect to SPAMIs partly or wholly situated on the high seas, the neighbouring Parties concerned shall consult each other with a view to ensuring the consistency of the proposed protection and management measures, as well as the means for their implementation.[194] In this case, the decision to include the area in the SPAMI list shall be taken by consensus by the Contracting Parties under Article 9 (4) (c). Currently the first twelve SPAMIs have been inscribed in the List: the island of Alborán, the sea bottom of the Levante de Almería, the Cape of Gata-Nijar, Mar Menor and the oriental coast of Murcia, the Cape of Cresus, the Medas island, the Coulembretes island (proposed by Spain), Port-Cros (proposed by France), the Kneiss island, La Galite, Zembra and Zembretta (proposed by Tunisia), and the French-Italian-Monegasque Sanctuary (jointly proposed by the three States concerned as a result of the trilateral agreement in 1999 on the creation of a sanctuary for marine mammals). The last SPAMI covers areas of the high seas.[195]

---

191 Article 9 (3) of the 1995 Protocol.

192 Article 9 (3) (b) of the 1995 Protocol.

193 C (3) of Annex I of the 1995 Protocol.

194 Article 9 (3) (a). This procedure is also applicable where a proposed area is situated in areas where the limits of national sovereignty or jurisdiction have not yet been defined.

195 Scovazzi, above note 163, pp. 114–15.

A second treaty establishing MPAs on the high seas in the broad sense is the 1999 Sanctuary Agreement.[196] Article 2 of the 1999 Agreement calls for the Parties to establish a marine sanctuary within the area of the Mediterranean Sea as defined in Article 3, whose biological diversity and richness represent an indispensable attribute for the protection of marine mammals and their habitats. Under Article 3, the sanctuary is composed of marine areas situated within the internal waters and territorial seas of the French Republic, Italian Republic and the Principality of Monaco, as well as portions of adjacent high seas. The Sanctuary extends over 96,000 square kilometres and is habited by the eight cetacean species regularly found in the Mediterranean.[197] It is of particular interest that Article 16 seeks to link the Sanctuary with SPAMIs once the 1995 Protocol enters into force for the States Parties. Within the Sanctuary, the Parties shall prohibit any deliberate take or intentional disturbance of marine mammals. Nevertheless, the non-lethal take of individuals shall be authorised in case of emergency situations or within the scope of scientific activities carried out in situ and in compliance with the terms of this Agreement.[198]

With respect to the implementation of this Agreement, Article 14 (2) provides that:

> In the other parts of the sanctuary [on the high seas], each of the State Parties is responsible for the application of the provisions of the present Agreement with respect to ships flying its flag as well as, within the limits provided for by the rules of international law, with respect to ships flying the flag of third States.

Hence, importantly, this provision appears to empower the States Parties to enforce the provisions of the 1999 Agreement on vessels of third States 'within the limits established by the rules of international law'. A question arising is how one should consider the relationship between this provision and the fundamental rule of treaty law, *res inter alios acta*. In this regard, it must be remembered that even though the areas covered by these agreements remain high seas, they will fall under the potential EEZ of either of the Parties to the conventions. In other words, the coastal States have potential by a legal title of EEZ over the area concerned. It would seem to follow that the coastal States have jurisdiction over conservation of living resources, although technically those areas remain the high seas. Hence, when taking conservation measures on high seas in the broad sense, it may be argued that the coastal States are only exercising jurisdiction to a lesser degree than that in an EEZ. In accordance with this interpretation, such measures will not necessarily

---

196 With respect to the 1999 Sanctuary Agreement, see Scovazzi, above note 47, pp. 132–41. The text of the Agreement is reproduced in *ibid.*, pp. 142–5.

197 These species are: the fin whale, the sperm whale, Cuvier's beaked whale, the long-finned pilot whale, the striped dolphin, the common dolphin, the bottlenose dolphin and Risso's dolphin. Scovazzi, above note 163, p. 115.

198 Article 7 (a).

be contrary to international law, since arguably those who can do more can also do less.[199] A typical example is the exclusive fishery zone. The concept of exclusive fishery zone is more limited than that of EEZ in the sense that exclusive fishery zone relates only to fisheries, whereas the concept of the EEZ also includes activities in the seabed. While in reality several States have created 200-nautical mile exclusive fishery zones, the validity of such a zone has not been disputed. Similarly, it might be argued that a coastal State may exercise the same jurisdiction which is exercisable in an EEZ, that is, jurisdiction concerning the conservation of marine biological diversity, in the marine spaces within 200 nautical miles, even if that State has not claimed an EEZ. Hence, it appears that, arguably at least, the coastal State may be entitled to establish MPAs on the high seas in the broad sense.

MPAs on the High Seas in a Strict Sense   To date, there are few treaties creating MPAs on the high seas in a strict sense. A possible instance is the 1986 Convention for the Protection of the Natural Resources and Environment of the South Pacific Region (hereafter 1986 Noumea Convention). Article 14 of the 1986 Noumea Convention places an obligation upon the Parties to take all appropriate measures to protect and preserve rare or fragile ecosystems and depleted, threatened or endangered flora and fauna, as well as their habitat in the Convention Area. To this end, Article 14 obliges Parties to establish protected areas, such as parks and reserves, and prohibit or regulate any activity likely to have adverse effects on the species, ecosystems or biological processes that such areas are designed to protect. In relation to this, the Convention Area contains:

> (i) the 200 nautical mile zones established in accordance with international law off: […]; (ii) *those areas of high seas which are enclosed from all sides by the 200 nautical mile zones referred to in sub-paragraph (i)*; (iii) areas of the Pacific Ocean which have been included in the Convention Area pursuant to article 3.[200]

It would seem to follow that textually the Parties establish protected areas in the Convention Area, which contains part of the high seas in a strict sense. It must be noted, however, that Article 14 immediately adds that: 'The establishment of such areas shall not affect the rights of other Parties or third States under international law.' It follows that regulatory measures of the coastal State are applicable only to its nationals. Hence, it is debatable whether the 1986 Noumea Convention provides a proper precedent for establishing MPAs on the high seas in a strict sense.

In reality, it would seem that the establishment of MPAs on the high seas in a strict sense will encounter considerable difficulties in theory and practice. A first difficulty relates to the lack of specific rules of international law in this matter. Currently there is no global treaty which provides for the creation of MPAs on the

---

199 Scovazzi, above note 78, p. 15.
200 Article 2 of the 1986 Noumea Convention. Emphasis added.

high seas in a strict sense. It is true that States are obliged to protect and preserve the marine environment, including rare or fragile ecosystems, by virtue of Articles 192 and 194 (5) of the 1982 LOSC. Furthermore, all States have the duty to take, or co-operate with other States in taking, such measures for their respective nationals as may be necessary for the conservation of the living resources of the high seas in conformity with Article 117 of the 1982 LOSC. States are also under the obligation to co-operate with each other in the conservation and management of living resources in the areas of the high seas in accordance with Article 118. Nonetheless, it appears that these general obligations do not directly provide for any right of States with regard to the establishment of MPAs on the high seas in a strict sense.[201] Due to their nature, to establish high seas MPAs is to close a part of the marine spaces of the high seas. Given that no State can claim territorial sovereignty or sovereign rights over parts of the high seas in a strict sense, however, it must be said that no State can unilaterally establish MPAs in the high seas.[202] Hence, the conclusion appears inevitable that the creation of MPAs on the high seas in a strict sense remains highly controversial in positive international law.[203]

A second difficulty pertains to the incompatibility with the principle of the freedom of the high seas. It would seem that the establishment of MPAs on the high seas in a strict sense may run the risk of limiting the freedom of the high seas, in particular, the freedom of navigation, freedom to lay submarine cables and pipelines, freedom of fishing and of scientific research. Considering that various actors and activities are involved on the high seas, it is foreseeable that the proper balance between the protection of marine biological diversity on the high seas in a strict sense and other legitimate use of the oceans will be highly difficult to achieve. Historically the freedom of the high seas has been formulated by oceanic powers with a view to promoting their national interests through free navigation. It would appear that the essential nature of freedom of the high seas remains intact

---

201 The AHTEG has considered that high seas areas presented a special situation in which existing legal instruments, including the Rio Convention, did not necessarily provide an adequate basis for the establishment of protected areas; therefore, the establishment of protected areas in the high seas would out of necessity need to be based on collaboration and co-operation between all user nations of a given area. Convention on Biological Diversity, *Ad Hoc* Technical Expert Group on Protected Areas, *The Role of Protected Areas within the Convention on Biological Diversity*, UNEP/CBD/AHTEG-PA/1/INF/1, 6 June 2003, paras 54–61.

202 Scovazzi, above note 78, p. 5.

203 The delegation of Norway advocated, in the Fourth Meeting of the United Nations Open-ended Informal Consultative Process on Oceans and the Law of the Sea, which was convened in 2003, that the establishment of protected areas in the high seas would appear to be in conflict with the prohibition of Article 89 of the LOSC, under which 'no State may validly purport to subject any part of the high seas to its sovereignty'. *United Nations Open-ended Informal Consultative Process on Oceans and the Law of the Sea, Protection and Conservation of Vulnerable Marine Ecosystems in Areas Beyond National Jurisdiction, Submitted by the Delegation of Norway*, A/AC.259/10, 4 June 2003, p. 2, paras 3–4.

today. Should MPAs affect the navigation of vessels including submarines, it is foreseeable that the creation of MPAs on the high seas will encounter strong opposition from naval powers.[204] It is true that any principle, including the freedom of the high seas, must be understood in relation to the evolution of legal systems and in the light of the peculiar circumstances under which it should apply.[205] In reality, however, States will accept legal regulation only if it will adequately reflect their national interests. It would seem that this condition is not yet fulfilled with respect to the creation of MPAs on the high seas in a strict sense.

A third difficulty relates to the procedural legitimacy of MPAs on the high seas in a strict sense. Considering that the creation of MPAs on the high seas in a strict sense may restrict the traditional freedoms of the high seas, the legitimacy of those MPAs is of central importance. In order to ensure such legitimacy, much consideration should be given to the formulation of objective criteria identifying the need to establish MPAs on the high seas in a strict sense. To this end, it will be advisable to establish a global institutional mechanism to evaluate scientific data as objectively as possible. In this respect, the universality and transparency of the decision-making process will become particularly important.

Fourthly, it appears that MPAs on the high seas in a strict sense will face considerable difficulty as to their practical implementation. Even if some States agreed to conserve marine biological diversity on the high seas by establishing MPAs, such an agreement could not be applicable to ships flying the flag of non-Parties. No State can claim that vessels flying a foreign flag must abide by the relevant provisions in positive international law.[206] In this regard, it must be remembered that under Article 194 (4) of the LOSC, States shall refrain from unjustifiable interference with activities carried out by other States in the exercise of their rights and in pursuance of their duties in conformity with the LOSC in taking measures to protect the marine environment, including rare or fragile marine ecosystems. Hence, further reflection will be needed with respect to the universal participation of States in the scheme of MPAs. Overall the conclusion seems inescapable that the validity and effectiveness of MPAs on the high seas in a strict sense remain a matter for discussion.

MPAs in the Area

The 1982 LOSC contains no specific provision with respect to MPAs in the Area. On the other hand, it should be noted that the Council of the International Seabed Authority (hereafter the Authority) may disapprove areas for exploitation by contractors or the Enterprise where there is the risk of serious harm to the marine environment. Furthermore, Regulation 31 (7) of the Mining Code requires

---

204　S. Kaye, 'Implementing High Seas Biodiversity Conservation: Global Geopolitical Considerations' (2004) 28 *Marine Policy*, pp. 223–4.

205　Scovazzi, above note 78, p. 6.

206　Scovazzi, above note 78, p. 5. See also Article 87 (2) of the LOSC.

the Contractor to propose areas to be set aside and used exclusively as impact reference zones and preservation reference zones.[207] Given that cold-water coral reefs are attached to the seabed, it would seem that the creation of those zones may serve for the protection of marine ecosystems in the deep seabed.[208] In the case of deep seabed genetic resources, however, caution is required, as a complete prohibition on access to the deep seabed area would be counterproductive in restricting scientific advancement or industrial and medicinal processes.[209]

A difficult question arising here relates to the regulation of fishing activities causing adverse impacts upon marine ecosystems of the Area. This problem is a serious one since marine ecosystems in seamounts and deep-water corals – which contain genetic resources – are mainly threatened by fishing activities, including bottom trawling.[210] In this respect, the UN General Assembly Resolution 60/30 called upon States and international organisations to urgently take action to address, in accordance with international law, destructive practices that have adverse impacts on marine biodiversity and ecosystems, including seamounts, hydrothermal vents and cold-water corals.[211] Nevertheless, under the 1982 LOSC, the Authority has no jurisdiction regulating fishing activities in superjacent waters to the Area. In order to prevent adverse impacts arising from fishing activities, there is an urgent need to enhance co-operation among the fishing States, regional fisheries bodies and the Authority.

Conclusion

The results of the survey in this chapter can be summarised in four points.

(i) In the light of the increasing importance of the conservation of marine biological diversity, the need to establish MPAs is increasingly voiced in various documents. At the global level, MPA-related concepts are reflected in the 1982 LOSC ('clearly defined area' in Article 211 (6) as well as 'ice-covered areas' in Article 234), MARPOL 73/78 ('special areas'), IMO Guidelines ('PSSA'), Montreal Guidelines ('specially protected areas'), and the Rio Convention

---

207 The 2000 Mining Code is reproduced in E.D. Brown, *Sea-bed Energy and Minerals: The International Legal Regime, Vol. 3, Selected Documents* (The Hague, Nijhoff, 2001) pp. 256–310.

208 T. Scovazzi, 'Mining, Protection of the Environment, Scientific Research and Bioprospecting: Some Considerations on the Role of the International Sea-Bed Authority' (2004) 19 *IJMCL*, p. 396.

209 Convention on Biological Diversity, SBSTTA, *Marine and Coastal Biodiversity: Review, Further Elaboration and Refinement of the Programme of Work*, UNEP/CBD/SBSTTA/8/INF/3/Rev.1, 22 February 2003, p. 23, para. 90.

210 United Nations, *Report of the Secretary-General, Oceans and the Law of the Sea*, A/59/62, 4 March 2004, p. 62, para. 245; pp. 60–61, paras 236–8.

211 UN General Assembly, *Oceans and Law of the Sea*, A/RES/60/30, 8 March 2006, pp. 13–14, para. 77.

('protected area'). It should be noted, however, that apart from 'protected area' in the Rio Convention, these concepts relate in essence to the regulation of vessel-source pollution, and they are not designed directly to protect marine biological diversity. While the effectiveness of these MPAs must be verified through State practice, it would seem that at the present stage, the practical role of the 'clearly defined area', 'ice-covered areas', 'PSSA' and 'specially protected areas' remains modest.

(ii) As threats to marine biological diversity may vary depending on the regions, a regional legal framework which contains more specific rules will assume considerable importance in this field. In fact, there are many agreements creating MPAs at the regional level. In this respect, the evolutionary approach of the OSPAR Convention and the development of a network of MPAs in the North-East Atlantic are worth noting.

(iii) On the other hand, concern is voiced that MPAs often fail to meet their objectives because of a lack of effectiveness. In order to enhance efficacy of MPAs, there is a strong need to strengthen the inter-linkage between MPAs on the one hand and the protection of the marine environment as well as the regulation of fisheries on the other hand. Hence, it is argued that the integrated management approach is required in the effective management of MPAs.

(iv) With respect to MPAs in marine spaces beyond the limits of national jurisdiction, a clear distinction should be drawn between MPAs on the high seas in the broad sense, those on the high seas in a strict sense, and those in the Area. Arguably, the coastal State has a right to create MPAs on the high seas in the broad sense in accordance with international law, since those areas fall under the potential EEZ of the coastal State, and, thus, the coastal State potentially has a legal title of EEZ over the area concerned. On the other hand, it appears that the creation of MPAs on the high seas in a strict sense represents considerable legal and practical difficulties. Such difficulties include:

– the lack of specific rules of international law;
– the possible incompatibility with the principle of the freedom of the high seas;
– the lack of procedural legitimacy identifying MPAs on the high seas; and
– the difficulty to ensure the universal participation of States in the scheme of MPAs on the high seas.

The conclusion seems inevitable that, at the present stage at least, the establishment of MPAs on the high seas in a strict sense remains a matter for discussion in positive international law.

PART III
Marine Scientific Research as a Foundation of Ocean Governance

The Obligation to Co-operate in Marine Scientific Research and Conservation of Marine Living Resources and Biological Diversity

Introduction

Nature of the Problem

There is little doubt that rules regulating the use of the ocean must be based on the sound scientific understanding of the marine environment. It is no exaggeration to say that marine scientific research is a foundation of ocean governance.[1] Indeed, the proper conservation of living resources and biological diversity in the oceans becomes possible only on the basis of sufficient and credible scientific data relating to marine species and ecosystems. It must also be noted that the assessment of the marine scientific data directly influences the determination of maximum sustainable yield (MSY) and the allocation of total allowable catch

---

1 The following are of particular interest on this issue. F.H.T. Wegelein, *Marine Scientific Research: The Operation and Status of Research Vessels and Other Platforms in International Law* (Leiden and Boston, Kluwer, 2005); M. Gorina-Ysern, *An International Regime for Marine Scientific Research* (New York, Transnational Publishers, 2003); J.A. Roach, 'Marine Scientific Research and the New Law of the Sea' (1996) 27 *ODIL*, pp. 59–72; E. Jarmache, 'Sur quelques difficultés de la recherche scientifique marine', in *La mer et son droit: Mélanges offerts à Laurent Lucchini et Jean-Pierre Quéneudec* (Paris, Pedone, 2003) pp. 303–14; A. de Marffy, 'Marine Scientific Research', in R-J. Dupuy and D. Vignes (eds), *A Handbook on the New Law of the Sea*, Vol. 2 (Dordrecht, Nijhoff, 1991) pp. 1127–46; A. de Marffy, 'Les difficultés posées par la mise en application du nouveau régime de la recherche scientifique marine avant l'entrée en vigueur de la Convention des Nations Unies sur le droit de la mer' (1989) 35 *AFDI*, pp. 736–51; T. Treves, 'Principe du consentement et nouveau régime juridique de la recherche scientifique marine', in D. Bardonnet and M. Virally (eds), *Le nouveau droit international de la mer* (Paris, Pedone, 1983) pp. 269–85; A.H.A. Soons, *Marine Scientific Research and the Law of the Sea* (Antwerp, Kluwer Law and Taxation Publishers, 1982); L. Caflisch and J. Piccard, 'The Legal Régime of Marine Scientific Research and the Third United Nations Conference on the Law of the Sea' (1978) 38 *ZaöRV*, pp. 848–901; United Nations, Office for Ocean Affairs and the Law of the Sea, *The Law of the Sea: Marine Scientific Research, A Guide to the Implementation of the Relevant Provisions of the United Nations Convention on the Law of the Sea* (New York, United Nations, 1991).

(TAC). In particular, as typically shown in the *Southern Bluefin Tuna* case of 1999, divergence in opinions concerning scientific evidence may produce international disputes concerning TAC. Hence the conducting of marine scientific research to obtain credible scientific data is of critical importance with a view to taking proper conservation measures and preventing disputes in this field.

It would appear that due to the highly complex nature of the ocean, even the strongest countries with the strongest marine scientific capacity could not clarify mechanisms of the ocean alone. Hence, it is natural that international co-operation is required in marine scientific research.[2] In light of the increasing need for such co-operation, it is important to examine the questions to what extent the legal basis for such co-operation exists in international law and how it is possible to promote international scientific co-operation.

Against this background, this chapter seeks to examine the obligation to co-operate in marine scientific research in the context of the conservation of living resources and biological diversity in the oceans. After briefly clarifying the concept of marine scientific research in the first section, the second section will address obligations to co-operate in marine scientific research in treaties concerning marine living resources and marine biological diversity. The next section will study the linkage between marine scientific research and the ecosystem approach, as well as the precautionary approach. The fourth section will examine the conditions to enhance effectiveness of the obligation to co-operate in marine scientific research. Finally, conclusions will be added.

The Concept of Marine Scientific Research in International Law

In the ordinary meaning, the term 'marine scientific research' may be defined as any scientific study or related investigation, wherever conducted, having the marine environment as its object.[3] The term 'marine environment' is understood to cover three elements, that is, seabed and the subsoil, adjacent water column and the atmosphere above the sea.[4] Obviously the marine environment contains marine

---

2 R.J.H. Beverton, 'Introduction', in E.D. Brown and R.R. Churchill (eds), *The UN Convention on the Law of the Sea: Impact and Implementation, Proceedings of Law of the Sea Institute Nineteenth Annual Conference* (Honolulu, University of Hawaii, 1987) p. 363.

3 Soons, above note 1, pp. 6–7 and 124. See also T. Treves, 'Marine Research', in R. Bernhardt (ed.), *Encyclopedia of Public International Law*, Vol. 3 (Amsterdam, Elsevier,1997) p. 295.

4 A.H.A. Soons, 'Marine Scientific Research Provisions in the Convention on the Law of the Sea: Issues of Interpretation', in Brown and Churchill, above note 2, p. 366. In particular, it is important to note that the marine environment includes the atmosphere above the oceans. For instance, the concepts of internal waters and territorial seas cover the air space above these waters. Concerning the EEZ, Article 58 (1) of the LOSC stipulates that '[i]n the exclusive economic zone', all States enjoy the freedoms of overflight. It follows that the airspace over the EEZ is to be considered part of the EEZ. Soons and Kuwahara

life. It would seem to follow that the concept of marine scientific research covers any scientific investigation, however and wherever, which concerns the marine environment as well as its organisms.[5] On the other hand, scientific research not concerning the marine environment, such as astronomical observations carried out at sea, is not regarded as marine scientific research.[6]

In international law of the sea, marine scientific research is usually divided into two rubrics: 'fundamental' or 'pure' research, and 'applied' or 'resource-oriented' research. This distinction dates back to the 1958 Geneva Convention on the Continental Shelf,[7] and is maintained in the 1982 UN Convention on the Law of the Sea (hereafter the 1982 LOSC). Although the 1982 LOSC does not define the precise meaning of the two types of research, 'fundamental research' may be regarded as research which is carried out 'exclusively for peaceful purposes and in order to increase scientific knowledge of the marine environment for the benefit of all mankind'.[8] On the other hand, 'applied research' can be considered that which is of 'direct significance for the exploration and exploitation of natural resources'.[9] Examples of applied research include chemical oceanographic investigations conducted for the purpose of the regulation of marine pollution, physical oceanographic investigations carried out for the purpose of enhancing long-range weather forecasting, and marine biological investigations for the purpose of the management of marine living resources.[10] As embodied in the 1958 Geneva Convention on the Continental Shelf as well as the 1982 LOSC, usually the concept of marine scientific research covers both kinds of research. Thus, the

---

in particular stress this point. Soons, above note 1, p. 177; T. Kuwahara, *Introduction to International Law of the Sea* (in Japanese) (Tokyo, Shinzansha, 2002) p. 121.

5   *Cf.* Soons, above note 4, p. 366.

6   *Ibid.*, p. 367.

7   Caflisch and Piccard, above note 1, p. 849. On this point, Article 5 (1) of the Geneva Convention on the Continental Shelf provides that the exploration and exploitation of the continental shelf must not result in 'any interference with fundamental oceanographic or other scientific research carried out with the intention of open publication', while Article 5 (8) stipulates that the consent of the coastal states shall be obtained in respect of 'any research concerning the continental shelf and undertaken there'. Article 5 (8) further adds that such consent shall not be 'normally' withheld 'if the request is submitted by a qualified institution with a view to purely scientific research into the physical or biological characteristics of the continental shelf'.

8   Article 246 (3) of the LOSC.

9   R. Churchill and V. Lowe, *The Law of the Sea*, 3rd edn (Manchester, Manchester University Press, 1999) pp. 405–6. With respect to the distinction between fundamental research and applied research, see Caflisch and Piccard, above note 1, pp. 848–53; Soons, above note 1, pp. 6–7 and124. See also Soons, above note 4, pp. 366–7.

10   Soons, above note 1, p. 7.

reference to 'marine scientific research' in this study also refers to the two types of research.[11]

For the purpose of this study, 'international co-operation in marine scientific research' may be understood in a broad sense to cover collaboration in the conduct of marine scientific research *per se* as well as the contribution or exchange of scientific information.[12] As almost all scientific work is conducted on the basis of the results of earlier investigations, the exchange of data has become an important condition for the progress of marine scientific research. In this regard, it is notable that the recent expansion of marine scientific research and the use of newly developed techniques have produced an enormous increase in the volume of oceanographic data.[13] Consequently, international co-operation is required in the exchange and management of marine scientific data. In addition, it should be noted that in certain circumstances, international collaboration between States and international organisations, such as the International Seabed Authority (hereafter the Authority), is also needed in the conduct of marine scientific research.

The Obligation to Co-operate in Marine Scientific Research in the Conservation of Marine Living Resources and Marine Biological Diversity

Global Instruments

The UN Convention on the Law of the Sea (1982)   In section 2 of Part XIII, the 1982 LOSC provides an obligation to co-operate in marine scientific research in a general manner. In this regard, Article 242 (1) stipulates: 'States and competent international organisations shall, in accordance with the principle of respect for sovereignty and jurisdiction and on the basis of mutual benefit, promote

---

11 Marine scientific research should be distinguished from the exploration (and exploitation) of natural resources, since the latter is governed by a legal framework different from that regulating marine scientific research. In this regard, Soons defines exploitation as 'data-collecting activities (scientific research) concerning natural resources, whether living or non-living, conducted specifically in view of the exploitation (i.e., economic utilization) of those natural resources'. Soons, above note 4, p. 367. In practice, however, it often appears difficult to make this distinction since the techniques used may sometimes be identical. Soons, above note 1, p. 7. See also Wegelein, above note 1, pp. 82–9.

12 In fact, as indicated in the text, the obligation to promote the flow of scientific data as well as the transfer of scientific knowledge is provided in section 2 of Part XIII concerning international co-operation in marine scientific research.

13 Soons, above note 1, p. 17. In this regard, there is a problem that in particular old scientific data could be lost from scientific memory because of poor data management or major political and social disruptions. On this issue, see D. Zeller, R. Froese and D. Pauly, 'On Losing and Recovering Fisheries and Marine Science Data' (2005) 29 *Marine Policy*, pp. 69–73.

international co-operation in marine scientific research for peaceful purposes.'[14] More specifically, Article 243 requires States and competent international organisations to co-operate 'to create favourable conditions for the conduct of marine scientific research in the marine environment and to integrate the efforts of scientists in studying the essence of phenomena and processes occurring in the marine environment and the interrelations between them'. Such co-operation is to be undertaken through the conclusion of international agreements. The need for co-operation in marine scientific research is further amplified in Article 255, which requires States to adopt reasonable rules and procedures to promote marine scientific research.[15] Article 244 (2) also ensures that States, both individually and in co-operation with other States and with competent international organisations, shall actively promote the flow of scientific data and the transfer of knowledge resulting from marine scientific research, especially to developing States. This obligation is also reflected in Annex VI of the Final Act of the UNCLOS III.[16] These obligations become particularly important in the conservation and management of marine living resources since reliable data concerning species to be harvested is a prerequisite for the establishment of an effective management scheme.

Article 2 of the 1982 LOSC provides that: '[t]he sovereignty of a coastal State extends beyond its land territory and internal waters and, in the case of an archipelagic State, its archipelagic waters, to an adjacent belt of sea, described as the territorial sea'. Except for the right of innocent passage of foreign ships in the territorial sea, therefore, the internal waters and territorial sea, including its seabed and subsoil and the superjacent air space, fall under the exclusive jurisdiction of the coastal State.[17] Consequently, any research to be conducted in internal waters or territorial sea by foreign States or by international organisations requires the

---

14 It appears that a duty of co-operation in a general context is implicit in Article 251 which requires States to 'promote through competent international organisations the establishment of general criteria and guidelines to assist States in ascertaining the nature and implications of marine scientific research'; and in Article 255 that obliges States to 'endeavour to adopt reasonable rules, regulations and procedures to promote and facilitate marine scientific research [...]'. On this point, see M.C.W. Pinto, 'The Duty of Co-operation and the United Nations Convention on the Law of the Sea', in A. Bos and H. Siblesz (eds), *Realism in Law-Making: Essays on International Law in Honour of Willem Riphagen* (Dordrecht, Nijhoff, 1986) p. 143.

15 M.H. Nordquist, S.N. Nandan and S. Rosenne (eds), *United Nations Convention on the Law of the Sea 1982: A Commentary*, Vol. IV (The Hague, Centre for Oceans Law and Policy, University of Virginia School of Law, Nijhoff, 1991, 1993, hereafter the Virginia Commentary) p. 477.

16 Annex VI is entitled 'Resolution on Development of National Marine Science, Technology and Ocean Service Infrastructures'.

17 Article 21 (1) (g) of the LOSC provides that the coastal State may adopt laws and regulations in respect of marine scientific research and hydrographic survey.

express consent of the coastal State.[18] Similarly, archipelagic waters are under the territorial sovereignty of the archipelagic States, and, thus, the conduct of marine scientific research in archipelagic waters calls for the authorisation of the archipelagic States. It follows that in marine spaces under territorial sovereignty, coastal States enjoy decisive powers over marine scientific research. It should be noted, however, that in enclosed or semi-enclosed seas, bordering States should co-operate to co-ordinate their scientific research policies and undertake where appropriate joint programmes of scientific research in the area in accordance with Article 123 (c).

In the EEZ and on the continental shelf, marine scientific research shall also be conducted with the consent of the coastal State. Nonetheless, coastal States shall, 'in normal circumstances', grant their consent for marine scientific research projects by other States or competent international organisations, which are 'exclusively for peaceful purposes and in order to increase scientific knowledge of the marine environment for the benefit of all mankind'.[19] In order to achieve the purpose of increasing 'scientific knowledge of the marine environment for the benefit of all mankind', arguably international scientific co-operation will be essential.[20] In connection with this, Article 249 (1) provides certain conditions that shall be complied with by foreign States or international organisations in undertaking marine scientific research with the approval of the coastal State. Such conditions include: ensuring the right of the coastal State to participate in the marine scientific project; providing the coastal State with the final results and conclusions; providing access for the coastal State to all data and samples derived from the marine scientific research project; providing the coastal State with an assessment of such data, samples and research results; ensuring that the research results are made internationally available, and so on. These conditions are provided with a view to balancing the interests of the coastal State and the interests of researching States or international organisations.[21] At the same time, it would appear that to some extent, these conditions may contribute to enhancing international co-operation by ensuring the participation of the coastal States as well as the publication of the results.[22]

---

18 See also Article 19 (2) (j). It should be remembered that Article 242 (1) of the LOSC prudently adds the words 'in accordance with the principle of respect for sovereignty and jurisdiction'. In addition, being the territorial sea, international straits are also under the sovereignty of the coastal State. Thus the same conclusion applies to the conduct of marine scientific research in international straits.

19 Article 246 (3). Under Article 297 (2) (a) (i), however, the coastal State is not obliged to accept the submission to the compulsory procedures embodied in Part XV of any disputes arising out of the exercise by the coastal State of a right or discretion in accordance with Article 246.

20 Jarmache, above note 1, p. 308.

21 *Virginia Commentary*, Vol. IV, above note 15, p. 540.

22 It should be noted that the coastal State enjoys full discretion as regards the granting of consent to publish the research results under Article 249 (2).

Furthermore, it would seem that international scientific co-operation in a broad sense may be required in the conservation of living resources in the EEZ. Whereas the coastal State has sovereign rights over natural resources in its EEZ, the coastal State is obliged to properly conserve the living resources 'taking into account the best scientific evidence available'.[23] In this respect, Article 61 (5) stipulates that available scientific information relevant to the conservation of fish stocks shall be contributed and exchanged on a regular basis through international organisations with participation by all States concerned, including States whose nationals are allowed to fish in the EEZ.[24] Those obligations may stimulate international co-operation in the exchange of scientific data, and diminish the risk of unilateral manipulation of data.[25] In addition to this, Part V of the 1982 LOSC concerning the EEZ adopts a distinct species-specific approach concerning each of the following categories: straddling fish stocks (Article 63), highly migratory species (Article 64), marine mammals (Article 65), anadromous stocks (Article 66), catadromous species (Article 67). In order to conserve these species, it is necessary to investigate their migrations across EEZs and high seas. In particular, it would seem that considerable studies will be needed with respect to movements of anadromous and catadromous species between their rivers of origin, internal and territorial seas, EEZs and, as appropriate, high seas. Such studies will necessitate international scientific co-operation between the coastal States and other States seeking access to such fishing.[26] In fact, conventions concerning the conservation of anadromous stocks explicitly oblige Contracting Parties to co-operate in marine scientific research on these species.[27]

On the high seas, all States enjoy freedom of scientific research. At the same time, States are required to promote the exchange of marine scientific data on the high seas. In this regard, Article 119 (2) of the 1982 LOSC calls upon all States to contribute available scientific information with respect to the conservation of the living resources of the high seas through competent international organisations.[28] It is argued that the obligation embodied in paragraph 2 is linked to the obligation in paragraph 1 (a) of the same provision, requiring all States to take conservation measures on the basis of 'the best scientific evidence available to the States concerned'. It is suggested that scientific information should include biological

---

23 Article 61 (2).

24 There is a parallel to this as regards Article 119 (2) relating to conservation of the living resources on the high seas.

25 F. Orrego Vicuña, *The Changing International Law of High Seas Fisheries* (Cambridge, Cambridge University Press, 1999), p. 27.

26 P. Birnie, 'Law of the Sea and Ocean Resources: Implications for Marine Scientific Research' (1995) 10 *IJMCL*, p. 238.

27 See, for instance, the 1999 Treaty between Canada and the United States concerning Pacific Salmon, and the 1992 Convention for the Conservation of Anadromous Stocks in the North Pacific Region.

28 *Virginia Commentary*, above note 15, Vol. III, 1995, p. 312.

data, the migratory habitats of the species in question, the fishing gear and methods utilised in harvesting those species, and the landing of each species, including incidental catches. Considering that statistics on high seas fisheries are still sporadic at best, the exchange of data is an important condition for the conservation of marine living resources.[29]

Furthermore, currently special attention should be drawn to marine scientific research in the Area, that is, the seabed and ocean floor and subsoil thereof, beyond the limits of national jurisdiction. As explained earlier, genetic resources contained in the deep seabed ecosystems have a considerable scientific and economic value.[30] Nonetheless, evidence suggests that communities surrounding the deep sea benthic ecosystems, in particular, hydrothermal vent ecosystems, are threatened primarily by marine scientific research as well as bioprospecting.[31] Research activities which may cause adverse impacts upon deep seabed ecosystems include: the removal of chimneys and rocks for geological investigations or chemical sampling; environmental manipulation; the clearing of fauna; the transplanting of fauna between locations; the placement of instruments that may disturb fauna and change water flows; the deleterious effects of light used for observation purposes on photosensitive organisms; and the use of manned submersibles and remotely operated vehicles which can damage fauna by landing on them or causing damage by the use of thrusters.[32] In order to minimise any impact on the deep seabed ecosystems from scientific investigation, there is a need for better co-operation and co-ordination among marine scientific research programmes.[33]

Considering this issue, it should be noted that under Article 143 (1) of the 1982 LOSC, marine scientific research in the Area shall be carried out exclusively for peaceful purposes and for the benefit of mankind as a whole, in accordance with Part XIII. Furthermore, Article 143 (3) makes clear that States Parties shall

---

29 *Ibid.*

30 See Chapter 4.

31 United Nations, *Report of the Secretary-General, Oceans and the Law of the Sea*, A/59/62, 4 March 2004, p. 62, para. 245. In this regard, the Secretary-General of the Authority warned that:

The international scientific community has concluded that deep sea hydrothermal vents are particularly sensitive because of their high percentage of endemic species and the unique nature of many of the species found there. Several such sites are already under potential threat either from intensive scientific exploration, including bioprospecting or from future mining activities.

International Seabed Authority, *Report of the Secretary-General of the International Seabed Authority under Article 166, paragraph 4, of the United Nations Convention on the Law of the Sea*, ISBA/8/A/5, 7 June 2002, p. 12, para. 50.

32 United Nations, *Report of the Secretary-General, Oceans and the Law of the Sea*, A/59/62, 4 March 2004, pp. 62–3, paras 245–6.

33 International Seabed Authority, *Report of the Secretary-General of the International Seabed Authority under Article 166, paragraph 4, of the United Nations Convention on the Law of the Sea*, ISBA/10/A/3, 31 March 2004, p. 43, para. 134.

promote international co-operation in marine scientific research in the Area by: (a) participating in international programmes and encouraging co-operation in marine scientific research by personnel of different countries and of the Authority; (b) ensuring that programmes are developed through the Authority or other international organisations as appropriate for the benefit of developing States and technologically less developed States; and (c) effectively disseminating the results of research and analysis when available, through the Authority or other international channels when appropriate. At the same time, the Authority itself is under the duty to promote and encourage the conduct of marine scientific research in the Area, and to co-ordinate and disseminate the results of such research and analysis when available under Article 143 (2). In fact, the Authority has promoted international collaboration with recognised scientists, representatives of contractors, the offshore mining industry and Member States in the collection and dissemination of data through a series of workshops since 1998. For instance, in 2002, the Authority convened a workshop on the prospects for international collaboration in marine scientific research.[34] The Authority is also collaborating in the Kaplan project, which is an international research project carried out in the Clarion-Clipperton zone nodule province in the Pacific Ocean.[35] This project seeks to measure biodiversity, species ranges and gene flow in the zone.[36] It can be observed that the promotion of co-ordination and co-operation of marine scientific research in the Area is becoming an important aspect of the work of the Authority.[37] Overall it appears that the Authority has a valuable role to play in organising marine scientific research of the Area in a proper manner.

---

34 The workshop focused on four key issues: (a) levels of biodiversity, species range and gene flow in abyssal nodule provinces; (b) disturbance and recolonisation processes at seafloor following mining track creation and plume resedimentation; (c) mining plume impacts on the water column ecosystems; and (d) natural variability in nodule province ecosystems. *Ibid.*, p. 41, para. 128.

35 International Seabed Authority, *Report of the Secretary-General of the International Seabed Authority under Article 166, paragraph 4, of the United Nations Convention on the Law of the Sea*, ISBA/12/A/2, 26 June 2006, p. 17, para. 69.

36 *Ibid.*

37 *Ibid.*, pp. 39–44. paras 122–36. In this respect, the Secretary-General of the Authority stated that: 'One of the most important, but so far unrealized functions of the Authority is to promote and encourage the conduct of marine scientific research in the Area, and to coordinate and disseminate the results of such research and analysis.' International Seabed Authority, *Report of the Secretary-General of the International Seabed Authority under Article 166, paragraph 4, of the United Nations Convention on the Law of the Sea*, ISBA/8/A/5, 7 June 2002, p. 9, para. 38. See also T. Scovazzi, 'Mining, Protection of the Environment, Scientific Research and Bioprospecting: Some Considerations on the Role of the International Sea-Bed Authority' (2004) 19 *IJMCL*, pp. 383–409 (in particular, pp. 397–9).

The FAO Code of Conduct for Responsible Fisheries (1995)   Since the adoption of the 1982 LOSC, the need for international co-operation in marine scientific research has been increasingly stressed in various international instruments relating to the conservation of marine living resources. For instance, the 1989 General Assembly Resolution 44/225, entitled 'Large-scale Pelagic Driftnet Fishing and Its Impact on the Living Marine Resources of the World's Oceans and Seas', calls upon all those involved in large-scale pelagic driftnet fishing to co-operate fully with the international community in the enhanced collection and sharing of statistically sound scientific data.[38] Growing concern for international co-operation in marine scientific research can also be detected in the 1995 FAO Code of Conduct for Responsible Fisheries. It is important to note that the 1995 FAO Code of Conduct sets out a dual requirement relating to marine scientific research: the requirement of the conduct of marine scientific research by each State and the requirement to co-operate on this matter.[39]

First, with respect to the requirement to conduct marine scientific research, Article 6.4 of the Code of Conduct states that: 'States should assign priority to undertake research and data collection in order to improve scientific and technical knowledge of fisheries including their interaction with the ecosystem.'[40] Article 7.4 stresses the need to compile fishery-related and other supporting scientific data relating to fish stocks by States as well as regional fisheries organisations or arrangements. More specifically, Article 12.5 provides that States should be able to monitor and assess the state of the stocks under their jurisdiction, including the impacts of ecosystem changes resulting from fishing pressure, pollution or habitat alteration; that States should also establish the research capacity necessary to assess the effects of climate or environment change on fish stocks and aquatic ecosystems. To this end, the Code of Conduct requires that States should establish a research capacity and support and strengthen national research capabilities to meet acknowledged scientific standards pursuant to Article 12.6. The results of such research should be made publicly available.[41]

Secondly, the Code of Conduct further calls for international co-operation in marine scientific research. Article 7.3.4 of the Code of Conduct requires States as well as regional fisheries management organisations and arrangements to foster and promote international co-operation and co-ordination in all matters related to fisheries, including information gathering and exchange, fisheries research, management and development. Furthermore, States are required to 'develop collaborative technical and research programmes to improve understanding of

---

38 UN General Assembly Resolution, *Large-scale Pelagic Driftnet Fishing and Its Impact on the Living Marine Resources of the World's Oceans and Seas*, A/RES/44/225, 22 December 1989, para. 2. For the text of the resolution, see <http://www.oceanlaw.net/texts/ga44_225.htm>.

39 The Code is a voluntary instrument relating to fisheries. See Article 1.1.

40 Article 6.4.

41 Article 12.8.

the biology, environment and status of transboundary aquatic stocks'.[42] At the same time, competent international organisations should, upon request, render technical and financial support to States in their research efforts.[43] It is logical that international marine scientific co-operation presupposes the action of each State to undertake marine scientific research. Hence it may be said that the two requirements are closely interconnected.

The Straddling and Highly Migratory Fish Stocks Agreement (1995)   Significantly, the dual requirement set out in the Code of Conduct was clearly enshrined as a legal obligation in the 1995 Straddling and Highly Migratory Fish Stocks Agreement (hereafter the 1995 Fish Stocks Agreement).[44] Realising that there are problems of unreliable databases and lack of sufficient co-operation between States,[45] this Agreement places an explicit obligation upon each State to undertake marine scientific research. Thus, Article 5 (k) calls for coastal States as well as States fishing on the high seas to 'promote and conduct scientific research and develop appropriate technologies in support of fishery conservation and management'.[46] Furthermore, States are under obligation not only to collect and exchange scientific, technical and statistical data with respect to fisheries for straddling and highly migratory fish stocks,[47] but also to obtain and evaluate scientific advice, review the status of the stocks and assess the impact of fishing on non-target and associated or dependent species.[48] States are also obliged to ensure that data are collected in sufficient detail to facilitate effective stock assessment and are provided in a timely manner to fulfil the requirements of subregional or regional fisheries management organisations.[49] Standard requirements for the collection and sharing of data are specified in detail in Annex I of the Agreement.[50] In so doing, it is argued that

---

42 Article 12.17.

43 Articles 12.19 and 12.20.

44 The full title of this agreement is: Agreement for the Implementation of the Provisions of the United Nations Convention on the Law of the Sea of 10 December 1982 Relating to the Conservation and Management of Straddling Fish Stocks and Highly Migratory Fish Stocks. For the text of the agreement, see (1995) 34 *ILM*, p. 1547.

45 Preamble of the 1995 Fish Stocks Agreement.

46 See also Article 10 (g).

47 Articles 14 (1) (a) and 10 (f).

48 Article 10 (d).

49 Article 14 (1) (b).

50 Such requirements include: (a) the need to ensure that data are collected from vessels flying their flag on fishing activities according to the operational characteristics of each fishing method and in sufficient detail to facilitate effective stock assessment; (b) the need to ensure that fishery data are verified through an appropriate system; (c) the need to compile fishery-related and other supporting scientific data and provide them in an agreed format and in a timely manner to the relevant subregional or regional fisheries management organisation or arrangement where one exists; (d) the need to agree on the specification of data and the format; (e) the need for regional organisations to compile data

the 1995 Fish Stocks Agreement greatly strengthens the obligations of States to collect and share marine scientific information enshrined in Articles 119 (2) and 61 (5) of the 1982 LOSC.[51] In connection with this, it is notable that Article 1 of Annex I requires that data collected should also include information on non-target and associated or dependent species. This requirement will be significant in implementing the ecosystem approach.

Due to their transfrontier nature, international co-operation is essential to the conservation of straddling and highly migratory species; and marine scientific research, which provides basic data concerning conservation, is no exception. Thus Article 14 (3) explicitly obliges States to co-operate to strengthen scientific research capacity in the field of fisheries and promote scientific research related to the conservation and management of straddling and highly migratory fish stocks for the benefit of all. Arguably the obligation to co-operate in the development of marine scientific capacity is particularly important for promoting scientific and technical assistance to developing countries. Moreover, Article 3 (2) of Annex I of the 1995 Agreement requires States to collect and provide to the relevant subregional or regional fisheries management organisation information to support stock assessment. Such information includes: (i) composition of the catch according to length, weight and sex; (ii) other biological information supporting stock assessments; and (iii) other relevant research, including surveys of abundance, biomass surveys, hydro-acoustic surveys, research on environmental factors affecting stock abundance, and oceanographic and ecological studies. It is worth noting that the 1995 Fish Stocks Agreement attempts to specify the contents of international scientific co-operation in some detail. In so doing, it may be said that the Agreement further amplifies the obligation to co-operate in marine scientific research enshrined in the 1982 LOSC.[52]

Convention on Biological Diversity (1992) The obligation to co-operate in scientific research can also be detected in the context of the conservation of (marine) biological diversity. In fact, the 1992 Convention on Biological Diversity

---

and make them available in a timely manner and in an agreed format to all interested States under the terms and conditions established by the organisation or arrangement; and (f) the need for scientists of the flag State and from the relevant regional fisheries management organisations to analyse the data separately or jointly.

51 M. Hayashi, 'The 1995 UN Fish Stocks Agreement and the Law of the Sea', in D. Vidas and W. Østreng (eds), *Order for the Oceans at the Turn of the Century* (The Hague, Kluwer, 1999) p. 40.

52 M. Hayashi, 'The Straddling and Highly Migratory Fish Stocks Agreement', in E. Hey (ed.), *Development in International Fisheries Law* (The Hague, Kluwer, 1999) p. 73. See also by the same author, 'The 1995 Agreement on the Conservation and Management of Straddling and Highly Migratory Fish Stocks: Significance for the Law of the Sea Convention' (1995) 29 *Ocean and Coastal Management*, p. 55.

(hereafter the Rio Convention), which is also applicable to marine biological diversity, sets out the dual obligation relating to scientific research.

First, with respect to the obligation to conduct scientific research, Article 12 (b) of the Rio Convention obliges the Contracting Parties to promote and encourage research which contributes to the conservation and sustainable use of biological diversity, particularly in developing countries. In this relation, the Subsidiary Body on Scientific, Technical and Technological Advice (SBSTTA) requested that Parties report on research activities related to deep seabed genetic resources beyond the limits of national jurisdiction, and ensure that the results of marine scientific research and analysis are effectively disseminated through international channels in accordance with Article 143 of the 1982 LOSC.[53]

Secondly, concerning the obligation to co-operate in scientific research, Article 12 (c) places an obligation upon the Contracting Parties to promote and co-operate in the use of scientific advances in biological diversity research in developing methods for conservation and sustainable use of biological resources. Each Contracting Party is also obliged to take measures to provide for the effective participation in biotechnological research activities by those Contracting Parties, especially developing countries under Article 19 (1). Article 18 (1) of the Rio Convention obliges the Contracting Parties to promote international technical and scientific co-operation in the field of conservation and sustainable use of biological diversity. Such co-operation includes the training of personnel and exchange of experts under Article 18 (4). In relation to this, it is notable that the Conference of the Parties (COP) requested the Executive Secretary, in consultation with Parties and other governments and the Authority, and in collaboration with international organisations, to compile information on the methods for the identification, assessment and monitoring of genetic resources of the Area.[54] In light of the primordial role of the Authority in marine scientific research in the Area, it appears that co-operation between the Contracting Parties to the Rio Convention and the Authority will be increasingly important in this field.

Regional Treaties

The obligation of co-operation in marine scientific research is also increasingly reflected in regional agreements concerning conservation of marine living

---

53 Convention on Biological Diversity, SBSTTA, *Marine and Coastal Biological Diversity: Status and Trends of, and Threats to, Deep Seabed Genetic Resources Beyond National Jurisdiction, and Identification of Technical Options for Their Conservation and Sustainable Use,* UNEP/CBD/SBSTTA/11/11, 22 July 2005, p. 6, para. 6.

54 Convention on Biological Diversity, Conference of the Parties, Decision VII/5, *Marine and Coastal Biological Diversity: Review of the Programme of Work on Marine and Coastal Biodiversity,* UNEP/CBD/COP/7/21, February 2004, p. 140, para. 54.

Table 6.1   Obligation to co-operate in marine scientific research in international instruments concerning the management of marine living resources

Year	Title	Relevant Provisions
1959	Convention Concerning Fishing in the Black Sea	Articles 1, 7
1962	Agreement Concerning Co-operation in Marine Fishing	Article 1
1980	Convention on the Conservation of Antarctic Marine Living Resources	Articles 3, 20[1]
1982	Protocol Concerning Mediterranean Specially Protected Areas	Articles 13, 14, 15
1982	United Nations Convention on the Law of the Sea	Articles 242, 61 (5), 119 (2), 143 (3)
1991	Convention on Fisheries Co-operation among African States Bordering the Atlantic Ocean	Articles 3, 15
1992	Convention for the Conservation of Anadromous Stocks in the North Pacific Ocean	Article 7
1992	Agenda 21*	Paras 17.57, 17.87.
1992	Convention on Biological Diversity	Articles 17, 18
1992	Agreement on the Conservation of Small Cetaceans of the Baltic and North Sea	Article 2 of Annex
1993	Convention for the Conservation of Southern Bluefin Tuna	Article 5 (3)
1994	Convention on the Conservation and Management of Pollock Resources Central Bering Sea	Articles 2 (3), 10
1995	FAO Code of Conduct for Responsible Fisheries*	Articles 7.3.4, 12.17
1995	Straddling Fish Stocks and Highly Migratory Fish Stocks Agreement	Article 14
1995	Protocol Concerning Specially Protected Areas and Biological Diversity in the Mediterranean	Articles 20, 22
1996	Agreement on the Conservation of Cetaceans of the Black Sea, Mediterranean Sea and Contiguous Atlantic Area	Articles 4 and 5 of Annex 2
1997	Protocol on the Conservation, Rational Utilisation and Management of Norwegian Spring Spawning Herring (Atlanto-Scandian Herring) in the North-East Atlantic	Article 5

1998	Agreement on the International Dolphin Conservation Program	Article 11 and Annex 6
1999	Treaty between Canada and the United States Concerning Pacific Salmon	Articles 3, 10, 14
1999	Agreement Concerning the Creation of a Marine Mammal Sanctuary in the Mediterranean	Article 12
2001	Convention on the Conservation and Management of Fishery Resources in the South-East Atlantic Ocean	Articles 13, 21(4)
2003	Treaty between Australia and France on Co-operation in the Maritime Areas Adjacent to the French Southern and Antarctic Territories (TAAF), Heard Island and the McDonald Islands	Article 2 and Annex II

* voluntary instrument

(Footnotes)
1 Article 3 of this convention provides that the Contracting Parties are bound by the obligation contained in Articles I and V of the Antarctic Treaty. Article III of the latter makes explicit the obligation to co-operate in scientific investigation in the Antarctic.

resources.[55] Such regional agreements concern various species, such as anadromous stocks, cetaceans, highly migratory fish species and marine biological diversity. Considering that these species are transboundary in nature, it is understandable that marine scientific co-operation is required in investigating them. At the same time, these regional treaties cover a variety of areas, such as the Black Sea, the Mediterranean Sea, the Antarctic, the Atlantic Ocean, the North Pacific Ocean, the Baltic and the North Sea, the Central Bering Sea, the North-East Atlantic as well as the South-East Atlantic Ocean. This factual situation shows that the need for international co-operation in marine scientific research is widely accepted in the conservation of various species as well as in various regions.[56] As the examination of each and every regional agreement is beyond the scope of this study, only two examples will be provided here.

Concerning a bilateral agreement, an interesting example is offered by the 1999 Treaty between Canada and the United States Concerning Pacific Salmon.[57] Article X of this treaty places an obligation upon the Parties to conduct research to investigate the migratory and exploitation patterns, the productivity and the status of stocks of common concern and the extent of interceptions. Furthermore, Parties shall allow nationals, equipment and vessels of the other Party conducting research approved by the Commission to have access to its waters for the purpose of carrying out such research. Interestingly, the Commission may make recommendations to the Parties regarding the conduct and co-ordination of research under Article X (2). Moreover, Article XIV (c) of the 1999 Treaty obliges each Party to exchange fisheries statistics and any other relevant information on a current and regular basis in order to facilitate the implementation of the Treaty. In so doing, it may be said that the 1999 Treaty clearly reflects the dual obligation relating to marine scientific research.

With respect to multilateral treaties on this issue, a typical example may be furnished by the 1992 Convention for the Conservation of Anadromous Stocks in the North Pacific Ocean (hereafter the 1992 North Pacific Convention). The remit of this Convention is to promote the acquisition, analysis and dissemination of scientific information pertaining to anadromous stocks and ecologically related species in the North Pacific Ocean. Thus Article VII (1) imposes on the Parties to co-operate in the conduct of scientific research in the North Pacific Ocean and its adjacent seas beyond 200 nautical miles, for the purpose of the conservation of anadromous stocks, including scientific research on other ecologically related species. Article VII (2) places an obligation upon the Parties to co-operate, as appropriate, in collecting, reporting and exchanging biostatistical information, fisheries data, including catch and fishing effort statistics, biological samples and other relevant data pertinent to the purposes of the Convention. In accordance with

---

55 See Table 6.1, which contains global as well as regional treaties. This list is not exhaustive.

56 Institutional mechanisms for international co-operation in marine scientific research will be studied later in the chapter.

57 The text of the treaty is available at <http://www.oceanlaw.net/texts/pcs.htm>.

Article VII (4), the Parties are under a duty to develop appropriate co-operation programmes, including scientific observer programmes, to collect fishing information in the Convention Area for the purpose of scientific research on anadromous stocks and, as appropriate, ecologically related species. The Parties shall further endeavour to co-operate in scientific exchanges such as seminars, workshops and, as appropriate, exchanges of scientific personnel necessary to achieve the objectives of this Convention pursuant to Article VII (5). Significantly, such scientific co-operation is controlled through a Commission, which is established in Article VIII. The controlling mechanisms through the Commission are worth noting, and will be studied later in the chapter.

Interrelationship between Marine Scientific Research and New Approaches to Ocean Governance

The above discussion demonstrates that the obligation to co-operate in marine scientific research is widely reflected in treaties concerning marine living resources as well as the protection of the marine environment at global and regional levels. It appears that this trend is *not* an isolated phenomenon, but is closely linked to the emergence of new approaches to the conservation of marine living resources and marine biological diversity in international law. In this respect, the interrelationship between the conduct of marine scientific research and the ecosystem approach as well as precautionary approach is worth examining.

Linkage between Marine Scientific Research and the Ecosystem Approach

As discussed earlier, the ecosystem approach is currently highlighted in a number of international instruments as a backbone of an integrated management approach.[58] It is obvious that conservation measures based on the ecosystem approach must be based on sound scientific understanding of marine ecosystems.[59] Considering that the knowledge of marine ecosystems is still inadequate, there will be a need for considerable marine scientific research concerning marine ecosystems in the application of this approach.

---

58 See Chapter 3. See also H. Wang, 'Ecosystem Management and Its Application to Large Marine Ecosystems: Science, Law, and Politics' (2004) 35 *ODIL*, pp. 41–74; S.M. Garcia and M. Hayashi, 'Division of the Oceans and Ecosystem Management: A Contrastive Spatial Evolution of Marine Fisheries Governance' (2000) 43 *Ocean and Coastal Management*, pp. 461–3.

59 For instance, the 1980 Convention on the Conservation of Antarctic Marine Living Resources (CCAMLR) clearly stated in its Preamble that 'it is essential to increase knowledge of the Antarctic marine ecosystem and its components so as to be able to base decisions on harvesting on sound scientific information'.

In this respect, science shows that the uniqueness of marine ecosystems frequently crosses maritime delimitation lines.[60] This is particularly true in the case of large marine ecosystems (LMEs), which are becoming a focal topic in ocean management.[61] According to Alexander, LMEs are extensive aggregates of fish populations which are linked together in predator–prey relationships.[62] LMEs are relatively large areas in the order of 200,000 square kilometres, and they annually produce 95 per cent of the world's fish catch.[63] The factual situation is that LMEs often cover maritime spaces under the national jurisdiction of several States.[64] Due to the transboundary nature of marine ecosystems, international co-operation is needed in the conduct of marine scientific research. In this regard, Article 6.4 of the Code of Conduct states that: 'In recognising the transboundary nature of many aquatic ecosystems, States should encourage bilateral and multilateral co-operation in research, as appropriate.' In practice, the linkage between marine scientific research and the ecosystem approach is clearly supported by the International Council for the Exploration of the Sea (ICES).[65] The ICES, established in 1902, is the world's oldest intergovernmental scientific organisation to co-ordinate scientific research,[66] and provides scientific information and advice relating to fish stocks to relevant institutions.[67] Since the early 1980s, ICES has assumed a leading position

---

60 L. Juda, 'Considerations in Developing a Functional Approach to the Governance of Large Marine Ecosystems' (1999) 30 *ODIL*, pp. 93–4.

61 Garcia and Hayashi, above note 58, p. 461. The concept of LMEs enjoys strong support from many international institutions, such as UNEP, UNDP, Global Environment Facility (GEF) and the World Bank. *Ibid.*, p. 465; L.M. Alexander, 'Large Marine Ecosystems: A New Focus for Marine Resources Management' (1993) 17 *Marine Policy*, p. 197.

62 *Ibid.*, p. 186. With respect to the large marine ecosystem, see M.H. Belsky, 'Management of Large Marine Ecosystems: Developing a New Rule of Customary International Law' (1985) 22 *San Diego Law Review*, pp. 733–63; K. Sherman, 'Achieving Regional Co-operation in the Management of Marine Ecosystems: The Use of the Large Marine Ecosystem Approach' (1995) 29 *Ocean and Coastal Management*, pp. 165–85; A.M. Duda and K. Sherman, 'A New Imperative for Improving Management of Large Marine Ecosystems' (2002) 45 *Ocean and Coastal Management*, pp. 797–833; Wang, above note 58, pp. 45–6. Information on LMEs is also available at <http://woodsmoke.edc. uri.edu/Portal/>.

63 Duda and Sherman, above note 62, p. 802.

64 Maps of LMEs are available at <http://woodsmoke.edc.uri.edu/Portal/>.

65 With respect to the structure and functions of ICES, see E.D. Anderson, 'The International Council for the Exploration of the Sea', in R. Platzöder and P. Verlaan (eds), *The Baltic Sea: New Developments in National Policies and International Co-operation* (The Hague, Kluwer, 1996) pp. 271–87.

66 Later, the ICES was given a new constitution by the 1964 Convention as well as its 1970 Protocol.

67 The ICES is the officially recognised scientific advisory body to the following organisations: North-East Atlantic Fisheries Commission (NEAFC); International Baltic

in developing the ecosystem approach.[68] In particular, the Advisory Committee on Ecosystems (ACE) was established in 2000 as the Council's official body for the provision of scientific information and advice on marine ecosystems, and on exploitation of living marine resources in an ecosystem context. Since 2001, ACE provides information and advice on marine ecosystems in accordance with requests from ICES member countries as well as other organisations.[69] By offering such scientific data and advice, the ICES assists policy-making concerning the management of marine living resources.

As an example, a close relationship between the ICES and the North-East Atlantic Fisheries Commission (NEAFC) may be noted. Article 14 of the Convention on Future Multilateral Co-operation in North-East Atlantic Fisheries requires the NEAFC to seek information and advice from the ICES on such matters as the biology and population dynamics of the fish stocks concerned, the state of the fish stocks, the effect of fishing on those stocks, and measures for their conservation and management. On the basis of such information provided by ICES, the NEAFC adopts management measures concerning fish stocks.[70] Overall it may be argued that the conduct of marine scientific research takes on a new meaning with the emergence of the ecosystem approach.

Linkage between Marine Scientific Research and the Precautionary Approach

Another issue which needs to be examined is the relationship between marine scientific research and the precautionary approach. The precautionary nature of this approach does not render scientific data unnecessary. There must be some scientific basis for predicting the possibility of harmful effects before applying the

---

Sea Fishery Commission (IBSFC); North Atlantic Salmon Conservation Organisation (NASCO); and Commission of the European Communities.

68 Anderson, above note 65, p. 279; Alexander, above note 61, p. 187.

69 *ICES Co-operation Research Report*, No. 249, *Report of the ICES Advisory Committee on Ecosystems*, 2001; *ICES Co-operation Research Report*, No. 254, *Report of the ICES Advisory Committee on Ecosystems*, 2002; *ICES Co-operation Research Report*, No. 262, *Report of the ICES Advisory Committee on Ecosystems*, 2003. These reports are available at the homepage of ICES, <http://www.ices.dk/index.asp>.

70 On this point, see in particular Articles 5, 6, 7, 8, 9 and 10 of the NEAFC Convention. Such measures, known technically as 'recommendations', are legally binding on members unless objected to during a specified period following their adoption in accordance with Article 12 of the NEAFC Convention. With respect to the linkage between the NEAFC and the ICES, see R.R. Churchill, 'Managing Straddling Fish Stocks in the North-East Atlantic: A Multiplicity of Instruments and Regime Linkage – but How Effective a Management?', in O. Schram Stokke (ed.), *Governing High Seas Fisheries: The Interplay of Global and Regional Regimes* (Oxford, Oxford University Press, 2001) p. 238. The EC is also a major 'client' of the ICES. Concerning interplay between the ICES and the common fishery policy of the EC, see O. Schram Stokke and C. Coffey, 'Precaution, ICES and the Common Fisheries Policy: A Study of Regime Interplay' (2004) 28 *Marine Policy*, pp. 117–26.

precautionary approach.[71] Hence adequate marine scientific research is required
in order to determine whether or not there is a risk of serious harm which may
trigger the application of the precautionary approach. On this point, the EC's
Communication on the Precautionary Principle clearly states that:

> Recourse to the precautionary principle presupposes that potentially dangerous
> effects deriving from a phenomenon, product or process have been identified, and that
> scientific evaluation does not allow the risk to be determined with sufficient certainty.
>   The implementation of an approach based on the precautionary principle should start
> with a scientific evaluation, as complete as possible, and where possible, identifying at
> each stage the degree of scientific uncertainty.[72]

Furthermore, the Communication unequivocally states that '[b]efore the
precautionary principle is invoked, the scientific data relevant to the risks must
first be evaluated'.[73] Similarly, in relation to the conservation of marine living
resources, the 2000 Convention on the Conservation and Management of Highly
Migratory Fish Stocks in the Western and Central Pacific Ocean makes clear
that: '[i]n applying the precautionary approach, the members of the Commission
shall: (c) develop data collection and research programmes to assess the impact of
fishing on non-target and associated or dependent species and their environment
[…].'[74] Considering that the precautionary approach may restrict activities by
States in the oceans, arguably adequate marine scientific research and reliable data
are prerequisites in the application of this approach.[75]

   In summary, the above considerations reveal that there exists a close relationship
between three elements, that is to say, marine scientific research, the ecosystem
approach and the precautionary approach. It may be said that the importance of
international co-operation in marine scientific research is underscored by the
emergence of these novel approaches to conservation of living resources and
biological diversity in the oceans.

---

71 P. Birnie and A. Boyle, *International Law and the Environment*, 2nd edn (Oxford,
Oxford University Press, 2002), p. 117; J. Wettestad, 'Science, Politics and Institutional
Design: The Case of the North-East Atlantic Land-based Pollution Regime' (1994) 18
Marine Policy, p. 226.

72 Commission of the European Communities, *Communication From the Commission
on the Precautionary Principle*, COM (2000) 1, 2 February 2000, p. 3, para. 4.

73 *Ibid.*, p. 13, para. 5.1.1.

74 Article 6 (1).

75 Birnie states that: '[t]he precautionary approach now required cannot be implemented
without maximum scientific knowledge and the gathering, evaluating and dissemination of
data.' Above note 26, p. 250.

Conditions to Enhance Effectiveness of the Obligation to Co-operate in Marine Scientific Research

On the other hand, one question arising is how it is possible to enhance the effectiveness of the implementation of the obligation to co-operate in marine scientific research in reality. In this respect, one may point to at least three issues which need further consideration.

Specification of Contents of the Obligation

The first issue pertains to the specification of the obligation to co-operate in marine scientific research. A possible criticism concerning the obligation to co-operate in general may be that the contents of this obligation are so vague as not to be very useful. It is undeniable that specific conducts required in fulfilment of the obligation of co-operation are left obscure, and that a breach of such an obligation is difficult to prove.[76] It appears that, to some extent, this criticism may be applicable to the obligation to co-operate in marine scientific research. Hence, further specification of the contents of this obligation becomes important.

In relation to this, special attention should be drawn to the quality of information. There are concerns that effective management of marine capture fisheries has been hindered by unreliable information.[77] UN General Assembly Resolution 60/31 noted with concern that 'effective management of marine capture fisheries has been made difficult in some areas by unreliable information and data caused by unreported and misreported fish catch and fishing effort and the contribution this lack of data makes to continued overfishing in some areas'.[78] Thus, UN General Assembly Resolution A/RES/S-19/2 of 1997, Programme for the Further Implementation of Agenda 21, calls for governments 'to take actions, individually and through their participation in competent global and regional forums, to improve the quality and quantity of scientific data as a basis for effective decisions related to the protection of the marine environment and the conservation and management of marine living resources'.[79] Furthermore, the FAO Committee on Fisheries adopted the FAO Strategy for Improving Information on Status and Trends of Capture Fisheries on 23 February 2003.[80] This FAO Strategy

---

76 Pinto, above note 14, p. 138.

77 United Nations, *Report of the Secretary-General, Oceans and the Law of the Sea*, A/59/62, 4 March 2004, p. 55, para. 215.

78 UN General Assembly Resolution, *Sustainable Fisheries, including through the 1995 Agreement for the Implementation of the Provisions of the United Nations Convention of the Law of the Sea of 10 December 1982 relating to the Conservation and Management of Straddling Fish Stocks and Highly Migratory Fish Stocks, and Related Instruments*, A/RES/60/31, 10 March 2006, p. 2.

79 UN General Assembly Resolution, A/RES/S-19/2, 19 September 1997, para. 36 (g)

80 The text of this Strategy is available at the homepage of FAO <http://www.fao.org/>.

explicitly requires States to enhance their capacities to collect data to ensure that the coverage of fisheries information is as complete as possible.[81] The Strategy also ensures that States should co-operate through their regional fishery bodies and arrangements to develop and adopt effective and pragmatic standards and systems for data collection, which should be compatible with FAO systems.[82] On the basis of the FAO Strategy, effort should be made to specify a criterion to enhance the quality of marine scientific information.

Institutional Mechanisms for the Implementation of the Obligation

A second issue relates to institutional mechanisms ensuring effective implementation of the obligation to co-operate in marine scientific research. It is argued that the obligation of co-operation requires action in good faith with a view to pursuing a common objective.[83] As Pinto has pointed out, co-operative obligations, whether express or implied, undertaken by the Parties to an international agreement would be a mere sham, if they were not recognised as being obligations to act.[84] There is no doubt that the obligation of international marine scientific co-operation has a legal basis at the treaty level, and that States Parties to treaties providing this obligation shall implement this obligation in good faith. It follows that *a priori* refusal to act to co-operate in marine scientific research is contrary to the obligation. In this respect, an issue that needs to be examined is how it is possible to ensure the implementation of this obligation.

The 1982 LOSC and the 1995 Fish Stocks Agreement do not contain specific institutional mechanisms, merely referring to co-operation through 'competent international organisations' or 'subregional or regional organisations'. It is presumed that the FAO is such a competent international organisation.[85] It is also acknowledged that other specialised UN agencies, such as UNESCO/IOC and UNEP, also play an important role for international co-operation in marine scientific research.[86] In this respect, special mention should be made of the role of regional fisheries organisations in ensuring international marine scientific co-operation. It is notable that many regional agreements relating to the management

---

81 FAO, *The Strategy for Improving Information on Status and Trends of Capture Fisheries* (Rome, FAO, 2003) p. 6, para. 25.

82 *Ibid.*, para. 27.

83 Scovazzi, above note 37, p. 132.

84 Pinto, above note 14, p. 145. See also N.Q. Dinh, P. Daillier and A. Pellet, *Droit international public*, 6th edn (Paris, L.G.D.J., 1999) p. 432.

85 Regarding the activities of the FAO on law of the sea, see M.H. Nordquist and J.N. Moore (eds), *Current Fisheries Issues and the Food and Agriculture Organization of the United Nations* (The Hague, Nijhoff, 2000).

86 The examination of the activities of these international organisations is beyond the scope of this study due to limited space. With respect to this issue, see Gorina-Ysern, above note 1, pp. 551–62. See also B. Kwiatkowska, *The 200 Mile Exclusive Economic Zone in the New Law of the Sea* (Dordrecht, Nijhoff, 1989) pp. 153–4.

of marine living resources seek to enhance marine scientific co-operation through fisheries commissions established in these regional agreements. To this end, the principal functions of such commissions can be summarised in four points:

(i)   to encourage, promote and co-ordinate scientific research;
(ii)   to compile, disseminate and analyse statistical and biological information;
(iii) to oblige parties to submit statistical and biological data;
(iv)   to provide a forum for consultation and exchange of information.

First, a number of regional fisheries commissions are empowered to promote and co-ordinate the conduct of marine scientific research.[87] In this respect, it is worth mentioning that the North Pacific Anadromous Fish Commission requires the Parties to submit to the Commission's scientific research programmes to be conducted by their nationals or vessels involving fishing for anadromous fish in the Convention Area. The catches of anadromous fish taken in conjunction with any scientific research in the Convention Area should be reported to the Commission within nine months.[88] In so doing, the conduct of marine scientific research is subject to the Commission's control. For this purpose, the Commission established the Committee on Scientific Research and Statistics (CSRS). At the CSRS, as well as at the Research Planning and Co-ordinating Meeting, the Parties discuss scientific research co-operation on the basis of their scientific research plans for salmon, the results of their previous researches as well as statistical data of their

---

87 Examples may be furnished by the following commissions: Indo-Pacific Fisheries Commission (Article 4 (f) of 1948 Indo-Pacific Fisheries Commission Agreement amended in 1996); General Fisheries Commission for the Mediterranean (Article 3 (1) (e) of the 1949 Agreement for the Establishment of a General Fisheries Commission for the Mediterranean most recently amended in 1997); Mixed Commission in the Black Sea (Article 9 (3) of the 1959 Convention Concerning Fishing in the Black Sea); International Baltic Sea Fishery Commission (Article 9 (1) (b) of the 1973 Convention on Fishing and Conservation of the Living Resources in the Baltic Sea and Belts); Scientific Committee of the Commission for the Conservation of Antarctic Marine Living Resources (Article 15 (1) of the 1980 CCAMLR); Indian Ocean Tuna Commission (Articles 5 (2) (b) and 12 (4) (c) of the 1993 Agreement for the Establishment of the Indian Ocean Tuna Commission); Scientific Committee of the Commission for the Conservation of Southern Bluefin Tuna (Article 9 (2) (b) of the 1993 Convention for the Conservation of Southern Bluefin Tuna); Regional Commission for Fisheries (Article 3 (1) (e) of the 1999 Agreement for the Establishment of the Regional Commission for Fisheries); the Pacific Salmon Commission (Article 10 (2) of the 1999 Treaty between the Government of Canada and the Government of the United States of America Concerning Pacific Salmon); the South-East Atlantic Fisheries Commission (Article 6 (f) of the 2001 Convention on the Conservation and Management of Fishery Resources in the South-East Atlantic Ocean).
88 Article VII (7) of the 1992 Convention for the Conservation of Anadromous Stocks in the North Pacific Ocean.

catches and fry releases.[89] Thus, international collaboration in marine scientific research is being enhanced through these activities of the Commission.

Secondly, regional fisheries bodies are often required to compile, disseminate and analyse relevant information by agreements.[90] For example, the Commission for the Conservation of Antarctic Marine Living Resources is under an obligation to compile data on the status, and changes in the population, of Antarctic marine living resources in accordance with Article 9 (1) (b). In connection with this, the Scientific Committee, which is established as a consultative body to the Commission, is empowered to analyse data concerning the direct and indirect effects of harvesting on the populations of Antarctic marine living resources under Article 15 (2) (c). Furthermore, it is worth noting that some regional commissions are empowered to conduct marine scientific research in their own right. For instance, the Commission for the Conservation and Management of Highly Migratory Fish Stocks in the Western and Central Pacific Ocean may engage the services of scientific experts to provide information and advice on the fishery resources covered by this Convention and related matters that may be relevant to the conservation and management of those resources. The scientific experts may, as directed by the Commission, conduct scientific research and analyses in support of the work of the Commission.[91] In carrying out their work, the scientific experts may undertake the collection, compilation and dissemination of fisheries data according to agreed principles and procedures established by the Commission, as well as investigate such other scientific matters as may be referred to them by the Commission.[92]

---

89 With respect to scientific activities of the North Pacific Anadromous Fish Commission, see <http://www.npafc.org>.

90 For instance, such power is provided in the following commissions: the Inter-American Tropical Tuna Commission (Article 2 (2) of the 1949 Convention for the Establishment of an Inter-American Tropical Tuna Commission); the International Commission for the Conservation of Atlantic Tunas (Article 4 (2) (a) of the 1966 International Convention for the Conservation of Atlantic Tunas); the Northwest Atlantic Fisheries Organisation (Article 6 (1) (b) of the 1978 Convention on Future Multilateral Co-operation in the Northwest Atlantic Fisheries); the South Pacific Forum Fisheries Agency (Article 7 (a) of the 1979 South Pacific Forum Fisheries Agency Convention); the Commission for the Conservation of Antarctic Marine Living Resources (Articles 9 (1) (b) (d) and 15 (2) (c) of the 1980 CCAMLR); the North Atlantic Salmon Conservation Organisation (Article 12 (2) (b) of the 1982 Convention for the Conservation of Salmon in the North Atlantic Ocean); the North Pacific Anadromous Fish Commission (Article 10 (2) (b) of the 1992 Convention for the Conservation of Anadromous Stocks in the North Pacific Ocean); the Indian Ocean Tuna Commission (Articles 5 (2) (a) and 12 (4) (b) of the 1993 Agreement for the Establishment of the Indian Ocean Tuna Commission).

91 Article 13 (1) and (2) of the 2000 Convention on the Conservation and Management of Highly Migratory Fish Stocks in the Western and Central Pacific Ocean.

92 Article 13 (3) (a) and (e) of the 2000 Convention on the Conservation and Management of Highly Migratory Fish Stocks in the Western and Central Pacific Ocean.

Thirdly, the regular submission of data from the Parties becomes essential in order to collect relevant data. Thus regional agreements often oblige the Parties to submit, regularly or on request, any available scientific and statistical information to fisheries commissions or associated scientific committees.[93] As an example, Article 13 (1) (d) of the Convention on the Conservation and Management of Fishery Resources in the South-East Atlantic Ocean of 2001 provides that each Contracting Party shall 'provide annually to the Organisation [South-East Atlantic Fisheries Organisation] such statistical, biological and other data and information as the Commission may require'. Such a reporting system can be an appropriate means of promoting the exchange of scientific information by the commissions. On the other hand, it is suggested that many States fail to fulfil the reporting obligation or report superficially to the relevant international institutions.[94] A solution to this problem may be to specify the content of the reports in detail or to provide commitments of Contracting Parties or commissions to information.[95]

Finally, there is little doubt that regional fisheries commissions can provide fora for the consultation and exchange of information by undertaking the three functions mentioned above. The above considerations lead to the conclusion that regional fisheries commissions have an important role to play in enhancing international co-operation in marine scientific research.

In relation to this, the issue arises that the proliferation of international institutions may produce problems regarding overlaps of jurisdiction.[96] With

---

93 Such examples include: Article 9 (2) (a) of the 1966 International Convention for the Conservation of Atlantic Tunas; Article 12 (3) of the 1973 Convention on Fishing and Conservation of the Living Resources in the Baltic Sea and Belts; Article 6 (3) of the 1978 Convention on Future Multilateral Co-operation in the Northwest Atlantic Fisheries; Article 9 (c) of the 1979 South Pacific Forum Fisheries Agency Convention; Article 16 (2) of the 1980 Convention on Future Multilateral Co-operation in North-East Atlantic Fisheries; Article 20 of the 1980 CCAMLR; Article 15 (1) (2) (3) of the 1982 Convention for the Conservation of Salmon in the North Atlantic Ocean; Article 7 (3) of the 1992 Convention for the Conservation of Anadromous Stocks in the North Pacific Ocean; Article 11 (1) of the 1993 Agreement for the Establishment of the Indian Ocean Tuna Commission; Article 10 (2) of the 1994 Convention on the Conservation and Management of Pollock Resources Central Bering Sea; Article 13 (1) (d) of the 2001 Convention on the Conservation and Management of Fishery Resources in the South-East Atlantic Ocean.

94 P. Sands, *Principles of International Environmental Law*, 2nd edn (Cambridge, Cambridge University Press, 2003) pp. 181–2.

95 Some treaties concerning the protection of the marine environment adopt this solution. See, for instance, the Helsinki Convention (Article 16), and the OSPAR Convention (Articles 9 and 22).

96 R.R. Churchill, 'Levels of Implementation of the Law of the Sea Convention: An Overview', in Vidas and Østreng, above note 51, p. 319. In fact, co-ordination between relevant international bodies is currently becoming an important issue in international law in general. Annick de Marffy presents her misgivings with respect to the sectoral approach which lacks a global basis for managing marine affairs. In her view, co-operation between international organisations is inadequate in this field. Thus de Marffy stresses the

respect to the protection of the marine environment, for instance, concern has already been voiced that collection, analysis and reporting of data is undertaken within overlapping frameworks.[97] It is of particular interest that, at the global level, the UN General Assembly agreed to the establishment of a new inter-agency co-ordination mechanism, the Oceans and Coastal Areas Network (UN-Oceans) in 2003. UN-Oceans seeks to enhance co-operation and co-ordination among the secretariats of the international organisations and bodies concerned with ocean-related activities, in particular by 'ensuring integrated ocean management at the international level'.[98] Thus it is hoped that the creation of UN-Oceans may provide a forum to co-ordinate various activities of international organisations with respect to ocean governance.

Scientific and Technical Assistance to Developing States

Last but not least, it is necessary to reflect upon scientific and technical assistance to developing States. Indeed, it is important to note that this issue is closely linked to the eradication of the poverty that is widespread in developing countries. In this respect, UN General Assembly Resolution 60/30 of 2005 recalled that:

> Marine science is important for eradicating poverty, contributing to food security, conserving the world's marine environment and resources, helping to understand, predict and respond to natural events and promoting the sustainable development of

---

importance of the 'global approach', which goes beyond each organisation. A. de Marffy, 'La place des organisations internationales compétentes dans la mise en application du régime de la ZEE', in E. Franckx and P. Gautier (eds), *La zone économique exclusive et la Convention des Nations Unies sur le droit de la mer, 1982–2000: un premier bilan de la pratique des Etats* (Bruxelles, Bruylant, 2003) pp. 51–63. See also Chapter 17 of Agenda 21, para. 17.116.

97 This concern was voiced in the First Joint Ministerial Meeting of the Helsinki and OSPAR Commissions. *Statement on the European Marine Strategy, What HELCOM and OSPAR Can Bring to the Development of the European Marine Strategy*, Record of the Meeting, Annex 6 (Ref. §6.1), Bremen, 25–26 June 2003, para. 3.

98 UN General Assembly Resolution 58/240. The first meeting of UN-Oceans was held at the headquarters of IOC of UNESCO from 25 to 29 January 2005. It was attended by the following representatives: the secretariat of the Convention on Biological Diversity, FAO, IAEA, IMO, IOC, International Seabed Authority, the UN Department of Economic and Social Affairs, UNDOALOS, UNDO, UNEP/the Co-ordination Office of the Global Programme of Action for the Protection of the Marine Environment from Land-Based Activities, WMO and the World Bank. For a brief outline of UN-Oceans, see International Seabed Authority, *Report of the Secretary-General of the International Seabed Authority under Article 166, paragraph 4, of the United Nations Convention on the Law of the Sea*, ISBA/11/A/4 and Corr. 1, 13 July 2005, p. 3, paras 14–15. The Report of the First Inter-Agency Meeting of UN-Oceans is available at the homepage of UN-Oceans <http://www.oceansatlas.org/www.un-oceans.org/Index.htm>.

the oceans and seas, by improving knowledge, through sustained research efforts and the evaluation of monitoring results, and applying such knowledge to management and decision-making.[99]

Considering that marine scientific facilities in developing countries remain insufficient, technical and financial assistance to these countries is imperative for promoting marine scientific research.[100] On this point, Annex VI of the Final Act of the UNCLOS III explicitly stated that 'unless urgent measures are taken, the marine scientific and technological gap between the developed and the developing countries will widen further and thus endanger the very foundations of the new regime'.[101] Thus Annex VI urged the industrialised countries to assist the developing countries in the preparation and implementation of their marine science, technology and ocean service development programmes.[102] In this regard, it should be remembered that Article 202 of the 1982 LOSC explicitly enunciates an obligation concerning scientific and technical assistance to developing States in the context of the protection of the marine environment.[103] Similarly, the Code of Conduct also pronounces the need for assistance to developing countries in Article 12.18. In particular, Article 12.20 states that '[r]elevant technical and financial international organisations should, upon request, support States in their research efforts, devoting special attention to developing countries, in particular the least-developed among them and small island developing countries'. In State practice, it is notable that Article 21 (4) (b) of the 2001 South-East Atlantic Convention provides the duty of co-operation with developing States in the South Atlantic region concerning stock assessment and scientific research.

In this respect, it is important to note that scientific and technical assistance to developing States is closely linked to the development and transfer of marine

---

99 UN General Assembly, *Oceans and the Law of the Sea*, A/RES/60/30, 8 March 2006, Preamble.

100 Some instruments make clear an obligation to assist developing States in marine scientific research. See, for instance, Articles 202 (a) (v) and 244 (2) of the 1982 LOSC; Articles 12.18, 12.20 of the FAO Code of Conduct; Article 21 (4) (b) of the 2001 Convention on the Conservation and Management of Fishery Resources in the South-East Atlantic Ocean; Article 30 (4) of the 2000 Convention on the Conservation and Management of Highly Migratory Fish Stocks in the Western and Central Pacific Ocean.

101 Preamble of Annex VI, 'Resolution on Development of National Marine Science, Technology and Ocean Service Infrastructures'.

102 *Ibid.*, paragraph 3.

103 Such assistance shall include, *inter alia*: (i) training of their scientific and technical personnel; (ii) facilitating their participation in relevant international programmes; (iii) supplying them with necessary equipment and facilities; (iv) enhancing their capacity to manufacture such equipment; (v) giving advice on and developing facilities for research, monitoring, educational and other programmes.

scientific technology embodied in Part XIV of the 1982 LOSC.[104] This point is clearly reflected in Article 266 (2) of the 1982 LOSC:

> States shall promote the development of the marine scientific and technological capacity of States which may need and request technical assistance in this field, particularly developing States, including land-locked and geographically disadvantaged States, with regard to the exploration, exploitation, conservation and management of marine resources, the protection and preservation of the marine environment, marine scientific research and other activities in the marine environment compatible with this Convention, with a view to accelerating the social and economic development of the developing States.

It is argued that this provision establishes objectives more than rules. Even so, it should be stressed that these objectives reflect the philosophy of the 1982 LOSC concerning 'a just and equitable international economic order which takes into account the interests and needs of mankind as a whole and, in particular, the special interests and needs of developing countries'.[105] In this sense, it may be said that the enhancement of international co-operation in marine scientific research is closely allied to the fundamental goal of the LOSC.

Conclusion

The above considerations can be summarised in four points.

(i) Currently there is a clear trend that the obligation to co-operate in marine scientific research is provided in treaties in those fields at the global and regional levels. At the global level, this obligation is explicitly reflected in the 1982 LOSC, the 1992 Rio Convention, the 1995 FAO Code of Conduct and the 1995 Fish Stocks Agreement. At the regional level, the need for international scientific co-operation is increasingly acknowledged in the conservation of various species as well as in various regions. In this respect, it is noteworthy that some treaties provide a dual obligation relating to marine scientific research, that is to say, an obligation on each State to conduct marine scientific research and an obligation for co-operation between States in marine scientific research. Considering that sufficient and credible scientific data is a prerequisite for the conservation of marine living resources, it is arguable that the dual obligation is of central importance in this matter.

---

104 Jarmache, above note 1, p. 309. Furthermore, as provided in Article 268, the development of human resources through training and education of nationals of developing States is also important. To this end, the IMO has established two educational organs: the World Maritime University (1983) and the IMO International Maritime Law Institute (1989).

105 Preamble. See *Virginia Commentary*, Vol. IV, above note 15, p. 677.

(ii) The emergence of the obligation to co-operate in marine scientific research is *not* an isolated phenomenon, but is closely linked to the new approaches to the conservation of marine living resources and biological diversity: the ecosystem and precautionary approaches. In applying the ecosystem approach, considerable studies will be needed with a view to investigating marine ecosystems. Such studies will necessitate international scientific co-operation, owing to the transboundary nature of marine ecosystems. Furthermore, marine scientific research is also required in order to determine the existence of serious threats which may trigger the application of the precautionary approach. As the application of the precautionary approach may restrict States' activities in the oceans, adequate marine scientific research before applying this approach is particularly important. It would follow that the conduct of marine scientific research is a prerequisite for the application of two key approaches in conservation of living resources and biological diversity in the oceans.

(iii) It needs to be stressed that at least three conditions should be fulfilled to effectively implement the obligation to co-operate in marine scientific research:

– further specification of the contents of the obligation, including the enhancement of the quality of information as well as the credibility of data assessment;
– establishment of institutional mechanisms ensuring the implementation of this obligation;
– scientific and technical assistance to developing countries.

With respect to the first issue, it is necessary to elaborate a criterion enhancing the quality of scientific data as required by the 2003 FAO Strategy. Furthermore, it would seem that the establishment of an independent scientific process may be useful to enhance the credibility of data assessment. Concerning the second issue, it is notable that specialised UN agencies as well as regional fisheries commissions have a primordial role to play. In relation to the third point, it has to be stressed that scientific and technical assistance to developing countries is particularly important to achieve an objective of the 1982 LOSC, to realise 'a just and equitable international economic order' which takes into account the special interests and needs of developing countries.

(iv) The above survey appears to show that interplay between law and science is increasingly important in the international law of the sea. As the ocean is a dynamic natural system, it is arguable that the law must take the dynamics of nature into account. Thus, further consideration will be required with respect to the growing interaction of law and marine science. This issue will highlight a need for an interdisciplinary approach in international law of the sea. There seems to be a general sense that close co-operation between lawyers and scientists will be further required in the conservation of living resources and biological diversity in the oceans.[106]

---

106 It should also be noted that accurate scientific data is essential in establishing an effective scheme for the protection of the marine environment. To this end, it is necessary to identify substances which may harm the marine environment and assess their impact on the ocean as well as its living organisms. In this respect, it should be noted that due to its nature, marine pollution may be transported beyond man-made delimitation lines. Consequently, international collaboration will be required in investigating the pathways as well as effects of pollutants on the oceans and marine life. See Soons, above note 1, p. 14; Meng Quing-Nan, *Land-based Marine Pollution* (London, Nijhoff, 1987) pp. 134–5.

Chapter 7
General Conclusion

This study has examined the limitations of the traditional zonal management approach and the possibility of a new integrated management approach in conservation of marine living resources and marine biological diversity. For that purpose, we have considered three principal issues: the dual approach to conservation of marine living resources; the dual approach to conservation of marine biological diversity; and marine scientific research as a foundation of ocean governance. These considerations lead to the following conclusions.

(i) Historically, one of the principal functions of international law concerns the spatial distribution of States' jurisdiction with a view to ensuring co-existence between States. Hence, traditionally, international law of the sea has purported to spatially distribute States' jurisdiction by dividing the ocean into several sectors. The zonal management approach is the result of the historical process of the law. It is particularly important to note the close connection between this approach and the principal function of international law.

(ii) The zonal management approach relies on two basic principles of the law of the sea: the principle of freedom and the principle of sovereignty. The principle of freedom attempts to safeguard national interest on the basis of the freedom of the use of the oceans, including navigation and fisheries, while the principle of sovereignty promotes national interest deriving from the control of offshore resources by the coastal State. The primary function of the traditional zonal management approach is to reconcile opposing national interests. Thus this approach is strongly characterised by national interests.

(iii) Currently, the zonal management approach, which was clearly established in the 1982 LOSC, provides the principal legal framework governing the oceans in international law. On the one hand, this framework is of central importance in establishing the legal order regulating the use of the oceans. On the other hand, it is becoming apparent that the zonal management approach encounters an inherent difficulty in the conservation of migratory species and biological diversity in the oceans, that is to say, the divergence between the law and nature. As marine spaces under this approach are in principle defined *spatially*, on the basis of distance from the coast, it is inevitable that maritime limits and delimitation lines divide the range of straddling and highly migratory species and marine ecosystems. This creates considerable difficulties in the conservation of migratory marine species and marine biological diversity since they are transboundary in nature.

(iv) In response to problems which cannot be easily resolved by the traditional approach, the need for an integrated management approach is increasingly highlighted in various international documents as well as in scholarly publications.

The considerations in this study appear to show that, to a certain extent, basic elements supporting the integrated management approach are developing in treaties as well as in various non-binding documents concerning conservation of marine living resources and marine biological diversity. Such elements include:

- The concept of sustainable development;
- The ecosystem approach;
- The precautionary approach;
- International supervision through international institutions;
- Non-flag State enforcement.

It is arguable that sustainable development, which seeks to reconcile the requirement of environmental protection and that of development, may provide a cardinal concept in this field. Furthermore, it is argued that the ecosystem approach, together with the precautionary approach, can be the backbone of an integrated management approach. It may also be argued that, to some extent, international supervision through international institutions and non-flag State enforcement can be useful legal techniques to secure the application of relevant rules in an integrated manner. In addition to this, it is notable that the inter-linkage between relevant treaties and institutions is being formulated through State practice, as the North-East Atlantic region demonstrates.

(v) At the same time, it must be pointed out that the normativity of three substantive elements, that is to say, the concept of sustainable development, the ecosystem approach and the precautionary approach, remains modest in international law. Considering that sustainable development is closely linked to national policy, it will be difficult if not impossible for international courts and tribunals to determine whether or not the conduct of a State is contrary to sustainable development. For the same reason, it is debatable whether and to what extent the concept of sustainable development would constrain the behaviour of States. Owing to the limited understanding of marine ecosystems as well as their variability, it appears difficult for a third party to evaluate whether or not conservation measures of a State are in conformity with the ecosystem approach. It is also argued that the determination of the precautionary approach is the political process, and the application of this approach may be qualified by economic, political and social factors. Given that the precautionary approach may restrict the economic and industrial development of States, it remains to be seen to what extent this approach constrains their behaviour. In relation to this, it must be noted that international courts and tribunals are still cautious in the application of this approach. Thus it may be appropriate to regard these elements as a factor orienting the behaviour of States and guiding proper interpretation of relevant rules in the judicial process.

(vi) It is important to note that, like environmental protection in general, rules of international law relating to conservation of marine living resources and biological diversity are essentially qualified by economic, technological and political factors.

Since conservation measures inevitably affect national development, there is a need to reconcile these measures with the economic, technological and political circumstances of each State. This is particularly true of fisheries, which are an important part of the economic activity of States. This may be the reason why the normativity of basic elements stimulating the integrated management approach remains weak. In any case, it has to be stressed that the validity and effectiveness of rules of international law in this field rely in essence on the sound balance between the requirement for conservation and the need for economic, social and political development of each State.

(vii) Another important question underlying international law in this field relates to the paucity of our knowledge of marine ecosystems and the environments that support them. It will be difficult to take proper conservation measures without adequate and reliable scientific data. Hence it could well be said that marine scientific research is a foundation of ocean governance. In this respect, it is worth noting that treaties in this field increasingly set out the dual obligation in marine scientific research, that is to say, the obligation to conduct marine scientific research and the obligation to co-operate in marine scientific research.

(viii) The above results appear to reveal that, while it is becoming apparent that the validity of the traditional zonal management approach is in need of reconsideration in the conservation of marine living resources and marine biological diversity, the integrated management approach is still embryonic. This does not mean, however, that the idea of an integrated management approach is merely an illusion in international law. As Georges Scelle stressed, the unity of the ocean is an undeniable truth.[1] It follows that the holistic viewpoint in ocean governance will not lose its importance. Thus, the reconciliation between the zonal and the integrated management approaches to ocean governance will be an important issue in international law, in order to preserve sound marine ecosystems and the environments that support them for future generations.

---

1 See Chapter 1 of this study.

Selected Bibliography

I. Documents and Reports

1. League of Nations

Rosenne, S. (ed.), *League of Nations, Committee of Experts for the Progressive Codification of International Law (1925–1928)*, Vol. 2, Documents (New York, Oceana, 1972).

———, *League of Nations, Conference for the Codification of International Law* (1930), Vol. 2 (New York, Oceana, 1975).

2. United Nations

Report of the International Law Commission, Covering the Work of Its Eighth Session 23 April–4 July 1956, General Assembly, *Official Records: Eighth Session*, Supplement No. 9 (A/3159) (New York, United Nations, 1956).

Report of the Review Conference on the Agreement for the Implementation of the Provisions of the United Nations Convention on the Law of the Sea of 10 December 1982 relating to the Conservation and Management of Straddling Fish Stocks and Highly Migratory Fish Stocks, A/CONF.210/2006/15, 5 July 2006.

Report of the UN Conference on Environment and Development, UN Doc. A/CONF. 151/26/REV. 1, Vols. I–III (1992).

United Nations Division for Ocean Affairs and the Law of the Sea, Office of Legal Affairs, *The Law of the Sea: Practice of States at the Time of Entry into Force of the United Nations Convention on the Law of the Sea* (New York, United Nations, 1994).

UN General Assembly, *Report on the Work of the United Nations Open-ended Informal Consultative Process Established by the General Assembly in Its Resolution 54/33 in Order to Facilitate the Annual Review by the Assembly of Developments in Ocean Affairs at Its Third Meeting*, A/57/80, 2 July 2002.

———, *Report of the Secretary-General, Oceans and the Law of the Sea*, A/58/65, 3 March 2003.

———, *United Nations Open-ended Informal Consultative Process on Oceans and the Law of the Sea, Protection and Conservation of Vulnerable Marine Ecosystems in Areas Beyond National Jurisdiction, Submitted by the Delegation of Norway*, A/AC.259/10, 4 June 2003.

——, *Report on the Work of the United Nations Open-ended Informal Consultative Process on Oceans and the Law of the Sea*, A/58/95, 26 June 2003.

——, *Report of the Secretary-General, Oceans and the Law of the Sea*, A/59/62, 4 March 2004.

——, *Report on the Work of the United Nations Open-ended Informal Consultative Process on Oceans and the Law of the Sea at its Fifth Meeting*, A/59/122, 1 July 2004.

——, *Report of the Secretary-General, Oceans and the Law of the Sea*, A/59/62/ Add.1, 18 August 2004.

——, *Report of the Secretary-General, Oceans and the Law of the Sea*, A/60/63, 4 March 2005.

——, *Report of the Secretary-General, Oceans and the Law of the Sea*, A/61/63, 9 March 2006.

——, *Report of the Ad Hoc Open-ended Informal Working Group to Study Issues Relating to the Conservation and Sustainable Use of Marine Biological Diversity beyond Areas of National Jurisdiction*, A/61/65, 20 March 2006.

——, *Report on the Work of the United Nations Open-ended Informal Consultative Process on Oceans and the Law of the Sea at its Seventh Meeting*, A/61/156, 17 July 2006.

——, *Report on the Work of the United Nations Open-ended Informal Consultative Process on Oceans and the Law of the Sea at its Eighth Meeting*, A/62/169, 30 July 2007.

UN General Assembly Resolution, *Report of the World Commission on Environment and Development*, A/RES/42/187, 11 December 1987.

——, *Possible Adverse Effects of Sea-level Rise on Islands and Coastal Areas, Particularly Low-lying Coastal Areas*, A/RES/44/206, 22 December 1989.

——, *Large-scale Pelagic Driftnet Fishing and Its Impact on the Living Marine Resources of the World's Oceans and Seas*, A/RES/44/225, 22 December 1989.

——, *Oceans and the Law of the Sea*, A/RES/56/12, 13 December 2001.

——, *Oceans and the Law of the Sea*, A/RES/57/141, 21 February 2003.

——, *Large-scale Pelagic Driftnet Fishing, Unauthorized Fishing in Zones of National Jurisdiction and on the High Seas/Illegal, Unreported and Unregulated Fishing, Fisheries By-catch and Discards, and Other Developments*, A/ RES/57/142, 26 February 2003.

——, *Promoting an Integrated Management Approach to the Caribbean Sea Area in the Context of Sustainable Development*, A/RES/57/261, 27 February 2003.

——, *Oceans and Law of the Sea*, A/RES/58/240, 5 March 2004.

——, *Oceans and Law of the Sea*, A/RES/60/30, 8 March 2006.

——, *Sustainable Fisheries, Including through the 1995 Agreement for the Implementation of the Provisions of the United Nations Convention on the Law of the Sea of 10 December 1982 Relating to the Conservation and Management of Straddling Fish Stocks and Highly Migratory Fish Stocks, and Related Instruments*, A/RES/60/31, 10 March 2006.

——, *Sustainable Fisheries, Including through the 1995 Agreement for the Implementation of the Provisions of the United Nations Convention on the Law of the Sea of 10 December 1982 Relating to the Conservation and Management of Straddling Fish Stocks and Highly Migratory Fish Stocks, and Related Instruments*, A/RES/61/105, 6 March 2007.

United Nations Conference on the Law of the Sea, *Official Records, Vol. II, Plenary Meetings, Summary Records of Meetings and Annexes*, Geneva, 24 February–27 April 1958.

United Nations Legislative Series, *Laws and Regulations on the Regime of the Territorial Sea* (New York, United Nations, 1957).

3. Food and Agriculture Organisation

FAO, *The Code of Conduct for Responsible Fisheries*, 31 October 1995.

——, *The Rome Declaration on the Implementation of the Code of Conduct for Responsible Fisheries*, 1999.

——, *International Plan of Action to Prevent, Deter and Eliminate Illegal, Unreported and Unregulated Fishing*, 2001.

——, *Reykjavik Declaration on Responsible Fisheries in the Marine Ecosystem*, C 2001/INF/25, 2001.

——, *The Strategy for Improving Information on Status and Trends of Capture Fisheries* (Rome, FAO, 2003).

——, *The State of World Fisheries and Aquaculture* (Rome, FAO, 2004).

——, *Rome Declaration on Illegal, Unreported and Unregulated Fishing*, 12 March 2005.

——, *Model Scheme on Port State Measures to Combat Illegal, Unreported and Unregulated Fishing*, 2007.

FAO Committee on Fisheries, *Implementation of Ecosystem Approach to Fisheries Management to Achieve Responsible Fisheries and to Restore Fisheries Resources and Marine Environments*, COFI/2003/10, 2003.

——, *Marine Protected Areas (MPAs) and Fisheries*, COFI/2005/8, 7–11 March 2005.

FAO Fisheries Department, *Review of the State of World Marine Fishery Resources*, *FAO Fisheries Technical Paper* 457 (Rome, FAO, 2005).

4. International Maritime Organisation

IMO, IMO Resolution A.720 (17), *Guidelines for the Designation of Special Areas and the Identification of Particularly Sensitive Sea Areas* (adopted on 6 November 1991).

——, IMO Resolution A.927 (22), *Guidelines for the Designation of Special Areas under MARPOL 73/78 and Guidelines for the Identification and Designation of Particularly Sensitive Sea Areas* (adopted on 29 November 2001), A22/Res.927, 15 January 2002.

——, *MARPOL 73/78 Consolidated Edition 2002* (London, IMO, 2002).

——, IMO Resolution MEPC.121 (52) *Designation of the Western European Waters as a Particularly Sensitive Sea Area* (adopted on 15 October 2004).

——, IMO Resolution A.982 (24), *Revised Guidelines for the Identification and Designation of Particularly Sensitive Sea Areas* (adopted on 1 December 2005), A24/Res.982, 6 February 2006.

——, *Particularly Sensitive Sea Areas: Compilation of Official Guidance Documents and PSSAs adopted since 1990* (London, IMO, 2007).

——, *Particularly Sensitive Sea Areas: Compilation of Official Guidance Documents and PSSAs Adopted Since 1990* (London, IMO, 2007).

5. UNEP/Convention on Biological Diversity

Convention on Biological Diversity, SBSTTA, *Recommendation I/8: Scientific, Technical and Technological Aspects of the Conservation and Sustainable Use of Coastal and Marine Biological Diversity*, UNEP/CBD/COP/2/5, 1995.

——, Conference of the Parties, Decision IV/5, *Conservation and Sustainable Use of Marine and Coastal Biological Diversity, including a Programme of Work*, Annex, Section B-2.

——, Conference of the Parties, Decision V/6, *Ecosystem Approach*, UNEP/CBD/COP/5/23, 15–16 May 2000.

——, *Climate Change and Biological Diversity: Cooperation between the Convention on Biological Diversity and the United Nations Framework Convention on Climate Change, Note by the Executive Secretary of the Convention on Biological Diversity Submitted to the Conference of the Parties to the United Nations Framework Convention on Climate Change (UNFCCC) at its Sixth Session and the UNFCCC Subsidiary Body on Scientific and Technological Advice at the Second Part of its Thirteenth Session*, The Hague, 13–24 November 2000.

——, Meeting of the Biodiversity Committee (BDC), Dublin, 20–24 January 2003, *Summary Record BDC 2003*, BDC 03/10/1-E, Annex 13.

——, *Ad Hoc* Technical Expert Group on Biodiversity and Climate Change, *Interlinkages between Biological Diversity and Climate Change and Advice on the Integration of Biodiversity Considerations into the Implementation of the United Nations Framework Convention on Climate Change and its Kyoto Protocol, Draft Report for Experts and Government Review*, 17 February 2003.

——, SBSTTA, *Marine and Coastal Biodiversity: Review, Further Elaboration and Refinement of the Programme of Work*, UNEP/CBD/SBSTTA/8/INF/3/Rev.1, 22 February 2003.

——, *Ad Hoc* Technical Expert Group on Marine and Coastal Protected Areas (AHTEG), *Report of the Ad Hoc Technical Expert Group on Marine and Coastal Protected Areas*, UNEP/CBD/AHTEG-PA/1/INF/5, 6 June 2003.

——, *Ad Hoc* Technical Expert Group on Protected Areas, *The Role of Protected Areas within the Convention on Biological Diversity*, UNEP/CBD/AHTEG-PA/1/INF/1, 6 June 2003.

——, *The Role of Protected Areas within the Convention on Biological Diversity*, UNEP/CBD/AHTEG-PA/1/INF/1, 6 June 2003.

——, SBSTTA, *Biological Diversity and Climate Change, Report of the Ad Hoc Technical Expert Group on Biodiversity and Climate Change*, UNEP/CBD/SBSTTA/9/INF12, 30 September 2003.

——, *Ad Hoc* Technical Expert Group on Biodiversity and Climate Change, *Interlinkages between Biological Diversity and Climate Change and Advice on the Integration of Biodiversity Considerations into the Implementation of the United Nations Framework Convention on Climate Change and its Kyoto Protocol, Draft Executive Summary* (CBD Technical Series 10) (Montreal, Secretary of the Convention on Biological Diversity, 2003).

——, Conference of the Parties, Decision VII/5, *Marine and Coastal Biological Diversity: Review of the Programme of Work on Marine and Coastal Biodiversity*, UNEP/CBD/COP/7/21, February 2004.

——, *Ad Hoc* Technical Expert Group on Marine and Coastal Protected Areas (AHTEG), *Technical Advice on the Establishment and Management of a National System of Marine and Coastal Protected Areas* (CBD Technical Series No. 13, 2004).

——, *Ad Hoc* Open-ended Working Group on Protected Areas, *Options for Cooperation for the Establishment of Marine Protected Areas in Marine Areas Beyond the Limits of National Jurisdiction*, UNEP/CBD/WG-PA/1/2, 20 April 2005.

——, SBSTTA, *Marine and Coastal Biological Diversity: Status and Trends of, and Threats to, Deep Seabed Genetic Resources Beyond National Jurisdiction, and Identification of Technical Options for Their Conservation and Sustainable Use*, UNEP/CBD/SBSTTA/11/11, 22 July 2005.

——, Conference of the Parties, Decision VIII/21, *Marine and Coastal Biological Diversity: Conservation and Sustainable Use of Deep Seabed Genetic Resources Beyond the Limits of National Jurisdiction*, March 2006.

——, Conference of the Parties, COP Decision VIII/24, *Protected Area*, UNEP/CBD/COP/ 8/31, 2006.

6. OSPAR Commission

First Joint Ministerial Meeting of the Helsinki and OSPAR Commissions, *Statement on the Ecosystem Approach to the Management of Human Activities*, Record of the Meeting, Annex 5 (Ref. §6.1), Bremen, 25–26 June 2003.

——, *Statement on the European Marine Strategy, What HELCOM and OSPAR Can Bring to the Development of the European Marine Strategy*, Record of the Meeting, Annex 6 (Ref. §6.1), Bremen, 25–26 June 2003.

Meeting of the Biodiversity Committee, *Draft OSPAR Recommendation on a Network of Marine Protected Areas*, BDC/03/10/1-E Annex 10, 20–24 January 2003, Dublin.

Ministerial Meeting of the OSPAR Commission, *The Sintra Statement*, 23 July 1998.

——, *Strategies of the OSPAR Commission for the Protection of the Marine Environment of the North-East Atlantic (Reference number: 2003-21)*, Summary Record OSPAR 03/17/1-E, Annex 31 (Ref. B-4.2), Bremen, 25 June 2003.

The OSPAR Commission, *Quality Status Report 2000* (London, OSPAR Commission, 2000).

——, *Draft Letter to Fisheries Authorities*, Summary Record OSPAR 2001, OSPAR 01/18/1, Annex 12 (Ref. § 6.25), Valencia, 25–29 June 2001.

——, *OSPAR Recommendation 2003/3 on a Network of Marine Protected Areas*, Summary Record OSPAR 2003, OSPAR 03/17/1-E, Annex 9 (Ref. § A-4.44a), Bremen, 23–27 June 2003.

——, *Guidelines for the Identification and Selection of Marine Protected Areas in the OSPAR Maritime Area*, Summary Record OSPAR 2003, OSPAR 03/17/1-E, Annex 10 (Ref. § A-4.44b(i)), Bremen, 23–27 June 2003.

——, *Guidelines for the Management of Marine Protected Areas in the OSPAR Maritime Area*, Summary Record OSPAR 2003, OSPAR 03/17/1-E, Annex 11 (Ref. §A-4.44b (ii)), Bremen, 23–27 June 2003.

——, *Draft Letter to NEAFC*, Summary Record OSPAR 2004, OSPAR 04/23/1-E, Annex 6 (Ref. § 5.14a), Reykjavik, 18 June–1 July 2004.

7. Fisheries Organisations

Commission for the Conservation of Antarctic Marine Living Resources, *Conservation Measure 118/XX Scheme to Promote Compliance by Non-Contracting Party Vessels with CCAMLR Conservation Measures*.

Commission for the Conservation of Southern Bluefin Tuna, *Report of the Special Meeting*, 16–18 November 2000.

——, *Report of the Sixth Meeting of the Scientific Committee*, 28–31 August 2001.

——, *Report of the Extended Commission of the Tenth Annual Meeting of the Commission*, 7–10 October 2003.

Indian Ocean Tuna Commission, *Resolution 01/03 Establishing a Scheme to Promote Compliance by Non-Contracting Party Vessels with Resolutions Established by IOTC*, 2001.

——, *Resolution 02/01 Relating to the Establishment of an IOTC Programme of Inspection in Port*, 2002.

International Commission for the Conservation of Atlantic Tunas, *Recommendation by ICCAT Concerning the Ban on Landings and Transshipments of Vessels from Non-Contracting Parties Identified as Having Committed a Serious Infringement*, 21 June 1999.

North-East Atlantic Fisheries Commission, *Scheme of Control and Enforcement*, May 2007.

North-West Atlantic Fisheries Organisation, *Conservation and Enforcement Measures*, NAFO/FC Doc. 07/1 (Revised), Serial No. N5335.

8. Other Documents

Commission of the European Communities, *Communication from the Commission to the Council and the European Parliament, Fisheries Management and Nature Conservation in the Marine Environment*, COM (1999) 363 final, 14 July 1999.

——, *Communication from the Commission on the Precautionary Principle*, COM (2000) 1, 2 February 2000.

——, *Communication from the Commission on the Precautionary Principle*, COM (2001) 1.

——, *Communication from the Commission to the Council and the European Parliament, Towards a Strategy to Protect and Conserve the Marine Environment*, COM (2002) 539 final, 2 October 2002.

EC, Council Directive 92/43/EEC on the Conservation of Natural Habitats and Wild Flora and Fauna.

EC, Council Regulation No 2371/2002 of 20 December 2002 on the Conservation and Sustainable Exploitation of Fisheries Resources under the Common Fisheries Policy.

International Law Association, *Final Report of the Committee on Coastal State Jurisdiction Relating to Marine Pollution*, International Law Association, London Conference (2000).

——, *The Second Report of the Committee on International Law on Sustainable Development*, ILA Toronto Conference (2006).

International North Sea Conference, *Ministerial Declaration of the Second International Conference on the Protection of the North Sea*, London, 24–25 November 1987.

——, *Ministerial Declaration of the Third International Conference on the Protection of the North Sea*, The Hague, 8 March 1990.

——, *Esbjerg Declaration, Ministerial Declaration of the Fourth International Conference on Protection of the North Sea*, 8–9 June 1995.

——, *Bergen Declaration, Fifth International Conference on the Protection of the North Sea*, 20–21 March 2002.

International Seabed Authority, *Report of the Secretary-General of the International Seabed Authority under Article 166, paragraph 4, of the United Nations Convention on the Law of the Sea*, ISBA/8/A/5, 7 June 2002.

——, *Report of the Secretary-General of the International Seabed Authority under Article 166, paragraph 4, of the United Nations Convention on the Law of the Sea*, ISBA/10/A/3, 31 March 2004.

——, *Report of the Secretary-General of the International Seabed Authority under Article 166, paragraph 4, of the United Nations Convention on the Law of the Sea*, ISBA/11/A/4 and Corr. 1, 13 July 2005.

——, *Report of the Secretary-General of the International Seabed Authority under Article 166, paragraph 4, of the United Nations Convention on the Law of the Sea*, ISBA/12/A/2, 26 June 2006.

IUCN, *Recommendations of the 5th IUCN World Parks Congress*, 2003, WPC Rec 5.23.

UNESCO, *Case Studies on Climate Change and World Heritage* (Paris, UNESCO World Heritage Centre, 2007).

World Trade Organization, *Chile – Measures Affecting the Transit and Importation of Swordfish, Request for the Establishment of a Panel by the European Communities*, WT/DS193/2, 7 November 2000.

World Trade Organization, *Chile – Measures Affecting the Transit and Importation of Swordfish, Arrangement between the European Communities and Chile, Communication from the European Communities*, WT/DS193/3, 6 April 2001 (01-1770).

II. Books and Articles

Abi-Saab, G., 'Cours général de droit international public' (1987-VII) 207 *RCADI*, 9–464.

——, 'Whither the International Community?' (1998) 9 *EJIL*, 248–65.

Agardy, T.S., *Marine Protected Areas and Ocean Conservation* (California and London, Academic Press, 1997).

Alexander, L.M., 'Large Marine Ecosystems: A New Focus for Marine Resources Management' (1993) 17 *Marine Policy*, 186–98.

Allen, C.H., 'Protecting the Oceanic Gardens of Eden: International Law Issues in Deep-Sea Vent Resource Conservation and Management' (2000–2001) 13 *The Georgetown International Environmental Law Review*, 563–660.

Anand, R.P., *Origin and Development of the Law of the Sea: History of International Law Revisited* (The Hague, Nijhoff, 1983).

——, 'Changing Concepts of Freedom of the Seas: A Historical Perspective', in J.M. Van Dyke, D. Zaelke and G. Hewison (eds), *Freedom for the Seas in the*

21st Century: Ocean Governance and Environmental Harmony (Washington, DC, Island Press, 1993) 72–86.

Anderson, D.H., 'The Straddling Stocks Agreement of 1995: An Initial Assessment' (1996) 45 *ICLQ*, 463–75.

Anderson, E.D., 'The International Council for the Exploration of the Sea', in R. Platzöder and P. Verlaan (eds), *The Baltic Sea: New Developments in National Policies and International Co-operation* (The Hague, Kluwer, 1996) 271–87.

Anderson, S., 'The North Sea and Beyond: Lessons Learned', in M.J. Valencia (ed.), *Maritime Regime Building: Lessons Learned and Their Relevance for Northeast Asia* (The Hague, Nijhoff, 2001) 51–72.

Ansari, A.H. and Jamal, P., 'The Convention on Biological Diversity: A Critical Appraisal with Special Reference to Malaysia' (2000) 40 *Indian Journal of International Law*, 137–77.

Anton, D.K., 'Law for the Sea's Biological Diversity', in J.I. Charney, D.K. Anton and M.E. O'Connell (eds), *Politics, Values and Functions : International Law in the 21st Century. Essays in Honour of Professor Louis Henkin* (The Hague, Nijhoff, 1997) 325–52.

Applebaum, B., 'The Straddling Stocks Problem: The Northwest Atlantic Situation, International Law, and Options for Coastal State Action', in A.H.A. Soons (ed.), *Implementation of the Law of the Sea Convention Through International Institutions, Proceedings of the 23rd Annual Conference of the Law of the Sea Institute 1989* (Honolulu, The Law of the Sea Institute, University of Hawaii, 1990) 282–317.

Armas Pfirter, F.M., 'Straddling Stocks and Highly Migratory Stocks in Latin American Practice and Legislation: New Perspectives in Light of Current International Negotiations' (1995) 26 *ODIL*, 127–50.

Asebey, E.J. and Kempenaar, J.D., 'Biodiversity Prospecting: Fulfilling the Mandate of the Biodiversity Convention' (1995) 28 *Vanderbilt Journal of Transnational Law*, 703–54.

Attard, D., *The Exclusive Economic Zone in International Law* (Oxford, Clarendon Press, 1987).

Baillie, J.E.M., Hilton-Taylor, C. and Stuart, S.N. (eds), *2004 IUCN Red List of Threatened Species. A Global Species Assessment* (Gland, IUCN, 2004).

Balton, D.A., 'The Compliance Agreement', in E. Hey (ed.), *Developments in International Fisheries Law* (The Hague, Kluwer, 1999) 31–53.

Balton, D.A. and Zbicz, D.C., 'Managing Deep-Sea Fisheries: Some Threshold Questions' (2004) 19 *IJMCL*, 247–58.

Bardonnet, D. and Virally, M. (eds), *Le nouveau droit international de la mer* (Paris, Pedone, 1983).

Barnes, R., 'The Convention on the Law of the Sea: An Effective Framework for Domestic Fisheries Conservation?', in D. Freestone, R. Barnes and D. Ong (eds), *The Law of the Sea: Progress and Prospects* (Oxford, Oxford University Press, 2006) 233–60.

Barston, R., 'The Law of the Sea and Regional Fisheries Organisations' (1999) 14 *IJMCL*, 333–52.

Baslar, K., *The Concept of the Common Heritage of Mankind in International Law* (The Hague, Martinus Nijhoff Publishers, 1998).

Bastid, Mme P., *Cours de droit international public* (*Les Cours de Droit*, Paris, Université de Paris, 1976–77).

Bayitch, S.A., *Interamerican Law of Fisheries: An Introduction with Documents* (New York, Oceana, 1957).

Beckman, R. and Coleman, B., 'Integrated Coastal Management: The Role of Law and Lawyers' (1999) 14 *IJMCL*, 491–522.

Beer-Gabel, J. and Lestang, V., *Les commissions de pêche et leur droit: La conservation et la gestion des ressources marines vivantes* (Bruxelles, Bruylant, 2003).

Belsky, M.H., 'Management of Large Marine Ecosystems: Developing a New Rule of Customary International Law' (1985) 22 *San Diego Law Review*, 733–63.

Beverton, R.J.H., 'Introduction', in E.D. Brown and R.R. Churchill (eds), *The UN Convention on the Law of the Sea: Impact and Implementation, Proceedings of Law of the Sea Institute Nineteenth Annual Conference* (Honolulu, University of Hawaii, 1987) 363–64.

Beyerlin, U., Stoll, P-T. and Wolfrum, R. (eds), *Ensuring Compliance with Multilateral Environmental Agreement: A Dialogue between Practitioners and Academia* (Leiden and Boston, Nijhoff, 2006).

Bindi, A-L., 'La création et la gestion des aires marines spécialement protégées (AMSP)' (2000) 5 *Annuaire du droit de la mer*, 165–75.

Birnie, P.W., 'Problems Concerning Conservation of Wildlife in the North Sea' (1991) 9 *Ocean Yearbook*, 339–68.

——, 'Reflagging of Fishing Vessels on the High Seas' (1993) 2 *RECIEL*, 270–76.

——, 'Law of the Sea and Ocean Resources: Implications for Marine Scientific Research' (1995) 10 *IJMCL*, 229–51.

——, 'The European Community and Preservation of Biological Diversity', in C. Redgwell and M. Bowman (eds), *International Law and the Conservation of Biological Diversity* (The Hague, Kluwer, 1996) 211–34.

——, 'Are Twentieth-Century Marine Conservation Conventions Adaptable to Twenty-First Century Goals and Principles?: Part I' (1997) 12 *IJMCL*, 307–39.

——, 'New Approaches to Ensuring Compliance at Sea: The FAO Agreement to Promote Compliance with International Conservation and Management Measures by Fishing Vessels on the High Seas' (1999) 8 *RECIEL*, 48–55.

——, 'Marine Mammals: Exploiting the Ambiguities of Article 65 of the Convention on the Law of the Sea and Related Provisions: Practice under the International Convention for the Regulation of Whaling', in D. Freestone, R. Barnes and D. Ong (eds), *The Law of the Sea: Progress and Prospects* (Oxford, Oxford University Press, 2006) 261–80.

——, 'Comment on the Compliance Control Mechanism within the Framework of the International Whaling Convention', in U. Beyerlin, P-T. Stoll and R. Wolfrum (eds), *Ensuring Compliance with Multilateral Environmental Agreement: A Dialogue between Practitioners and Academia* (Leiden and Boston, Nijhoff, 2006) 175–200.

Birnie, P.W. and Boyle, A. (eds), *Basic Documents on International Law and the Environment* (Oxford, Oxford University Press, 1995).

——, *International Law and the Environment*, 2nd edn (Oxford, Oxford University Press, 2002).

Bliss, M., 'The Emerging Concepts for Developing and Strengthening the Legal Regime of the Oceans: Integrated Ocean Management, the Ecosystem-Based Approach and Marine Protected Areas', *Commemoration of the Twentieth Anniversary of the Adoption of the United Nations Convention on the Law of the Sea*, 9 December 2002, 1–13.

Böckenförde, M., 'The Operationalization of the Precautionary Approach in International Environmental Law Treaties: Enhancement or Façade Ten Years After Rio?' (2003) 63 *ZaöRV*, 313–31.

Bodansky, D., 'Remarks', in *The American Society of International Law, Proceedings of the 85th Annual Meeting*, Washington, DC, 17–20 April 1991, 413–17.

Boehlert, G.W., 'Biodiversity and the Sustainability of Marine Fisheries' (1996) 9 *Oceanography*, 28–35.

Boisson de Chazournes, L., 'Technical and Financial Assistance and Compliance: The Interplay', in U. Beyerlin, P-T. Stoll and R. Wolfrum (eds), *Ensuring Compliance with Multilateral Environmental Agreement: A Dialogue between Practitioners and Academia* (Leiden and Boston, Nijhoff, 2006) 273–300.

Bothe, M., 'International Obligations, Means to Secure Performance', in R. Bernhardt (ed.), *Encyclopedia of Public International Law*, Vol. 2 (Amsterdam, North-Holland Elsevier, 1995) 1278–84.

——, 'The Protection of the Marine Environment Against the Impacts of Seabed Mining: An Assessment of the New Mining Code of the International Seabed Authority', in P. Ehlers, E. Mann-Borgese and R. Wolfrum (eds) *Marine Issues: From a Scientific, Political and Legal Perspective* (The Hague, Kluwer, 2002) 221–32.

Boyle, A.E., 'The Convention on Biological Diversity', in L. Campiglio, L. Pineschi, D. Siniscalco, T. Treves and F.E.E. Mattei (eds), *The Environment after Rio: International Law and Economics* (London, Graham & Trotman and Nijhoff, 1994) 111–27.

——, 'The Rio Convention on Biological Diversity', in C. Redgwell and M. Bowman (eds), *International Law and the Conservation of Biological Diversity* (The Hague, Kluwer, 1996) 33–49.

——, 'The *Gabčíkovo-Nagymaros* Case: New Law in Old Bottles' (1997) 8 *Yearbook of Environmental Law*, 13–20.

——, 'Dispute Settlement and the Law of the Sea Convention: Problems of Fragmentation and Jurisdiction' (1997) 46 *ICLQ*, 37–54.

——, 'Problems of Compulsory Jurisdiction and the Settlement of Disputes Relating to Straddling Fish Stocks' (1999) 14 *IJMCL*, 1–25.

——, 'The Southern Bluefin Tuna Arbitration' (2001) 50 *ICLQ*, 447–52.

——, 'Further Development of the Law of the Sea Convention: Mechanisms for Change' (2005) 54 *ICLQ*, 563–84.

Boyle, A.E. and Freestone, D. (eds), *International Law and Sustainable Development: Past Achievements and Future Challenges* (Oxford, Oxford University Press, 1999).

Brierly, J.L., *The Outlook for International Law* (Oxford, Clarendon Press, 1944).

Brown, C., 'Provisional Measures before the ITLOS: The MOX Plant Case' (2002) 17 *IJMCL*, 267–88.

Brown, E.D., *The International Law of the Sea*, Vol. II (Documents, Cases and Tables) (Aldershot, Dartmouth, 1994).

——, *Sea-bed Energy and Minerals: The International Legal Regime, Vol. 3, Selected Documents* (The Hague, Nijhoff, 2001).

Burhenne-Guilmin, F. and Casey-Lefkowitz, S., 'The Convention on Biological Diversity: A Hard Won Global Achievement' (1992) 3 *Yearbook of International Environmental Law*, 43–59.

Burke, W.T., 'U.S. Fishery Management and the New Law of the Sea' (1982) 76 *AJIL*, 24–55.

——, 'UNCED and the Oceans' (1993) 17 *Marine Policy*, 519–33.

——, 'Unregulated High Seas Fishing and Ocean Governance', in J.M. Van Dyke, D. Zaelke and G. Hewison (eds), *Freedom for the Seas in the 21ˢᵗ Century: Ocean Governance and Environmental Harmony* (Washington, DC, Island Press, 1993) 235–71.

——, *The New International Law of Fisheries: UNCLOS 1982 and Beyond* (Oxford, Clarendon Press, 1994).

——, 'State Practice, New Ocean Uses, and Ocean Governance under UNCLOS', in T.A. Mensah (ed.), *Ocean Governance: Strategies and Approaches for the 21st Century: Proceedings of The Law of the Sea Institute Twenty-eighth Annual Conference, Honolulu, Hawaii, July 11–14, 1994* (Honolulu, University of Hawaii, 1996) 219–34.

——, 'Evolution in the Fisheries Provisions of UNCLOS', in N. Ando, E. McWhinney and R. Wolfrum (eds), *Liber Amicorum Judge Shigeru Oda* (The Hague, Kluwer, 2002) 1355–62.

Bury, C. and Sack, J., 'The European Union', in E. Franckx and P. Gautier (eds), *La zone économique exclusive et la Convention des Nations Unies sur le droit de la mer, 1982–2000: un premier bilan de la pratique des Etats* (Bruxelles, Bruylant, 2003) 65–77.

Caddy, J.F. and Cochrane, K.L., 'A Review of Fisheries Management Past and Present and Some Future Perspectives for the Third Millennium' (2001) 44 *Ocean and Coastal Management*, 653–82.

Caflisch, L., 'La convention des Nations Unies sur le droit de la mer adoptée le 30 avril 1982' (1983) 39 *ASDI*, 39–104.

——, 'Fisheries in the Exclusive Economic Zone: An Overview', in U. Leanza (ed.), *The International Legal Regime of the Mediterranean Sea* (Milan, Giuffrè, 1987) 149–71.

Caflisch, L. and Piccard, J., 'The Legal Régime of Marine Scientific Research and the Third United Nations Conference on the Law of the Sea' (1978) 38 *ZaöRV*, 848–901.

Cameron, J. and Abouchar, J., 'The Status of the Precautionary Principle in International Law', in D. Freestone and E. Hey (eds), *The Precautionary Principle and International Law: The Challenge of Implementation* (The Hague, Kluwer Law International, 1996) 29–52.

Cameron, J., Werksman, J. and Roderick, P. (eds), *Improving Compliance with International Environmental Law* (London, Earthscan Publications Ltd, 1996).

Caminos, H., 'The Regime of Fisheries in the Exclusive Economic Zone', in F. Orrego Vicuña (ed.), *The Exclusive Economic Zone, A Latin American Perspective* (Boulder, Colorado, Westview Press, 1984), 143–58.

Caron, D.D. and Scheiber H.N. (eds), *Bringing New Law to Ocean Waters* (Leiden, Brill, 2004).

Carroz, J., 'Les problèmes de la pêche dans la convention sur le droit de la mer et la pratique des Etats', in D. Bardonnet and M. Virally (eds), *Le nouveau droit international de la mer* (Paris, Pedone, 1983) 177–229.

Cassese, A., 'Remarks on Scelle's Theory of "Role Splitting" (*dédoublement fonctionnel)* in International Law' (1990) 1 *EJIL*, 210–31.

Cataldi, G., 'La pêche dans les eaux soumises à la souveraineté ou à la juridiction des Etats côtiers', in D. Vignes, G. Cataldi and R.C. Raigón (eds), *Le droit international de la pêche maritime* (Bruxelles, Bruylant, 2000) 47–116.

Chandler, M., 'The Biodiversity Convention: Selected Issues of Interest to the International Lawyer' (1993) 4 *Colorado Journal of International Environmental Law and Policy*, 141–175.

Charlier, R-E., 'Résultats et enseignements des conférences du droit de la mer' (Genève 1958 and 1960) (1960) 6 *AFDI*, 63–76.

Churchill, R.R., 'The Fisheries Jurisdiction Cases: The Contribution of the International Court of Justice to the Debate on Coastal States' Fisheries Rights' (1975) 24 *ICLQ*, 82–105.

——, 'Legal Uncertainties in International High Seas Fisheries Management' (1998) 37 *Fisheries Research*, 225–37.

——, 'Levels of Implementation of the Law of the Sea Convention: An Overview', in D. Vidas and W. Østreng (eds), *Order for the Oceans at the Turn of the Century* (The Hague, Kluwer, 1999) 317–25.

——, 'International Tribunal for the Law of the Sea: The Southern Bluefin Tuna Cases (New Zealand v Japan; Australia v Japan): Order for Provisional Measures of 27 August 1999' (2000) 49 *ICLQ*, 979–90.

——, 'Managing Straddling Fish Stocks in the North-East Atlantic: A Multiplicity of Instruments and Regime Linkage – but How Effective a Management?', in O. Schram Stokke (ed.), *Governing High Seas Fisheries: The Interplay of Global and Regional Regimes* (Oxford, Oxford University Press, 2001) 235–72.

——, '10 Years of the UN Convention on the Law of the Sea: Towards a Global Ocean Regime? A General Appraisal' (2005) 48 *GYIL*, 81–116.

——, 'The Impact of State Practice on the Jurisdictional Framework Contained in the LOS Convention', in Alex G. Oude Elferink (ed.), *Stability and Change in the Law of the Sea: The Role of the LOS Convention* (Leiden and Boston, Nijhoff, 2005) 91–143.

——, 'The Management of Shared Fish Stocks: The Neglected "Other" Paragraph of Article 63 of the UN Convention on the Law of the Sea', in A. Strati, M. Gavouneli and N. Skourtos (eds), *Unresolved Issues and New Challenges to the Law of the Sea: Time Before and Time After* (Leiden and Boston, Nijhoff, 2006) 3–19.

Churchill, R.R. and Lowe, A.V., *The Law of the Sea*, 3rd edn (Manchester, Manchester University Press, 1999).

——, 'The International Tribunal for the Law of the Sea: Survey for 2001' (2002) 17 *IJMCL*, 477–84.

Churchill, R. and Scott, J., 'The MOX Plant Litigation: The First Half-Life' (2004) 53 *ICLQ*, 643–76.

Cicin-Sain, B., 'Sustainable Development and Integrated Coastal Management' (1993) 21 *Ocean and Coastal Management*, 11–43.

Cicin-Sain, B., Knedht, R.W., Bowman, L.D. and Fisk, G.W., 'Emerging Policy Issues in the Development of Marine Biotechnology' (1996) 12 *Ocean Yearbook*, 179–206.

Cicin-Sain, B. and Knecht, R.W., *Integrated Coastal and Ocean Management: Concepts and Practices* (Washington, DC, Island Press, 1998).

Combacau, J., *Le droit international de la mer, (Que sais-je?)* (Paris, PUF, 1985).

Curran, P.A. and Long, R.J., 'Fishery Law, Unilateral Enforcement in International Waters: The Case of the "Estai"' (1996) 5 *Irish Journal of European Law*, 123–63.

Dahl, A.L., 'Land-Based Pollution and Integrated Coastal Management' (1993) 17 *Marine Policy*, 561–72.

Dalton, J.G., 'The Chilean Mar Presencial: A Harmless Concept or a Dangerous Precedent?' (1993) 8 *IJMCL*, 397–418.

Damrosch, L.F., 'Enforcing International Law Through Non-Forcible Measures' (1997) 269 *RCADI*, 9–250.

Davies, P.G.G. and Redgwell, C., 'The International Legal Regulation of Straddling Fish Stocks' (1996) 67 *BYIL*, 199–274.

Daw, T. and Gray, T., 'Fisheries Science and Sustainability in International Policy: A Study of Failure in the European Union's Common Fisheries Policy' (2005) 29 *Marine Policy*, 189–97.

De Fontaubert, A.C., 'The Politics of Negotiation at the United Nations Conference on Straddling Fish Stocks and Highly Migratory Fish Stocks' (1995) 29 *Ocean and Coastal Management*, 79–91.

De Fontaubert, A.C., Downes, D.R. and Agardy, T.S., 'Biodiversity in the Seas: Implementing the Convention on Biological Diversity in Marine and Coastal Habitats' (1998) 10 *Georgetown International Environmental Law Review*, 753–854.

De Klemm, C., *Biological Diversity Convention and the Law: Legal Mechanisms for Conserving Species and Ecosystems*, (Gland, IUCN-The World Conservation Union, 1993).

De Lapradelle, A.G., 'Le droit de l'État sur la mer territoriale' (1898) 5 *RGDIP*, 264–84; 309–47.

De La Fayette, L., 'The OSPAR Convention Comes into Force: Continuity and Progress' (1999) 14 *IJMCL*, 247–97.

——, 'The Fisheries Jurisdiction Case (Spain v Canada), Judgment on Jurisdiction of 4 December 1998' (1999) 48 *ICLQ*, 664–72.

De Marffy, A., 'Les difficultés posées par la mise en application du nouveau régime de la recherche scientifique marine avant l'entrée en vigueur de la Convention des Nations Unies sur le droit de la mer' (1989) 35 *AFDI*, 736–51.

——, 'Marine Scientific Research', in R-J. Dupuy and D. Vignes (eds), *A Handbook on the New Law of the Sea*, Vol. 2 (Dordrecht, Nijhoff, 1991) 1127–46.

——, 'La place des organisations internationales compétentes dans la mise en application du régime de la ZEE', in E. Franckx and P. Gautier (eds), *La zone économique exclusive et la Convention des Nations Unies sur le droit de la mer, 1982–2000: un premier bilan de la pratique des Etats* (Bruxelles, Bruylant, 2003) 51–63.

——, 'Ocean Governance: A Process in the Right Direction for the Effective Management of the Oceans' (2004) 18 *Ocean Yearbook*, 162–92.

De Martens, F., 'Le Tribunal d'Arbitrage de Paris et la mer territoriale' (1894) 1 *RGDIP*, 32–43.

De Santo, E.M. and Jones, P.J.S., 'Offshore Marine Conservation Policies in the North East Atlantic: Emerging Tensions and Opportunities' (2007) 31 *Marine Policy*, 336–47.

De Vattel, E., *Le droit des gens ou principes de la loi naturelle, Appliqués à la conduite et aux affaires des Nations et des Souverains*, Vol. 1 (Reproduction of Books I and II of Edition of 1758) (Washington, Carnegie Institution of Washington, 1916). Translated by J. Chitty, *The Law of Nations; or, Principles of the Law of Nature, Applied to the Conduct and Affairs of Nations and Sovereigns* (Philadelphia, T. & J.W. Johnson and Co., Law Booksellers, 1863).

De Yturriaga, J.A., 'Fishing in the High Seas : From the 1982 UN Convention on the Law of the Sea to the 1995 Agreement on Straddling and Highly Migratory Fish Stocks' (1996) 3 *African Yearbook of International Law*, 151–81.

——, *The International Regime of Fisheries: From UNCLOS 1982 to the Presential Sea* (The Hague, Nijhoff, 1997).

Detjen, M., 'The Western European PSSA – Testing a Unique International Concept to Protect Imperilled Marine Ecosystems' (2006) 30 *Marine Policy*, 442–53.

Dinh, N.Q., 'La revendication des droits préférentiels de pêche en haute mer devant les Conférences des Nations Unies sur le droit de la mer de 1958 et 1960' (1960) 6 *AFDI*, 77–110.

——, *Droit international public*, 1st edn (Paris, L.G.D.J., 1975).

Dinh, N.Q., Daillier, P. and Pellet, A., *Droit international public*, 6th edn (Paris, L.G.D.J., 1999).

Duda, A.M. and Sherman, K., 'A New Imperative for Improving Management of Large Marine Ecosystems' (2002) 45 *Ocean and Coastal Management*, 797–833.

Dupuy, P-M., 'Humanité, communauté et efficacité du droit', in *Humanité et droit international, Mélanges René-Jean Dupuy* (Paris, Pedone, 1991) 133–48.

——, 'Où en est le droit international de l'environnement à la fin du siècle' (1997) 101 *RGDIP*, 873–903.

——, 'L'unité de l'ordre juridique international: Cours général de droit international public (2000)' (2002) 297 *RCADI*, 9–490.

——, 'Le principe de précaution et le droit international de la mer', in *La mer et son droit: Mélanges offerts à Laurent Lucchini et Jean-Pierre Quéneudec* (Paris, Pedone, 2003) 205–20.

——, *Droit international public*, 8th edn (Paris, Dalloz, 2006).

Dupuy, R-J., 'Communauté internationale et disparités de développement: Cours général de droit international public' (1979) 165 *RCADI*, 9–232.

——, 'The Sea Under National Competence', in R-J. Dupuy and D. Vignes (eds), *A Handbook on the New Law of the Sea*, Vol. 1 (Dordrecht, Nijhoff, 1991) 247–313.

——, 'La notion de patrimoine commun de l'humanité appliquée aux fonds marins', in R-J. Dupuy, *Dialectiques du droit international: souveraineté des Etats, communauté internationale et droits de l'humanité* (Paris, Pedone, 1999) 189–94.

——, *Le droit international public, Que sais-je?*, 11th edn (Paris, PUF, 2001).

Dzidzornu, D.M., 'Four Principles in Marine Environment Protection: A Comparative Analysis' (1998) 29 *ODIL*, 91–123.

——, 'Marine Environment Protection under Regional Conventions: Limits to the Contribution of Procedural Norms' (2002) 33 *ODIL*, 291–8.

Ebbesson, J., 'A Critical Assessment of the 1992 Baltic Sea Convention' (2000) 43 *GYIL*, 38–64.

——, 'Protection of the Marine Environment of the Baltic Sea Area: The Impact of the Stockholm Declaration', in M.H. Nordquist, J.N. Moore and S. Mahmoudi (eds), *The Stockholm Declaration and Law of the Marine Environment* (The Hague, Nijhoff, 2003) 155–64.

Edeson, W., 'Sustainable Use of Marine Living Resources' (2003) 63 *ZaöRV*, 355–75.

Ehlers, P., Mann-Borgese, E. and Wolfrum, R. (eds), *Marine Issues: From a Scientific, Political and Legal Perspective* (The Hague, Kluwer, 2002).

Engelhardt, E.D., 'De l'exécution de la sentence arbitrale de 1893 sur les pêcheries de Behring' (1898) 5 *RGDIP*, 193–207.

Epiney, A., 'The Role of NGO in the Process of Ensuring Compliance with MEAs', in U. Beyerlin, P-T. Stoll and R. Wolfrum (eds), *Ensuring Compliance with Multilateral Environmental Agreement: A Dialogue between Practitioners and Academia* (Leiden and Boston, Nijhoff, 2006) 319–52.

Erceg, D., 'Deterring IUU Fishing through State Control over Nationals' (2006) 30 *Marine Policy*, 173–9.

Evans, M.D. (ed.), *Blackstone's International Law Documents*, 6th edn (Oxford, Oxford University Press, 2003).

Fanning, L., Mahon, R., McConney, P., Angulo, J., Burrows, F., Chakalall, B., Gil, D., Haughton, M., Heileman, S., Maritínez, S., Ostine, L., Oviedo, A., Parsons, S., Phillips, T., Santizo Arroya, C., Simmons, B. and Toro, C., 'A Large Marine Ecosystem Governance Framework' (2007) 31 *Marine Policy*, 434–43.

Favoreu, L., 'Les affaires de la compétence en matière de pêcheries (Royaume-Uni c. Islande et Allemagne Fédérale c. Islande) Arrêts du 25 juillet 1974 (fond)' (1974) 20 *AFDI*, 253–85.

Feintuck, M., 'Precautionary Maybe, but What's the Principle? The Precautionary Principle, the Regulation of Risk, and the Public Domain' (2005) 32 *Journal of Law and Society*, 371–98.

Fisher, E., 'Is the Precautionary Principle Justiciable?' (2001) 13 *Journal of Environmental Law*, 315–34.

——, 'Precaution, Precaution Everywhere: Developing a "Common Understanding" of the Precautionary Principle in the European Community' (2002) 9 *Maastricht Journal of European and Comparative Law*, 7–28.

Fitzmaurice, M.A., 'International Protection of the Environment' (2001) 293 *RCADI*, 9–488.

Fleischer, C.A., 'Fisheries and Biological Resources', in R-J. Dupuy and D. Vignes (eds), *A Handbook on the New Law of the Sea*, Vol. 2 (Dordrecht, Nijhoff, 1991) 989–1126.

Floit, C., 'Reconsidering Freedom of the High Seas: Protection of Living Marine Resources on the High Seas', in J.M. Van Dyke, D. Zaelke and G. Hewison (eds), *Freedom for the Seas in the 21ˢᵗ Century: Ocean Governance and Environmental Harmony* (Washington, DC, Covelo, California, Island Press, 1993) 310–26.

Fortier, L.Y., 'From Confrontation to Cooperation on the High Seas: Recent Developments in International Law Concerning the Conservation of Marine

Resources,' in N. Ando, E. McWhinney and R. Wolfrum (eds), *Liber Amicorum Judge Shigeru Oda* (The Hague, Kluwer, 2002) 1377–90.

Fosså, J.H., Mortensen, P.B. and Furevik, D.M., 'The Deep-Water Coral *Lophelia Pertusa* in Norwegian Waters: Distribution and Fishery Impacts' (2002) 471 *Hydrobiologa*, 1–12.

Foster, C.E., 'The "Real Dispute" in the Southern Bluefin Tuna Case: A Scientific Dispute?' (2001) 16 *IJMCL*, 571–601.

Francioni, F. and Scovazzi,T. (eds), *Biotechnology and International Law* (Oxford and Portland, Oregon, Hart Publishing, 2006).

Franckx, E., '*Pacta Tertiis* and the Agreement for the Implementation of the Provisions of the United Nations Convention on the Law of the Sea of 10 December 1982 relating to the Conservation and Management of Straddling Fish Stocks and Highly Migratory Fish Stocks' (2000) 8 *FAO Legal Papers Online*, 2–28.

Franckx, E. (ed.), *Vessel-source Pollution and Coastal State Jurisdiction: The Work of the ILA Committee on Coastal State Jurisdiction Relating to Marine Pollution (1991–2000)* (The Hague, Kluwer, 2001).

Franckx, E. and Gautier, P. (eds), *La zone économique exclusive et la Convention des Nations Unies sur le droit de la mer, 1982–2000: un premier bilan de la pratique des États* (Bruxelles, Bruylant, 2003).

Frank, V., 'Consequences of the Prestige Sinking for European and International Law' (2005) 20 *IJMCL*, 1–64.

Freestone, D., 'International Law and Sea Level Rise', in R. Churchill and D. Freestone (eds), *International Law and Global Climate Change* (London, Nijhoff, 1991) 109–25.

——, 'The Conservation of Marine Ecosystems under International Law', in C. Redgwell and M. Bowman (eds), *International Law and the Conservation of Biological Diversity* (The Hague, Kluwer, 1996) 91–107.

——, 'International Fisheries Law Since Rio: The Continued Rise of the Precautionary Principle,' in A. Boyle and D. Freestone, *International Law and Sustainable Development: Past Achievements and Future Challenges* (Oxford, Oxford University Press, 1999) 135–64.

Freestone, D., Barnes, R. and Ong, D. (eds), *The Law of the Sea: Progress and Prospects* (Oxford, Oxford University Press, 2006).

Freestone, D. and Hey, E., 'Origin and Development of the Precautionary Principle', in D. Freestone and E. Hey (eds), *The Precautionary Principle and International Law: The Challenge of Implementation* (The Hague, Kluwer, 1996) 3–15.

Freestone, D. and Hey, E. (eds), *The Precautionary Principle and International Law: The Challenge of Implementation* (The Hague, Kluwer Law International, 1996).

Freestone, D. and Ijlstra, T. (eds), *The North Sea: Basic Legal Documents on Regional Environmental Co-operation* (Dordrecht, Graham and Trotman/ Nijhoff, 1991).

Freestone, D. and Makuch, Z., 'The New International Environmental Law of Fisheries: The 1995 United Nations Straddling Stocks Agreement' (1996) 7 *Yearbook of International Environmental Law*, 3–51.

Freiwald, A., Fosså, J.H., Grehan, A., Koslow, T. and Roberts, J.M., *Cold-Water Coral Reefs* (Cambridge, UNEP World Conservation Monitoring Centre, 2004).

Friedmann, W., *The Changing Structure of International Law* (London, Stevens and Sons, 1964).

——, 'General Course in Public International Law' (1969) 127 *RCADI*, 39–246.

——, 'Selden Redivivus: Toward a Partition of the Seas?' (1971) 65 *AJIL*, 757–70.

Frid, C., Paramor, O. and Scott, C., 'Ecosystem-based Fisheries Management: Progress in the NE Atlantic' (2005) 29 *Marine Policy*, 461–9.

Fulton, T.W., *The Sovereignty of the Sea* (Edinburgh and London, William Blackwood and Sons, 1911).

Fur Seal Arbitration, *Proceedings of the Tribunal of Arbitration Convened at Paris under the Treaty Between the United States of America and Great Britain, Concluded at Washington, February 29, 1892, for the Determination of Questions between the Two Governments Concerning the Jurisdictional Rights of the United States in the Waters of the Bering Sea*, 16 Vols (Washington, DC, Government Printing Office, 1895).

Garcia, S.M., 'The Precautionary Principle: Its Implications in Capture Fisheries Management' (1994) 22 *Ocean and Coastal Management*, 99–125.

Garcia, S.M. and Hayashi, M., 'Division of the Oceans and Ecosystem Management: A Contrastive Spatial Evolution of Marine Fisheries Governance' (2000) 43 *Ocean and Coastal Management*, 445–74.

Gaston, K.J. and Spicer, J.I., *Biodiversity: An Introduction*, 2nd edn (Oxford, Blackwell Publishing, 2004).

Gauci, G.M., 'Protection of the Marine Environment through the International Ship-Source Oil Pollution Compensation Regimes' (1999) 8 *RECIEL*, 29–36.

Gautier, P., 'L'Etat du pavillon et la protection des intérêts liés au navire', in M.G. Kohen (ed.), *Promoting Justice, Human Rights and Conflict Resolution through International Law, Liber Amicorum Lucius Caflisch* (Leiden, Nijhoff, 2007) 717–45.

Gherari, H., 'L'accord du 4 août 1995 sur les stocks chevauchants et les stocks de poissons grands migrateurs' (1996) 100 *RGDIP*, 367–90.

Gidel, G., *Le droit international public de la mer: Le temps de paix*, Tome 3, La mer territoriale et la zone contiguë, Fascicule I (Paris, Edouard Duchemin, reprint 1981).

Ginther, K., Denters, H. and de Waart, P.J.I.M. (eds), *Sustainable Development and Good Governance* (Dordrecht, Kluwer, 1995).

Gjerde, K.M., 'High Seas Marine Protected Areas' (2001) 16 *IJMCL*, 515–28.

——, 'Ecosystems and Biodiversity in Deep Waters and High Seas' (2006) 178 *UNEP Regional Sea Report and Studies*, 22–32.

Gjerde, K.M. and Breide, C., *Towards a Strategy for High Seas Marine Protected Areas*, Proceedings of the IUCN, WCPA and WWF Experts Workshop on High Seas Marine Protected Areas, 15–17 January 2003, Malaga, Spain (Gland, IUCN, 2003).

Gjerde, K. and Freestone, D., 'Particularly Sensitive Sea Areas: An Important Environmental Concept at a Turning-point' (1994) 9 *IJMCL*, 431–68.

——, 'Unfinished Business: Deep-Sea Fisheries and the Conservation of Marine Biodiversity Beyond National Jurisdiction, Editors' Introduction' (2004) 19 *IJMCL*, 209–22.

Glowka, L., 'The Deepest of Ironies: Genetic Resources, Marine Scientific Research, and the Area' (1996) 12 *Ocean Yearbook*, 154–78.

——, 'Genetic Resources, Marine Scientific Research and the International Seabed Area' (1999) 8 *RECIEL*, 56–66.

——, 'Beyond the Deepest of Ironies: Genetic Resources, Marine Scientific Research and International Seabed Area', in J-P. Beurier, A. Kiss and S. Mahmoudi (eds), *New Technologies and Law of the Marine Environment* (The Hague, Kluwer, 2000) 75–93.

Gonzalez-Laxe, F., 'The Precautionary Principle in Fisheries Management' (2005) 29 *Marine Policy*, 495–505.

Goote, M.M., 'Convention on Biological Diversity: The Jakarta Mandate on Marine and Coastal Biological Diversity' (1997) 12 *IJMCL*, 377–95.

Gorina-Ysern, M., *An International Regime for Marine Scientific Research* (New York, Transnational Publishers, 2003).

Gowlland-Debbas, V., 'Judicial Insights into Fundamental Values and Interests of the International Community,' in A.S. Muller, D. Raič and J.M. Thuránszky (eds), *The International Court of Justice: Its Future Role after Fifty Years* (The Hague, Nijhoff, 1997) 327–66.

Goy, R., 'L'affaire du thon à nageoire bleue: Tribunal International du Droit de la Mer, Ordonnance du 27 août 1999 et sentence arbitrale du 4 août 2000' (2001) 14 *Espaces et ressources maritimes*, 47–73.

Gros, A., 'La convention sur la pêche et la conservation des ressources biologiques de la haute mer' (1959-II) 97 *RCADI*, 1–88.

Gross, L., 'The Peace of Westphalia 1648–1948' (1948) 42 *AJIL*, 20–41.

Gubbay, S., 'Marine Protected Areas – Past, Present and Future', in S. Gubbay (ed.), *Marine Protected Areas: Principles and Techniques for Management* (London, Chapman and Hall, 1995) 1–14.

——, (ed.), *Marine Protected Areas: Principles and Techniques for Management* (London, Chapman and Hall, 1995).

——, 'Protecting the Natural Resources of the High Seas', Scientific Document in *IUCN, WCPA and WWF High Seas Marine Protected Areas Workshop*, Malaga, 15–17 January 2003, 1–29.

Gündling, L., 'Compliance Assistance in International Environmental Law: Capacity-Building through Financial and Technology Transfer' (1996) 56 *ZaöRV*, 796–809.

Haeuber, R., 'Setting the Environmental Policy Agenda: The Case of Ecosystem Management' (1996) 36 *Natural Resources Journal*, 1–28.

Hahn, H.J., 'International Control', in R. Bernhardt (ed.), *Encyclopedia of Public International Law*, Vol. 2 (Amsterdam, North-Holland, 1995) 1079–84.

Handl, G., 'Environmental Security and Global Change: The Challenge to International Law' (1990) 1 *Yearbook of International Environmental Law*, 3–33.

Hassan, D., *Protecting the Marine Environment from Land-Based Sources of Pollution: Towards Effective International Cooperation* (Hampshire, Ashgate, 2006).

Haward, M., 'IUU Fishing: Contemporary Practice', in A.G. Oude Elferink and D.R. Rothwell (eds), *Oceans Management in the 21st Century: Institutional Frameworks and Responses* (Leiden, Nijhoff, 2004) 87–105.

Hayashi, M., 'The 1995 Agreement on the Conservation and Management of Straddling and Highly Migratory Fish Stocks: Significance for the Law of the Sea Convention' (1995) 29 *Ocean and Coastal Management*, 51–69.

——, 'Enforcement by Non-Flag States on the High Seas Under the 1995 Agreement on Straddling and Highly Migratory Fish Stocks' (1996) 9 *The Georgetown International Environmental Law Review*, 1–36.

——, 'The 1995 UN Fish Stocks Agreement and the Law of the Sea', in D. Vidas and W. Østreng (eds), *Order for the Oceans at the Turn of the Century* (The Hague, Kluwer, 1999) 37–53.

——, 'The Straddling and Highly Migratory Fish Stocks Agreement', in E. Hey (ed.), *Developments in International Fisheries Law* (The Hague, Kluwer, 1999) 55–83.

——, 'Three Decades' Progress in High Seas Fisheries Governance: Towards a Common Heritage Regime?', in M.H. Nordquist, J.N. Moore and S. Mahmoudi (eds), *The Stockholm Declaration and Law of the Marine Environment* (The Hague, Nijhoff, 2003) 375–98.

——, 'New Developments in International Fisheries Law and the Freedom of High Seas Fishing' (in Japanese) (2003) 102 *The Journal of International Law and Diplomacy*, 156–77.

——, 'High Seas Fisheries' (in Japanese) in C. Mizukami (ed.), *The Contemporary Law of the Sea* (Tokyo, Yushindo, 2003) 3–39.

——, 'Global Governance of Deep-Sea Fisheries' (2004) 19 *IJMCL*, 289–98.

Heintschell von Heinegg, W., 'The Development of Environmental Standards for the North-East Atlantic, including the North Sea', in P. Ehlers, E. Mann-Borgese and R. Wolfrum (eds), *Marine Issues: From a Scientific, Political and Legal Perspective* (The Hague, Kluwer, 2002) 135–53.

Hendrickx, F., Koester, V. and Prip, C., 'Convention on Biological Diversity, Access to Genetic Resources: A Legal Analysis' (1993) 23 *Environmental Policy and Law*, 250–58.

Henne, G. and Fakir, S., 'The Regime Building of the Convention on Biological Diversity on the Road to Nairobi' (1999) 3 *Max Planck Yearbook of United Nations Law*, 314–61.

Henriksen, T., Hønneland, G. and Sydnes, A., *Law and Politics in Ocean Governance: The UN Fish Stocks Agreement and Regional Fisheries Management Regimes* (Leiden and Boston, Nijhoff, 2006).

Hentrich, S. and Salomon, M., 'Flexible Management of Fishing Rights and a Sustainable Fisheries Industry in Europe' (2006) 30 *Marine Policy*, 712–20.

Hermitte, M-A., 'La convention sur la diversité biologique' (1992) 38 *AFDI*, 844–70.

Hewison, G.J., 'The Precautionary Approach to Fisheries Management: An Environmental Perspective' (1996) 11 *IJMCL*, 301–32.

Hey, E., 'The Precautionary Approach: Implications of the Revision of the Oslo and Paris Conventions' (1991) *Marine Policy*, 244–54.

——, 'A Healthy North Sea Ecosystem and a Healthy North Sea Fishery: Two Sides of the Same Regulation?' (1992) 23 *ODIL*, 217–38.

——, 'Global Fisheries Regulations in the First Half of the 1990s' (1996) 11 *IJMCL*, 459–90.

——, 'The Protection of Marine Ecosystems, Science, Technology and International Law' (1997) 10 *Hague Yearbook of International Law*, 69–84.

—— (ed.), *Developments in International Fisheries Law* (The Hague, Kluwer, 1999).

——, 'The International Regime for the Protection of the North Sea: From Functional Approaches to a More Integrated Approach' (2002) 17 *IJMCL*, 325–50.

Hey, E., Ijlstra, T. and Nolkaemper, A., 'The 1992 Paris Convention for the Protection of the Marine Environment of the North-East Atlantic: A Critical Analysis' (1993) 8 *IJMCL*, 1–76.

Hilf, J., 'The Convention for the Protection of the Marine Environment of the North-East Atlantic: New Approaches to an Old Problem?' (1995) 55 *ZaöRV*, 580–603.

Hohmann, H., *Basic Documents of International Environmental Law*, 3 Vols (London, Nijhoff, 1992).

Hyvarinen, J., Wall, E. and Lutchman, I., 'The United Nations and Fisheries in 1998' (1998) 29 *ODIL*, 323–38.

International Maritime Organisation, *MARPOL 73/78 Consolidated Edition 2002* (London, IMO, 2002).

——, *Particularly Sensitive Sea Areas: Compilation of Official Guidance Documents and PSSAs Adopted Since 1990* (London, IMO, 2007).

Iudicello, S. and Lytle, M., 'Marine Biodiversity and International Law: Instruments and Institutions that can be Used to Conserve Marine Biological Diversity Internationally' (1994) 8 *Tulane Environmental Law Journal*, 123–61.

Iwama, T., 'On the Precautionary Principle in International Environmental Law' (in Japanese) (2004) 1264 *Jurist*, 54–63.

Jameson, S.C., Tupper, M.H. and Ridley, J.M., 'The Three Screen Doors: Can Marine "Protected" Areas Be Effective?' (2002) 44 *Marine Pollution Bulletin*, 1177–83.

Jarmache, E., 'Sur quelques difficultés de la recherche scientifique marine', in *La mer et son droit: Mélanges offerts à Laurent Lucchini et Jean-Pierre Quéneudec* (Paris, Pedone, 2003) 303–14.

Jessup, P.C., *The Law of Territorial Waters and Maritime Jurisdiction* (New York, G.A. Jennings Co., Inc, 1927).

Johnston, D.M., 'Is Coastal State Fishery Management Successful or Not?' (1991) 22 *ODIL*, 199–208.

——, 'Vulnerable Coastal and Marine Areas: A Framework for the Planning of Environmental Security Zones in the Ocean' (1993) 24 *ODIL*, 63–79.

Johnston, S, 'The Convention on Biological Diversity: The Next Phase' (1997) 6 *RECIEL*, 219–30.

Joyner, C.C., 'Biodiversity in the Marine Environment: Resource Implications for the Law of the Sea' (1995) 28 *Vanderbilt Journal of Transnational Law*, 635–87.

Joyner, C.C. and De Cola, P.N., 'Chile's Presential Sea Proposal: Implications for Straddling Stocks and the International Law of Fisheries' (1993) 24 *ODIL*, 99–121.

Juda, L., *International Law and Ocean Use Management: The Evolution of Ocean Governance* (London and New York, Routledge, 1996).

——, 'Considerations in Developing a Functional Approach to the Governance of Large Marine Ecosystems' (1999) 30 *ODIL*, 89–125.

——, 'Rio Plus Ten: The Evolution of International Marine Fisheries Governance' (2002) 33 *ODIL*, 109–44.

——, 'Changing Perspectives on the Oceans: Implications for International Fisheries and Oceans Governance', in D.D. Caron and H.N. Scheiber (eds), *Bringing New Law to Ocean Waters* (Leiden, Brill, 2004) 17–27.

Kagami, Y., 'Developing MPAs under the UNCLOS Regime: Focusing on the Practice in the Exclusive Economic Zone' (in Japanese) (2005) 1 *Ocean Policy Studies*, 153–220.

Kanehara, A., 'A Critical Analysis of Changes and Recent Developments in the Concept of Conservation of Fishery Resources on the High Seas' (1998) 41 *The Japanese Annual of International Law*, 1–29.

Kaye, S.B., *International Fisheries Management* (The Hague, Kluwer, 2001).

——, 'Implementing High Seas Biodiversity Conservation: Global Geopolitical Considerations' (2004) 28 *Marine Policy*, 221–6.

Kelleher, G. (ed.), *Guidelines for Marine Protected Areas* (Gland, IUCN-The World Conservation Union, 1999).

Kesteven, G.L., 'MSY Revisited: A Realistic Approach to Fisheries Management and Administration' (1997) 21 *Marine Policy*, 73–82.

Kimball, L.A., 'Institutional Linkages Between the Convention on Biological Diversity and Other International Conventions' (1997) 6 *RECIEL*, 239–48.

——, 'Deep-Sea Fisheries of the High Seas: The Management Impasse' (2004) 19 *IJMCL*, 259–87.

Kingsbury, B., 'The Concept of Compliance as a Function of Competing Conceptions of International Law' (1998) 19 *Michigan Journal of International Law*, 345–72.

Kirchner, A. (ed.), *International Marine Environmental Law* (The Hague, Kluwer, 2003).

Kirk, E.A., 'Maritime Zones and the Ecosystem Approach: A Mismatch?' (1999) 8 *RECIEL*, 67–72.

Kiss, A-C., 'La notion de patrimoine commun de l'humanité' (1982-II) 175 *RCADI*, 101–256.

Kiss, A., 'The Rights and Interests of Future Generations and the Precautionary Principle', in D. Freestone and E. Hey (eds), *The Precautionary Principle and International Law: The Challenge of Implementation* (The Hague, Kluwer Law International, 1996), 19–28.

——, 'Reporting Obligations and Assessment of Reports', in U. Beyerlin, P-T. Stoll and R. Wolfrum (eds), *Ensuring Compliance with Multilateral Environmental Agreement: A Dialogue between Practitioners and Academia* (Leiden and Boston, Nijhoff, 2006), 229–45.

Kiss, A-C. and Doumbe-Bille, S., 'La conférence des Nations Unies sur l'environnement et le développement (Rio de Janeiro, 3–14 Juin 1992)' (1992) 38 *AFDI*, 823–43.

Kiss, A. and Shelton D., *Manual of European Environmental Law*, 2nd edn (Cambridge, Cambridge University Press, 1997).

Klein, N., *Dispute Settlement in the UN Convention on the Law of the Sea* (Cambridge, Cambridge University Press, 2005).

Kopelmanas, L., 'Le contrôle international' (1950-II) 77 *RCADI*, 57–147.

Krämer, L., *EC Environmental Law*, 4th edn (London, Sweet and Maxwell, 2000).

Kullenberg, G., 'Reflections on Marine Science Contributions to Sustainable Development' (1995) 29 *Ocean and Coastal Management*, 35–49.

Kuribayashi, T., *Chukai Kokuren Kaiyoho Jyoyaku* (in Japanese) (*Commentary on the United Nations Convention on the Law of the Sea*) (Tokyo, Yuhikaku, 1994).

Kuwabara, S., *The Legal Regime of Protection of the Mediterranean Against Pollution from Land-Based Sources* (Dublin, Tycooly International Publishing Ltd, 1984).

Kuwahara, T., 'La notion de domaine public international' (in Japanese) (1987) 97 *The Hitotsubashi Review*, 867–77.

——, *International Law of the Sea* (in Japanese) (Tokyo, Kokusaishoin, 1992).

——, *Introduction to International Law of the Sea* (in Japanese) (Tokyo, Shinzansha, 2002).

Kwiatkowska, B., *The 200 Mile Exclusive Economic Zone in the New Law of the Sea* (Dordrecht, Nijhoff, 1989).

——, 'The Role of Regional Organizations in Development Cooperation in Marine Affairs', in A.H.A. Soons, *Implementation of the Law of the Sea Convention Through International Institutions, Proceedings of the 23rd Annual Conference of the Law of the Sea Institute, June 12–15, 1989* (Honolulu, University of Hawaii, 1990) 38–138.

——, 'The High Seas Fisheries Regime: At a Point of No Return?' (1993) 8 *IJMCL*, 327–55.

——, 'The Southern Bluefin Tuna (New Zealand v Japan; Australia v Japan) Cases' (2000) 15 *IJMCL*, 1–36.

——, 'The Australia and New Zealand v Japan Southern Bluefin Tuna (Jurisdiction and Admissibility) Award of the First Law of the Sea Convention Annex VII Arbitral Tribunal' (2001) 16 *IJMCL*, 239–93.

——, 'The Southern Bluefin Tuna Award (Jurisdiction and Admissibility)', in N. Ando, E. McWhinney and R. Wolfrum (eds), *Liber Amicorum Judge Shigeru Oda* (The Hague, Kluwer, 2002) 697–730.

——, 'The Ireland v United Kingdom (MOX Plant) Case: Applying the Doctrine of Treaty Parallelism' (2003) 18 *IJMCL*, 1–58.

Labat, B., 'Le concept chilien de "Mer presencielle" et ses conséquences sur le régime de la pêche dans la partie de la haute mer adjacente à la limite des 200 milles marins' (1997) 2 *Annuaire du droit de la mer*, 29–52.

Lagoni, R., 'Principles Applicable to Living Resources Occurring Both Within and Without the Exclusive Economic Zone or in Zones of Overlapping Claims', in International Law Association, *Report of the Sixty-Fifth Conference at Cairo in 1992* (1993) 254–85.

——, 'Monitoring Compliance and Enforcement of Compliance Through the OSPAR Commission', in P. Ehlers, E. Mann-Borgese and R. Wolfrum (eds), *Marine Issues: From a Scientific, Political and Legal Perspective* (The Hague, Kluwer, 2002), 155–63.

——, 'Marine Protected Areas in the Exclusive Economic Zone', in A. Kirchner (ed.), *International Marine Environmental Law: Institutions, Implementation and Innovations* (The Hague, Kluwer, 2003) 157–67.

——, 'Regional Protection of the Marine Environment in the Northeast Atlantic Under the OSPAR Convention of 1992', in M.H. Nordquist, J.N. Moore and S. Mahmoudi (eds), *The Stockholm Declaration and Law of the Marine Environment* (The Hague, Nijhoff, 2003) 183–203.

Lang, W. (ed.), *Sustainable Development and International Law* (Dordrecht, Nijhoff, 1995).

——, 'Compliance Control in International Environmental Law: Institutional Necessities' (1996) 56 *ZaöRV*, 685–95.

Langavant, E. and Pirotte, O., 'L'affaire des pêcheries islandaises: L'arrêt de la Cour Internationale de Justice du 25 juillet 1974' (1976) 80 *RGDIP*, 55–103.

Leary, D.K., *International Law and the Genetic Resources of the Deep Sea* (Leiden and Boston, Nijhoff, 2007).

Lévy, J-P., 'L'autorité des fonds marins à cinq ans' (1999–2000) 13 *Espaces et ressources maritimes*, 1–20.

——, 'La première décennie de l'autorité internationale des fonds marins' (2005) 109 *RGDIP*, 101–22.

Lochte, K., 'The Deep Sea Floor: New Discoveries and Visions', in P. Ehlers, E. Mann-Borgese and R. Wolfrum (eds), *Marine Issues: From a Scienfitic, Political and Legal Perspective* (The Hague, Kluwer, 2002) 233–40.

Lodge, M., 'New Approaches to Fisheries Enforcement' (1993) 2 *RECIEL*, 277–84.

——, 'Improving International Governance in the Deep Sea' (2004) 19 *IJMCL*, 299–316.

Long, R. and Grehan, A., 'Marine Habitat Protection in Sea Areas under the Jurisdiction of a Coastal Member State of the European Union: The Case of Deep-Water Coral Conservation in Ireland' (2002) 17 *IJMCL*, 235–61.

Lowe, A.V., 'The Development of the Concept of the Contiguous Zone' (1981) 52 *BYIL*, 109–69.

——, 'Sustainable Development and Unsustainable Arguments', in A.E. Boyle and D. Freestone (eds), *International Law and Sustainable Development: Past Achievements and Future Challenges* (Oxford, Oxford University Press, 1999) 19–37.

Lucchini, L., 'La loi canadienne du 12 mai 1994: la logique extrême de la théorie du droit préférentiel de l'Etat côtier en haute mer au titre des stocks chevauchants' (1994) 40 *AFDI*, 864–75.

——, 'Le principe de précaution en droit international de l'environnement: ombres plus que lumières' (1999) 45 *AFDI*, 710–31.

Lucchini, L. and Vœlckel, M., *Droit de la mer,* Tome 2 *Délimitation, Navigation et Pêche* Volume 2 *Navigation et Pêche* (Paris, Pedone, 1996).

Lyster, S., *International Wildlife Law: Analysis of International Treaties Concerned with the Conservation of Wildlife* (Cambridge, Grotius Publications Limited, 1985).

Macdonald, J.M., 'Appreciating the Precautionary Principle as an Ethical Evolution in Ocean Management' (1995) 26 *ODIL*, 255–86.

Malanczuk, P., 'Sustainable Development: Some Critical Thoughts in the Light of the Rio Conference', in K. Ginther, H. Denters and P.J.I.M. de Waart (eds), *Sustainable Development and Good Governance* (Dordrecht, Kluwer, 1995) 23–52.

——, *Akehurst's Modern Introduction to International Law*, 7th revised edn (London, Routledge, 1997).

Mann-Borgese, E., 'The Common Heritage of Mankind: From Non-living to Living Resources and Beyond', in N. Ando, E. McWhinney and R. Wolfrum (eds), *Liber Amicorum Judge Shigeru Oda* (The Hague, Kluwer, 2002) 1313–34.

Mann-Borgese, E. and Saigal, K., 'Managerial Implications of Sustainable Development in the Ocean' (1996) 12 *Ocean Yearbook*, 1–18.

Marauhn, T., 'Towards a Procedural Law of Compliance Control in International Environmental Relations' (1996) 56 *ZaöRV*, 696–731.

Marr, S., *The Precautionary Principles in the Law of the Sea: Modern Decision Making in International Law* (The Hague, Nijhoff, 2003).

Martin-Bidou, P., 'Le principe de précaution en droit international de l'environnement', (1999) 103 *RGDIP*, 631–66.

Masterson, W.E., *Jurisdiction in Marginal Seas with Special Reference to Smuggling* (New York, The Macmillan Company, 1929).

Matsui, Y., 'The Road to Sustainable Development: Evolution of the Concept of Development in the UN', in K. Ginther, H. Denters and P.J.I.M. de Waart (eds), *Sustainable Development and Good Governance* (Dordrecht, Kluwer, 1995) 53–71.

——, 'The Principle of "Common But Differentiated Responsibilities"', in N. Schrijver and F. Weiss (eds), *International Law and Sustainable Development, Principles and Practice* (The Hague, Brill, 2004) 73–96.

Matz, N., 'Marine Biological Resources: Some Reflections on Concepts for the Protection and Sustainable Use of Biological Resources in the Deep Sea' (2002) 2 *Non-State Actors and International Law*, 279–300.

——, 'The Interaction Between the Convention on Biological Diversity and the UN Convention on the Law of the Sea', in P. Ehlers, E. Mann-Borgese and R. Wolfrum (eds) *Marine Issues: From a Scientific, Political and Legal Perspective* (The Hague, Kluwer, 2002) 203–20.

McConnell, F., *The Biodiversity Convention: A Negotiating History* (London, Kluwer, 1996).

McGoldrick, D., 'Sustainable Development and Human Rights: An Integrated Conception' (1996) 45 *ICLQ*, 796–818.

McIntyre, O. and Mosedale, T., 'The Precautionary Principle as a Norm of Customary International Law' (1997) 9 *Journal of Environmental Law*, 221–41.

Mengozzi, P., 'Fishing and International Cooperation in the Light of New Developments in the Law of the Sea', in B. Vukas (ed.), *Essays on the New Law of the Sea* (Zagreb, Sveučilišna naklada Liber, 1985) 261–75.

Mensah, T.A., 'The Dispute Settlement Regime of the 1982 United Nations Convention on the Law of the Sea' (1998) 2 *Max Planck Yearbook of United Nations Law*, 307–23.

Meseguer, J.L., 'Le régime juridique de l'exploitation de stocks communs de poissons au-delà des 200 milles (article 63, paragraphe 2, de la Convention sur le droit de la mer' (1982) 28 *AFDI*, 885–99.

Mgbeoji, I., '(Under) Mining the Seabed? Between the International Seabed Authority Mining Code and Sustainable Bioprospecting of Hydrothermal Vent Ecosystems in the Seabed Area: Taking Precaution Seriously' (2004) 18 *Ocean Yearbook*, 413–52.

Mitchell, R.B., 'Compliance Theory: An Overview', in J. Cameron, J. Werksman and P. Roderick (eds), *Improving Compliance with International Environmental Law* (London, Earthscan Publications Ltd, 1996) 3–28.

Molenaar, E.J., *Coastal State Jurisdiction over Vessel-Source Pollution* (The Hague, Kluwer, 1998).

——, 'The Concept of "Real Interest" and Other Aspects of Co-operation through Regional Fisheries Management Mechanisms' (2000) 15 *IJMCL*, 475–531.

——, 'Ecosystem-Based Fisheries Management, Commercial Fisheries, Marine Mammals and the 2001 Reykjavik Declaration in the Context of International Law' (2002) 17 *IJMCL*, 561–95.

——, 'Regional Fisheries Management Organizations: Issues of Participation, Allocation and Unregulated Fishing', in A.G. Oude Elferink and D.R. Rothwell (eds), *Oceans Management in the 21st Century: Institutional Frameworks and Responses* (Leiden, Nijhoff, 2004) 69–86.

——, 'Unregulated Deep-Sea Fisheries: A Need for a Multi-Level Approach' (2004) 19 *IJMCL*, 223–46.

——, 'Addressing Regulatory Gaps in High Seas Fisheries' (2005) 20 *IJMCL*, 533–70.

——, 'Managing Biodiversity in Areas Beyond National Jurisdiction' (2007) 22 *IJMCL*, 89–124.

Momtaz, D., 'L'accord relatif à la conservation et la gestion des stocks de poissons chevauchants et grands migrateurs' (1995) 41 *AFDI*, 676–99.

Moore, G., 'The Food and Agriculture Organisation of the United Nations Compliance Agreement' (1995) 10 *IJMCL*, 412–25.

——, 'The Code of Conduct for Responsible Fisheries', in E. Hey (ed.), *Developments in International Fisheries Law* (The Hague, Kluwer, 1999) 85–105.

——, 'The FAO Compliance Agreement', in M.H. Nordquist and J.N. Moore (eds), *Current Fisheries Issues and the Food and Agriculture Organisation of the United Nations* (The Hague, Kluwer, 2000) 77–91.

Moore, J.B., *History and Digest of the International Arbitrations to Which the United States Has Been a Party*, Vol. I (Washington, DC, Government Printing Office, 1898).

——, *A Digest of International Law*, Vol. I (Washington, DC, Government Printing Office, 1906).

Morgan, D.L., 'Implications of the Proliferation of International Legal Fora: The Example of the *Southern Bluefin Tuna Cases*' (2002) 43 *Harvard International Law Journal*, 541–51.

Morita, A., *Le contrôle international: théorie et pratique* (in Japanese) (Tokyo, Tokyo Daigaku Shuppan Kai, 2000).

Mossop, J., 'Protecting Marine Biodiversity on the Continental Shelf Beyond 200 Nautical Miles' (2007) 38 *ODIL*, 283–304.

Murawski, S.A., 'Ten Myths Concerning Ecosystem Approaches to Marine Resource Management' (2007) 31 *Marine Policy*, 681–90.

Naeve, H. and Garcia, S.M., 'The United Nations System Responds to Agenda 21.17: Oceans' (1995) 29 *Ocean and Coastal Management*, 23–33.

National Research Council, *Marine Protected Areas: Tools for Sustaining Ocean Ecosystems* (Washington, DC, National Academy Press, 2001).

Navid, D., 'Compliance Assistance in International Environmental Law: Capacity-Building, Transfer of Finance and Technology' (1996) 56 *ZaöRV*, 810–19.

Nishiumi, M., 'Dédoublement fonctionnel de l'Etat et droit international contemporain: d'après la pensée de Georges Scelle' (in Japanese) (2001) 20 *Yearbook of World Law*, 77–106.

Nollkaemper, A., 'The Precautionary Principle in International Environmental Law: What's New Under the Sun?' (1991) 22 *Marine Pollution Bulletin*, 107–10.

——, '"What You Risk Reveals What You Value" and Other Dilemmas Encountered in the Legal Assaults on Risks', in D. Freestone and E. Hey (eds), *The Precautionary Principle and International Law* (The Hague, Kluwer, 1996) 73–94.

——, 'Balancing the Protection of Marine Ecosystems with Economic Benefits from Land-Based Activities: The Quest for International Legal Barriers' (1996) 27 *ODIL*, 153–79.

——, 'Habitat Protection in European Community Law: Evolving Conceptions of a Balance of Interests' (1997) 9 *Journal of Environmental Law*, 271–86.

Nordquist, M.H., Nandan, S.N. and Rosenne, S. (eds), *United Nations Convention on the Law of the Sea 1982: A Commentary*, Vol. II and Vol. IV (The Hague, Centre for Oceans Law and Policy, University of Virginia School of Law, Nijhoff, 1991, 1993).

Nordquist, M.H. and Moore, J.N. (eds), *Current Maritime Issues and the International Maritime Organization* (The Hague, Nijhoff, 1999).

——, (eds), *Current Fisheries Issues and the Food and Agriculture Organization of the United Nations* (The Hague, Nijhoff, 2000).

Nouzha, C., 'L'affaire de l'usine MOX (Irlande c. Royaume-Uni) devant le Tribunal international du droit de la mer: quelles mesures conservatoires pour la protection de l'environnement?' [PDF version] (2002) mars *Actualité et Droit International* <http://www.ridi.org/adi> 1–12.

Obata, K., '"Stratification of International Law" as the Construction of a World Public Sphere: The Legal Project of Wolfgang Friedmann in His Later Period' (in Japanese) (2001) 20 *Yearbook of World Law*, 151–76.

O'Connell, D.P. (Shearer, I.A., ed.), *The International Law of the Sea* (Oxford, Clarendon Press, 1982).

Oda, S., 'New Trends in the Regime of the Seas: A Consideration of the Problems of Conservation and Distribution of Marine Resources (I) (II)', (1957–58) 18 *ZaöRV*, 61–102; 261–86.

—— (ed.), *The International Law of the Ocean Development: Basic Documents* (Leiden, Sijthoff, 1972).

——, 'Sharing of Ocean Resources: Unresolved Issues in the Law of the Sea' (1981) 3 *Journal of International and Comparative Law*, 1–14.

——, 'Fisheries under the United Nations Convention on the Law of the Sea' (1983) 77 *AJIL*, 739–55.

——, *Chukai Kokuren Kaiyoho Jyoyaku* (Commentary on the UN Convention on the Law of the Sea, in Japanese) (Tokyo, Yuhikaku, 1985).

——, *International Control of Sea Resources* (Dordrecht, Nijhoff, 1989).

——, 'The 1958 Geneva Convention on Fishing and Conservation of the Living Resources of the High Seas: Its Immaturities', in S. Oda (ed.), *Fifty Years of the Law of the Sea, with a Special Section on the International Court of Justice, Selected Writings of Shigeru Oda* (The Hague, Kluwer, 2003) 139–62.

——, 'Recent Problems of International High Seas Fisheries: Allocation of Fishery Resources', in S. Oda (ed.), *Fifty Years of the Law of the Sea, With a Special Section on the International Court of Justice, Selected Writings of Shigeru Oda* (The Hague, Kluwer, 2003) 227–38.

Oral, N., 'The Black Sea: A Case Study in Regional Cooperation', in M.H. Nordquist, J.N. Moore and S. Mahmoudi (eds), *The Stockholm Declaration and Law of the Marine Environment* (The Hague, Nijhoff, 2003) 237–56.

——, 'Protection of Vulnerable Marine Ecosystems in Areas Beyond National Jurisdiction: Can International Law Meet the Challenge?', in A. Strati, M. Gavouneli and N. Skourtos (eds), *Unresolved Issues and New Challenges to the Law of the Sea: Time Before and Time After* (Leiden and Boston, Nijhoff, 2006) 85–108.

Orellana, M.A., 'The Swordfish Dispute between the EU and Chile at the ITLOS and the WTO' (2002) 71 *Nordic Journal of International Law*, 55–81.

Orrego Vicuña, F. (ed.), *The Exclusive Economic Zone, A Latin American Perspective* (Boulder, Colorado, Westview Press, 1984).

——, *The Exclusive Economic Zone: Regime and Legal Nature under International Law* (Cambridge, Cambridge University Press, 1989).

——, 'The "Presential Sea": Defining Coastal States' Special Interests in High Seas Fisheries and Other Activities' (1992) 35 *GYIL*, 264–92.

——, 'New Approaches Under International Law to the Issue of High Seas Fisheries', in *International Law in an Evolving World, Liber Amicorum in Tribute to Professor Eduardo Jiménez de Aréchaga*, II (Montevideo, Fundacion de cultura universitaria, 1994) 745–61.

——, 'Coastal States' Competences over High Seas Fisheries and the Changing Role of International Law' (1995) 55 *ZaöRV*, 520–35.

——, *The Changing International Law of High Seas Fisheries* (Cambridge, Cambridge University Press, 1999).

——, 'The International Law of High Seas Fisheries: From Freedom of Fishing to Sustainable Use', in O.S. Stokke (ed.), *Governing High Seas Fisheries: The Interplay of Global and Regional Regimes* (Oxford, Oxford University Press, 2001) 24–52.

——, 'The Law Governing High Seas Fisheries: In Search of New Principles' (2004) 18 *Ocean Yearbook*, 383–94.

Otani, Y., 'Quelques réflexions sur la juridiction et la recevabilité vis-à-vis de l'*Affaire du thon à nageoire bleue*', in N. Ando, E. McWhinney and R. Wolfrum (eds), *Liber Amicorum Judge Shigeru Oda* (The Hague, Kluwer, 2002) 731–42.

Ottesen, P., Sparkes, S. and Trinder, C., 'Shipping Threats and Protection of the Great Barrier Reef Marine Park – The Role of the Particularly Sensitive Sea Area Concept' (1994) 9 *IJMCL*, 507–34.

Oude Elferink, A.G., 'The Impact of Article 7 (2) of the Fish Stocks Agreement on the Formulation of Conservation and Management Measures for Straddling and Highly Migratory Fish Stocks' (1999) 4 *FAO Legal Papers Online*, 13–18.

——, 'The Determination of Compatible Conservation and Management Measures for Straddling and Highly Migratory Fish Stocks' (2001) 5 *Max Planck Yearbook of United Nations Law*, 551–607.

—— (ed.), *Stability and Change in the Law of the Sea: The Role of the LOS Convention* (Leiden and Boston, Nijhoff, 2005).

Oxman, B.H.,'Coastal States' Competences over High Seas Fisheries and the Changing Role of International Law: Comment' (1995) 55 *ZaöRV*, 536–43.

Parsons, L.S., Powles, H. and Comfort, M.J., 'Science in Support of Fishery Management: New Approaches for Sustainable Fisheries' (1998) 39 *Ocean and Coastal Management*, 151–66.

Partsch, K.J., 'Reporting Systems in International Relations', in R. Bernhardt (ed.), *Encyclopedia of Public International Law*, Vol. 4 (Amsterdam, North-Holland Elsevier, 2000) 191–5.

Pastor Ridruejo, J.A., 'Le droit international à la veille du vingt et unième siècle: Normes, faits et valeurs: Cours général de droit international public' (1998) 274 *RCADI*, 9–308.

Peet, G., 'Particularly Sensitive Sea Areas: A Documentary History' (1994) 9 *IJMCL*, 469–506.

Pinto, M.C.W., 'The Duty of Co-Operation and the United Nations Convention on the Law of the Sea', in A. Bos and H. Siblesz (eds), *Realism in Law-Making: Essays on International Law in Honour of Willem Riphagen* (Dordrecht, Nijhoff, 1986) 131–54.

Prideaux, M., *Conserving Cetaceans: The Convention on Migratory Species and its Relevant Agreements for Cetacean Conservation* (Munich, WDCS, 2003).

Quing-Nan, M., *Land-based Marine Pollution* (London, Nijhoff, 1987).

Raigón, R.C., 'Règlement des différends', in D. Vignes, G. Cataldi and R.C. Raigón (eds), *Le droit international de la pêche maritime* (Bruxelles, Bruylant, 2000) 316–65.

——, 'La pêche en haute mer', in D. Vignes, G. Cataldi and R.C. Raigón (eds), *Le droit international de la pêche maritime* (Bruxelles, Bruylant, 2000), 117–242.

Ranjeva, R., 'Les organisations non gouvernementales et la mise en oeuvre du droit international' (1997) 270 *RCADI*, 9–106.

Rayfuse, R.G., *Non-Flag State Enforcement in High Seas Fisheries* (Leiden, Nijhoff, 2004).

——, 'Regulation and Enforcement in the Law of the Sea: Emerging Assertions of a Right to Non-Flag State Enforcement in the High Seas Fisheries and Disarmament Contexts' (2005) 24 *Australian Yearbook of International Law*, 181–200.

——, 'To Our Children's Children's Children: From Promoting to Achieving Compliance in High Seas Fisheries' (2005) 20 *IJMCL*, 509–32.

Redgwell, C. and Bowman, M. (eds), *International Law and the Conservation of Biological Diversity* (The Hague, Kluwer, 1996).

Rieser, A., 'International Fisheries Law, Overfishing and Marine Biodiversity' (1997) 9 *The Georgetown International Environmental Law Review*, 251–79.

Roach, J.A., 'Marine Scientific Research and the New Law of the Sea' (1996) 27 *ODIL*, 59–72.

——, 'Particularly Sensitive Sea Areas: Current Developments', in M.H. Nordquist, J.N. Moore and S. Mahmoudi (eds), *The Stockholm Declaration and Law of the Marine Environment* (The Hague, Nijhoff, 2003) 311–50.

Roach, J.A. and Smith, R.W., *United States Responses to Excessive Maritime Claims*, 2nd edn (The Hague, Nijhoff, 1996).

Robb, C.A.R. (ed.), *International Environmental Law Reports*, Vol. 1, Early Decisions (Cambridge, Cambridge University Press, 1999).

Röben, V., 'The Order of the UNCLOS Annex VII Arbitral Tribunal to Suspend Proceedings in the Case of the MOX Plant at Sellafield: How Much Jurisdictional Subsidiarity?' (2004) 73 *Nordic Journal of International Law*, 223–45.

Roberts, J., 'Protecting Sensitive Marine Environments: The Role and Application of Ships' Routeing Measures' (2005) 20 *IJMCL*, 135–59.

——, *Marine Environment Protection and Biodiversity Conservation: The Application and Future Development of the IMO's Particularly Sensitive Sea Area Concept* (Berlin, Springer, 2007).

Roberts, J., Tsamenyi, M., Workman, T. and Johnston, L., 'The Western European PSSA Proposal: A "Politically Sensitive Sea Area"' (2005) 29 *Marine Policy*, 431–40.

Romano, C.P.R., *The Peaceful Settlement of International Environmental Disputes: A Pragmatic Approach* (The Hague, Kluwer Law International, 2000).

Rose, G., 'Marine Biodiversity Protection through Fisheries Management: International Legal Developments' (1999) 8 *RECIEL*, 284–90.

Ruzié, D., *Droit international public*, 7th edn (Paris, Dalloz, 1987).

Sachariew, K., 'Promoting Compliance with International Environmental Legal Standards: Reflections on Monitoring and Reporting Mechanisms' (1991) 2 *Yearbook of International Environmental Law*, 31–52.

Salchow, R., 'The Quality Status Report (QSR 2000) for the North East Atlantic', in P. Ehlers, E. Mann-Borgese and R. Wolfrum (eds), *Marine Issues: From a Scientific, Political and Legal Perspective* (The Hague, Kluwer, 2002) 119–34.

Salm, R.V., Clark, J. and Siirila, E., *Marine and Coastal Protected Areas: A Guide for Planners and Managers*, 3rd edn (Gland, IUCN, 2000).

Salmona, P. and Verardi, D., 'The Marine Protected Area of Portofino, Italy: A Difficult Balance' (2001) 44 *Ocean and Coastal Management*, 39–60.

Sand, P.H., 'Institution-Building to Assist Compliance with International Environmental Law: Perspectives' (1996) 56 *ZaöRV*, 774–95.

——, 'The Precautionary Principle: Coping with Risk' (2000) 40 *Indian Journal of International Law*, 1–13.

Sands, P., 'International Law in the Field of Sustainable Development' (1994) 65 *BYIL*, 303–81.

——, 'Compliance with International Environmental Obligations: Existing International Legal Arrangements', in J. Cameron, J. Werksman and P. Roderick (eds), *Improving Compliance with International Environmental Law* (London, Earthscan Publications Ltd, 1996).

——, 'International Courts and the Application of the Concept of "Sustainable Development"' (1999) 3 *Max Planck Yearbook of United Nations Law*, 389–405.

——, *Principles of International Environmental Law*, 2nd edn (Cambridge, Cambridge University Press, 2003).

Sands, P., Tarasofsky, R. and Weiss, M. (eds), *Documents in International Environmental Law: Principles of International Environmental Law IIA* (Manchester, Manchester University Press, 1994).

Sanwal, M., 'Sustainable Development, the Rio Declaration and Multilateral Cooperation' (1993) 4 *Colorado Journal of International Environmental Law and Policy*, 45–68.

Sato, T., 'International Supervision by International Organizations with Regard to States' (in Japanese) (1995) 114 *The Hitotsubashi Review*, 99–115.

Savini, M., 'La règlementation de la pêche en haute mer par l'assemblée générale des Nations Unies (A Propos de la résolution 44/225 sur les grands filets maillants dérivants)' (1990) 36 *AFDI*, 777–817.

Scelle, G., *Manuel élémentaire de droit international public (avec les Textes essentiels)* (Paris, Les éditions Domat-Montchrestien, 1943).

——, 'Plateau continental et droit international,' (1955) 63 *RGDIP*, 5–62.

——, 'Le phénomène juridique du dédoublement fonctionnel', in *Rechtsfragen der internationalen Organisation, Festschrift für Hans Wehberg zu seinem Geburtstag* (Frankfurt am Main, Vittorio Klostermann, 1956) 324–42.

——, 'Obsession du territoire', *Symbolae Verzijl* (The Hague, Nijhoff, 1958) 347–61.

Scheiber, H.N., 'U.S. Policy, the Pacific Tuna Economy, and Ocean Law Innovation: The Post-World War II Era, 1945 to 1970', in D.D. Caron and H.N. Scheiber (eds), *Bringing New Law to Ocean Waters* (Leiden, Brill, 2004) 29–53.

Schram Stokke, O., 'Managing Straddling Stocks: The Interplay of Global and Regional Regimes' (2000) 43 *Ocean and Coastal Management*, 205–34.

—— (ed.), *Governing High Seas Fisheries: The Interplay of Global and Regional Regimes* (Oxford, Oxford University Press, 2001).

Schram Stokke, O. and Coffey, C., 'Precaution, ICES and the Common Fisheries Policy: A Study of Regime Interplay' (2004) 28 *Marine Policy*, 117–26.

Schrank, W.E., 'Is There Any Hope for Fisheries Management?' (2007) 31 *Marine Policy*, 299–307.

Schrijver, N. and Weiss, F. (eds), *International Law and Sustainable Development, Principles and Practice* (The Hague, Brill, 2004).

Schwarz, P., 'Sustainable Development in International Law' (2005) 5 *Non-State Actors and International Law*, 127–52.

Schwebel, S.M., 'The Southern Bluefin Tuna Case', in N. Ando, E. McWhinney and R. Wolfrum (eds), *Liber Amicorum Judge Shigeru Oda* (The Hague, Kluwer, 2002) 743–8.

Scott, S.V., 'The Inclusion of Sedentary Fisheries within the Continental Shelf Doctrine' (1992) 41 *ICLQ*, 788–807.

Scovazzi, T., 'Biodiversity in the Deep Seabed' (1996) 7 *Yearbook of International Environmental Law*, 481–7.

——, 'La liberté de la mer: vers l'affaiblissement d'un principe vénérable?' (1998) 3 *Annuaire du droit de la mer*, 13–29.

—— (ed.), *Marine Specially Protected Areas: The General Aspects and the Mediterranean Regional System* (The Hague, Kluwer, 1999).

——, 'The Evolution of International Law of the Sea: New Issues, New Challenges' (2000) 286 *RCADI*, 39–243.

——, 'The Mediterranean Marine Mammals Sanctuary' (2001) 16 *IJMCL*, 132–45.

——, 'Les zones côtières en Méditerranée: évolution et confusion' (2001) 4 *Annuaire du droit de la mer*, 95–108.

——, 'Marine Protected Areas on the High Seas: Some Legal and Policy Considerations' (2004) 19 *IJMCL*, 1–17.

——, 'Mining, Protection of the Environment, Scientific Research and Bioprospecting: Some Considerations on the Role of the International Sea-Bed Authority' (2004) 19 *IJMCL*, 383–409.

——, 'New International Instruments for Marine Protected Areas in the Mediterranean Sea', in A. Strati, M. Gavouneli and N. Skourtos (eds), *Unresolved Issues and New Challenges to the Law of the Sea: : Time Before and Time After* (Leiden and Boston, Nijhoff, 2006) 109–20.

——, 'Bioprospecting on the Deep Seabed: A Legal Gap Requiring to be Filled', in F. Francioni and T. Scovazzi (eds), *Biotechnology and International Law* (Oxford and Portland, Oregon, Hart Publishing, 2006), 81–97.

Secretariat of the Convention on Biological Diversity, *Handbook of the Convention on Biological Diversity* (London and Sterling, Earthscan, 2001).

Sen, S., 'The Evolution of High-Seas Fisheries Management in the North-East Atlantic' (1997) 35 *Ocean and Coastal Management*, 85–100.

Serdy, A., 'One Fin, Two Fins, Red Fins, Bluefins: Some Problems of Nomenclature and Taxonomy Affecting Legal Instruments Governing Tuna and Other Highly Migratory Species' (2004) 28 *Marine Policy*, 235–47.

Sherman, K., 'Achieving Regional Cooperation in the Management of Marine Ecosystems: The Use of the Large Marine Ecosystem Approach' (1995) 29 *Ocean and Coastal Management*, 165–85.

Simcock, A., 'OSPAR Convention on the Protection of the Marine Environment of the North-East Atlantic', in U. Beyerlin, P-T. Stoll and R. Wolfrum (eds), *Ensuring Compliance with Multilateral Environmental Agreements: A Dialogue between Practitioners and Academia* (Leiden and Boston, Nijhoff, 2006) 97–113.

Simma, B., 'From Bilateralism to Community Interest in International Law' (1994-IV) 250 *RCADI*, 217–384.

——, 'Reciprocity', in R. Bernhardt (ed.), *Encyclopedia of Public International Law*, Vol. 4 (Amsterdam, North-Holland Elsevier, 2000) 29–33.

Simma, B. and Paulus, A.L., 'The "International Community": Facing the Challenge of Globalization' (1998) 9 *EJIL*, 266–77.

Simmonds, K.R. (ed.), *Cases on the Law of the Sea*, 3 Vols (New York, Oceana, 1976, 1977 and 1980).

Skjærseth, J.B., 'Protecting the North-East Atlantic: Enhancing Synergies by Institutional Interplay' (2006) 30 *Marine Policy*, 157–66.

Sohn, L.B., 'Managing the Law of the Sea: Ambassador Pardo's Forgotten Second Idea', in J.I. Charney, D.K. Anton and M.E. O'Connell (eds), *Politics, Values and Functions: International Law in the 21st Century. Essays in Honor of Professor Louis Henkin* (The Hague, Kluwer, 1997) 275–93.

Sohnle, J., 'Irruption du droit de l'environnement dans la jurisprudence de la C.I.J.: l'affaire *Gabčíkovo-Nagymaros*' (1998) 102 *RGDIP*, 85–121.

Soons, A.H.A., *Marine Scientific Research and the Law of the Sea* (Antwerp, Kluwer Law and Taxation Publishers, 1982).

——, 'Marine Scientific Research Provisions in the Convention on the Law of the Sea: Issues of Interpretation', in E.D. Brown, and R.R. Churchill, *The UN Convention on the Law of the Sea: Impact and Implementation Proceedings*, Law of the Sea Institute Nineteenth Annual Conference (Honolulu, University of Hawaii, 1987) 365–72.

Speer, L. and Chasis, S., 'The Agreement on the Conservation and Management of Straddling and Highly Migratory Fish Stocks: An NGO Perspective' (1995) 29 *Ocean and Coastal Management*, 71–7.

Stephens, T., 'The Limits of International Adjudication in International Environmental Law: Another Perspective on the Southern Bluefin Tuna Case' (2004) 19 *IJMCL*, 177–97.

Sugihara, T., 'The Dispute Settlement Procedure of the United Nations Convention on the Law of the Sea: Its Applicability to Other Treaty Disputes concerning the Law of the Sea' (in Japanese) (2000) 146 *Kyoto Law Review*, 1–25.

Symes, D., 'North Atlantic Fisheries: Trends, Status, and Management Issues' (1997) 35 *Ocean and Coastal Management*, 51–67.

——, 'Conclusion: Towards a Regionalised Management System for the North Atlantic' (1997) 35 *Ocean and Coastal Management*, 217–24.

——, 'The European Community's Common Fisheries Policy' (1997) 35 *Ocean and Coastal Management*, 137–55.

Tahindro, A., 'Conservation and Management of Transboundary Fish Stocks: Comments in Light of the Adoption of the 1995 Agreement for the Conservation and Management of Straddling Fish Stocks and Highly Migratory Fish Stocks' (1997) 28 *ODIL*, 1–58.

——, 'Conservation et gestion des stocks de poissons chevauchants et des stocks de poissons grands migrateurs: une étude préliminaire du régime juridique de l'Accord aux fins de l'application des dispositions de la Convention des Nations Unies sur le droit de la mer du 10 décembre 1982 relatives à la conservation et à la gestion des stocks de poissons dont les déplacements s'effectuent tant à l'intérieur qu'au-delà de zones économiques exclusives (stocks chevauchants) et des stocks de poissons grands migrateurs' (1999–2000) 13 *Espaces et ressources maritimes*, 186–206.

Takabayashi, H., *Ryokai Seido no Kenkyu* (Study of Territorial Sea, in Japanese), 3rd edn (Tokyo, Yushindo, 1987).

——, *A Study of the UN Convention on the Law of the Sea* (in Japanese) (Tokyo, Toshindo, 1996).

Takamura, Y., 'The Precautionary Principle in International Environmental Law: Its Current Status and Functions' (in Japanese) (2005) 104 *The Journal of International Law and Diplomacy*, 235–62.

Takashima, T., 'Sustainable Development and International Law' (in Japanese) (2002) 75 *Hogaku Kenkyu* (*Journal of Law, Politics and Sociology*) 223–47.

Takei, Y., 'Unfinished Business: Review Conference on the 1995 UN Fish Stocks Agreement' (2006) 21 *IJMCL*, 551–68.

Tanaka, N. (ed.), 'Kaiyo hogoku no kokusaiho teki kento' (Reflections on Marine Protected Areas in International Law) (in Japanese) (Tokyo, Ministry of Foreign Affairs, 2004), 1–96.

Tanaka, Y., 'Zonal and Integrated Management Approaches to Ocean Governance: Reflections on a Dual Approach in International Law of the Sea' (2004) 19 *IJMCL*, 483–514.

——, 'Obligation to Co-operate in Marine Scientific Research and the Conservation of Marine Living Resources' (2005) 65 *ZaöRV*, 937–65.

——, 'Regulation of Land-Based Marine Pollution in International Law: A Comparative Analysis Between Global and Regional Legal Frameworks' (2006) 66 *ZaöRV*, 535–74.

——, *Predictability and Flexibility in the Law of Maritime Delimitation* (Oxford, Hart Publishing, 2006).

——, 'Reflections on the Conservation and Sustainable Use of Genetic Resources in the Deep Seabed Beyond the Limits of National Jurisdiction' (2008) 38 *ODIL*, 129–149.

Thébaud, O., 'Transboundary Marine Fisheries Management: Recent Developments and Elements of Analysis' (1997) 21 *Marine Policy*, 237–53.

Thiel, H., 'Approaches to the Establishment of Protected Areas on the High Seas', in A. Kirchner (ed.), *International Marine Environmental Law: Institutions Implementation and Innovations* (The Hague, Kluwer, 2003) 169–92.

Tomuschat, C., 'Obligations Arising for States Without or Against Their Will' (1993) 241 *RCADI*, 209–40.

——, 'International Law: Ensuring the Survival of Mankind on the Eve of A New Century' (1999) 281 *RCADI*, 9–438.

Treves, T., 'Principe du consentement et nouveau régime juridique de la recherche scientifique marine', in D. Bardonnet and M. Virally (eds), *Le nouveau droit international de la mer* (Paris, Pedone, 1983) 269–85.

——, 'Codification du droit international et pratique des Etats dans le droit de la mer' (1990-IV) 223 *RCADI*, 9–302.

——, 'Marine Research', in R. Bernhardt (ed.), *Encyclopedia of Public International Law*, Vol. 3 (Amsterdam, Elsevier, 1997) 295–8.

Trindade, A.A.C., 'International Law for Humankind: Towards a New *Jus Gentium* (I): General Course on Public International Law' (2005) 316 *RCADI*, 9–440.

Trouwborst, A., *Evolution and Status of the Precautionary Principle in International Law* (The Hague, Kluwer Law International, 2002).

Tsimplis, M., 'Alien Species Stay Home: The International Convention for the Control and Management of Ships' Ballast Water and Sediments 2004' (2004) 19 *IJMCL*, 411–45.

Uggla, Y., 'Environmental Protection and the Freedom of the High Seas: The Baltic Sea as a PSSA from a Swedish Perspective' (2007) 31 *Marine Policy*, 251–7.

Ulfstein, G. (ed.), *Making Treaties Work: Human Rights, Environment and Arms Control* (Cambridge, Cambridge University Press, 2007).

United Nations, *The Law of the Sea: Marine Scientific Research, A Guide to the Implementation of the Relevant Provisions of the United Nations Convention on the Law of the Sea* (New York, United Nations, 1991).

——, *The Law of the Sea: The Regime for High-Seas Fisheries, Status and Prospects* (New York, United Nations, 1992).

——, *The Law of the Sea: Concept of the Common Heritage of Mankind, Legislative History of Articles 133 to 150 and 311 (6) of the United Nations Convention on the Law of the Sea* (New York, United Nations, 1996).

——, *The Law of the Sea: Declarations and Statements with Respect to the United Nations Convention on the Law of the Sea and to the Agreement Relating to the Implementation of Part XI of the United Nations Convention on the Law of the Sea of 10 December 1982* (New York, United Nations, 1997).

United States General Accounting Office, *International Environment, International Agreements Are Not Well Monitored*, Report to Congressional Requesters (GAO/RCED-92-43, January 1992).

——, *International Environment, Options for Strengthening Environmental Agreements*, Testimony (GAO/RCED-92-83, For Immediate Release).

——, *International Environment: Strengthening the Implementation of Environmental Agreements*, Report to Congressional Requesters (GAO/RCED-92-188, August 1992).

Vanderzwaag, D., 'The Precautionary Principle and Marine Environmental Protection: Slippery Shores, Rough Seas, and Rising Normative Tide' (2002) 33 *ODIL*, 165–88.

Van Dyke, J.M., Zaelke, D. and Hewison, G. (eds), *Freedom for the Seas in the 21st Century: Ocean Governance and Environmental Harmony* (Washington, DC, Covelo, California, Island Press, 1993).

Van Ettinger, J., 'Oceans, Climate Change, and Energy' (1993) 10 *Ocean Yearbook*, 132–46.

Verzijl, J.H.W., 'The United Nations Conference on the Law of the Sea, Geneva, 1958 (I) and (II)' (1959) 6 *NILR*, 1–42; 115–39.

Vice, D., 'Implementation of Biodiversity Treaties: Monitoring, Fact-Finding, and Dispute Resolution' (1997) 29 *New York University Journal of International Law and Politics*, 577–639.

Vidas, D. and Østreng, W. (eds), *Order for the Oceans at the Turn of the Century* (The Hague, Kluwer, 1999).

Vignes, D., 'La formation historique du droit international de la pêche', in D. Vignes, G. Cataldi and R.C. Raigón (eds), *Le droit international de la pêche maritime* (Bruxelles, Bruylant, 2000) 11–45.

Vignes, D., Cataldi, G. and Raigón, R.C. (eds), *Le droit international de la pêche maritime* (Bruxelles, Bruylant, 2000).

Virally, M., 'Le principe de réciprocité dans le droit international contemporain' (1967-III) 122 *RCADI*, 1–105.

——, 'Panorama du droit international contemporain: Cours général de droit international public' (1983-V) 183 *RCADI*, 9–382.

Vœlckel, M., 'Comment vit la zone économique exclusive?' (2001) 4 *Annuaire du droit de la mer*, 111–14.

Vukas, B., 'State Practice in the Aftermath of the UN Convention on the Law of the Sea: The Exclusive Economic Zone and the Mediterranean Sea', in A. Strati, M. Gavouneli and N. Skourtos (eds), *Unresolved Issues and New Challenges to the Law of the Sea: Time Before and Time After* (Leiden and Boston, Nijhoff, 2006) 251–8.

Wang, H., 'Ecosystem Management and Its Application to Large Marine Ecosystems: Science, Law, and Politics' (2004) 35 *ODIL*, 41–74.

Warner, R., 'Marine Protected Areas Beyond National Jurisdiction – Existing Legal Principles and Future Legal Frameworks', paper presented at the *Expert Workshop on Managing Risks to Biodiversity and the Environment on High*

Seas, including Tools such as MPAs, Scientific Requirement and Legal Aspects (Federal Agency for Nature Conservation, Isle of Vilm, Germany, February 2001).

Warren, L.M., 'The Role of *Ex Situ* Measures in the Conservation of Biodiversity', in C. Redgwell and M. Bowman (eds), *International Law and the Conservation of Biological Diversity* (The Hague, Kluwer, 1996) 129–44.

Weil, P., 'Le principe de la juridiction consensuelle à l'épreuve du feu: à propos de l'arrêt de la Cour internationale de Justice dans l'affaire de la compétence en matière de pêcheries (Espagne c. Canada)', in C.A. Armas Barea, J.A. Barberis, J. Barboza, H. Caminos, E. Candioti, E. de La Guardia, H.D.T. Gutiérrez Posse, G. Moncayo, E.J. Rey Caro and R.E. Vinuesa (eds), *Liber Amicorum 'In Memoriam' of Judge José Maria Ruda* (The Hague, Kluwer 2000) 157–78.

Wegelein, F.H.T., *Marine Scientific Research: The Operation and Status of Research Vessels and Other Platforms in International Law* (Leiden and Boston, Nijhoff, 2005).

Wettestad, J., 'Science, Politics and Institutional Design: The Case of the North-East Atlantic Land-based Pollution Regime' (1994) 18 *Marine Policy*, 219–32.

Whiteman, M.M., *Digest of International Law*, Vol. 4 (Washington, DC, Department of State Publication, 1965).

Williams, W., 'Reminiscences of the Bering Sea Arbitration' (1943) 37 *AJIL*, 562–84.

Wilson, E.O., *The Diversity of Life* (London, Penguin Books, 1992, reprinted 2001).

Wold, C., 'The Futility, Utility, and Future of the Biodiversity Convention' (1998) 9 *Colorado Journal of International Environmental Law and Policy*, 1–41.

Wolf, S., 'Neue Tendenzen zur Ausdehnung küstenstaatlicher Umweltkompetenzen auf See: Eine Untersuchung am Beispiel der französischen "zone de protection écologique" im Mittelmeer' (2006) 66 *ZaöRV*, 73–141.

Wolfrum, R., 'Fishery Commissions', in R. Bernhardt (ed.), 11 *Encyclopedia of Public International Law* (Amsterdam, Elsevier, 1989) 117–21.

——, 'Means of Ensuring Compliance with and Enforcement of International Environmental Law' (1998) 272 *RCADI*, 9–154.

——, 'The Protection and Management of Biological Diversity', in F.L. Morrison and R. Wolfrum (eds), *International, Regional and National Environmental Law* (The Hague, Kluwer, 2000) 355–72.

Wolfrum, R. and Matz, N., 'The Interplay of the United Nations Convention on the Law of the Sea and the Convention on Biological Diversity' (2000) 4 *Max Planck Yearbook of United Nations Law*, 445–80.

——, *Conflicts in International Environmental Law* (Berlin, Springer, 2003).

World Commission on Environment and Development, *Our Common Future* (Oxford, Oxford University Press, 1987).

Xue, G., *China and International Fisheries Law and Policy* (Leiden and Boston, Nijhoff, 2005).

Yamada, C., 'Priority Application of Successive Treaties Relating to the Same Subject Matter: The Southern Bluefin Tuna Case', in N. Ando, E. McWhinney and R. Wolfrum (eds), *Liber Amicorum Judge Shigeru Oda* (The Hague, Kluwer, 2002) 763–71.

Yankov, A., 'The Concept of Protection and Sustainable Development of the Marine Environment' (2004) 18 *Ocean Yearbook*, 267–83.

Young, T.R., 'Developing a Legal Strategy for High Seas Marine Protected Areas', Legal Document in *IUCN, WCPA and WWF High Seas Marine Protected Areas Workshop*, Malaga, 15–17 January 2003, 1–36.

Yusuf, A.A., 'International Law and Sustainable Development: The Convention on Biological Diversity' (1994) 2 *African Yearbook of International Law*, 109–37.

Zeller, D., Froese, R. and Pauly, D., 'On Losing and Recovering Fisheries and Marine Science Data' (2005) 29 *Marine Policy*, 69–73.

Zhang, X., 'Issues Concerning Precautionary Principle in Environmental Protection: A Chinese Perspective' (in Japanese) (2007) 26 *Yearbook of World Law*, 69–81.

Index